本书出版得到《大中华文库》出版经费资助

大中华文库

LIBRARY
OF CHINESE CLASSICS

大中华文库

汉英对照

LIBRARY OF CHINESE CLASSICS

Chinese-English

汉书选

CHRONICLES OF THE HAN DYNASTY

II

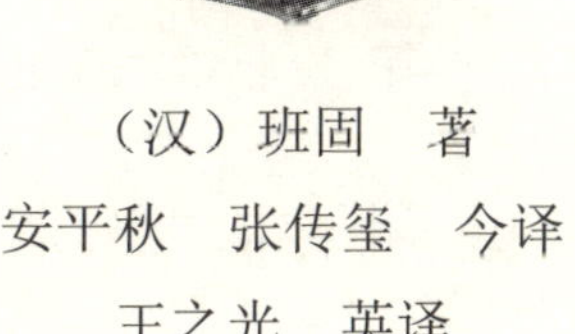

（汉）班固　著

安平秋　张传玺　今译

王之光　英译

Written by Ban Gu (Han Dynasty)

Edited by An Pingqiu, Zhang Chuanxi

Translated by Wang Zhiguang

外文出版社

Foreign Languages Press

目　录

CONTENTS

晁错传

【原文】

晁错，颍川人也。学申商刑名于轵张恢生所，与洛阳宋孟及刘带同师。以文学为太常掌故。

错为人陗直刻深。孝文时，天下亡治《尚书》者，独闻齐有伏生，故秦博士，治《尚书》，年九十馀，老不可征。乃诏太常，使人受之。太常遣错受《尚书》伏生所，还，因上书称说。诏以为太子舍人，门大夫，迁博士。又上书言："人主所以尊显，功名扬于万世之后者，以知术数也。故人主知所以临制臣下而治其众，则群臣畏服矣；知所以听言受事，则不欺蔽矣；知所以安利万民，则海内必从矣；知所以忠孝事上，则臣子之行备矣：此四者，臣窃为皇太子急

【今译】

晁错是颍川人。曾经在轵县张恢先生那里学习过申不害、商鞅的刑名学说，与雒阳人宋孟和刘带同师。因为通晓文献典籍，担任了太常掌故。

晁错为人严峻刚直而又苛刻。汉文帝时，朝廷没有研究《尚书》的人，只听说齐国有伏生，原是秦朝的博士，精通《尚书》，已经九十多岁了，年老不能征召，文帝于是下令太常派人前往学习。太常派遣晁错到伏生那里学习《尚书》，回来后，趁机上书报告学习情况，称赞解说《尚书》。文帝下诏先后任命他担任太子舍人、门大夫，后升为博士。晁错又上书说："君王所以地位尊贵显赫，功名传播万代之后，是因为懂得运用刑名之术。因此知道怎样控制臣下、治理众人，那么群臣便畏惧顺从了；懂得怎样听取各种言论，那么便不被欺骗蒙蔽了；懂得怎样安定社会，使百姓富裕，那么天下百姓就会服从；懂得怎样对尊长尽忠尽孝，那么臣子的行为就具备了。这四条，臣自以为是皇太子的当务之急。人臣的议论有人认为皇太子

Chapter 9

Biography of Chao Cuo

Chao Cuo was from Yingchuan. He had studied the Legalists Shen Buhai and Shang Yang's criminal law theory at Mr. Zhang Hui's residence in Zhi County, with the same teacher as Song Meng and Liu Dai from Luoyang. Because of his knowledge of literary classics, he served as a clerk to the Chamberlain for Ceremonials.

By nature Chao Cuo was straightforward, but harsh. In the reign of Emperor Wendi, there was no one in the whole land expert in the *Book of Documents*, apart from a Mr. Fu in Qi. He had originally been a Qin erudite, and was proficient in the *Book of Documents*, but already a nonagenarian, he was too old to be pressed into service. So the Emperor ordered the Chamberlain for Ceremonials to send people to learn it. The Chamberlain for Ceremonials then sent Chao Cuo to learn the *Book of Documents* at Mr. Fu's residence.When he came back, Chao took the opportunity to report on his study, extoling the *Book*. The Emperor ordered him appointed as a secretary of the Crown Prince, then grand master of the prince, and then promoted him to an erudite. Chao Cuo said in another memorial: "The Lord has so noble a position, and his fame spreads to a thousand later generations because of his mastery of laws and punishment. Therefore, the Lord knows how to control his subjects and manage the people, so that the ministers are awed and obedient; he knows how to listen to all kinds of opinions, so is not deceived; he knows how to maintain social stability, benefiting the multitude, so that the common people within the seas have to obey; he knows how to faithfully fulfill his filial duties to the Emperor, thus he achieves the conduct of a courtier. These four items I think should be the priority

【原文】

之。人臣之议或曰皇太子亡以知事为也，臣之愚，诚以为不然。窃观上世之君，不能奉其宗庙而劫杀于其臣者，皆不知术数者也。(皇太子所读书多矣，而未深知术数者也。)皇太子所读书多矣，而未深知术数者，不问书说也。夫多诵而不知其说，所谓劳苦而不为功。臣窃观皇太子材智高奇，驭射伎艺过人绝远，然于术数未有所守者，以陛下为心也。窃愿陛下幸择圣人之术可用今世者，以赐皇太子，因时使太子陈明于前。唯陛下裁察。”上善之，于是拜错为太子家令。以其辩得幸太子，太子家号曰“智囊”。

是时匈奴强，数寇边，上发兵以御之。错上言兵事，曰：

臣闻汉兴以来，胡虏数入边地，小入则小利，大入则大利；高后时再入陇西，攻城屠邑，驱略畜产；其后复入陇西，杀吏卒，大寇盗。窃闻战胜之威，民气百倍；败兵之卒，没世不复。

【今译】

没有必要知道干什么事，臣虽然愚笨，实在认为并非如此。看看上世君王，不能供奉宗庙而被臣子所胁迫杀害的原因，就在于不懂得刑名之术这门学问。皇太子所读书很多了，所以没有深入掌握刑名之术的原因，在于不深究书中论说的义理。多读而不知其中论述的道理，这就是劳而无功。臣看到皇太子才智高奇，驾驭、骑射技艺超绝出众，然而对于刑名之学还没有掌握，这与陛下的心思是有关的。臣希望陛下选择一些圣人之术，又可用于今世的，用以赐教皇太子，根据情况让太子陈述出来。望陛下明察、裁决。”皇上称善，于是拜授晁错为太子家令。由于他的善辩才能得宠于太子，在太子家中号称为“智囊”。

这时匈奴正强大，多次侵边，皇上发兵抵御。晁错上书论兵事，说：

臣听说汉兴以来，胡人多次侵入边地，小规模侵入就获得小利，大规模侵入就有大利；高后时再侵入陇西，攻城抢劫邑镇，驱掠畜产；之后又侵入陇西，杀害官兵，大举抢掠。臣听说战胜的威力，可使民气百倍；失败的兵卒，至死也不能振奋。从高后

of the Crown Prince. Some ministers may say that the Crown Prince does not need to know what things to do. Although I am a stupid minister, I truly believe the opposite. Looking at rulers of previous generations and why they could not preserve their ancestral temple but were coerced and killed by their courtiers, I find the reason to be that they did not understand the art of government and divination. The Crown Prince has read a lot, but he has no deep understanding of the art of government and divination, because he does not go into the principles in the books. To read much without knowing the principles is futile labor. I find that the Crown Prince is highly intelligent and extremely outstanding at riding and bowmanship, but he does not keep to the art of government and divination, and this has to do with Your Majesty's own attitude. I suggest that Your Majesty selects some of the arts of the sages appropriate for the present day, in which the Crown Prince may be instructed, so that he can make presentations according to the situation. I hope Your Majesty will observe this clearly and adjudicate." The Emperor approved the ideas, and appointed Chao Cuo as the household provisioner of the Prince. Because of his eloquence he became a favorite of the Prince, and was known to the family as "Brains."

At this time, the Huns were strong, invading the border area many times, so the emperor sent soldiers to resist them. Cuo submitted a memorial on military matters:

I heard that since the rise of Han, the barbarians have made incursions into the border areas, with a small profit after a small-scale invasion, and huge gains after a large-scale invasion. They invaded Longxi again in the time of Empress Gaozu, attacking and massacring towns, driving and looting livestock; later they invaded Longxi again, killing officials and soldiers, in addition to wholesale looting. They say that the power of victory can boost the people's morale a hundred times, while the soldiers after failure cannot be cheered up

【原文】

自高后以来，陇西三困于匈奴矣，民气破伤，亡有胜意。今兹陇西之吏，赖社稷之神灵，奉陛下之明诏，和辑士卒，底厉其节，起破伤之民以当乘胜之匈奴，用少击众，杀一王，败其众而(法曰)大有利。非陇西之民有勇怯，乃将吏之制巧拙异也。故兵法曰："有必胜之将，无必胜之民。"繇此观之，安边境，立功名，在于良将，不可不择也。

臣又闻用兵，临战合刃之急者三：一曰得地形，二曰卒服习，三曰器用利。兵法曰：丈五之沟，渐车之水，山林积石，经川丘阜，屮木所在，此步兵之地也，车骑二不当一。土山丘陵，曼衍相属，平原广野，此车骑之地，步兵十不当一。平陵相远，川谷居间，仰高临下，此弓弩之地也，短兵百不当一。两陈相近，平地浅(草)[屮]，可前可后，此长戟之地也，剑楯三不当一。(雚)[萑]苇竹萧，屮木蒙茏，支叶茂接，此矛鋋之地也，长

【今译】

以来，陇西三次被匈奴困扰，民气受到摧折伤害，没有取胜的信心。今天陇西的官吏，仰仗先祖神灵，奉行陛下明诏，和睦团结士卒，激励他们的气节意志，唤起受伤害的百姓来抵挡正气盛的匈奴，以少击众，杀死匈奴一王，对于击败众多士兵十分有利。不是陇西之民有勇怯之分，而是将吏表现得巧妙、拙笨有不同而已。因此兵法说："有必胜的将领，没有必胜的百姓。"由此看来，安定边境，建立功业，在于良将，不可不加以选择。

臣又听说用兵，临战交锋最紧急的有三件事：一是占领有利地形，二是士兵服从命令、训练有素，三是兵器精良、使用便利。兵法说：宽有丈五的沟渠，漫过车的水，山林和垒集的石块，长流之水、大的丘陵，草木生长之地，这是步兵用武之地，车兵骑兵在这里战斗二不当一。土山丘陵，连绵不断，平原旷野，是车、骑的用武之地，步兵在这里交战十不当一。高低悬殊，河谷居其中，居高临下，这是弓弩的用武之地，使用短兵器百不当一。两阵相临近，平地短草，可前可后，这是长戟兵器用武之地，使用剑盾三不当一。萑苇竹萧，草木葱茏，枝叶茂密，这是长矛短矛用武之地，使用长戟二不当一。道路曲屈，险阻交

all their lives. From the time of the Empress, Longxi has been plagued three times by the Huns, and the national morale has been injured, not confident of victory. Today's Longxi officials, relying on the gods of land and grains, carried out the wise imperial edicts, gathered soldiers, inspired their fine character, and aroused the low-spirited people to resist the triumphant Huns. They attacked the enemy though outnumbered, killing a king, gaining tremendously by defeating the Hun army. This was not due to the courage or cowardliness of the local people, but the different performance, clever or inept, of the generals and officials. As it says in the Art of War: "There are winning generals, but not winning commoners." From this, we see that the stability of the border, and the establishment of meritorious titles, depend on good generals, and we cannot but select them. I also heard that in the deployment of military forces, there are three most urgent affairs in a battle: first is to occupy a favorable terrain, second, disciplined and well-trained soldiers, third, excellent weapons, easy to use. The Art of War *says: when there are ditches ten feet and five wide, water just submerging the carriages, mountains and piled stones, long streams, large hills, the land with brush growth, these are used for infantry, one infantry soldier being the equal of two cavalry and chariots in fighting here. Undulating continuous hills, plains and wilderness are used for cavalry and chariots, one against ten infantry for fighting here. The mountaintop high above flat ground, with a river valley in between, looking down from above, this is the arena for crossbows, one is the equal of 100 short arms. When two front formations are close to each other on short-grass plains, this is fit for advance and reverse maneuvers, and is the terrain for long halberds, one the equal of three swords and shields. Reeds, bamboo, wormwood, this lush vegetation and dense foliage is used for spears short*

【原文】

戟二不当一。曲道相伏，险陒相薄，此剑楯之地也，弓弩三不当一。士不选练，卒不服习，起居不精，动静不集，趋利弗及，避难不毕，前击后解，与金鼓之(音)[指]相失，此不习勒卒之过也，百不当十。兵不完利，与空手同；甲不坚密，与袒裼同；弩不可以及远，与短兵同；射不能中，与亡矢同；中不能入，与亡镞同：此将不省兵之祸也，五不当一。故兵法曰：器械不利，以其卒予敌也；卒不可用，以其将予敌也；将不知兵，以其主予敌也；君不择将，以其国予敌也。四者，(国)[兵]之至要也。

臣又闻小大异形，强弱异势，险易异备。夫卑身以事强，小国之形也；合小以攻大，敌国之形也；以蛮夷攻蛮夷，中国之形也。今匈奴地形技艺与中国异。上下山阪，出入溪涧，中国之马

【今译】

错，这是剑盾的用武之地，使用弓弩三不当一。士不经选拔、训练，卒不熟练兵器，起居动作不精，动静不协调、不稳定，争夺利益不能到手，躲避灾难不迅速，前面攻击后面懈怠，与金鼓指挥脱节，这些都是不熟习训练管理部队的过错，这种士兵交战时百不当十。兵器不锐利，与空手相同；铠甲不坚硬，与袒肉露体相同；弩不能射到远处，与短兵器相同；射箭不中目标，与没有箭相同；中目标而不能入内，与没有箭头相同：这些是将领没有察看检查兵器所造成的灾祸，在这些情况下交战，五不当一。因此兵法说：兵器不锐利，就是把士兵交给了敌人；卒不可用，就是把将领交给了敌人；将领不知用兵谋略，就是把国君交给了敌人；国君不懂择将，就是把国家交给了敌人。这四方面，就是用兵要领。

臣又听说小与大形状是不同的，强与弱力量是不同的，险与易具有不同的防备。以低微之身去事奉强者是小国所表现的形态；联合小国攻打大国，是势均力敌之国的形态；以夷攻夷，是中原之国的形态。如今匈奴地形技艺与中原不同。上下山坡，出

and long, one for two against long halberds. Zigzagging roads hiding repeated evil obstacles are used for swords and shields, so one for three against crossbows. The sergeants are not selected, soldiers not trained, with their personal life unrefined, their movements uncoordinated and chaotic; failing to seize opportunities or avoid disasters completely, attacking in the front though vulnerable in the rear, out of touch with the command signals of drums and gongs; these are the bad results of not training and managing soldiers; 100 soldiers like this in battle equate to only 10. When weapons are not sharp, it is the same as empty-handedness; when armor is not hard, it is the same as a naked body; when crossbows cannot reach the distance, it is the same as short weapons; when the archer does not hit the target, it is the same as no arrows; when the arrow cannot penetrate, it is the same as no arrowhead; these are the dire results of generals not checking their weapons, worth one per five weapons in fighting. So The Art of War *says: "Without sharp weapons, it is to give soldiers to the enemy; with soldiers not available, it is to give generals to the enemy; when the generals do not know military strategy, it is to give the lord to the enemy; when the monarch does not select his generals, it is to hand over the state to the enemy." These four areas are the essentials of military service.*

I was also told that there are different shapes, small and large, different forces strong and weak, and different armaments, risky and easy. To humble the self to serve the strong power means the form of a small country; to attack a large state by uniting small countries is the form of an evenly-matched country; to attack barbarians with barbarians is the form of the kingdom of the Central Plains. Now the lands of the Huns are different from the Central Plains in terrain and their skills are different too. For riding constantly uphill and

【原文】

弗与也；险道倾仄，且驰且射，中国之骑弗与也；风雨罢劳，饥渴不困，中国之人弗与也：此匈奴之长技也。若夫平原易地，轻车突骑，则匈奴之众易挠乱也；劲弩长戟，射疏及远，则匈奴之弓弗能格也；坚甲利刃，长短相杂，游弩往来，什伍俱前，则匈奴之兵弗能当也；材官驺发，矢道同的，则匈奴之革笥木荐弗能支也；下马地斗，剑戟相接，去就相薄，则匈奴之足弗能给也：此中国之长技也。以此观之，匈奴之长技三，中国之长技五。陛下又兴数十万之众，以诛数万之匈奴，众寡之计，以一击十之术也。

虽然，兵，凶器；战，危事也。以大为小，以强为弱，在俛卬之间耳。夫以人之死争胜，跌而不振，则悔之亡及也。帝王之道，出于万全。今降胡义渠蛮夷之属来归谊者，其众数千，饮食

【今译】

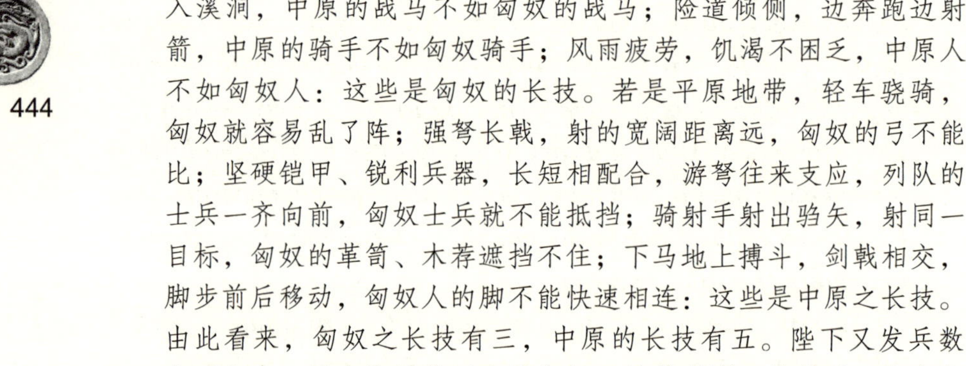

入溪涧，中原的战马不如匈奴的战马；险道倾侧，边奔跑边射箭，中原的骑手不如匈奴骑手；风雨疲劳，饥渴不困乏，中原人不如匈奴人：这些是匈奴的长技。若是平原地带，轻车骁骑，匈奴就容易乱了阵；强弩长戟，射的宽阔距离远，匈奴的弓不能比；坚硬铠甲、锐利兵器，长短相配合，游弩往来支应，列队的士兵一齐向前，匈奴士兵就不能抵挡；骑射手射出驺矢，射同一目标，匈奴的革笥、木荐遮挡不住；下马地上搏斗，剑戟相交，脚步前后移动，匈奴人的脚不能快速相连：这些是中原之长技。由此看来，匈奴之长技有三，中原的长技有五。陛下又发兵数十万之众，用来诛杀数万人的匈奴，计算众寡，就是以一击十之术了。

虽然是这样，兵器还是凶器；战争还是危险的事情。不懂用兵之道和方法，就会以大为小，由强变弱，这种变化也仅仅在于俯仰之间那样容易。用人的死亡换取胜利，就会失足而不振，悔之不及。帝王成功之道，立足于万全之策。今天来投降的胡人义渠蛮夷等是归义的，部众有几千人，他们的饮食、长技与匈奴相

downhill, in and out of streams, our battle horses are inferior to theirs; shooting arrows while riding on dangerous steep roads, our riders are no match for theirs; braving storms without fatigue, not wearying in hunger and thirst, our people are not as good as the Huns: these are the Huns' superior skills. However, if it is easy, level terrain, using fleet horses and light chariots, the Hun throngs will be easy to disrupt; with our strong crossbows and long halberds, shot across the wide distance, the Hun bows cannot match ours; with our hard armor and sharp blades, swords of different lengths, crossbow maneuvering, advances of massed marched ranks, the Hun soldiers cannot resist us; with our strong archers shooting arrows simultaneously at the same targets, the leather armor and wooden shields of the Huns could not resist; when we dismount for fighting on the ground, and engage with swords and halberds, moving forward and then back, the Huns cannot order their feet fast enough: these are our people's superior skills. From this, we find the Huns to have three superior skills, while we are superior in five. Your Majesty has sent hundreds of thousands of soldiers to wipe out tens of thousands of Huns. In terms of the number of troops, this is a scheme to blow out ten with one.

Despite this, weapons are dangerous tools; and a war is a risky affair. And it is the matter of a twinkling of an eye to turn a large country into a smaller one, or go from strong to weak. To sacrifice the lives of people in exchange for victory, will cause the nation to stumble and slump, and it will be too late for regrets. The Imperial Way to success is based on a surefire plan. Now the Yiqu barbarians who once surrendered to the Huns have been converted to righteousness; they are thousands in number, and their diet and special skills are the same as the Huns. We could give them hard armor and padded coats,

【原文】

长技与匈奴同，可赐之坚甲絮衣，劲弓利矢，益以边郡之良骑。令明将能知其习俗和辑其心者，以陛下之明约将之。即有险阻，以此当之；平地通道，则以轻车材官制之。两军相为表里，各用其长技，衡加之以众，此万全之术也。

传曰："狂夫之言，而明主择焉。"臣错愚陋，昧死上狂言，唯陛下财择。

文帝嘉之，乃赐错玺书宠答焉，曰："皇帝问太子家令：上书言兵体三章，闻之。书言'狂夫之言，而明主择焉'。今则不然。言者不狂，而择者不明，国之大患，故在于此。使夫不明择于不狂，是以万听而万不当也。"

错复言守边备塞，劝农力本，当世急务二事，曰：

臣闻秦时北攻胡貉，筑塞河上，南攻杨粤，置戍卒焉。其起兵而攻胡、粤者，非以卫边地而救民死也，贪戾而欲广大也，故功未立而天下乱。且夫起兵而不知其势，战则为人禽，屯则卒积

【今译】

同，可以赐给他们硬铠甲棉衣，强弓利矢，再增加边郡的良骑。让明将能知他们的习俗，使他们和睦相处，就在于用陛下之明智去节制统帅。要是有了险阻，用这一办法对付；平地通道，就用轻车骑手去对付。两军互相配合，协同作战，各用其长技，横向上使用众多士兵，这就是万全之策。

书传上说："狂夫之言，请明主选择。"臣晁错愚笨鄙陋，冒犯死罪进上狂言，望陛下裁择。

文帝十分赞扬晁错的陈述，便赐给他玺书回答，说："皇帝问太子家令：上书所讲兵事三章，听到了。书曰'狂夫之言，而明主择焉'。如今不是这样。言者不狂，而择取的人却不明智，国家的大患，就在于此。要是让不明智去选择不狂，就是听一万条上书也是有一万次对付不了。"

晁错又论守边备塞，鼓励农耕，致力本业，当世的二件紧急要务，说：

臣听说秦朝北攻胡、貉，在黄河上修筑工事，南攻杨、粤，安置了戍守士卒。他们发兵攻胡、粤的目的，并非保卫边地、救助死亡，而是贪图扩大，因此功业尚未建立天下就大乱起来。要

strong bows and sharp arrowheads, and then add good cavalry from the frontier prefectures. So order your wise generals that understand their practices and desires to win their hearts and minds and so command them under Your Majesty's wise covenant. If there are risky obstacles, combat them with these reserves; on flat ground and wide roads, just contain them with light chariots and strong bow strikers. The two armed forces, each with special skills, would complement each other, then deploy the massed ranks in crosswise fashion. This is a surefire plan.

According to a book: "The words of a mad man, the wise monarch will select." Your servant is stupid and shallow, but I take the liberty to submit my mad words, and I hope the wise monarch will choose at his discretion.

Emperor Wendi praised Chao Cuo, and gave him his sealed edict as his answer. It read: "The Emperor asked the Household Provisioner of the Prince, and heard the three chapters on military matters in the memorial. The book reads: 'The words of a mad man, the wise monarch will select.' This is not the present case. The speaker is not mad, nor is the selector wise: that is the tragedy of the country. If the unwise man is to select a man not mad then even if he heard 10,000 proposals he would fail to deal with any one of them."

Chao Cuo also elaborated on what he saw as the urgent priorities of the age - guarding the frontiers and preparing frontier garrisons, as well as encouraging agriculture as the primary occupation. He argued:

I heard that Qin attacked the Huns and the Mo in the north, constructing fortifications on the Yellow River; it attacked Yang and Yue in the south, placing frontier garrisons there. They invaded north and south, with no thought of defending the frontier, or saving the people from death, but greedily seeking to expand, so before any meritorious deeds had been established

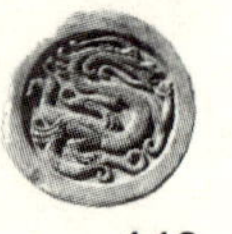

【原文】

死。夫胡貉之地，积阴之处也，木皮三寸，冰厚六尺，食肉而饮酪，其人密理，鸟兽毳毛，其性能寒。杨粤之地少阴多阳，其人疏理，鸟兽希毛，其性能暑。秦之戍卒不能其水土，戍者死于边，输者偾于道。秦民见行，如往弃市，因以谪发之，名曰“谪戍”。先发吏有谪及赘婿、贾人，后以尝有市籍者，又后以大父母、父母尝有市籍者，后入闾，取其左。发之不顺，行者深怨，有背畔之心。凡民守战至死而不降北者，以计为之也。故战胜守固则有拜爵之赏，攻城屠邑则得其财卤以富家室，故能使其众蒙矢石，赴汤火，视死如生。今秦之发卒也，有万死之害，而亡铢两之报，死事之后不得一算之复，天下明知祸烈及已也。陈胜行戍，

【今译】

是发兵而不知道所处的形势，交战就会被人擒获，屯守就会让士卒老死在边地。胡、貉之地是阴寒之处，草木生长出三寸，而冰冻厚达六尺，食肉饮酪，人们肌肉紧密，鸟兽长着细毛，很能耐寒。杨、粤之地少阴多阳，人们的肌肉疏松，鸟兽长着稀毛，性能耐暑热。秦朝的戍卒不能适应边地水土，戍守士卒死在边境，运输的士卒、民工跌死在路上。秦民上路，如赴刑场，因此政府就强制征发，名曰“谪戍”。先征发有罪被贬官吏及上门女婿、小商贩，然后征发曾经入过商人户籍的，又往后是征发祖父母、父母曾经入过商人户籍的，最后征发居住在闾左的所有穷人。征发不顺利，上路的服役人深切怨恨，有背叛之心。凡是百姓在防守、攻战中宁死而不降敌，就是用计谋实现的。因此战胜固守就应有拜爵之赏赐，攻城掠地就要夺取战利品使士兵家室富足，所以能让士众甘愿冒着箭矢和石块，赴汤蹈火，视死如归。今天秦朝征发士卒，有万死的灾害，而无铢两之报赏，战死之后不能免除一算钱的赋税，天下人清楚地看到灾祸的火焰已经烧到身边。

the empire was in chaos. If you send your troops without knowing the situation, you are likely to be taken captive, or have them die of old age garrisoned at the frontier. The Huns and Mo live in a chilly place, where the ground freezes six feet thick and vegetation grows only three inches high. With their diet of meat and yoghurt, the people there have solid muscles, and the birds and beasts there have thick plumages and coats, to endure the bitter cold. Yang and Yue are more yang *than* yin, *and people there have loose muscles, while the birds and beasts are lightly plumed and coated, so they can all endure heat. Qin's soldiers garrisoned on the frontier were not accustomed to the local environment and climate, so soldiers died on the border, and transport workers fell to their death on the roads. Qin people went on the road, as if they were headed to the execution ground, so the Qin government would force the disgraced to go, hence the name "exile garrison." They first sent banished officials, uxorilocal husbands and small traders, and then former merchants, then those whose grandparents or parents had been merchants, then at last all the poor people living in the left gateways of the villages. The levy did not go smoothly, and those on the road forced into service harbored deep resentment, were minded to betray. All those who defend or attack to the utmost, preferring death to surrender or retreat, are those who have been treated with strategy. Therefore, those who win or hold out should be rewarded by raising their ranks and posts; having conquered and taken new territories they could seize booty to enrich the soldiers, and thus the army would be willing to brave bombardment, ready to go through hell and high water, unafraid of death. But when Qin drafted soldiers, they faced 10,000-death disasters, without being awarded a single cash; dying for the country did not bring exemption from one* suan *in taxes, so all under Heaven clearly saw the severe scourge which*

【原文】

至于大泽，为天下先倡，天下从之如流水者，秦以威劫而行之之敝也。

胡人衣食之业不著于地，其势易以扰乱边竟。何以明之？胡人食肉饮酪，衣皮毛，非有城郭田宅之归居，如飞鸟走兽于广壄，美草甘水则止，草尽水竭则移。以是观之，往来转徙，时至时去，此胡人之生业，而中国之所以离南晦也。今使胡人数处转牧行猎于塞下，或当燕代，或当上郡、北地、陇西，以候备塞之卒，卒少则入。陛下不救，则边民绝望而有降敌之心；救之，少发则不足，多发，远县才至，则胡又已去。聚而不罢，为费甚大；罢之，则胡复入。如此连年，则中国贫苦而民不安矣。

陛下幸忧边境，遣将吏发卒以治塞，甚大惠也。然令远方之卒守塞，一岁而更，不知胡人之能，不如选常居者，家室田作，

【今译】

陈胜前往戍边，到了大泽乡，为天下率先倡导起义，天下人从之如流水，就是因为秦朝用暴力强行征发劳役的恶果。

胡人衣食之业不固定在土地上，这就自然形成了轻易来扰乱边境的形势。怎么证明呢？胡人食肉饮酪，穿皮衣，没有城市田宅去居住，像飞鸟走兽在旷野，遇到甜美水草便停下来，草尽水竭便移走。由此看来，转移不定，时而到达，时而离去，这就是胡人的生存的职业，而在中原就会造成离开耕地的局面。如今让胡人在几处转移放牧，在塞边行猎，有时到燕、代，有时到上郡，有时到北地，有时到陇西，以便窥伺防守的戍卒，卒少就侵入。陛下不救，边民就绝望而产生降敌之心；去救，派兵少不足以抵抗胡人，多派，路途遥远，刚刚到达，胡人便已经离开。屯聚不退，费用太大，退回来，胡人又来入侵。如此连年，中原就贫苦而百姓不得安宁了。

陛下幸好担忧边界，遣将派兵整治边塞，大有好处。然而让远道而来的士卒守边塞，一年便轮换，不了解胡人的特长，不如

would hit them. When Chen Sheng was drafted to garrison the frontiers, arriving at Da Ze, he rose up, showing the rest of the country a lead, and all under Heaven followed him like streams. And this was the consequence of violent forced conscription by Qin.

The Huns do not depend on a fixed piece of land to provide food and clothing, and this makes it easy to disrupt our border regions. How to prove it? Barbarians eat meat and drink dairy, wear fur; they are without cities, fields and houses to return to live in, existing like animals and birds in the wilderness. When they encounter thick grass and sweet water they stop, moving on when the grass and water are exhausted. From this, we see the barbarians subsist by migrating to and fro, sometimes coming, and sometimes leaving, and the reason why the people in the Central Plains have to leave their farmland. Now we have the Huns on the move, grazing in several places and hunting under the Great Wall, sometimes in Yan and Dai, and sometimes in Shangjun, Beidi, and Longxi, watching for the defending troops at the fortress, and invading if our soldiers are few. If Your Majesty does not save them, the people living on the frontiers will be desperate and harbor thoughts of surrender to the enemy; if you do come to their aid, small detachments will not be enough to resist; if you send more, the Huns will have left before they cover the distance. If the troops are built up and have to stay there, the cost will be huge; if you call them off, the Huns will again invade. So year after year, the Central Plains will be destitute and the people restless.

Fortunately, Your Majesty is concerned about the border area, and has sent generals, officials and troops to consolidate the frontier, and there is much that is good about this. However, expeditionary soldiers are ordered to hold this frontier, on an annual rotation basis, which means they do not get to

【原文】

且以备之，以便为之高城深堑，具蔺石，布渠答，复为一城其内，城间百五十步。要害之处，通川之道，调立城邑，毋下千家，为中周虎落。先为室屋，具田器，乃募罪人及免徒复作令居之；不足，募以丁奴婢赎罪及输奴婢欲以拜爵者；不足，乃募民之欲往者，皆赐高爵，复其家。予冬夏衣，廪食，能自给而止。郡县之民得买其爵，以自增至卿。其亡夫若妻者，县官买予之。人情非有匹敌，不能久安其处。塞下之民，禄利不厚，不可使久居危难之地。胡人入驱而能止其所驱者，以其半予之，县官为赎其民。如是，则邑里相救助，赴胡不避死。非以德上也，欲全亲戚而利其财也。此与东方之(戎)[戍]卒不习地势而心畏胡者，功

【今译】

选拔常居的士卒，建立家室，耕种田地，就此守边。为了防守之便，就建造高城深沟。准备垒石，布下铁蒺藜，再造一城于城内，两城之间相距一百五十步。要害之处，河流经的路口，规划并建立城邑，计算城邑中居民不少于千家，城周围应设置防盗用的竹篾，先造居室，准备好农具，然后招募罪人及免去徒刑处罚一年劳役的人居住下来；不够数，招募用成丁奴婢赎罪的和用奴婢买爵的；再不够，便招募百姓想去的，一律赐给高爵位，免除全家赋役。发给冬夏衣服，供给饮食，能自给时停止供应。郡县百姓可以买爵位，可以买到高级爵位，可同列卿。他们有丧失丈夫或妻子的，由官府给买奴、买妻子、买衣服。人情上说，非有匹配，不能久居其处。塞下之民，利禄不厚，不可让他们永久居住在危难之地。胡人入侵抢掠，能阻止其抢掠的将被抢的一半财物奖给他，官府出价赎回被抢掳的百姓。这样，邑里就会互相救助，与胡人去交战就不怕死。所有这些，并不是让皇上立德义的，而是想保护亲戚生命财产。与东方戍卒不熟习地势又心畏胡

understand the Huns' skills. It is better to select soldiers for permanent residence, together with their families and allocated farmland, and protect the border by this means. To this end they will dig deep moats and construct high city walls, preparing with catapults and thorn-topped poles. We will build an inner wall within the wall, separated by 150 paces. At vulnerable points, the intersections by the rivers, we will plan and build cities and towns designed for no fewer than 1,000 resident households, to be protected with bamboo fences around the walls. We will first build houses, ready with farming tools, to be occupied by criminals and convicts impressed for labor service in lieu of prison punishment; if not enough, then slaves given by their masters to purchase pardons or aristocratic ranks, and then all those commoners who desire to go. They will all be given high titles of honorary nobility, exempt from family taxation or corvee. They will be supplied with winter and summer clothes, food from the official warehouse, until they become self-sufficient. The people in prefectures and counties can buy the titles, up to the high titles on ministerial level. Those who have lost a husband or wife will be remarried at the expense of the imperial government. It is human nature that without a spouse, people will not remain settled long in their place. People near the border are not well paid and endowed, so we should not allow them to live permanently in the land of distress. Those who are able to stop the Huns from raiding and looting will be awarded half of what is taken from the Huns, and the government will redeem who are taken captive by them. Thus, the neighborhoods and villages will aid each other, not fearing death by doing battle with the Huns. And this they will do, not for the grace of the Emperor, but to protect the life and property of their kin. Compared to the soldiers from the east who are unfamiliar with the terrain and fear the barbarians at

【原文】

相万也。以陛下之时，徙民实边，使远方无屯戍之事，塞下之民父子相保，亡系虏之患，利施后世，名称圣明，其与秦之行怨民，相去远矣。

上从其言，募民徙塞下。错复言：

陛下幸募民相徙以实塞下，使屯戍之事益省，输将之费益寡，甚大惠也。下吏诚能称厚惠，奉明法，存恤所徙之老弱，善遇其壮士，和辑其心而勿侵刻，使先至者安乐而不思故乡，则贫民相募而劝往矣。臣闻古之徙远方以实广虚也，相其阴阳之和，尝其水泉之味，审其土地之宜，观其屮木之饶，然后营邑立城，制里割宅，通田作之道，正阡陌之界，先为筑室，家有一堂二内，门户之闭，置器物焉，民至有所居，作有所用，此民所以轻

【今译】

人的情况相比，功劳要高出万倍。陛下这个时候，徙民充实边塞，让远方的百姓没有屯戍负担，边塞的百姓又父子相保，没有被俘虏的后患，好处流传给后世，陛下就是圣明之君，这和秦朝去服役的怨民相比，利害相差太大了。

皇上听从了晁错的建议，募民迁徙到边塞去。晁错又说：

陛下幸好募民迁徙到边塞去，使屯戍之事大大节省，运送物资的费用更加减少，益处显著。下面官吏真能称得起厚惠，执行英明办法，关心迁来的老弱，善待壮士，对他们宽柔和睦而不侵害，让先来的安乐而不思念故土，那么贫民便互相招请、勉励。臣闻古代迁徙到远方去充实空虚之地，要察看阴阳的调和，尝尝水泉之味，查一查土地好坏，观察草木的长势，然后营造城邑，编制里区，划割住宅，开通通向田地的道路，确定田间边界，先造住室，一家有一堂二室，有门窗的开闭，设置家具，百姓来就可以居住，耕作有农具，这就是百姓所以肯轻易离乡而乐意到新

heart, their merits will be 10,000 times higher. At this time in Your Majesty's reign, you should resettle people to stiffen the frontier, so that the distant people are freed from the burden of sending soldiers to garrison, and the frontier people can protect their sons and fathers, without worrying about being captured. Then the benefits will spread to future generations, and Your Majesty will be called a wise monarch. This will be in enormous contrast to Qin, with its mobilization of resentful and discontented conscripts.

The Emperor listened to his proposal, and recruited people to relocate to the frontier. Chao Cuo followed up with these further ideas:

Happily, Your Majesty mobilized people to be moved to the frontier region to strengthen our borders, thereby making great savings in terms of frontier defenses and reducing the cost of transporting goods. The benefits are plain to see. If the lower officials are really kind and beneficial in implementing the wise decree and care for the elderly and weak migrants, treat the warriors well, treat them generously and harmoniously rather than exploit them, so that the first-comers are happy and do not miss the homeland, then the poor will recruit each other, and persuade others to go there. I heard that in ancient times, migration to distant lands in order to populate the empty places took place only after looking at the harmony of yin *and* yang*, trying the taste of the spring water, checking out the adequacy of the land, observing the luxuriance of vegetation; then they created castle towns, zoned neighborhoods, prepared residential areas, opened roads into the fields, and determined the field boundaries. But first they built accommodation, giving each family one living room and two bedrooms, with opening and closing doors and windows and furniture and utensils all provided. When people arrived they had a place to live,*

【原文】

去故乡而劝之新(色)[邑]也。为置医巫，以救疾病，以修祭祀，男女有昏，生死相恤，坟墓相从，种树畜长，室屋完安，此所以使民乐其处而有长居之心也。

臣又闻古之制边县以备敌也，使五家为伍，伍有长；十长一里，里有假士；四里一连，连有假五百；十连一邑，邑有假候：皆择其邑之贤材有护，习地形知民心者，居则习民于射法，出则教民于应敌。故卒伍成于内，则军正定于外。服习以成，勿令迁徙，幼则同游，长则共事。夜战声相知，则足以相救；昼战目相见，则足以相识；驩爱之心，足以相死。如此而劝以厚赏，威以重罚，则前死不还踵矣。所徙之民非壮有材力，但费衣粮，不可

【今译】

邑去的原因。要给他们准备医生巫师，以便治疗疾病，祭祀祖先、神灵，男婚女嫁，生死相照应，坟墓相跟从，种树养畜，室屋完整安全，这些足以让百姓乐于居其处而有长住久留之心。

臣又听说古代设置边地县城是为了防备敌人侵犯的，让五家为一伍，有伍长；十长为一里，里有假士；四里一连，连有假五百；十连一邑，邑有假侯：各长都是邑中贤才又有保护能力，熟习地形和民心，闲居就让百姓练习射箭，外出就教民如何应敌。因此对内是卒伍编制，对外就是军政制度。训练完成之后，就不许再迁徙，幼年时同游，成年后就共事。夜战凭声音认出自己人，便足以互相救护；白天作战眼睛能看到，便足以相认；爱护之心，足以拼死相救。这样，用厚赏劝导，用重罚威慑，那么死亡在前面也不会转回身退逃。所迁徙之民不是健壮有材力的人，只是消耗衣粮者，不能使用；虽然有勇力，没有良好官吏，

complete with farming implements; and this is why the people so easily left their hometowns and were happy to go to the new garrisons. They were provided with doctors and shamans to cure their diseases, and to help worship their ancestors and gods. Men and women could marry, to take care of each other in life and death, and their graves would lie next to each other. They grew trees and raised livestock, so their rooms and houses were complete and secure. Through these measures the people were happy to live there and intended to remain there long term.

I was also told that the ancient frontier county towns were set up to prepare against an enemy assault, with five households to a wu, *led by a corporal; ten of these* wu *made a neighborhood, led by a village commandant; four neighborhoods made a company, led by an aggregation commandant; ten companies made one city, led by a district commandant: all of them were talented people chosen from the whole city because of their moral rectitude, and knowledge of the terrain and public opinion. In the slack season, they had the people practice archery; outside, they taught them how to meet the enemy. So domestically the army units were established, and externally the military and political system was complete. Once training was complete, they were not allowed to move from the area, so they would play together as children, and become comrades as adults. During night fighting, they would recognize the voices of their own side, sufficient to aid each other; in daylight combat, they could see with their eyes and be able to recognize each other; loving each other, they would be happy to die to rescue others. In this way, together with the incentive of heavy rewards, and the deterrence of severe penalties, they would die charging forward rather than turn back in retreat. If the migrants were not robust and muscular, but mere consumers of food and*

【原文】

用也；虽有材力，不得良吏，犹亡功也。

陛下绝匈奴不与和亲，臣窃意其冬来南也，壹大治，则终身创矣。欲立威者，始于折胶，来而不能困，使得气去，后未易服也。愚臣亡识，唯陛下财察。

后诏有司举贤良文学士，错在选中。上亲策诏之，曰：

惟十有五年九月壬子，皇帝曰：昔者大禹勤求贤士，施及方外，四极之内，舟车所至，人迹所及，靡不闻命，以辅其不逮；近者献其明，远者通厥聪，比善戮力，以翼天子。是以大禹能亡失德，夏以长楙。高皇帝亲除大害，去乱从，并建豪英，以为官师，为谏争，辅天子之阙，而翼戴汉宗也。赖天之灵，宗庙之福，方内以安，泽及四夷。今朕获执天子之正，以承宗庙之祀，朕既不德，又不敏，明弗能烛，而智不能治，此大夫之所著闻

【今译】

和无功是一样的。

陛下断绝与匈奴和亲，臣估计今冬胡人会南来，重创胡人一次，便永久受创。想确立威严，必须从使用弓弩开始，来犯而不能重创，让敌人得胜而去，以后就不易降服了。愚臣无识，希望陛下裁察。

后来下诏朝廷官员推荐贤良文学之士，晁错也在推举之列。皇上亲自策诏，说：

十五年九月壬子日，皇帝说："以前大禹广求贤士，扩及到境外，四方边远的尽头以内，舟车所能达到的地方，人迹能去之处，无不听命，以弥补其施政之缺陷；近者献出明亮，远者献出智慧，和善勉力，以助天子。所以大禹能不失去德政，夏朝长久盛美。高皇帝亲除大害，去祸乱之踪迹，选拔豪杰英才，作为一官之长，极尽力争提出劝谏，弥补天子朝政的缺陷，而拥戴汉家王朝。幸赖上天之灵，宗庙之福，天下安定，延及到四方边界各民族。今朕即天子正位，以继承宗庙的祭祀，朕既没有高德，又不聪敏，明亮度不能照射、洞察，智慧不能使国家大治，这是诸

clothing, they could not be used; although there was valor, without good officials it would be equivalent to uselessness.

Your Majesty has broken with the policy of marriage alliances to pacify the Huns. I privately estimate that the Huns will come south this winter. Once punished severely, the barbarians will be permanently traumatized. To show our invincible might, we must start from the making of crossbows. If we allow the invaders to win, without inflicting heavy casualties on them, it will not be easy to subjugate them in the future. I humbly await Your Majesty's judgment of my foolish ideas.

Later, an edict ordered the officials in charge to recommend the worthy, excellent and learned, and Chao Cuo was among those selected. The emperor himself quizzed them on policy, saying:

On the 29th day of the ninth moon of the 15th year (165 BC), the Emperor said: "In the past, King Yu used frequently to seek talents, even as far as to the outside world, within the four remote territories, in order to compensate for his imperfect policy, and nobody disobeyed in the areas reached by the boats and chariots or visited by human beings; the people nearby gave their wisdom, and the remote people contributed their intelligence, and they harmoniously cooperated to help the Son of Heaven. That was why King Yu was able to maintain his benevolent rule, and the Xia Dynasty flourished long. Our Emperor Gaodi personally eliminated the great despot and the remains of chaos, set up gallant and outstanding figures as officials and remonstrators, to make up for the faults in the Son of Heaven's government, and support the House of Han. Thanks to the spirits of Heaven, the blessing of the ancestral temple, we enjoy domestic stability, and extend our grace to the four borders. Now I am formally enthroned as the Son of Heaven, to continue the ancestral worship, but I am neither virtuous or smart, nor wise enough to discern or intelligent enough to

【原文】

也。故诏有司、诸侯王、三公、九卿及主郡吏，各帅其志，以选贤良明于国家之大体，通于人事之终始，及能直言极谏者，各有人数，将以匡朕之不逮。二三大夫之行当此三道，朕甚嘉之，故登大夫于朝，亲谕朕志。大夫其上三道之要，及永惟朕之不德，吏之不平，政之不宣，民之不宁，四者之阙，悉陈其志，毋有所隐。上以荐先帝之宗庙，下以兴愚民之休利，著之于篇，朕亲览焉，观大夫所以佐朕，至与不至。书之，周之密之，重之闭之。兴自朕躬，大夫其正论，毋枉执事。乌虖，戒之！二三大夫其帅志毋怠！

错对曰：

平阳侯臣窋、汝阴侯臣灶、颍阴侯臣何、廷尉臣宜昌、陇西太守臣昆邪所选贤良太子家令臣错昧死再拜言：臣窃闻古之贤主莫不求贤以为辅翼，故黄帝得力牧而为五帝[先]，大禹得咎繇而

【今译】

大夫看得见的。因此下诏有司、诸侯王、三公、九卿及郡守，各凭自己的意志，选出贤良优秀人才，深明国家大体，通晓人事的变化，敢于直言极力劝谏的，各有若干人数，将用来辅佐匡正朕的不完备之处。有二三名大夫可以论述国体、人事、劝谏三方面的道理，朕十分嘉许，因此让诸大夫登朝，亲自告谕朕的旨意。大夫应陈述国体、人事、直谏三道要领，深思朕德之缺乏之处，官吏办事不公正，政事不宣通，百姓不安宁，四者缺漏、错误之处，全部讲出自己的意见，不要隐瞒。上可以进献先帝之宗庙，下可以兴办愚民的美好利益，写成篇章，朕要亲自阅览，观察大夫用来辅佐朕的建议，是尽到了责任还是没有把话说完、说透。写下来，周密慎重地封闭起来，由朕亲自拆封，大夫们应正言直论，不要顾忌当权官吏的阻挠。啊，要切戒啊！被推荐来的二三位大夫应抒发自己的意志，不要怠慢！”

晁错回答说：

平阳侯臣曹窋、汝阴侯臣夏侯灶、颍阴侯臣灌何、廷尉臣宜昌、陇西太守臣公孙昆邪所推荐贤良太子家令臣晁错冒死再拜说：臣听说古代英贤之主无不求贤士来辅佐自己，因此黄帝得

create national peace and order. This is clearly visible to all the grand masters. So the officers in charge, princes, great nobles of the realm, chief ministers of the state, and prefecture governors are hereby ordered, each of their own will, to select the worthy and excellent, well versed in the state affairs in general, with knowledge of human vicissitudes, outspoken and insistent remonstrators, and a certain number in each category, ready to remedy my imperfect policy. Two or three grand masters could deal with these three aspects, and I very much appreciate them, so I promoted the grand masters to the Court, and personally told them my intention. The grand masters should demonstrate the essentials of the three aspects - state affairs, human vicissitudes, and remonstration - and ponder my lack of virtue, the officials' injustice, inconsistent policies, and the unease of the people. About inadequacy in these four areas, you should all speak your mind, and not hide anything. You can offer them in the ancestral temple of late emperors; and promote the benefits of the ignorant masses. Prepare them in written essays, and I will personally read them, and observe the grand masters' supportive suggestions, to see if you have done your duties or not. Write them down, carefully considered and fully sealed, to be opened by me personally. The grand masters should be upright and straightforward. Do not be deterred by the officials in power. Be on guard! You should express your own will. Do not neglect!

Chao Cuo answered:

Chao Cuo, Household Provisioner of the Prince, a worthy and excellent recommended by Marquis of Pingyang Cao Zhu, Marquis of Ruyin Xiahou Zhao, Marquis of Yingyin Guan He, Chamberlain of Law Enforcement Yichang, Governor of Longxi Prefecture Gongsun Hunye, makes bold to say: I heard that all the ancient sage kings sought talents for assistance,

【原文】

为三王祖，齐桓得筦子而为五伯长。今陛下讲于大禹及高皇帝之建豪英也，退托于不明，以求贤良，让之至也。臣窃观上世之传，若高皇帝之建功业，陛下之德厚而得贤佐，皆有司之所览，刻于玉版，藏于金匮，历之春秋，纪之后世，为帝者祖宗，与天地相终。今臣窋等乃以臣错充赋，甚不称明诏求贤之意。臣错草茅臣，亡识知，昧死上愚对，曰：

诏策曰"明于国家大体"，愚臣窃以古之五帝明之。臣闻五帝神圣，其臣莫能及，故自亲事，处于法宫之中，明堂之上；动静上配天，下顺地，中得人，故众生之类亡不覆也，根著之徒亡不载也；烛以光明，亡偏异也；德上及飞鸟，下至水虫，草木诸产，皆被其泽。然后阴阳调，四时节，日月光，风雨时，膏露降，五谷孰，祅孽灭，贼气息，民不疾疫，河出图，洛出书，神

【今译】

力牧而在五帝中名列首位，大禹得咎繇成了三王的鼻祖，齐桓公得管仲成了五霸之长。今陛下讲到从大禹至高皇帝之选拔豪杰英才，自谦不明，以求贤士辅佐，责备之至。臣观上世史传，像高皇帝一样建功立业，陛下之大德从而得到贤士辅佐，都是有司看到的，刻在记录功勋的玉版上，藏在金匮之中，经历年月，传至后世，为帝王所宗仰，与天地相终始。今臣曹窋等把晁错拿来充数，很不合明诏寻求贤良的旨意。臣晁错草茅之臣，没有见识，冒死献上愚对，说：

诏策曰："明于国家大体"，愚臣自以古代的五帝来说明它。臣闻五帝神智圣明，那些大臣都不如五帝圣明，因此亲自处理政务，在正殿之中，宣明政教的明堂之上。处事上符合天时，下顺应地利，中得人和。因此众生之类无不被覆盖，生长在土地中的万物无不被托载；用光明来照耀，没有偏异；恩德上及飞鸟，下至水虫，草木诸产物，都受到润泽。然后阴阳调和，四季有节，日月生光，风雨适时，膏露普降，五谷丰登，妖孽灭绝，毒气息灭，民不生疾病，黄河现出图，洛水现出书，神龙到来，

so the Yellow Emperor recruited Li Mu, and ranked first in the Five Emperors, King Yu got Gaoyao and became the originator of Three Kings, Duke Huan of Qi became the first of Five Hegemons because of Master Guan. Your Majesty talked about the selection of gallant and outstanding figures by King Yu and Emperor Gaodi on pretext of inadequate wisdom, in order to recruit the worthy and excellent, and the modesty is extreme. I read the history of the previous reigns, and just as Gaodi performed meritorious deeds in establishing his empire, so Your Majesty has virtue in abundance to be assisted by the talents, which is seen by officials in charge and carved on jade pages hidden in Golden Closets. And this record will endure through the ages, to be communicated to future generations, as the example to emperors, lasting as long as heaven and earth. Today Cao Zhu and others took Chao Cuo to make up the numbers, quite unworthy of the wise edict seeking out virtuous talents. Chao Cuo, a rustic courtier with little insight, hereby makes bold to present a stupid policy reply, and says:

The imperial policy topic is: "well versed in state affairs in general." I will humbly try to illustrate this with the Five Emperors in ancient times. I heard that the Five Emperors were sages, and their policy was beyond their ministers, so they dealt with government affairs in person, in the main palace or the Hall of Enlightened Rule. They acted in line with Heaven above, following Earth below, and humanely in the middle. Therefore, all living beings were protected, and all things grown in all land were supported. They used light to shine without exception; and their grace extended to the birds of the air above and water bugs and vegetation below; all received nurture. Then yin *and* yang *were in harmony, the seasons were normal, the sun and the moon bright, wind and rain timely, manna fell, harvests were bumper, the supernatural extinct, toxic* qi *stopped, the*

【原文】

龙至，凤鸟翔，德泽满天下，灵光施四海。此谓配天地，治国大体之功也。

诏策曰“通于人事终始”，愚臣窃以古之三王明之。臣闻三王臣主俱贤，故合谋相辅，计安天下，莫不本于人情。人情莫不欲寿，三王生而不伤也；人情莫不欲富，三王厚而不困也；人情莫不欲安，三王扶而不危也；人情莫不欲逸，三王节其力而不尽也。其为法令也，合于人情而后行之；其动众使民也，本于人事然后为之。取人以己，内恕及人。情之所恶，不以强人；情之所欲，不以禁民。是以天下乐其政，归其德，望之若父母，从之若流水；百姓和亲，国家安宁，名位不失，施及后世。此明于人情终始之功也。

【今译】

凤凰飞翔，德泽遍布天下，灵光施至四海。这就是配天应地，治国大体的基本内容。

诏策曰“通于人事终始”，愚臣用古代三王来说明。臣闻三王君臣都贤明，因此合谋相辅助，计谋安定天下，无不从人情出发。人情无不想长寿，三王保护人们的生命而不加以伤害；人情无不想富，三王让人们财富丰厚而不使人穷困；人情无不想安宁，三王维持社会秩序而不去危害人民；人情无不想舒适，三王节省人力而不竭尽民力。三王制订法令，合于人情然后执行；发动民众兴办事业，从人事出发然后去实行。以己之心为根据来要求别人，把自己的好恶也用到别人身上。自己心里讨厌的，不可强加于人；自己心里想要办的，不要禁止人们去办。这样的话天下就欢迎政府的政令，佩服政府的恩德，敬仰他们就像父母一样，像流水一样跟从他们；百姓和睦亲爱，国家安宁，名分地位的秩序不混乱，延续到后代。这些就是明了人事终始的人事之道。

people did not get diseases; then a fairy horse carried the Map out of the Yellow River, and the divine turtle showed the Diagram from Luohe River; the Dragon arrived, Phoenix flew, and their grace filled all under heaven, and their aura covered the four seas. This means the achievement of government in general, in line with heaven and earth.

The imperial policy topic is: "knowledge of human vicissitudes." I will humbly try to illustrate this with reference to the ancient Three Kings. I heard that the Three Kings and their courtiers were all worthy, so they discussed their plans with assistants and their schemes to stabilize the world were all based on human nature. No human being does not desire longevity, so the Three Kings protected people's lives without harming them; no human being does not desire wealth, so they enriched people without distressing them; no human being does not desire peace, so they supported people without endangering them; no human being does not desire comfort, so the Three Kings saved manpower without exhausting their resources. When the Three Kings formulated laws, they made them in conformity with human nature before implementing them; and when they mobilized the people, they started on the basis of human vicissitudes. What was required from others was based on their own heart, and they forgave others' weaknesses as they did their own. What they disliked for themselves they did not impose on others; what their own hearts wanted to do they did not forbid others from doing it. In this way, the world welcomed their government, submitted willingly to their kindness, respected them as parents, following them like a stream; the people lived harmoniously and affectionately, so there was peace in the nation, no disruption in birthright, status and precedence, which extended to future ages. This is the achievement of familiarity with human vicissitudes.

【原文】

诏策曰“直言极谏”，愚臣窃以五伯之臣明之。臣闻五伯不及其臣，故属之以国，任之以事。五伯之佐之为人臣也，察身而不敢诬，奉法令不容私，尽心力不敢矜，遭患难不避死，见贤不居其上，受禄不过其量，不以亡能居尊显之位。自行若此，可谓方正之士矣。其立法也，非以苦民伤众而为之机陷也，以之兴利除害，尊主安民而救暴乱也。其行赏也，非虚取民财妄予人也，以劝天下之忠孝而明其功也。故功多者赏厚，功少者赏薄。如此，敛民财以顾其功，而民不恨者，知与而安己也。其行罚也，非以忿怒妄诛而从暴心也，以禁天下不忠不孝而害国者也。故罪大者罚重，罪小者罚轻。如此，民虽伏罪至死而不怨者，知罪罚之至，自取之也。立法若此，可谓平正之吏矣。法之逆者，请而

【今译】

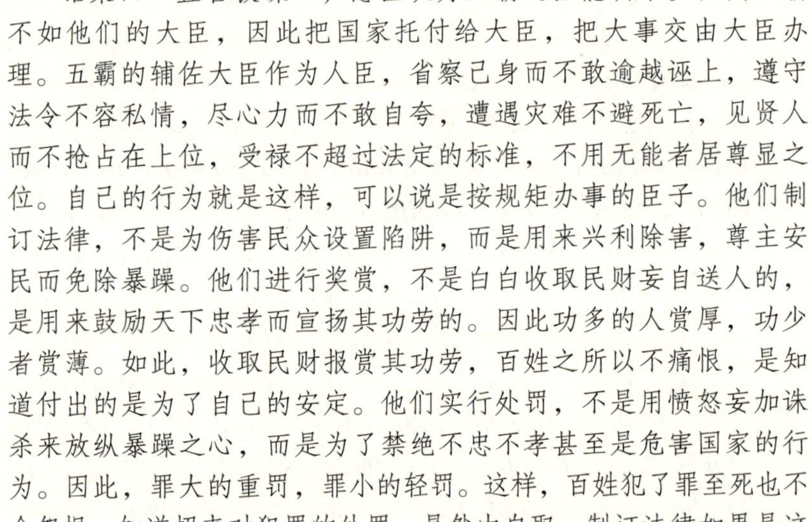

诏策曰“直言极谏”，愚臣认为五霸之臣能明了。臣闻五霸不如他们的大臣，因此把国家托付给大臣，把大事交由大臣办理。五霸的辅佐大臣作为人臣，省察己身而不敢逾越诬上，遵守法令不容私情，尽心力而不敢自夸，遭遇灾难不避死亡，见贤人而不抢占在上位，受禄不超过法定的标准，不用无能者居尊显之位。自己的行为就是这样，可以说是按规矩办事的臣子。他们制订法律，不是为伤害民众设置陷阱，而是用来兴利除害，尊主安民而免除暴躁。他们进行奖赏，不是白白收取民财妄自送人的，是用来鼓励天下忠孝而宣扬其功劳的。因此功多的人赏厚，功少者赏薄。如此，收取民财报赏其功劳，百姓之所以不痛恨，是知道付出的是为了自己的安定。他们实行处罚，不是用愤怒妄加诛杀来放纵暴躁之心，而是为了禁绝不忠不孝甚至是危害国家的行为。因此，罪大的重罚，罪小的轻罚。这样，百姓犯了罪至死也不会怨恨，知道招来对犯罪的处罚，是咎由自取。制订法律如果是这样，可以说是公平正直的官吏了。法律违背了情理，请求修改，

The imperial policy topic is: "outspoken and insistent remonstrators." I can elaborate this topic by reference to the ministers of the Five Hegemons. I heard that the Hegemons were not as capable as their ministers, so they entrusted their states to them and engaged them in their affairs. The Hegemons' assistants were their subjects, and so they did not dare to go further than mulling over issues nor did they cheat, but relied on compliance with laws instead of personal feelings; they dedicated their mental strength but dared not boast, nor tried to save their skin in the face of disasters; they did not lord it over talented people, or exceeded the statutory standards of salary; they did not employ incompetents in positions of respect. If their behavior was such, they could be said to be straightforward and upright scholars. They made laws, not to harm or set traps for people, but to promote what was beneficial and prevent what was harmful, to respect the monarch and reassure the public by preventing violent disorder. Their reward system relied not on unjustified requisitioning of people's property to squander in wanton gift giving, but to encourage and promote the loyal and filial by telling the world about their meritorious behavior. Therefore, the more deserving people enjoyed heavy rewards, and the less so were rewarded less. So, the people's wealth was collected to reward merit, but the practice was not resented, because they knew that they were paying for their own stability. They practiced punishments, not to indulge in violence by improper killing in anger, but in order to extirpate disloyal, unfilial behavior or even behavior endangering the nation. Therefore, those with more severe crimes got heavy penalties, while lesser offenders got light punishment. In this way, even those facing a death sentence could not complain , knowing that they themselves had invited it. If they made laws like this, they can be said to be fair

【原文】

更之，不以伤民；主行之暴者，逆而复之，不以伤国。救主之失，补主之过，扬主之美，明主之功，使主内亡邪辟之行，外亡骞污之名。事君若此，可谓直言极谏之士矣。此五伯之所以德匡天下，威正诸侯，功业甚美，名声章明。举天下之贤主，五伯与焉，此身不及其臣而使得直言极谏补其不逮之功也。今陛下人民之众，威武之重，德惠之厚，令行禁止之势，万万于五伯，而赐愚臣策曰“匡朕之不逮”，愚臣何足以识陛下之高明而奉承之！

诏策曰“吏之不平，政之不宣，民之不宁”，愚臣窃以秦事明之。臣闻秦始并天下之时，其主不及三王，而臣不及其佐，然功力不迟者，何也？地形便，山川利，财用足，民利战。其所与并者六国，六国者，臣主皆不肖，谋不辑，民不用，故当此

【今译】

不要用来伤民；君主执行的暴烈，就反过来恢复正确作法，不要用来伤害国家。补救国君的过失，发扬国君的美德，彰明国君的功劳，使国君内无邪僻行为，外无损害污秽的坏名声。侍奉国君到这种地步，可谓直言极力劝谏之士了。这正是五霸之所以用德政来扶正天下，威势校正诸侯，功业盛美，名声显赫的原因，举出天下贤明君主的话，五霸就是突出的代表，这是自己不如其臣而能用直言极谏弥补不足的办法。今天陛下统领人民的众多，威武的庄重，德惠的深厚，令行禁止之势，超过五霸万万倍，然而赐给愚臣的诏策说“弥补朕的不足”，愚臣怎么还能够认识到陛下的高明而要去奉承！

诏策曰“吏之不平，政之不宣，民之不宁”，愚臣用秦事来说明。臣闻秦开始兼并天下时，它的国君不及三王，而大臣也不及三王的辅臣，然而功业的建立并不迟慢，为什么？地形方便，山川有利，财富充足，民善于作战。它与并存的六国相比，六国臣主都是无能之辈，计谋不统一，民不能任使，因此，这时秦国

and honest officials. Laws contrary to reason, they requested to modify them so as not to harm the public; monarchs who performed violent acts, they guided back the correct approach, so as not to hurt the country. They remedied the faults of the monarchs, carried forward their virtues, and publicized their meritorious behavior, so that the monarchs perpetrated no evil behavior in their own domains, to harm and sully their reputation beyond. To serve the monarchs in this fashion, can be called outspoken and insistent remonstration. This is the reason why the Five Hegemons righted the world with their virtue, and corrected the other princes with their might; and why they had glorious exploits and illustrious names. Of worthy monarchs under heaven, the Five Hegemons were outstanding examples, and this is how they, although not as good as their ministers, could use outspoken and insistent remonstrators to make up for their own deficiencies. Today, Your Majesty's large population, military might, virtuous grace and strength in enforcing orders and prohibitions are a million times more than those of the Hegemons; even so, you gave your humble servant the imperial policy topic to "remedy my faulty policy." How could I comprehend Your Majesty's brilliant ideas and carry them out!

The imperial policy topic is: "the officials' injustice, the inconsistent policies, and the unease of the people." For this let me refer to Qin. I heard that when Qin was beginning to annex the world, its monarch was less wise than the Three Kings, and Qin ministers were not as capable as the kings' assistants. Even so, meritorious exploits came thick and fast; and why? Convenient terrain, advantageous mountains and rivers, sufficient wealth, and the people good at fighting. The six states coeval with Qin had incompetent ministers and monarchs and unconcerted planning, so that their people were not

【原文】

之时，秦最富强。夫国富强而邻国乱者，帝王之资也，故秦能兼六国，立为天子。当此之时，三王之功不能进焉。及其末涂之衰也，任不肖而信谗贼；宫室过度，耆欲亡极，民力罢尽，赋敛不节；矜奋自贤，群臣恐谀，骄溢纵恣，不顾患祸，妄赏以随(善)[喜]意，妄诛以快怒心，法令烦憯，刑罚暴酷，轻绝人命，身自射杀；天下寒心，莫安其处。奸邪之吏，乘其乱法，以成其威，狱官主断，生杀自恣。上下瓦解，各自为制。秦始乱之时，吏之所先侵者，贫人贱民也；至其中节，所侵者富人吏家也；及其末涂，所侵者宗室大臣也。是故亲疏皆危，外内咸怨，离散逋逃，人有走心。陈胜先倡，天下大溃，绝祀亡世，为异姓福。此吏不平，政不宣，民不宁之祸也。今陛下配天象地，覆露万民，绝秦

【今译】

最富强。国强而邻国混乱，最具备称帝的条件，所以秦国可以兼并六国，立为天子。当时，三王建立功业的办法不能被采纳．到后来衰败之时，任用不肖而听信谗贼；宫室超过限度，奢侈的欲望没有极限，民力疲尽，赋敛没有节制；妄自称贤，群臣因恐惧而争相阿谀，骄横放纵，不顾灾祸临头；妄赏以随个人喜好，妄诛以发泄怒心，法令烦苛残害下民，刑罚酷暴，轻易处决，亲自射杀人命；天下寒心，不能安定居住，奸邪官吏，利用乱法，横施威风，狱官判官，生杀专断。上下瓦解，各自为政。秦刚开始内乱时，官吏先侵夺的对象是贫人贱民；到中期，所侵害的是富人官吏之家；到了末路时，所侵害的是宗室大臣。因此，亲疏皆危，内外怨恨，离散逃亡，人有叛心。陈胜首倡，天下崩溃，断绝了宗庙祭祀，为异姓占有国家。这就是吏不平、政不宣、民不宁之祸。今陛下配天之时，象地之利，荫泽万民，除绝亡秦遗

available for use; thus the state of Qin was the most powerful and prosperous. When a state is powerful and prosperous and its neighbors in disarray, it is advantageous to its monarch. Therefore, Qin was able to swallow up the six states and establish its monarch as the Son of Heaven. At that time, the methods of the Three Kings could not have been adopted. Later, it went into terminal decline: it appointed unworthy people and listened to slanderous villains; its palaces were over-extravagant, with no limit to the luxurious desires; its popular resources were exhausted, taxation and corvee out of control. It arrogantly claimed itself to worthy, so its courtiers were intimidated into flattery. It was conceited and self-indulgent, oblivious to disaster on the threshold. It wantonly rewarded to humor personal preference, and jumped to punishment to vent grievance; its laws were complicated and harsh, regarding lives as cheap, with the penalty official shooting the convicted in person; the world was chilled at heart, not safe even at home. The treacherous officials made use of the arbitrary laws to effect their intimidation, and the prison officials passed judgment, having power over life at will. The hierarchy dissolved, all acting in their own way. At the beginning of civil unrest under Qin, it was the poor and the wretched whom the officials preyed on first. At the mid-stage of the unrest it was the turn of the rich and officials' families; in its final stage, it was the turn of the imperial clan and the ministers. Therefore, people, both close and distant, were in danger, and there was resentment both inside the court and outside. The people scattered and took flight, changing loyalties. Chen Sheng initiated the revolt, causing the collapse of the empire, cutting off the imperial ancestral worship, to the happiness of a different surname. This was the disaster of officials' injustice, the inconsistent policies, and the unease of the people. Now Your Majesty matches the

【原文】

之迹，除其乱法；躬亲本事，废去淫末；除苛解娆，宽大爱人；肉刑不用，罪人亡帑；非谤不治，铸钱者除；通关去塞，不孽诸侯；宾礼长老，爱恤少孤；罪人有期，后宫出嫁；尊赐孝悌，农民不租；明诏军师，爱士大夫；求进方正，废退奸邪；除去阴刑，害民者诛；忧劳百姓，列侯就都；亲耕节用，视民不奢。所为天下兴利除害，变法易故，以安海内者，大功数十，皆上世之所难及，陛下行之，道纯德厚，元元之民幸矣。

诏策曰“永惟朕之不德”，愚臣不足以当之。

诏策曰“悉陈其志，毋有所隐”，愚臣窃以五帝之贤臣明之。臣闻五帝其臣莫能及，则自亲之；三王臣主俱贤，则共忧

【今译】

迹，废去乱法；亲身提倡本业，杜禁奢侈末业；消除烦扰，宽厚爱人；肉刑不用，犯罪不及妻子；诽谤不治罪。废禁铸钱律；打通关塞，不猜疑诸侯；礼敬长老，抚恤少孤；罪人有期，后宫出嫁；尊敬赏赐孝悌，农民在朝廷足用时免租；明诏军中师长，爱惜士卒和官员；寻求正派官吏，废退奸邪之官；除去宫刑，害民者处死；慰问百姓，列侯回到封国；亲自耕田，节省用费，向百姓昭示不侈。为天下兴利除害，变法革旧，安定海内，大功数十项，都是上世所难以办到的，陛下实行了，道德纯厚，是天下百姓之大幸。

诏策曰“永远纠正朕的不合德义的言行”，愚臣不足以当此。

诏策曰“悉陈其志，毋有所隐”，愚臣用五帝的贤臣来说明。臣闻五帝之臣不如五帝，五帝便亲自去办；三王臣主皆贤，

evolution of heaven and the blessings of earth; you benefit the people by spreading manna, eliminating the traces of Qin by eradicating its arbitrary laws; you personally promote the fundamental and forbid the luxury of the secondary; you eliminate harassment and administer generous love; eschew corporal punishment, and do not extend punishment of criminals to wives and children; you do not punish those who libel and reverse the ban on coin minting; you open the passes and fortresses and bear no suspicion against the princes; you respect the elders, care for the orphans and those who are lonely; criminals have fixed terms of imprisonment, and the harem are sent out for marriage; you respect and reward filial sons and brothers, and when the court is fully supplied farmers are excused rent; wise edicts order the military leaders to value their ordinary soldiers and officials; you seek out the straightforward and upright, and dismiss the treacherous officials; abolish castration punishment and put to death those who harm the people; you worry about the people's toil, and send adjunct marquises back to their fiefs; you personally farm the land, and save expenses, to show the people your economy. Previous reigns cannot match your dozens of great merits to promote benefit and abolish harm for the empire, reform the old laws and customs to pacify the nation. What Your Majesty has done, out of your pure moral and honest virtue, is the great fortune of the common people.

The imperial policy topic is: "ponder my lack of virtue," but this is beyond your humble servant.

The imperial policy topic is: "you should all speak your mind, without hiding anything", I will illustrate this with the worthy ministers of the Five Emperors. I heard the ministers were not as able as the Five Emperors, so the emperors dealt with government affairs in person; the lords and ministers

【原文】

之；五伯不及其臣，则任使之。此所以神明不遗，而圣贤不废也，故各当其世而立功德焉。传曰“往者不可及，来者犹可待，能明其世者谓之天子”，此之谓也。窃闻战不胜者易其地，民贫穷者变其业。今以陛下神明德厚，资财不下五帝，临制天下，至今十有六年，民不益富，盗贼不衰，边竟未安，其所以然，意者陛下未之躬亲，而待群臣也。今执事之臣皆天下之选已，然莫能望陛下清光，譬之犹五帝之佐也。陛下不自躬亲，而待不望清光之臣，臣窃恐神明之遗也，日损一日，岁亡一岁，日月益暮，盛德不及究于天下，以传万世，愚臣不自度量，窃为陛下惜之。昧死上狂惑草茅之愚，臣言唯陛下财择。

时贾谊已死，对策者百馀人，唯错为高第，繇是迁中大夫。

错又言宜削诸侯事，及法令可更定者，书凡三十篇。孝文虽不尽听，

【今译】

便臣主共同操心；五霸不及其臣，便任使其臣。这便是不弃神明之德，不废圣贤之名，各在当世建立功德。传曰“以往的事追不回来，将来的事还可以等待，能明白世事者就是天子”，说的就是这个意思。我私下听说战不能取胜就改换他的封地，百姓贫穷就改变他的职业。今陛下神明厚德，素质之才不低于五帝，主宰天下，至今十六年，民不增富，盗贼不衰减，边境没有安定，其所以是这样，有人说陛下没有亲身办事，而在等待群臣去办。如今当政大臣都是从天下各地选拔上来的，然而不能望见陛下清明之光，就像五帝的辅佐之臣。陛下不亲自处理，而等待不望清明之光的臣子，臣私自以为神明之德就要被自己遗弃。日损失是一日，岁损失了是一岁，日月更加临近夜暮，盛德不普及到天下，来流传万世，愚臣不自量力，私下为陛下惋惜。冒死上狂惑草茅之愚见，臣言仅供陛下裁择。

当时贾谊已死，对策者百余人，只有晁错是最高等级，由是升为中大夫。

晁错又说宜削诸侯，还有法令应更改的，写出共三十篇。孝文帝

of the Three Kings were both worthy, so they pondered them together; the Five Hegemons were not as capable as their ministers, so they entrusted their state affairs to them. This means not dispensing with the virtue of brilliant minds, and not to waste the names of sages; all of them established their merit at their appropriate times. According to the classics: "Since it is impossible to recover the past, and things in the future can wait, the one who can enlighten his times is the Son of Heaven." That is what I mean. I heard that he who could not win battles had his fief changed, while a poor person had his occupation changed. Your Majesty, whose mind is brilliant and virtue profound, who is no less able than the Five Emperors, has ruled for 16 years now; but the people are not richer, thieves not weakened, and the border not stable; the reason, it is suggested, might be that Your Majesty does not attend to things personally, but leaves the responsibility to your ministers. The ministers now in charge are all selected from around the land, however, they cannot see Your Majesty's clear aura, like the ministers of the Five Emperors. Your Majesty does not deal with government affairs in person, but leaves it to the ministers who do not see the aura, so I am afraid that the virtue of your brilliant mind might be abandoned of your own will. Day after day, and year after year, there is loss; when the sun and the moon are near dusk, your flourishing virtue will not spread to the world for all posterity. Your humble servant will not conjecture, but I am in private sorry for Your Majesty. Your humble rustic servant will risk death to present my idiotic opinion, for Your Majesty's choice.

Jia Yi was dead by then, and among the hundred-odd people who had answered, only Chao Cuo was rated at the highest level, so he was promoted to a grand master of the palace. In a total of 30 memorials Chao Cuo also called for the power of the princes to be

【原文】

然奇其材。当是时，太子善错计策，爰盎诸大功臣多不好错。

景帝即位，以错为内史。错数请间言事，辄听，幸倾九卿，法令多所更定。丞相申屠嘉心弗便，力未有以伤。内史府居太上庙堧中，门东出，不便，错乃穿门南出，凿庙堧垣。丞相大怒，欲因此过为奏请诛错。错闻之，即请间为上言之。丞相奏事，因言错擅凿庙垣为门，请下廷尉诛。上曰："此非庙垣，乃堧中垣，不致于法。"丞相谢。罢朝，因怒谓长史曰："吾当先斩以闻，乃先请，固误。"丞相遂发病死。错以此愈贵。

迁为御史大夫，请诸侯之罪过，削其支郡。奏上，上[令]公卿列

【今译】

虽然不尽采纳，然而惊奇他的才华。当时，太子称善晁错的计策，袁盎诸大功臣多不喜欢晁错。

景帝登位后，用晁错作内史。晁错多次请求单独谈论政事，景帝每每听从，宠爱超过了九卿，法令被修改的很多。丞相申屠嘉心里不满，但又无力加以伤害。内史府建在太上庙围墙里的空地上，门向东开，进出不方便，晁错便向南边开了两扇门出入，凿开了太上庙的围墙。丞相申屠嘉听说后，非常生气，打算藉这个过失撰写奏章请求诛杀晁错。晁错听到这个消息，当夜请求单独进见皇上，原原本本地向皇上说了这件事。丞相上朝奏事，趁机说了晁错擅自凿开太上庙的墙作门，请求把他交给廷尉处死。皇上说："这不是庙墙，是庙外空地上的围墙，不牵涉到法律。"丞相谢罪，退朝后，生气地对长史说："我应该先杀掉他再报告皇上，却先奏请，反被这小子出卖，因此失误。"丞相于是发病死了，晁错因此更加显贵。

晁错被提升为御史大夫，陈述诸侯的罪过，请求削减他们的土地，收回他们的旁郡。奏章送上去，皇上命令公卿、列侯和皇族集会

curtailed, and that laws should be revised, Emperor Wendi admired his talent, although he did not adopt all his proposals. At that time, the Crown Prince liked the plans of Chao Cuo, but Yuan Ang and other meritorious heroes mostly did not like him.

After Emperor Jingdi came to the throne, Chao Cuo was appointed Chamberlain for the Capital City. Chao Cuo several times requested private audience about political matters, and the Emperor often accepted his proposals, favoring him more than the nine chamberlains, thus the laws were changed a lot. Despite his dissatisfaction at this, Prime Minister Shentu Jia was unable to hurt him. Chao Cuo's office building was in the open space inside the enclosing wall of the Temple of Super-Emperor, and its gate opened, inconveniently, to the east. Chao Cuo had a southern gate made, cutting through the temple perimeter wall. When informed of this, the prime minister was outraged, and prepared to submit a memorial demanding the death of Chao Cuo for this negligence. Chao Cuo heard the news, and requested a private night-time audience with the emperor about the matter. When the prime minister petitioned to hand Chao Cuo to the Chamberlain of Law Enforcement for execution on the grounds that he had, without authorization, cut a gate through the wall of the temple, the Emperor said: "This is not a temple wall, but the perimeter wall of the temple, and the law does not apply here." The prime minister apologized. After the court meeting, he said angrily to his aide: "I should have killed him first, before reporting to the Emperor, but I petitioned first, and the brat turned the tables on me! What a wrong move of mine." The prime minister then died of sickness, and Chao Cuo's star rose even higher.

Chao Cuo was promoted to censor-in-chief. Expounding the transgressions of the princes, he requested to reduce the size of their domains. When the memorial reached the Emperor, he ordered the high nobles, chief ministers, marquises and the imperial family to discuss it. Nobody dared raise objection, with the sole exception of

【原文】

侯宗室[杂议]，莫敢难，独窦婴争之，繇此与错有隙。错所更令三十章，诸侯讙哗。错父闻之，从颍川来，谓错曰："上初即位，公为政用事，侵削诸侯，疏人骨肉，口让多怨，公何为也！"错曰："固也。不如此，天子不尊，宗庙不安。"父曰："刘氏安矣，而晁氏危，吾去公归矣！"遂饮药死，曰："吾不忍见祸逮身。"

后十馀日，吴楚七国俱反，以诛错为名。上与错议出军事，错欲令上自将兵，而身居守。会窦婴言爰盎，诏召入见，上方与错调兵食。上问盎曰："君尝为吴相，知吴臣田禄伯为人乎？今吴楚反，于公意何如？"对曰："不足忧也，今破矣。"上曰："吴王即山铸钱，煮海为盐，诱天下豪桀，白头举事，此其计不百全，岂发乎？何以言其无能为也？"盎对曰："吴铜盐之利则有之，安得豪桀而诱之！诚令吴得豪桀，亦且辅而为谊，不反矣。吴所诱，皆亡赖子弟，亡命铸钱奸人，故相诱以乱。"错曰："盎策之善。"上问曰："计

【今译】

讨论，没有谁敢非难，只有窦婴不同意，从此和晁错有了隔阂。晁错修改的法令有三十章，诸侯哗然，憎恨晁错。晁错的父亲听到这个消息，从颍川赶来，对晁错说："皇上刚才即位，您执政掌权，侵害削弱诸侯，疏远人家的骨肉，人们都责怪怨恨您，为什么这样做呢？"晁错说："当然嘛。不这样，天子不会尊贵，国家不得安宁。"晁错的父亲说："刘家的天下安宁了，而晁家却危险了，我离开您回去了！"便服毒药死去，临死时说："我不忍看到大祸连累自己。"

十几天之后，吴、楚七国皆反，以诛晁错为名。皇上与晁错商议出兵事，晁错想让皇上亲自率兵，由他居守后方。当时窦婴正推举袁盎，受诏入见，皇上正与晁错筹划军粮。皇上问袁盎说："你曾担任吴国相，知道吴臣田禄伯的为人吗？今吴、楚反，你怎么看？"回答说："不足忧，今天就可以打败。"皇上说："吴王就山铸钱，煮海为盐，引诱天下豪杰，头裹白巾为号起事，这个计划还没有完善，那能放弃呢？为什么说他不足担忧呀？"袁盎回答说："吴国铜盐之利是有的，哪里去找豪杰来引诱！真是让吴国得到豪杰，也只是辅政为谊，不会反叛。吴国所引诱的人，都是一些无赖子弟，亡命铸钱奸人，所以招来后为乱。"晁错说："袁盎策很好。"皇上说："平乱

Dou Ying. Hence the two became estranged. Chao Cuo amended 30 chapters of the law, the princes protested loudly and their hatred of him grew. When Chao Cuo's father heard the news, he came from Yingchuan and told his son: "The Emperor has not long ascended the throne, and you are in power. You infringe on and weaken the princes, alienating people of the same flesh and blood, so people blame and hate you. Why do you do it?" He replied: "Of course. Without this, the Emperor would not be distinguished, and the ancestral temple would not be peaceful." Chao Cuo's father retorted: "The Liu empire enjoys peace, but the Chao family is in danger. I'll leave you here and go back!" He poisoned himself, and said dying: "I could not bear to see disaster embroil me."

A dozen days later, Wu and Chu led seven kingdoms in rebellion in the name of punishing Chao. The Emperor discussed plans to send troops against them; Chao Cuo wanted the Emperor to take personal command of the army, while he would guard the home front. At that time, Dou Ying recommended Yuan Ang, who was admitted to Court, where the Emperor was planning the army rations with Chao Cuo. The Emperor asked Yuan Ang: "You served as Wu's prime minister. What sort of man is the Wu minister Tian Lubo? Now Wu and Chu are in revolt. How do you think we can do?" Ang responded: "Do not worry. Today you can beat them." The Emperor said: "The Prince of Wu mints coin on the mountains, dries sea water for salt, and attracts the gallants of the land. Wearing white turbans they started an uprising. How would they have started if the program had not been perfect? Why do you say not to worry about them?" Yuan Ang replied: "Wu does have the profit from copper and salt, but where to find gallants to attract? Even if Wu got gallants, they would just assist towards righteousness rather than rebellion. The people Wu lured are all hooligans, desperados. There just to mint coins, their presence has just provoked chaos." Chao said: "This is good policy advice." The Emperor asked: "What

【原文】

安出？”盎对曰：“愿屏左右。”上屏人，独错在。盎曰：“臣所言，人臣不得知。”乃屏错。错趋避东箱，甚恨。上卒问盎，对曰：“吴楚相遗书，言高皇帝王子弟各有分地，今贼臣晁错擅適诸侯，削夺之地，以故反名为西共诛错，复故地而罢。方今计，独有斩错，发使赦吴楚七国，复其故地，则兵可毋血刃而俱罢。”于是上默然，良久曰：“顾诚何如，吾不爱一人谢天下。”盎曰：“愚计出此，唯上孰计之。”乃拜盎为太常，密装治行。

后十馀日，丞相青翟、中尉嘉、廷尉欧劾奏错曰：“吴王反逆亡道，欲危宗庙，天下所当共诛。今御史大夫错议曰：‘兵数百万，独属群臣，不可信，陛下不如自出临兵，使错居守。徐、僮之旁吴所未下者可以予吴。’错不称陛下德信，欲疏群臣百姓，又欲以城邑予吴，亡臣子礼，大逆无道。错当要斩，父母妻子同产无少长皆弃市。

【今译】

之计怎么订？”袁盎说：“请左右人等退下。”左右人退下，晁错一人留下。袁盎说：“臣要说的，人臣不得知。”于是让晁错退下。晁错忙避到东厢房，深恨袁盎。皇上急问袁盎，回答说：“吴、楚相送来书信，说高帝封子弟为王各有分地，今贼臣晁错擅罚诸侯，削夺他们的土地，所以反名是‘西进共诛晁错’，恢复原有封地就罢兵。如今的计策，只有斩晁错，派使者赦吴、楚七国，恢复故地，那么不会流血就可以全都罢兵。”于是皇上默不作声，很久才说：“看看情况如何，我不爱一人以谢天下。”袁盎说：“愚计拿出来，只能是皇上好好合计。”于是任袁盎为太常，秘密打点行装起程。

十几天后，丞相青翟、中尉嘉、廷尉欧劾上奏弹劾晁错说：“吴王反逆无道，想危害宗庙，天下应当共诛之。今御史大夫晁错建议说：‘兵几百万，单独交给群臣不可靠，陛下不如亲自率兵，让晁错留守。徐、僮周围未攻占的地方可以给吴。’晁错不称颂陛下德义诚信，想疏远群臣百姓，又想用城邑给吴，没有尽臣子之礼，大逆无道。晁错应当受腰斩刑罚，父母妻子兄弟无论老少都应处死。臣请按

is your anti-insurgency plan?" Yuan Ang said: "Please order your attendants away." All withdrew, apart from Chao Cuo. Yuan Ang said: "What I would say, no minister should know." So the Emperor ordered Chao to withdraw, and he retired to the east wing, annoyed. The Emperor then asked Yuan Ang, who answered: "Wu and Chu's prime ministers exchanged letters, saying that Gaodi granted his children and brothers their own fiefs as princes, but now the treacherous courtier Chao Cuo has downgraded the princes without authorization, depriving them of their land. Their rationale for rebellion is 'go west to jointly punish Chao Cuo,' and to stop once their original lands are restored. Today's plan is to behead only Cuo, and send a messenger to pardon Wu, Chu and the other princes, and restore their old fiefs. In this way you can prevent the war without any bloodshed at all." The Emperor was silent for a long time before speaking: "It depends on the actual circumstances. I do not like to apologize to the world by punishing one person." Yuan Ang said: "That was my stupid plan. If only the emperor would ponder on it." Yuan Ang was then appointed as chamberlain for ceremonials and he made secret preparations to leave.

A dozen days later, the prime minister Qingzhai, the chamberlain for the imperial insignia Jia, and the chamberlain for law enforcement Zhang Qu, impeached Chao Cuo: "The Prince of Wu rebels against the Way, wanting to harm the imperial temple, and the world should join together to wipe him out. Censor-in-Chief Chao Cuo recommends that, since it is not reliable for ministers alone to command millions of soldiers, it is better for His Majesty to take command personally, while he would stay behind at Court. Places in Xu and Tong near Wu which are not captured by Wu may be granted to Wu. Chao Cuo does not live up to His Majesty's virtue and integrity, wants to alienate the ministers and the people, and wants to give the cities to Wu, against the rite of being a courtier; it is treason and heresy. Chao Cuo should be executed by cutting

【原文】

臣请论如法。”制曰：“可。”错殊不知。乃使中尉召错，给载行市。错衣朝衣斩东市。

错已死，谒者仆射邓公为校尉，击吴楚为将。还，上书言军事，见上。上问曰：“道军所来，闻晁错死，吴楚罢不？”邓公曰：“吴为反数十岁矣，发怒削地，以诛错为名，其意不在错也。且臣恐天下之士拑口不敢复言矣。”上曰：“何哉？”邓公曰：“夫晁错患诸侯强大不可制，故请削之，以尊京师，万世之利也。计画始行，卒受大戮，内杜忠臣之口，外为诸侯报仇，臣窃为陛下不取也。”于是景帝喟然长息，曰：“公言善，吾亦恨之。”乃拜邓公为城阳中尉。

邓公，成固人也，多奇计。建元年中，上招贤良，公卿言邓先。

【今译】

法论处。”皇上批示说：“可以。”晁错毫无所知。便派中尉召晁错，骗上车经过街市，晁错穿着朝服在东市被斩。

晁错已死，谒者仆射邓公担任校尉，这时担任将领进攻吴、楚叛军。他回京师，上书报告军事情况，进见皇上。皇上问道：“你从军中来，听到晁错死了，吴、楚退兵没有？”邓公说：“吴王谋反已有几十年了，因削减他的封地而发怒，以诛杀晁错为名，他的本意不在晁错呀。而且我担心天下的士大夫闭口，不敢进言了！”皇上说：“为什么呢？”邓公说：“晁错忧虑诸侯强大了不能够制服，所以请求削减诸侯的封地，藉以尊崇朝廷，这是万世的好事。计划刚开始实行，竟然遭受杀戮，对内来说，堵塞了忠臣的口，对外来说，替诸侯报了仇，我私下认为您这样做是不可取的。”这时，景帝长声叹息，说道：“您说的对，我也悔恨这件事。”于是任命邓公担任城阳中尉。

邓公是成固人，多有奇特的谋略。建元年间，朝廷招纳贤良，公

in half, and his parents, wife, sons, brothers, both young and old, should be put to death. Let Chao Cuo be punished by law." The imperial instructions said: "Agreed." Chao Cuo did not have a clue this was going on. He was sent for by a chamberlain for the imperial insignia, and driven through the streets on a carriage. Chao Cuo was executed in the East Market wearing his court garments.

With Chao Cuo dead, Chief Receptionist Mr. Deng as Commandant then led the army to attack the Wu-Chu rebels. He returned to report on the military situation, and came before the Emperor, who asked: "You came from the army, so did Wu and Chu not retreat on hearing that Chao Cuo was dead?" Mr. Deng said: "The Prince of Wu has rebelled for decades. Furious at the reduction of his fief, he rose up in the name of condemning Chao, but this was merely a pretext. Now I worry that the literati and grand masters will keep their mouths shut, no longer daring to speak out!" Asked why, Mr. Deng replied: "Chao Cuo was worried about the powerful princes who cannot be contained, so he requested to reduce their fiefs, in order to respect the Court, a move that would produce benefits for all time. Just as the plan was being implemented, he was suddenly killed; at Court this caused the mouths of the loyal courtiers to fall silent, and outside it served the princes' revenge. I privately think that Your Majesty has done something not desirable." Emperor Jingdi sighed a long sigh: "You are right. I too regret this." He then appointed Mr. Deng as the secretary of war of the Princedom of Chengyang.

Mr. Deng was from Chenggu, was a resourceful and ingenious strategist. In the Jianyuan reign period (140-135 BC), the Emperor recruited the worthy and excellent, and the highest nobles and chief ministers selected Mr. Deng. At the time Deng had no post, and was

【原文】

邓先时免，起家为九卿。一年，复谢病免归。其子章，以修黄老言显诸公间。

——卷四十九《爰盎晁错传》第十九

【今译】

卿们推举邓公，这时邓公免了职，由平民起用做了九卿。一年后，邓公又托病辞职回家。他的儿子邓章因为研究黄帝、老子的学说，在朝廷大臣中间很有名望。

promoted from a commoner to one of the nine chamberlains. A year later, pleading illness, he resigned and returned to his home. His son Deng Zhang was a scholar of the pronouncements of the Yellow Emperor and Laozi and made a great name for himself among court ministers.

苏武传

【原文】

武字子卿，少以父任，兄弟并为郎，稍迁至栘中厩监。时汉连伐胡，数通使相窥观，匈奴留汉使郭吉、路充国等，前后十馀辈。匈奴使来，汉亦留之以相当。天汉元年，且鞮侯单于初立，恐汉袭之，乃曰："汉天子我丈人行也。"尽归汉使路充国等。武帝嘉其义，乃遣武以中郎将使持节送匈奴使留在汉者，因厚(赂)[赂]单于，答其善意。武与副中郎将张胜及假吏常惠等募士斥候百馀人俱。既至匈奴，置币遗单于。单于益骄，非汉所望也。

方欲发使送武等，会缑王与长水虞常等谋反匈奴中。缑王者，昆邪王姊子也，与昆邪王俱降汉，后随浞野侯没胡中。及卫律所将降者，

【今译】

苏武，字子卿，年轻时因父亲苏建为国立功，而与兄弟们一起被任用为郎，苏武后来逐渐升迁为栘中厩监。当时汉朝不断讨伐匈奴，双方多次派使者暗察对方情况，匈奴先后扣留了郭吉、路充国等十多批汉使者。匈奴使者到来，汉朝也扣留以相抵偿。天汉元年，且鞮侯单于刚刚即位，害怕汉朝袭击，于是说："汉朝的皇帝是我的长辈。"把扣留的汉朝使者路充国等全部放还。汉武帝称赞他明于大义，就派苏武以中郎将的身份带着汉朝符节护送被扣留在汉朝的匈奴使者，并赠送给单于许多财物，以报答他的好意。苏武与副使汉中郎将张胜以及临时兼任使者属吏的常惠等人招募士卒、斥候（侦察兵）一百多人同去匈奴。到达匈奴后，陈设财物赠送给单于。单于更加傲慢，完全不像汉朝所期望的那样。

单于正要派使者护送苏武等人返回，正赶上缑王和长水虞常等在匈奴谋反。缑王是昆邪王姐姐的儿子，曾与昆邪王一起投降汉朝，后来随同汉浞野侯讨伐匈奴，兵败而降。他们与随从卫律投降的人暗中

Chapter 10

Biography of Su Wu

As a young man, Su Wu, styled Ziqing, was appointed a court gentleman along with his brothers, because of his father Su Jian's meritorious service to the state. He was gradually promoted to Supervisor in the Imperial Stables. It was a time of continual military campaigning against the Huns. Both sides sent envoys to secretly investigate each other's situation, and the Huns had detained a dozen parties of Han envoys, among them Guo Ji, Lu Chongguo. So, when Hun envoys arrived, Han also detained them, to even the score. In the first year of the Tianhan reign period (100 BC), the Hun Chanyu Qiedihou had just ascended the throne, and fearful of being attacked by Han, he proclaimed: "The Han Emperor is my father." He set free all the detained Han envoys, including Lu Chongguo. The Emperor praised his reasonableness, and sent leader of the court gentlemen Su Wu as the imperial envoy to escort back the Hun envoys detained by Han. He presented the Chanyu with rich endowments to repay his kindness. Su Wu, his deputy Zhang Sheng, and acting entourage Chang Hui, recruited more than a hundred soldiers and scouts to go to the Huns. On their arrival, they displayed the presents to the Chanyu, who was all the more arrogant, contrary to all expectations.

Just as a protective escort was being appointed to take Su Wu and his men back, the King of Gou, together with Changshui Commandant Yu Chang and others among the Huns, was planning to rebel. Gou was the son of the king of Kunye tribe's sister. He had surrendered along with his father to the Han Dynasty, but along with Marquis Zhao of Zhuoye had later been captured by the Huns. Secretly planning with those who had surrendered under the

【原文】

阴相与谋劫单于母阏氏归汉。会武等至匈奴，虞常在汉时素与副张胜相知，私候胜曰："闻汉天子甚怨卫律，常能为汉伏弩射杀之。吾母与弟在汉，幸蒙其赏赐。"张胜许之，以货物与常。后月馀，单于出猎，独阏氏子弟在。虞常等七十余人欲发，其一人夜亡，告之。单于子弟发兵与战。缑王等皆死，虞常生得。

单于使卫律治其事。张胜闻之，恐前语发，以状语武。武曰："事如此，此必及我。见犯乃死，重负国。"欲自杀，胜、惠共止之。虞常果引张胜。单于怒，召诸贵人议，欲杀汉使者。左伊秩訾曰："即谋单于，何以复加？宜皆降之。"单于使卫律召武受辞，武谓惠等："屈节辱命，虽生，何面目以归汉！"引佩刀自刺。卫律惊，自抱持武，驰召医。凿地为坎，置煴火，覆武其上，蹈其背以出血。

【今译】

策划，要劫持单于的母亲阏氏返回汉朝，恰巧苏武等出使匈奴。虞常在汉朝时和副使张胜关系一直不错，就暗中拜访张胜，说："听说汉朝皇帝非常怨恨卫律，我能为汉朝暗设弓弩杀死他。我的母亲和弟弟在汉朝，希望他们能得到我为汉朝立功的赏赐。"张胜表示同意，并送给虞常财物。一个多月以后，单于出去打猎，只有阏氏及其侍从在家。虞常等七十多人准备下手，但其中一人晚上逃走，向单于告密，单于及其部下派兵与虞常等展开激战，缑王等都在战斗中被杀。虞常被活捉。

单于任用卫律审理这一事件。张胜听到这个消息，恐怕以前与虞常密谋之语被泄露，就把情况告诉给苏武。苏武说："事情已发展到这个地步，一定会牵涉到我。受到侮辱之后才死，将更加对不起国家。"于是便要自杀，张胜、常惠一起把他劝住。虞常果然供出张胜。单于大怒，召集匈奴贵族商议，要杀死汉朝使者。左伊秩訾说："如果有谋害单于的，该如何加重处罚？不如让他们全部投降。"单于便派卫律召来苏武审问。苏武对常惠等人说："使自己的节操和国家的使命受到屈辱，即使不死，还有什么脸面回到汉朝？"拔出佩刀自杀。卫律大吃一惊，亲自抱住苏武，派人骑马跑去找医生。医生在地上凿了一个坑，放进煴火，使苏武伏卧在火坑上，用手叩击他的背

command of Wei Lü, they wanted to kidnap the Chanyu's mother Queen Yanzhi and return to Han. This all coincided with the timing of Su Wu's diplomatic mission. Yu Chang had been on good terms at the Han Court with the deputy envoy Zhang Sheng, and visited him in secret with a dangerous suggestion: "I heard that the Han Emperor hates Wei Lü, but I can kill him on the Emperor's behalf, setting a crossbow archer to kill him in ambush. My mother and brother are in the Han Court, and I hope they will be rewarded by the Emperor for my meritorious deed." Zhang Sheng agreed and gave Yu Chang some property. More than a month later, the Chanyu went hunting, leaving Yanzhi and her young relatives alone at home. Yu Chang and 70-plus men got ready to start, but an informer among them escaped at night, so the Chanyu's young men fought them. King of Gou and others were killed in combat, but Yu Chang was taken alive.

The Chanyu appointed Wei Lü to hear the case. When Zhang Sheng got the news, he was terrified that his conversation with Yu Chang would come to light, and told Su Wu about it. Su Wu said: "As the situation goes, this would involve me. To be thus humiliated before death, my guilt to my country would be all the more." So he wanted to commit suicide, but Zhang Sheng and Chang Hui stopped him. Yu Chang did indeed implicate Zhang Sheng. The Chanyu was furious, and called a meeting of his nobles, intent on killing the Han envoys. The Left Yiyizi or king said: "If there was an attempt against the Chanyu, what is the worst punishment we could inflict? It would be better to make them all surrender." The Chanyu ordered Wei Lü to interrogate Su Wu, who said to Chang Hui and the others: "When my own integrity and the nation's diplomacy are humiliated, what face do we have to take back to Han, even if I do live?" He pulled out a knife, and stabbed himself in an attempt to commit suicide. Shocked, Wei clasped Su Wu to his own body, and sent a horse messenger to bring a doctor. The doctor dug a hole in the ground,

【原文】

武气绝，半日复息。惠等哭，舆归营。单于壮其节，朝夕遣人候问武，而收系张胜。

武益愈，单于使使晓武。会论虞常，欲因此时降武。剑斩虞常已，律曰："汉使张胜谋杀单于近臣，当死，单于募降者赦罪。"举剑欲击之，胜请降。律谓武曰："副有罪，当相坐。"武曰："本无谋，又非亲属，何谓相坐？"复举剑拟之，武不动。律曰："苏君，律前负汉归匈奴，幸蒙大恩，赐号称王，拥众数万，马畜弥山，富贵如此。苏君今日降，明日复然。空以身膏草野，谁复知之！"武不应。律曰："君因我降，与君为兄弟，今不听吾计，后虽欲复见我，尚可得乎？"武骂律曰："女为人臣子，不顾恩义，畔主背亲，为降虏于蛮夷，何以女为见？且单于信女，使决人死生，不平心持正，反

【今译】

使淤血从伤口中流出。苏武昏死过去，很久才苏醒。常惠等人哭着把他抬回营帐。单于非常佩服他的气节，派人早晚探问他的病情，并拘捕了张胜。

苏武的伤势日渐好转，单于派使者劝他投降，又共同审判虞常，想藉此机会迫使苏武投降。用剑杀死虞常之后，卫律说："汉朝使者张胜谋杀单于亲近的大臣，罪当处死，不过单于招募投降的人，赦免他的罪过。"举剑要杀张胜，张胜请求投降。卫律又对苏武说："副使有罪，你应当与他连坐。"苏武说："我本来没有参与密谋，又不是他的亲属，为什么要与他连坐？"卫律用剑比划着要刺苏武，苏武毫不动摇。卫律说："苏先生，我卫律从前背叛汉朝，归降匈奴，幸而承蒙单于恩德，赐给我王号，使我拥有部众数万，马畜满山，富贵如此。您今日投降，明天也会这样。否则被杀，白白葬身于荒野之中，有谁知道你为汉朝而死？"苏武不予理睬。卫律又说："您藉助我而投降，我与您结为兄弟；今天不听我的话，以后再想见到我，还有可能吗？"苏武痛斥卫律说："你作为汉朝臣民，不顾恩义廉耻，背叛皇帝和亲人，投降蛮夷，我见你干什么？况且单于信任你，让你裁决人的生死，你却不出于公心，主持平正，反而要使两国之主相互

lit a smoldering fire, and lay Su Wu over the fire pit, tapping on his back to squeeze blood from the wound. Su Wu went into a coma from which he did not emerge for a long time. Chang Hui and others wept and carried him back to camp on a cart. The Chanyu admired Su Wu's integrity, sending people twice daily to inquire about his condition. Zhang Sheng was arrested.

As Su Wu gradually recovered, the Chanyu sent messengers urging him to surrender; he would also make him stand trial with Yu Chang, hoping to take this opportunity to force Su Wu to surrender. After killing Yu Chang with his sword, Wei Lü said: "The Han envoy Zhang Sheng tried to murder the Chanyu's close minister and he deserves death, but the Chanyu pardons he who surrenders." He brandished his sword to kill Zhang Sheng, who begged to surrender. Wei then turned to Su Wu: "When your deputy is guilty, you should be punished for his guilt." Su Wu said: "Since I am neither a co-conspirator nor a relative, why should I be punished?" At this Wei brandished his sword again, pointing to stab Su Wu, who was unwavering. Wei said: "Mr. Su, I once turned my back on Han, but thanks to the fortunate benevolence of the Chanyu, I was made a king. So now I am rich and prosperous; I command tens of thousands of troops, and my horses fill the hills. If you surrender today, the same will be yours tomorrow. Otherwise, you will be killed, buried in the wilderness for no purpose at all, with no one to know your self-sacrifice for your Emperor." Su Wu did not respond. Wei urged: "Take my advice and submit to the Chanyu, then you and I will become brothers; if you do not, who knows if you will see my face again?" Su denounced: "You, a subject of Han, betrayed your lord and family, disregarding the gratitude you owe. You serve barbarians as a surrendered captive, so what purpose is there in seeing you? Moreover, the Chanyu trusts you to make a ruling of life or death, but you do not uphold justice out of any public spirit. No, your aim is to pit both rulers against each other, so as to observe

【原文】

欲斗两主，观祸败。南越杀汉使者，屠为九郡；宛王杀汉使者，头县北阙；朝鲜杀汉使者，即时诛灭。独匈奴未耳。若知我不降明，欲令两国相攻，匈奴之祸从我始矣。”

律知武终不可胁，白单于。单于愈益欲降之，乃幽武置大窖中，绝不饮食。天雨雪，武卧啮雪与旃毛并咽之，数日不死。匈奴以为神，乃徙武北海上无人处，使牧羝，羝乳乃得归。别其官属常惠等，各置他所。

武既至海上，廪食不至，掘野鼠去屮实而食之。杖汉节牧羊。卧起操持，节旄尽落。积五六年，单于弟於靬王弋射海上。武能网纺缴，檠弓弩，於靬王爱之，给其衣食。三岁馀，王病，赐武马畜服匿穹庐。王死后，人众徙去。其冬，丁令盗武牛羊，武复穷厄。

初，武与李陵俱为侍中，武使匈奴明年，陵降，不敢求武。久之，

【今译】

争斗以坐观双方混战所造成的祸乱。南越杀汉使者，被夷平成为汉朝的九个郡；大宛王杀汉使者，他的头颅已被悬于汉宫之北阙；朝鲜杀汉使者，立即遭到灭顶之灾。惟独匈奴未发生这种事。你明知我不投降，如果想让两国相攻伐，匈奴的祸败将从杀我开始。”

卫律知道最终不能威胁苏武投降，就把情况汇报给单于。单于越发想使苏武投降，便把他囚禁在大窖里，断绝向他供应饮食。天降大雪，苏武就卧在地上，吞食雪团与毡毛，得以好多天没饿死. 匈奴以为他是神人，就把他迁徙到北海没有人烟的地方，让他放牧公羊，直到公羊产乳生仔，才允许他回来，并把他与属吏常惠等分开，分别安置在不同的地方。

苏武被流放到北海以后，匈奴不供给他粮食，他只好挖掘野鼠所贮藏的草籽充饥。拄着汉朝节符牧羊，时时刻刻把汉朝节符带在身边，以致节符上的旄都脱落了。过了五六年，单于的弟弟於靬王到北海打猎，因苏武会制做猎网和箭缴，校正弓弩，於靬王很喜欢他，送给他衣服和食物。又过了三年多，於靬王病了，就赠送苏武牲畜、酒酪器皿和毡帐。於靬王死后，他的部众也都走了。这年冬天，丁令人偷走了苏武的牛羊，苏武再一次陷入了困境。

起初，苏武与李陵同在汉朝任侍中，苏武出使匈奴的第二年，李

the disaster that comes from their fighting. After South Yue killed Han envoys, it was annihilated and is now nine prefectures of Han; for killing Han envoys, the head of Dayuan's King was hung on the north gate of the Han Palace; when Gojoseon killed Han envoys ruin ensued immediately. Only the Huns have not killed Han diplomats. You know quite well that I will not surrender, if you want the two nations to attack each other, the Huns' demise will begin from the moment of my death."

Wei knew that he would never be able to coerce Su Wu into surrendering, and he reported accordingly to the Chanyu, but this made him ever the more determined to achieve his submission. He had Su Wu imprisoned in a large dungeon, cutting off all food to him. It was snowing, and Su Wu, lying on the ground, managed to survive starvation only by eating the wool from his clothes and drinking handfuls of snow. The Huns thought him a divine, and moved him to an uninhabited area near Lake Baikal, where he was made to herd rams until "such time as the rams gave birth to lambs." He was split from his deputy Chang Hui and the rest, who were settled in different places.

In his Lake Baikal exile, Su Wu was not supplied with food, so he had to dig into the holes where squirrels had stored their seeds and nuts. The Han ambassadorial staff, used as a shepherd's crook, never left his side until its decorative tassel wore off. After five or six years, the Chanyu's brother King Wujian came hunting around Baikal. As Su Wu was able to make hunting nets and silk-stringed arrows, and fix crossbows, the king took a liking to him, and gave him clothes and food. Then, more than three years later, when the king was sick he gifted Su Wu livestock, wine pots, and a yurt. After the king's death, his men were also gone. That winter, the Dingling tribe stole Su's cattle and sheep, plunging him once more into dire straits.

In earlier days, Su Wu and Li Ling had served together as

【原文】

单子使陵至海上，为武置酒设乐，因谓武曰："单于闻陵与子卿素厚，故使陵来说足下，虚心欲相待。终不得归汉，空自苦亡人之地，信义安所见乎？前长君为奉车，从至雍棫阳宫，扶辇下除，触柱折辕，劾大不敬，伏剑自刎，赐钱二百万以葬。孺卿从祠河东后土，宦骑与黄门驸马争船，推堕驸马河中溺死，宦骑亡，诏使孺卿逐捕不得，惶恐饮药而死。来时，大夫人已不幸，陵送葬至阳陵。子卿妇年少，闻已更嫁矣。独有女弟二人，两女一男，今复十馀年，存亡不可知。人生如朝露，何久自苦如此！陵始降时，忽忽如狂，自痛负汉，加以老母系保宫，子卿不欲降，何以过陵？且陛下春秋高，法令亡常，大臣亡罪夷灭者数十家，安危不可知，子卿尚复谁为乎？愿听

【今译】

陵投降匈奴，不敢求见苏武。过了很长时间，单于派李陵到北海，为苏武置办酒宴，陈设乐舞，趁机对苏武说："单于听说我与您平素交往很深，因此派我来劝您，单于将诚心待您。终究不能回到汉朝，白白地在这无人之地自找苦吃，谁能看见您的信义之心呢？从前您的哥哥苏嘉任奉车都尉，随皇帝到雍城棫阳宫，扶辇下殿阶，辇撞到柱子上，折断了辕，以大不敬罪受到弹劾，拔剑自杀，皇帝赐给了二百万钱的安葬费。你的弟弟苏贤随从皇帝去河东郡祭祀土神，宦骑与黄门驸马争船，驸马被推入河中淹死，宦骑逃跑，皇帝命令苏贤追捕宦骑，没能捉住，苏贤忧虑害怕，饮药自杀。我领兵离长安时，您的母亲不幸去世，我送葬到阳陵。您的妻子年轻，听说已改嫁了。只剩下两个妹妹、两个女儿和一个儿子，现在已过去十多年，不知是死是活。人生如同早上的露珠一样短促，何必长时间地折磨自己！我开始投降时，心神恍惚，如疯若狂，为自己背叛汉朝而痛心，加上老母亲被囚禁在保宫，您不想投降的心情怎么会超过我呢？况且皇帝年老，法令没有常规，大臣无罪而被诛灭的有数十家，安危难以预料，您还

imperial palace attendants. In the year after Su Wu's embassy to the Huns, Li Ling surrendered to them but never dared ask to see Su Wu. After a very long time, the Chanyu sent Li Ling to Baikal, bringing a banquet and music to Su Wu, and Li Ling said to him: "When the Chanyu heard that you and I were on good terms, he sent me to persuade you. The Chanyu will treat you honorably. After all, you cannot return to the Han Court and to be alone in this no man's land foraging for your foods serves no good purpose, for who can see your faithfulness? Your elder brother Su Jia, as Captain of the Imperial Carriage, followed the Emperor to Yuyang Palace in Yongcheng City. When he walked the palanquin down the steps, it hit a pillar, breaking its shaft. He was charged with the crime of disrespect to the Emperor, and committed suicide with his own sword; His Majesty granted two million cash in funeral expenses. Your younger brother Su Xian followed the Emperor to Hedong to worship the Spirit of Earth, when a riding eunuch guard fought over a ship with the Yellow-Door Commandant-Escort, and pushed him into the river to drown. The eunuch escaped, and the Emperor ordered Su Xian to hunt him down. Unable to catch him, Su Xian was so worried that he committed suicide by drinking poison. When I led troops from Chang'an, your mother died of grief and I followed the funeral procession to Yangling. I also heard that your wife, being young, has remarried. You are left only with two younger sisters, two daughters and a son, but now a dozen years have passed, so who knows if they are dead or alive. Life is as short as the morning dew, so why torture yourself for so long? When I just surrendered to the Huns, my mind was in a trance, like a crazy man, and I was sad to feel I had turned my back on Han. Besides, with my old mother imprisoned in the Palace, how can your unwillingness to surrender surpass my own? Moreover, the Emperor Wudi is getting old, his edicts become erratic, and dozens of guiltless ministers have been killed together with their clans, so our safety is difficult to predict.

【原文】

陵计，勿复有云。”武曰：“武父子亡功德，皆为陛下所成就，位列将，爵通侯，兄弟亲近，常愿肝脑涂地。今得杀身自效，虽蒙斧钺汤镬，诚甘乐之。臣事君，犹子事父也，子为父死亡所恨。愿勿复再言。”陵与武饮数日，复曰：“子卿壹听陵言。”武曰：“自分已死久矣！王必欲降武，请毕今日之欢，效死于前！”陵见其至诚，喟然叹曰：“嗟乎，义士！陵与卫律之罪上通于天。”因泣下沾衿，与武决去。

陵恶自赐武，使其妻赐武牛羊数十头。后陵复至北海上，语武：“区脱捕得云中生口，言太守以下吏民皆白服，曰上崩。”武闻之，南鄉号哭，欧血，旦夕临。

数月，昭帝即位。数年，匈奴与汉和亲。汉求武等，匈奴诡言武死。后汉使复至匈奴，常惠请其守者与俱，得夜见汉使，具自陈道。教使者谓单于，言天子射上林中，得雁，足有系帛书，言武等在某泽

【今译】

为谁守节呢？希望听从我的计策，什么也别说了。”苏武说：“我们父子无功无德，都是由于皇帝的提拔，才位列将军，爵至通侯，兄弟三人都为皇帝近臣，常愿为此肝脑涂地。现在如果能牺牲自己，报效国家，即使蒙受斧钺之诛、汤镬之刑，也甘心情愿。大臣侍奉君主，如同儿子侍奉父亲，儿子为父亲而死，毫无怨恨。希望您不要再说了。”李陵与苏武宴饮了几天之后，又劝苏武：“您一定要听我的话。”苏武说：“我早已心甘情愿去死，您一定要使我投降，就请结束今天的欢宴，让我死在您面前！”李陵见他对汉朝如此忠诚，长叹一声，说：“唉，真是义士！我和卫律的罪过，比天还高啊！”随之泪如雨下，沾湿了衣襟，与苏武告别离去。

李陵羞于亲自赠送苏武财物，就派他的妻子给苏武送去几只牛羊。后来，李陵又到北海，告诉苏武：“匈奴边塞哨所活捉云中汉人，说上自太守下至百姓都穿白色丧服，并说皇帝死了。”苏武听到这个消息，面对南方痛哭，以致吐血，每天早晚哭吊武帝。

几个月后，昭帝即位。过了几年，匈奴与汉朝和好。汉朝寻求苏武等人，匈奴诈说苏武死了。后来汉使者又到匈奴，常惠请求看守他的人和他一起晚上去见汉使者，详细叙述了事情的经过，又教汉使者对单于说，汉朝皇帝在上林苑打猎，射下一只雁，脚上系着一封帛书，说

So, for whom are you keeping the tally? Please take my advice, and don't contest it." Su Wu responded: "We father and sons were without deeds to our credit, and it is only due to elevation by the Emperor that we ranked as generals, with the title of marquis. We brothers were the Emperor's inner circle, therefore willing to lay down our lives. Now if we can sacrifice ourselves to serve the country, we are content even to suffer beheading and boiling. A minister serves his monarch, just as a son serves his father; if the son dies for his father, he does so without complaint. Let the matter now be dropped." Li Ling and Su Wu drank a few days, and then he advised Su Wu: "You really must take my advice." Su Wu said: "I was ready and willing to die long ago! If you insist on my surrender, then stop this feast right now, and let me die in your presence!" Seeing such loyalty to Han, Li Ling sighed: "Oh, this is true righteousness! The sins of Wei Lü and I are higher even than heaven!" His tears fell like rain, soaking his collar, as he bade farewell to Su Wu.

Too embarrassed to donate property personally, Li Ling sent his wife to give Su Wu dozens of cattle and sheep. Later, Li Ling came again to Baikal, and told him: "A Hun frontier post captured a Han from Yunzhong, who said that everybody there was wearing white mourning, from the governor down to the common people, and that Emperor Wudi is dead." At this, Su Wu turned to face south, and wept so bitterly that he coughed blood. He mourned the Emperor every morning and evening.

A few months later, Emperor Zhaodi ascended the throne. After a marriage alliance between the two ruling houses, the Han Court sought the return of Su Wu and others, but the Huns lied that Su Wu had died. Later, another Han envoy came to the Huns, and Chang Hui requested that his guard take him by night to the envoy, to whom he described every event in detail. He also coached the envoy to tell the Chanyu that the Han Emperor, while hunting in the Imperial Forest Park, had shot down a wild goose, on whose foot

【原文】

中。使者大喜，如惠语以让单于。单于视左右而惊，谢汉使曰："武等实在。"于是李陵置酒贺武曰："今足下还归，扬名于匈奴，功显于汉室，虽古竹帛所载，丹青所画，何以过子卿！陵虽驽怯，令汉且贯陵罪，全其老母，使得奋大辱之积志，庶几乎曹柯之盟，此陵宿昔之所不忘也。收族陵家，为世大戮，陵尚复何顾乎？已矣！令子卿知吾心耳。异域之人，壹别长绝！"陵起舞，歌曰："径万里兮度沙幕，为君将兮奋匈奴。路穷绝兮矢刃摧，士众灭兮名已陨。老母已死，虽欲报恩将安归！"陵泣下数行，因与武决。单于召会武官属，前以降及物故，凡随武还者九人。

武以(元始)[始元]六年春至京师。诏武奉一太牢谒武帝园庙，拜为典属国，秩中二千石，赐钱二百万，公田二顷，宅一区。常惠、徐

【今译】

苏武在某个大泽中。汉使者非常高兴，就按常惠所说的责问单于。单于左顾右盼，暗暗吃惊，只好向汉使者道歉说："苏武确实活着。"这时，李陵摆设酒宴庆贺苏武，说："您今天回去，美名传颂于匈奴，功勋显扬于汉朝，即使古代史书所载，图画所描绘的，有谁能胜过您！我李陵虽无能怯懦，假使汉朝暂且宽赦我的罪过，保全我的老母，使我能施展由于投降匈奴之耻辱而积蓄已久的志愿，或许能像曹沫那样寻找机会立功赎罪，这是我从前念念不忘的。皇帝灭了我全家，这是世上最大的侮辱，我还有什么可留恋的？算了吧！我只是让您知道我的心情罢了。你我各处异国，这一分手将永无相见之日了！"李陵起身舞蹈，唱道："驰骋万里啊横度沙漠，为皇帝领兵啊奋击匈奴。被困于狭谷啊矢尽刀折，士兵战死啊我名声扫地。老母已死，虽想报恩何处归！"李陵涕泪交流，与苏武诀别。单于召集苏武的属吏，除去已投降的和死去的，随苏武返回的总共九人。

苏武在昭帝始元六年春天回到都城长安。昭帝命令他供奉牛、羊、豕到武帝陵墓，又授予他典属国之职，官阶为中二千石，并赏赐二百万钱，公田二顷，宅地一处。常惠、徐圣、赵终根均被授予中郎

was tied a silk letter, saying Su Wu and others were in a wetland. The envoy was overjoyed, and questioned the Hun ruler according to Chang Hui's story. The Chanyu looked around in embarrassment and secret surprise, and was forced to apologize: "Su Wu and the others are really alive." At this time, Li Ling organized a celebration banquet for Su Wu, saying: "You'll go back today, with your good name on the lips of the Huns, and your deeds trumpeted in the Han Court. Even in the ancient histories and paintings, who of those portrayed within could surpass you! Although I am weak and cowardly, if Han had shown Li Ling a moment's clemency, pardoned my crime, and protected my mother, then I could have vented my resolve so long pent-up since the shame of my surrender. I might have sought redemption as meritorious as that of Cao Mo. This used to be my fixed obsession. But the Emperor arrested and exterminated my family, and this is the biggest insult in the world. What is there for me to miss back home? Let this be the end of it! I just wanted to impart my feelings. You and I will henceforth live in different lands; this parting is our last, since we shall never meet again!" Li Ling got up and danced, singing: "I galloped thousands of *li* across the desert,/ Ah, I led troops for the Emperor to strike the Huns./ Trapped in the valley, my arrows all shot and my blades all broken./ The soldiers killed, I was discredited./ My mother is dead, but where to go to pay my debt of gratitude!" Li Ling shed tears, and said farewell. The Chanyu called together Su Wu's deputy and soldiers, and the returning party totaled nine, leaving behind the dead and those who had surrendered.

Su Wu came back to the capital Chang'an in the spring of the year six of the Shiyuan reign period (81 BC). Emperor Zhaodi ordered him to sacrifice cattle, sheep, and pigs at Emperor Wudi's tomb and temple, and granted him the post of Vassal Reception Officer, of full 2,000 piculs rank. He rewarded him with two million cash, two hectares of official land, and a residence. Chang Hui, Xu Sheng, and

【原文】

圣、赵终根皆拜为中郎，赐帛各二百匹。其馀六人老归家，赐钱人十万，复终身。常惠后至右将军，封列侯，自有传。武留匈奴凡十九岁，始以强壮出，及还，须发尽白。

武来归明年，上官桀子安与桑弘羊及燕王、盖主谋反。武子男元与安有谋，坐死。

初桀、安与大将军霍光争权，数疏光过失予燕王，令上书告之。又言苏武使匈奴二十年不降，还乃为典属国，大将军长史无功劳，为搜粟都尉，光颛权自恣。及燕王等反诛，穷治党与，武素与桀、弘羊有旧，数为燕王所讼，子又在谋中，廷尉奏请逮捕武。霍光寝其奏，免武官。

数年，昭帝崩，武以故二千石与计谋立宣帝，赐爵关内侯，食邑

【今译】

之职，每人得赏赐绢帛二百匹。其余六人年老归家，每人得赏赐十万钱，免除终身徭役。常惠后来官至右将军，封为列侯，在《汉书》中有他的传记。苏武在匈奴被扣留十九年，出使时年富力强，等到返回时，已须发全白了。

苏武回来的第二年，上官桀的儿子上官安与桑弘羊及燕王、盖主谋反。苏武的儿子苏元与上官安有密谋，犯罪被杀。

起初上官桀、上官安父子与大将军霍光争权，多次逐条记录霍光的过失，送给燕王，让燕王上书昭帝，告发霍光。又扬言说苏武只因出使匈奴二十年不投降，回来才授予典属国之职，霍光的长史杨敞没有功劳，却任搜粟都尉，霍光专权，肆意妄为。等到燕王等因谋反被杀，穷究与他们同谋的人。苏武平素与上官桀、桑弘羊有交情，燕王也曾就苏武为国立功之事多次向皇帝申诉过，苏武的儿子又参与谋反，因此廷尉上奏请求逮捕苏武。霍光把这个奏章压下，只免除了苏武的官职。

几年以后，昭帝去世，苏武因曾以中二千石的身份参与朝臣迎立宣帝的计谋，被赐给关内侯的爵位和三百户的食邑。过了很长时间，

Zhao Zhonggen were all appointed court gentlemen, each receiving a reward of 200 rolls of silk. The remaining six retired to their homes, each one being awarded 100,000 cash, and exempted from labor service for life. Chang Hui later rose to the rank of general of the right, as an adjunct marquis, and his biography appears in the "Chronicles of the Han Dynasty." Su Wu was detained among the Hun for 19 years; he was a fit and strong young man when he accepted the mission, but was white-haired when he returned.

The year after Su Wu returned, Shangguan An, the son of Shangguan Jie, rebelled with Sang Hongyang, Prince of Yan and Princess Gai. Su Wu's son Su Yuan was a co-conspirator with Shangguan An, and was executed as an accomplice.

Originally, Shangguan Jie and Shangguan An were in a power struggle with General-in-Chief Huo Guang, and gave the Prince of Yan many detailed reports of the former's faults, asking the prince to write to Zhaodi, accusing Huo Guang. They also claimed that Su Wu's 20-year-long mission without surrender had earned him only the post of Vassal Reception Officer, whereas Yang Chang, General-in-Chief Huo Guang's aide, had been made Defender in Charge of Searching for Millet, not on the grounds of meritorious deeds but because of Guang's exercise of power and reckless acts. When the Prince of Yan and others were killed for rebelling, those accomplices were thoroughly punished. Since Su Wu had been on good terms with Shangguan Jie and the Prince of Yan, since the prince had often reminded the Emperor of Su Wu's merit, and since Su's son had actually been involved in the plot, the Chamberlain of Law Enforcement asked that Su Wu be apprehended. Huo Guang shelved the petition, but dismissed Su Wu from his post.

A few years later, Emperor Zhaodi died. As Su Wu, being a full 2,000 piculs official participated in the council of ministers to enthrone Emperor Xuandi, he was given the title of Marquis of Guannei with a fief of 300 households. After a very long time, he

【原文】

三百户。久之，卫将军张安世荐武明习故事，奉使不辱命，先帝以为遗言。宣帝即时召武待诏宦者署，数进见，复为右曹典属国。以武著节老臣，令朝朔望，号称祭酒，甚优宠之。

武所得赏赐，尽以施予昆弟故人，家不馀财。皇后父平恩侯、帝舅平昌侯、乐昌侯、车骑将军韩增、丞相魏相、御史大夫丙吉皆敬重武。武年老，子前坐事死，上闵之，问左右："武在匈奴久，岂有子乎？"武因平恩侯自白："前发匈奴时，胡妇适产一子通国，有声问来，愿因使者致金帛赎之。"上许焉。后通国随使者至，上以为郎。又以武弟子为右曹。武年八十馀，神爵二年病卒。

甘露三年，单于始入朝。上思股肱之美，乃图画其人于麒麟阁，法其形貌，署其官爵姓名，唯霍光不名，曰大司马大将军博陆侯姓霍

【今译】

卫将军张安世推荐苏武熟悉过去的典章制度，奉命出使不辱使命，昭帝生前常常提到这些。宣帝立即征召苏武在宦者署听候命令，苏武多次进见宣帝，又任右曹典属国。因为苏武是以有节操著名的老臣，宣帝命令他每逢初一、十五入朝，给予祭酒的尊号，非常优容、尊宠他。

苏武所得赏赐的财物，全都赠送给兄弟和旧友，家里不蓄积财产。皇后的父亲平恩侯许伯、宣帝的舅舅平昌侯王无故和乐昌侯王武、车骑将军韩增、丞相魏相、御史大夫丙吉都很敬重苏武。苏武年事已高，儿子苏元又犯罪被杀，宣帝很可怜他，就询问左右大臣："苏武在匈奴那么长时间，难道没有生子？"苏武通过平恩侯向宣帝陈述："当初从匈奴动身回来时，我的匈奴族妻子正好生下一个儿子，叫苏通国，刚好有音信传来，希望能通过使者用财物把他赎回来。"宣帝同意了。后来苏通国随使者回来，宣帝任命他为郎。又任用苏武的侄子为右曹。苏武终年八十多岁，于宣帝神爵二年病死。

宣帝甘露三年，单于开始入塞朝拜汉朝皇帝。宣帝思念那些辅佐自己的大臣的美德，便令人把他们的形体相貌画在麒麟阁上，并注明他们各自的官职、爵位和姓名，只有霍光不注名字，以示尊崇，称为

was recommended to the Emperor by Zhang Anshi, General of the Guards, as being familiar with the laws and institutions of the past, a former diplomat who had completed his mission with honor, and as often being mentioned for these things by the late Emperor Zhaodi. Xuandi immediately recruited Su Wu in the Office of Eunuchs pending orders. Su Wu had frequent audiences with the Emperor, and was again appointed Vassal Reception Officer as Head of the Right Section. Because Su Wu was a veteran well-known for his integrity, Emperor Xuandi ordered him to Court only every first and 15th day of the month. He gave him the honorific title of Libationer, and made a favorite of him.

Su Wu shared out all his rewards with his brothers and old friends, amassing no wealth of his own. He was much respected by Xu Bo the Empress's father and Marquis of Pingen, and by Xuandi's uncles Wang Wugu Marquis of Pingchang and Wang Wu Marquis of Lechang, by Chariot Horse General Han Zeng, by Prime Minister Wei Xiang, and by Censor-in-Chief Bing Ji. Since Su Wu was old, and his son Su Yuan had been killed as a criminal, Emperor Xuandi felt sorry for him, and asked the ministers: "Does Su Wu have no sons, since he was among the Huns for so long?" Su Wu made a statement through the Marquis of Pingen: "When I came back from the Huns, my Hun wife just gave birth to a son, called Tongguo. I just received news of him, and I hope it will be possible to redeem him with gold and silk through the envoy." The Emperor agreed. Later, Tongguo returned with the envoy, and he was made a court gentleman. The Emperor also appointed Su Wu's nephew for the Right Section. Su Wu died of illness in his eighties, in year two of the Shenjue reign period (60 BC). In year three of the Ganlu reign period (51 BC), the Chanyu began to pay respects to the Han emperor. Xuandi remembered the virtues of his assistants and his ministers, and decreed that their portraits be displayed in Kylin Pavilion, with their respective offices, titles and names indicated.

【原文】

氏，次曰卫将军富平侯张安世，次曰车骑将军龙额侯韩增，次曰后将军营平侯赵充国，次曰丞相高平侯魏相，次曰丞相博阳侯丙吉，次曰御史大夫建平侯杜延年，次曰宗正阳城侯刘德，次曰少府梁丘贺，次曰太子太傅萧望之，次曰典属国苏武。皆有功德，知名当世，是以表而扬之，明著中兴辅佐，列于方叔、召虎、仲山甫焉。凡十一人，皆有传。自丞相黄霸、廷尉于定国、大司农朱邑、京兆尹张敞、右扶风尹翁归及儒者夏侯胜等，皆以善终，著名宣帝之世，然不得列于名臣之图，以此知其选矣。

——卷五十四《李广苏建传》第二十四附

【今译】

大司马大将军博陆侯霍氏，以下依次为：卫将军富平侯张安世，车骑将军龙额侯韩增，后将军营平侯赵充国，丞相高平侯魏相，丞相博阳侯丙吉，御史大夫建平侯杜延年，宗正阳城侯刘德，少府梁丘贺，太子太傅萧望之，典属国苏武。这些人都功勋卓著品德高尚，为当世人所熟知，因此画名臣图来表彰他们，明确说明他们是汉宣帝中兴的辅佐之臣，可与辅佐周宣王中兴的名臣方叔、召虎、仲山甫媲美。共十一人，在《汉书》中各有传记。从丞相黄霸、廷尉于定国、大司农朱邑、京兆尹张敞、右扶风尹翁归到名儒夏侯胜等，都能善始善终，扬名于宣帝之时，却不能列于名臣图中，由此可知辅佐之臣的选择标准。

Only the name of Huo Guang was not shown in full, known as the Commander-in-Chief, General-in-Chief, Marquis of Bolu Mr. Huo. The order was as follows: General of Guards, Marquis of Fuping Zhang Anshi; Chariot Horse General, Marquis of Long'e Han Zeng; Posterior General, Marquis of Yingping Zhao Chongguo; Prime Minister, Marquis of Gaoping Wei Xiang; Prime Minister, Marquis of Boyang Bing Ji; Censor-in-General, Marquis of Jianping Du Yannian; Chamberlain for the Imperial Clan, Marquis of Yangcheng Liu De; Chamberlain of the Palace Revenues, Liang Qiuhe; Grand Mentor of the Heir Apparent Xiao Wangzhi; and Vassal Reception Officer Su Wu. These people were all meritorious and virtuous, well known to their age, and therefore recognized by inclusion in the Portraits of Famous Courtiers, clearly showing that they assisted in the resurgence of Xuandi's reign, and comparable to Fang Shu, Zhao Hu and Zhongshan Fu, the famous courtiers who had assisted in the resurgence of King Xuan of Zhou. A total of 11 people have their own biography in the "Chronicles of the Han Dynasty." Among their number are Huang Ba the prime minister, Yu Dingguo the chamberlain of law enforcement, Zhu Yi the chamberlain for the national treasury, Zhang Chang the metropolitan governor, Yin Wenggui the guardian of the right, and famous scholar Xiahou Sheng. All performed their jobs well from beginning to end, and were famous in the reign of Xuandi, but they could not rank among the Portraits of Famous Courtiers. Thus we can see the criteria by which the Emperor's assistant courtiers were selected.

董仲舒传

【原文】

董仲舒，广川人也。少治《春秋》，孝景时为博士。下帷讲诵，弟子传以久次相授业，或莫见其面。盖三年不窥园，其精如此。进退容止，非礼不行，学士皆师尊之。

武帝即位，举贤良文学之士前后百数，而仲舒以贤良对策焉。

制曰：朕获承至尊休德，传之亡穷，而施之罔极，任大而守重，是以夙夜不皇康宁，永惟万事之统，犹惧有阙。故广延四方之豪俊，郡国诸侯公选贤良修絜博习之士，欲闻大道之要，至论之极。今子大夫褎然为举首，朕甚嘉之。子大夫其精心致思，朕垂听而问焉。

【今译】

董仲舒，广川人。年轻时研究《春秋》，汉景帝时为博士。他在室内挂上帷幕，坐在帷幕后面讲学，弟子们先入学的对后入学的传授学业，有的学生竟然没有见过他。董仲舒三年不看园圃，精心钻研学问到如此的程度。他的进退仪容举止，不符合礼仪的不做，学士们都尊他为老师。

汉武帝继承帝位以后，下令荐举贤良文学先后一百多位，董仲舒作为贤良回答皇帝的策问。

汉武帝策问道：

我继承了先帝最崇高的地位和最美好的德行，要永久传下去，延长到无穷尽的未来，这项任务巨大而且职守重要，所以我从早到晚都没有时间来享乐休息，长久地思考一切事情的原委，惟恐有不周到的地方。因此广泛地邀请各地的豪杰俊才，郡守、国王、诸侯公正地推选出来的贤良、修德、博学的才士们，我想知道治国大道的纲要，安民理论的最高原则。现在大夫们卓然作为贤良的首选，我认为这很好。大夫们要精心思考，我很想知道和要问的如下。

Chapter 11

Biography of Dong Zhongshu

Dong Zhongshu, born in Guangchuan, studied the *Spring and Autumn Annals* when young, and became an erudite in the reign of Emperor Jingdi. He gave his lectures sitting behind the curtain, and his disciples who came first were to teach later students, so that some students never saw him at all. Dong did not look at his garden for a period of three years, which showed how carefully he studied. He never did anything indecorous, in terms of propriety, his appearance or manners, so that scholars all looked to him as their teacher.

After Emperor Wudi succeeded to the throne, he ordered local officials to recommend "the worthy and excellent, and the learned," over one hundred in number, and, as one of those selected, Dong answered the Emperor's policy questions.

Wudi asked about policy thus:

> *I inherited the late Emperor's most noble and virtuous position, and wish to pass it down for ever, extending to infinity. This is an important task and heavy duty, so I do not have time for rest or pleasure from morning till night, pondering all the time the basis of everything going on and fearing something amiss. So I have widely invited the gallants and brightest people from all quarters. The prefects, fiefs, and princes have properly selected the worthy and excellent, the virtuous and pure, and the learned people, as I want to know the outline of the Way of government, the highest principle of the theory of ruling. Now that you grand masters have excelled as leaders among the worthy and excellent, I think this is good. You must think carefully about it, and I would like to know and to ask the*

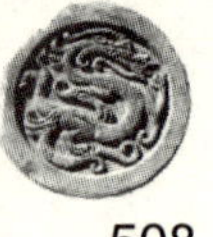

【原文】

盖闻五帝三王之道，改制作乐而天下洽和，百王同之。当虞氏之乐莫盛于《韶》，于周莫盛于《勺》。圣王已没，钟鼓筦弦之声未衰，而大道微缺，陵夷至乎桀纣之行，王道大坏矣。夫五百年之间，守文之君，当涂之士，欲则先王之法以戴翼其世者甚众，然犹不能反，日以仆灭，至后王而后止，岂其所持操或悖缪而失其统与？固天降命不可复反，必推之于大衰而后息与？乌虖！凡所为屑屑，夙兴夜寐，务法上古者，又将无补与？三代受命，其符安在？灾异之变，何缘而起？性命之情，或夭或寿，或仁或鄙，习闻其号，未烛厥理。伊欲风流而令行，刑轻而奸改，百姓和乐，政事宣昭，何脩何饬而膏露降，百谷登，德润四海，

【今译】

听说五帝三王治理国家之道，是改革制度，创作乐章，因而天下安定，后来的百位国王也都同样这么做。虞舜的乐以《韶》乐最美好，周朝的乐以《勺》最优美。圣明的君王死后，钟鼓管弦的声音依然存在，可是大道衰微，逐渐变坏到桀纣那样的所作所为，王道大大地败坏了。这五百年中间，遵守旧制度的国君和当权的士人，想学习先王的法制来辅助当时政治的很多，可是都没有扭转过来，而且王道还一天天走向灭亡，一直到后来的王兴起了，这种没落的趋势才得到制止。难道是他们所信奉的有错误，而失掉了道的传统吗？还是天命就是这样，不是人力所能扭转的，一定要衍变到国家危亡以后才停止呢？唉！所作的一切日夜勤劳，力求效法遥远的古代，难道都没有作用吗？那么，夏、商、周三代的君主承受天命，他们的依据在什么地方？灾异变故，又是因为什么而发生的呢？性命的实际，或者夭亡，或者长寿，或者仁德，或者鄙陋，常常听到这些名称，可是没能透彻地明晓其中的道理。想用风俗教化的力量使命令推行；使刑罚减轻，奸邪改变；使百姓和睦安乐，政治开明。应该怎样整顿政治才能使甘露普降，百谷丰收，使四海之内的人民都受到德泽，连

following.

I heard that the Five Emperors and Three Kings' Way of governing was to reform the system, creating music to stabilize the world, and so did the hundred kings after them. Yu Shun's most beautiful music was the "Shao," and the Zhou's most magnificent music was the "Zhuo." After the death of the sage kings, the orchestral sound, bells and drums remained still there, but the Way declined, gradually deteriorating to the kind of actions perpetrated by King Jie and King Zhou, and the royal Way was greatly undermined. During these 500 years, there have been many ruling monarchs complying with the old system and many scholars in office wanted to learn from the systems of the ancient kings to help the political issues of their day. But they were not able to revert, and the Way was still perishing day by day, until the rise of a later King. Could it be that what they persisted in was error, so they lost their tradition? Or was it the way of fate, not to be reversed by a human, that the state had to be pushed into peril, and only then stopped? Alas! These hectic days and nights consumed in hard work, and the endeavor to emulate the ancient times: can it be that this will not work? Then, wherefore did the monarchs of the Xia, Shang and Zhou Dynasties receive the mandate of heaven? What is the reason for calamities and visitations happening? The truths of life, a king's mandate, character and emotions, short-life or longevity, benevolent or mean: we often heard these terms, but we are not enlightened with their truth. Now we want to implement the law by the force of custom and moral education, and change the law-breakers with lighter penalties so that people live in happy harmony and the government is enlightened. How should we order our rule to make manna fall and farmland yield a bumper harvest, so that people within the four seas are permeated with virtue, and even grass and trees are nourished? How do we

【原文】

泽臻屮木，三光全，寒暑平，受天之祜，享鬼神之灵，德泽洋溢，施乎方外，延及群生？

子大夫明先圣之业，习俗化之变，终始之序，讲闻高谊之日久矣，其明以谕朕。科别其条，勿猥勿并，取之于术，慎其所出。乃其不正不直，不忠不极，枉于执事，书之不泄，兴于朕躬，毋悼后害。子大夫其尽心，靡有所隐，朕将亲览焉。

仲舒对曰：

陛下发德音，下明诏，求天命与情性，皆非愚臣之所能及也。臣谨案《春秋》之中，视前世已行之事，以观天人相与之际，甚可畏也。国家将有失道之败，而天乃先出灾害以谴告之，不知自省，又出怪异以警惧之；尚不知变，而伤败乃至。以此见

【今译】

草木也得到滋润？怎样才能使日、月、星三光完全不发生亏蚀，寒暑季节正常，能够得到天的福佑，为鬼神所歆享？使德泽洋溢，扩大到国外，普及到所有的生命呢？

大夫们通晓先代圣王的事业，熟悉风俗变化的道理，了解事物从发生、发展到结束的次序，而且你们研究高深道理的时间也很久了，希望把研究的成果明白地告诉我！要分清条理，不要笼统，不要混乱，提出的方案，也应慎密考虑。要是有不正直、不忠实、邪曲不守中道的官吏，你们大胆告诉我，决不会泄露出去，我亲自拆看，希望你们不要有后顾之忧。大夫们尽管说出所知道的一切，不要隐瞒，我要亲自看的啊！

董仲舒的对策说：

陛下发出有德的声音和英明的诏书，寻求天命和情性的解答，这两个问题都不是愚臣所能答复的。我谨慎地按照《春秋》中的记载，考察前代已经做过的事情，来研究天和人相互作用的关系，情况是很可怕的呀！国家将要发生违背道德的败坏事情，那么天就降下灾害来谴责和提醒它；如果不知道醒悟，天又生出一些怪异的事来警告和恐吓它；还不知道悔改，那么伤害和败亡就会降临。由此可以看出，天对人君是仁爱的，希望帮助人君消

prevent eclipses of the sun, moon and planets, bring normality to the seasons, so that we can enjoy blessings of heaven and rely on the spirits of the sacrifice gods? How, with virtue filled, we can apply it to distant lands, and spread it to all living things?

You grand masters understand the cause of the earlier sages, you are familiar with the changes of custom and culture, know the sequence of cause and effect, and you have long studied the profound meaning, so I hope you will tell me what you know clearly! Distinguish between entries, be neither multifarious nor confusing, and the proposed program should also be carefully considered and based on a proper theory. If there is a devious, dishonest, disloyal, or inactive minister, be courageous enough to write down his name, for I will never disclose it. I will personally unseal it. You do not have to look over your shoulder in fear. You may unbosom yourselves. Do not hide anything, as I shall read it in person!

Dong's response was:

Your Majesty issued a wise edict in virtuous voice, seeking to understand the Mandate of Heaven and emotions, but these are issues beyond your humble servant's competence to answer. I hereby propose to study the interaction between heaven and man in the light of what the previous dynasties have done, based on the records in the Spring and Autumn Annals. *But our situation is indeed most fearsome! When a nation is on the verge of ruin due to moral corruption, heaven visits a disaster to condemn and to remind it; if man does not wake up, heaven visits strange happenings to warn and threaten; if man still does not mend his ways, then damage and ruin will surely come. It can be seen that heaven is benevolent to the ruler, wanting to disperse chaos. Unless the era is a total stranger to the Way, heaven always wants to support and preserve the ruler, and what matters is the endeavor of the monarch.*

【原文】

天心之仁爱人君而欲止其乱也。自非大亡道之世者，天尽欲扶持而全安之，事在强勉而已矣。强勉学问，则闻见博而知益明；强勉行道，则德日起而大有功：此皆可使还至而(立)有效者也。《诗》曰“夙夜匪解”，《书》云“茂哉茂哉！”皆强勉之谓也。

道者，所繇适于治之路也，仁义礼乐皆其具也。故圣王已没，而子孙长久安宁数百岁，此皆礼乐教化之功也。王者未作乐之时，乃用先王之乐宜于世者，而以深入教化于民。教化之情不得，雅颂之乐不成，故王者功成作乐，乐其德也。乐者，所以变民风，化民俗也；其变民也易，其化人也著。故声发于和而本于情，接于肌肤，臧于骨髓，故王道虽微缺，而筦弦之声未衰也。夫虞氏之不为政久矣，然而乐颂遗风犹有存者，是以孔子在齐而闻《韶》也。夫人君莫不欲安存而恶危亡，然而政乱国危者甚众，所任者非其人，而所繇者非其道，是以政日以仆灭也。夫周道衰于幽厉，非道亡也，幽厉不繇也。至于宣王，思昔先王之德，

【今译】

弥祸乱。如果不是非常无道的世代，天总是都想扶持和保全他，事情在于君主发奋努力罢了。发奋努力钻研学问，就会见闻广博使才智更加聪明；奋发努力行道，德行就会日见崇高，而且越发成功，这些都是可以很快得到，并且是可以很快就有成效的。《诗经》上说：“从早到晚，不敢懈怠。”《尚书》中说：“努力呀！努力呀！”都是奋勉努力的意思。

“道”就是由此达到治理国家的道路，仁、义、礼、乐都是治理国家的工具。所以虽然圣明的君王死了，可是他的子孙还能长久统治，安宁数百年，这都是礼乐教化的功效啊。君王在自己没有制作乐章的时候，就选用先代君王乐章中能适合当时社会的，用它来深入教化人民。得不到教化的实效，典雅、歌颂的乐也就做不成，所以君王功成名就以后才作乐，用乐来歌颂他的功德。乐是用来改变民风，感化民俗的；乐改变民风容易，感化人民也有显著的功效。所以，乐的声音是从和谐的气氛中发出，依据于感情，接触到肌肤，深藏在骨髓。因此王道虽然衰微了，管弦之声却依然流传。虞舜的政治已经很久都没有了，可是流传下来的乐颂还依旧存在，所以孔子在齐国能听到《韶》乐。人君没有不希望国家安宁而憎恶危亡的，然而政治混乱、国家危亡的很多，这是由于任用的人不得当，言行举止不符合治理国家的“道”，所以政事一天天衰败下去。周代的“道”到了周厉王、周幽王时衰落了，不是“道”亡了，而是厉王和幽王不遵循这个

Endeavor in studying will result in a broader mind and deeper wisdom; with endeavor to implement the Way, his virtue will become more noble, and be more and more successful; these can be expeditious and can soon be effective. As it says in the Book of Odes*: "From morning to night, keep your nose to the grindstone." And in the* Book of Documents*: "Try hard! Try hard!" Both mean endeavor.*

The Way is thus the means to govern, while benevolence, righteousness, propriety, and music are all tools of government. Therefore, although the sage kings died, their descendants could maintain a long-term rule of peace for hundreds of years. This is the efficacy of ritual, music and moral education. When the monarchs have not made their own music, they first take what music of the earlier kings is suitable in society at that time, and use it to further educate the people. When moral education is ineffective, the making of elegant and praising music is not possible, so only when a monarch has success to his credit is music made, with which to praise his merits. Music is what is used to ameliorate people's ways and customs; moreover, it is remarkably effective at doing so. So, music is the sound emitted from the harmonious atmosphere, based on emotions, touching the skin, stored deep in the bone marrow. Therefore, even after the decline of the Way of the kings, the sounds of pipes and strings still circulate. The rule of Yu and Shun was long ago, but the music of their time has been handed down and still survives. That is why Confucius could hear Shao music in Qi. Every ruler wants national peace and hates national peril; but, political turmoil and national peril are all too frequent. This is because the wrong people were appointed to office, words and actions were not in accordance with the Way; and so governance declined day upon day. The Way of Zhou declined under King Li and King You. But though these kings did not

【原文】

兴滞补弊，明文武之功业，周道粲然复兴，诗人美之而作，上天祐之，为生贤佐，后世称诵，至今不绝。此夙夜不解行善之所致也。孔子曰“人能弘道，非道弘人”也。故治乱废兴在于己，非天降命不可得反，其所操持悖谬失其统也。

臣闻天之所大奉使之王者，必有非人力所能致而自至者，此受命之符也。天下之人同心归之，若归父母，故天瑞应诚而至。《书》曰“白鱼入于王舟，有火复于王屋，流为乌”，此盖受命之符也。周公曰“复哉复哉”，孔子曰“德不孤，必有邻”，皆积善絫德之效也。及至后世，淫佚衰微，不能统理群生，诸侯背畔，残贼良民以争壤土，废德教而任刑罚。刑罚不中，则生邪气；邪

【今译】

“道”走。周宣王思念先代圣君的德行，复兴久已停滞的事业，补救时弊，发扬周文王、周武王开创的功业，周代的“道”又灿烂复兴起来。诗人赞美他，为他作诗，认为上天保佑他，为他出生贤良的辅佐，后世称颂周宣王，至今不绝。这是周宣王日夜不懈地做好事得来的。孔子说“人能光大‘道’，不是‘道’光大人”。所以治和乱、废和兴，都在于自己。世遭衰乱并不是天命不可挽回，而是由于人君的行为荒谬，失掉了先王优良的传统啊。

臣听说受到天的尊重，天使他得到天下而成为王的人，必定有人力做不到而自然达到的事情，这就是王者承受天命的凭证。天下的人都同心归顺他，就像归顺父母一样，所以天感应到诚意，祥瑞就出现了。《尚书》中说：“白鱼跳进王乘坐的船里，有火覆盖着王屋，变成了乌鸦。”这就是承受天命的凭证啊。周公说：“应得善报呀！应得善报呀！”孔子说：“有德的人决不会孤立，一定会得到帮助。”这都是积善累德的效果啊。可是到了后世，君主淫逸奢侈，道德衰微，不能治理人民，诸侯背叛他，杀害良民，争夺土地，废弃道德教化，滥用刑罚。刑罚使用不适

practice this Way, it does not mean that it died out. As to Zhou's King Xuan, he remembered the earlier sage kings' virtuous doings and revived the long-stalled cause, remedying the ills of the day and proclaiming the achievements of King Wen and King Wu, so that the Way of Zhou went on to new brilliance. Poets praised him, wrote poetry about him, that heaven blessed him by providing him virtuous assistance and counsel. Later generations praised King Xuan, up to the present day. This is the result of King Xuan tirelessly doing good day and night. Confucius said: "A man can enlarge the Way which he follows, but the Way does not enlarge the man." So it depends on one's own acts whether one's kingdom is stable or troubled, wasted or prosperous. Decline and chaos is by no means decreed by heaven and not to be reversed by human deeds; they come about because of a ruler's persistence in error, and letting drop the tradition of the sage kings.

I heard that the person whom heaven respects, and allows to win the world and rule it as king must have something naturally inborn and not achievable by human effort; it is evidence of the Mandate of Heaven. All the people under heaven submit willingly to him, like to their parents, so that heaven, moved by their sincerity, causes an auspicious sight to appear. According to the Book of Documents*: "A white fish jumped into the boat of the King; a fiery object alighted above the King's tent and turned into a red bird." This is the Mandate of Heaven for sure. The Duke of Zhou said: "The good are rewarded! The good are rewarded!" Confucius said: "The virtuous man will never be alone, he will always have help." This is the effect of accumulating good deeds and virtue. But in the later generations, the monarch was given to luxury and debauchery, and moral decline led to inability to control the living things, so that the vassal kings rebelled. He killed innocent civilians,*

【原文】

气积于下，怨恶畜于上。上下不和，则阴阳缪盭而妖孽生矣。此灾异所缘而起也。

臣闻命者天之令也，性者生之质也，情者人之欲也；或夭或寿，或仁或鄙，陶冶而成之，不能粹美，有治乱之所生，故不齐也。孔子曰："君子之德风(也)，小人之德屮(也)，屮上之风必偃。"故尧舜行德则民仁寿，桀纣行暴则民鄙夭。夫上之化下，下之从上，犹泥之在钧，唯甄者之所为；犹金之在镕，唯冶者之所铸。"绥之斯俫，动之斯和"，此之谓也。

臣谨案《春秋》之文，求王道之端，得之于正。正次王，王次春。春者，天之所为也；正者，王之所为也。其意曰，上承天之所为，而下以正其所为，正王道之端云尔。然则王者欲有所为，

【今译】

当，就产生了邪气；邪气聚积在下面，怨恶聚集在上面，上下不和，就会阴阳错乱，妖孽滋生。这就是灾害怪异发生的原因。

臣听说，命就是天的命令，性就是生来的本质，情就是人的欲望。有的人夭折，有的人长寿，有的人仁慈，有的人卑鄙，好比造瓦铸金，不可能都是纯粹美好的，由于社会治、乱的影响，所以人的寿命、品行是不一致的。孔子说："君子的德行像风，小人的德行像草，风向哪边吹，草就向哪边倒。"所以尧、舜实行德政，人民就仁慈长寿；桀纣肆行暴虐，人民就贪鄙夭亡。在上的人君教化在下的人民，下面的人民服从在上的人君，好像泥土放在模型里，听凭陶匠的加工；也好像金属放在容器里，听凭冶匠的铸造。《论语》中说："使人民安定，人民就来归顺，使人民得到鼓舞，人民就会同心协力。"说的就是这样的意思。

臣仔细考察《春秋》里"春王正月"的意思，寻求王道的开端，得到了"正"。"正"次于"王"，"王"次于"春"。春是天的作为。正是王的作为。它的意思是说，君主上面奉承天的作为，下面用来端正自己的行为，"正"是王道的开端啊。可是，

fought over good land and abandoned moral education, resorting to abusive penalties instead, The inappropriate use of punishment gave rise to malaise, which accumulated at the bottom of society, and indignation at the top. When the two levels are not in harmony the order of yin *and* yang *is disrupted, breeding supernatural events. This is where calamity and visitation come from.*

They say that mandate is the decree of Heaven, character is the innate nature, while emotion is human desire. Some people die young, some people live longer; some people are kind, and others mean; just like the making of pottery and the casting of bronze, not every one can be pure and good. Because of different social governance and the impact of turmoil, people's lives and behavior are not identical. Confucius said: "The relation between superiors and inferiors is like that between the wind and the grass; when the wind blows, the grass must bend." Therefore, when Yao and Shun practiced rule by virtue, people were kind and lived longer; in the age of Jie and Zhou's wanton brutality, the people became mean, and died before their time. Moral education from the ruler above of the people below, and the obedience of the people below to the ruler above, are like the clay on the wheel, to be shaped by the potter; and like metal in the cast, to be smelted by the caster. As it is put in The Analects of Confucius*: "He would make them happy, and forthwith multitudes would resort to his dominions; he would stimulate them, and forthwith they would be harmonious." After a careful study of the text of the* Spring and Autumn Annals*, searching for the beginning of the Way of the King, I obtained the first month, which is inferior to King, and King is inferior to Spring. Spring is what heaven brings about; the first month is what the King brings about. This means that the monarch follows what heaven brings about from above, and uses this*

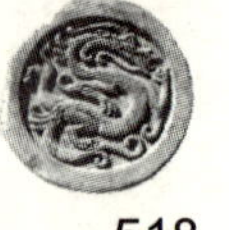

【原文】

宜求其端于天。天道之大者在阴阳。阳为德，阴为刑；刑主杀而德主生。是故阳常居大夏，而以生育养长为事；阴常居大冬，而积于空虚不用之处。以此见天之任德不任刑也。天使阳出布施于上而主岁功，使阴入伏于下而时出佐阳；阳不得阴之助，亦不能独成岁。终阳以成岁为名，此天意也。王者承天意以从事，故任德教而不任刑。刑者不可任以治世，犹阴之不可任以成岁也。为政而任刑，不顺于天，故先王莫之肯为也。今废先王德教之官，而独任执法之吏治民，毋乃任刑之意与！孔子曰："不教而诛谓之虐。"虐政用于下，而欲德教之被四海，故难成也。

臣谨案《春秋》谓一元之意，一者万物之所从始也，元者辞之所谓大也。谓一为元者，视大始而欲正本也。《春秋》深探其本，而反自贵者始。故为人君者，正心以正朝廷，正朝廷以正百官，

【今译】

王者想有所作为，应该向天去求到这个开端。天道最大的就是阴阳，阳作为德，阴作为刑，刑主杀，德主生。所以阳常常处在盛夏，把生育养长作为自己的事；阴经常处在严冬，积聚在空虚不起作用的地方。由此可以看出，天是任用德教，不任用刑罚的。天使阳出现，在上面布施，主管一年的收成；使阴入内，在下面藏伏，时常出来帮助阳；阳没有阴的帮助，也不能使年岁独自完成。从始至终阳是以完成年岁为名的，这是天意啊。王者秉承天意来做事，所以任用德教而不任用刑罚。刑不能任用来治理社会，就像阴不能用来完成年岁一样。执政而任用刑罚，是不顺从天意，所以先王没有肯这样做的。现在废除了先王掌管德教的官员，只任用执法官吏来治理人民，这难道是先王任用刑罚的本意吗？孔子说："不进行教育就杀人，叫做暴虐。"暴虐的政治施用到下面，却想使德教普及到四海，这是难以办到的啊。

臣认真考察《春秋》讲的"一元"的意义，"一"就是万物的开始，"元"就是辞语中所说的"大"。说"一"是"元"，显示了大的开始并且想正其根本。《春秋》深深地探究它的本源，原来却要从尊贵的人开始。所以做君主的，先正心才能正

to correct his own behavior down below, which is the starting point of the King's Way. However, if the king wants to make a difference, he should seek the starting point from heaven. The largest Way in heaven is that of yin *and* yang*;* yang *operates as virtue,* yin *as punishment; punishment means killing, and virtue is life-generating. So* yang *is often situated in the high summer, engaged in generating, raising, nourishing and growing as its business;* yin *is often in the deepest winter, accumulating in the empty and void places. It can be seen that heaven employs instruction through virtue instead of punishment. Heaven makes* yang *appear above, spreading, governing the year's harvest; heaven takes in* yin*, lying low but often coming out to help* yang*; without the help of* yin*,* yang *cannot make a year alone. It is heaven's will that* yang *is the name to complete the year after all. Kings do things by heaven's will, so they prefer moral education to penalty. Punishment cannot be appointed to govern society just as* yin *cannot be used to complete the year. Governing by penalty means not obeying heaven, so the early kings were not willing to do so. Now we have the abolition of the early kings' officials of moral indoctrination, and the appointment of only law enforcers to govern the people: is this the early king's purpose when he used punishments? Confucius said: "To put people to death without having instructed them; this is called brutality." So, for a brutal government below heaven, it is difficult to spread moral education to the whole world.*

I carefully examined the meaning of "one" and "head" in the Annals*. "One" is the beginning of all things, while "head" is what is called "great." To say that "one" is "head" indicated the starting point of greatness and the desire to get to the origin. The* Spring and Autumn Annals *deeply explores its origin, and actually it begins from the noble one. So the monarch should*

【原文】

正百官以正万民，正万民以正四方。四方正，远近莫敢不壹于正，而亡有邪气奸其间者。是以阴阳调而风雨时，群生和而万民殖，五谷孰而屮木茂，天地之间被润泽而大丰美，四海之内闻盛德而皆徕臣，诸福之物，可致之祥，莫不毕至，而王道终矣。

孔子曰："凤鸟不至，河不出图，吾已矣夫！"自悲可致此物，而身卑贱不得致也。今陛下贵为天子，富有四海，居得致之位，操可致之势，又有能致之资，行高而恩厚，知明而意美，爱民而好士，可谓谊主矣，然而天地未应而美祥莫至者，何也？凡以教化不立而万民不正也。夫万民之从利也，如水之走下，不以教化堤防之，不能止也。是故教化立而奸邪皆止者，其堤防完也；教化废而奸邪并出，刑罚不能胜者，其堤防坏也。古之王者

【今译】

朝廷，正朝廷才能正百官，正百官才能正万民，正万民才能正四方。四方正了，远近就没有敢不趋向于正的，而且没有邪气掺杂在里面。所以阴阳调和而风雨及时，万物和谐而人民长育，五谷丰收而草木茂盛，天地间都受到恩泽，并呈现出非常丰富美好的景象，四海之内听到君主的盛德都来称臣，一切幸福的东西，可以得到的祥瑞，无不毕至，这就是王道完成了。

孔子说："凤鸟不来到，'河图'不出现，我恐怕要完了吧！"这是他悲伤自己的德行可以招致这些祥瑞，却因为自己地位卑贱而不能招来。现在陛下贵为天子，富有四海，处在可以招致祥瑞的地位，掌握了可以招致祥瑞的形势，又有能招致祥瑞的资质，行为高尚而恩德广厚，才智聪明而意向美好，爱护人民而喜欢文士，可以说是有道义的君主了。然而天地没有感应，美好的祥瑞没有到来，这是什么原因呢？大概是教化没有建立，没有把人民纳入正道吧。万民追逐利益，就好像水向下流一样，不拿教化作他们的堤防，就不能制止。所以教化建立而奸邪停止，是因为它的堤防完好；教化废止而奸邪并出，用刑罚也不能制止，

first right his mind, so as to right his court; by righting the court he can right officialdom; by righting the officials he can right the populace; by righting all the people he can right all sides. When all sides are put right, no one far or near would dare not to tend to rightness, and nor is there any inner malaise. Therefore, yin *and* yang *are reconciled, so that wind and rain come in a timely manner; all living things are harmonious and people multiply, with a good harvest and rich vegetation; everything between heaven and earth receives grace, and shows a richly beautiful scene; all people within the four seas who hear the ruler's abundant virtue acknowledge allegiance; all the blessed things and all auspicious signs possible appear; this is the Way of the King completed.*

Confucius said: "The phoenix does not come; the River sends forth no Map; it will be all over with me!" He was sad that he might have had such good fortune with his own virtue, but because of his lowly status he could not. Now Your Majesty is the Emperor, rich owner of the four seas, in a position to get good fortune, poised to grasp the situation that can lead to good fortune, but also entitled to good fortune. We can say there is a monarch accomplished in the Way, with noble conduct and rich grace, with distinct intelligence and good intentions, loving the people and the literati. This being so, why is there no response from heaven and earth, and why no auspicious signs? Perhaps because moral education has not been established, and the people are not at one with the right Way. Now all the people are liable to pursue material interests, just as water flows downward, so they cannot be stopped without the dikes of moral education. Therefore, the establishment of moral culture and the ending of the malign is because the embankments have been well built; while the discontinuation of moral education encourages the return of the malign, something that

【原文】

明于此，是故南面而治天下，莫不以教化为大务。立大学以教于国，设庠序以化于邑，渐民以仁，摩民以谊，节民以礼，故其刑罚甚轻而禁不犯者，教化行而习俗美也。

圣王之继乱世也，埽除其迹而悉去之，复修教化而崇起之。教化已明，习俗已成，子孙循之，行五六百岁尚未败也。至周之末世，大为亡道，以失天下。秦继其后，独不能改，又益甚之，重禁文学，不得挟书，弃捐礼谊而恶闻之，其心欲尽灭先王之道，而颛为自恣苟简之治，故立为天子十四岁而国破亡矣。自古以来，未尝有以乱济乱，大败天下之民如秦者也。其遗毒馀烈，至今未灭，使习俗薄恶，人民嚚顽，抵冒殊扞，孰烂如此之甚

【今译】

这是它的堤防坏了。古代的王者明白这个道理，所以坐朝治理天下，没有不把教化当作主要任务的。在国都设立太学进行教育，在县邑设立县学、乡学实施教化，用仁来教育人民，用义来感化人民，用礼来节制人民，所以，虽然刑罚很轻，却没人违犯禁令，这是教化施行，习俗美好的缘故啊。

圣明的君王承继乱世，他把乱世所遗留的一切痕迹都扫除掉，恢复教化，并且给以特别推崇。到了教化已经明了，习俗已经养成，子孙遵循推行下去，遇五六百年仍然不会衰败。到周朝末世，君主非常无道，以致失去了天下。秦朝承继周朝以后，不但没有更改，反而比周朝末年更加无道，严禁文学，不许私自藏书，摒弃礼义，甚至厌恶听到礼义的话，他想把先王的道义完全毁灭掉，专门用自己放肆、苟且、简陋的一套办法来治理国家，所以做天子才十四年，国家就灭亡了。自古以来，还没有像秦朝这样用乱救乱，严重危害天下人民的。秦朝遗留下来的毒素像残余的火焰，到现在还没有熄灭，它使习俗薄恶，人民欺诈顽劣，抵触抗拒，犯法乱德，腐败达到如此严重的地步。孔子说：“腐朽的木头，不能雕饰啊；泥糊的墙，不能粉饰啊。”现在汉朝继

punishments cannot prevent, because the embankments are broken. The ancient kings understood this clearly, so when they governed the world, all of them without exception took moral education as their main task. The establishment of the Imperial College for the education of the whole country, and the county and town schools to teach the towns, were intended to move the people with benevolence, to influence the people with righteousness, and to control the people with the rites, so that although penalty was very light, no one violated taboos. This was because moral education was practiced and customs were good.

When the sage king succeeded, inheriting a troubled age, he removed all vestiges of those times, restored moral education, and gave it special praise. When moral education was obvious, and good customs developed, the later generations followed suit ensuring its endurance without decline for five or six centuries. At the end of the Zhou, the monarch was seriously incompetent and went against the Way, so that he lost the world. After succeeding Zhou, the Qin Emperor did not change for the better; in fact there was even less adherence to the Way than in the last days of Zhou. He strictly prohibited literature, allowing no unauthorized collection of books. He abandoned rites and righteousness, even hating to hear the words of propriety mentioned; he wanted to completely destroy the Way of the previous kings, sticking to his own unbridled, perfunctory and crude way of government, so his state perished only 14 years after he became the Son of Heaven. Since ancient times, there has been no such a regime as Qin to save chaos with more chaos, and to seriously endanger the people of the world. The residual toxicity remain, like smoldering embers. It makes customs mean and evil, people unruly and fraudulent, truculent, flouters of law and virtue, corrupted as never before. Confucius

【原文】

者也。孔子曰："腐朽之木不可雕也，粪土之墙不可圬也。"今汉继秦之后，如朽木粪墙矣，虽欲善治之，亡可奈何。法出而奸生，令下而诈起，如以汤止沸，抱薪救火，愈甚亡益也。窃譬之琴瑟不调，甚者必解而更张之，乃可鼓也；为政而不行，甚者必变而更化之，乃可理也。当更张而不更张，虽有良工不能善调也；当更化而不更化，虽有大贤不能善治也。故汉得天下以来，常欲善治而至今不可善治者，失之于当更化而不更化也。古人有言曰："临渊羡鱼，不如(蛛)[退]而结网。"今临政而愿治七十馀岁矣，不如退而更化；更化则可善治，善治则灾害日去，福禄日来。《诗》云："宜民宜人，受禄于天。"为政而宜于民者，固当受禄于天。夫仁谊礼知信五常之道，王者所当脩饬也；五者

【今译】

承秦朝之后，社会状况就像朽木和泥墙，虽然想很好地治理它，却没有好办法。法令一颁布，奸邪接着就发生，命令一下达，欺骗跟着就兴起，好像用热水去制止沸腾，抱着木柴去救火，只会越来越糟，没有任何益处。譬如琴瑟的音不协调，严重的必须把弦折下来重新安装，才能弹奏；处理政事不行，坏得厉害的，必须破旧立新，才能治理。应当重新张设琴弦而不改弦更张的，虽然有优秀技工也不能调理好；应当改革而不改革的，虽然有大贤人也不能整治好。所以汉朝得天下以来，常想好好治理，可是到现在还没治理好，问题就在于应当改革而没有改革。古人说过："站在潭边羡慕别人捕到了鱼，不如自己回去编织鱼网。"汉朝临政并且想把政事治理好，到现在已经七十多年了，不如回头来进行改革，改革了就能好好治理，国家治理好了，灾害就会一天天消除，福禄也就会一天天到来。《诗经》上说："适合于民，适合于人，接受天给予的福禄。"执政能适合人民，自然会得到天给予的福禄。仁、义、礼、智、信是五种恒久不变的道，这是

said: "Rotten wood cannot be carved; a wall of dirty earth will not receive the trowel." Now Han inherited the social conditions of Qin, like the rotten wood and muddy walls. Even though you aspire to good governance, you can do nothing about it. Every decree promulgated straightway produces a crafty response and every command gives rise to fraudulent acts; it is like using hot water to stop the water boiling, and to pile on firewood to put out a fire; things will only get worse, and no benefit will ensue. For example, when the notes of lute and zither are discordant, in serious cases the strings have to be removed and reinstalled before you can play them; when political affairs are not handled smoothly, if the condition is too bad they too must be overhauled and renewed, before you can control them. If you do not reset the strings when you should, you cannot tune the instruments although good tuners do exist; if you do not reform when you should, you cannot have good government despite the existence of great and worthy statesmen. Therefore, Han has often craved good government since it won the empire, but has not so far achieved this, the problem being that you have not reformed when you should have. The ancients said: "Better go back and make a net than stand by the fishpond envying other people's catches." Han has adopted this stance toward political affairs, longing for good government for 70 years and more, so it is better to go back and reform. Reform can bring good government, which means the gradual elimination of disasters and good fortune also will come day by day. According to The Book of Odes*: "Make the people comfortable, and receive good fortune from heaven." Since your government can make the people comfortable, you will naturally receive good fortune from heaven. The Way of the five constant virtues - benevolence, righteousness, propriety, wisdom and good faith - is what the monarch should nurture and strengthen. When these five virtues*

【原文】

修饬，故受天之祐，而享鬼神之灵，德施于方外，延及群生也。

天子览其对而异焉，乃复册之曰：

制曰：盖闻虞舜之时，游于岩郎之上，垂拱无为，而天下太平；周文王至于日昃不暇食，而宇内亦治。夫帝王之道，岂不同条共贯与？何逸劳之殊也？

盖俭者不造玄黄旌旗之饰。及至周室，设两观，乘大路，朱干玉戚，八佾陈于庭，而颂声兴。夫帝王之道岂异指哉？或曰良玉不瑑，又曰非文无以辅德，二端异焉。

殷人执五刑以督奸，伤肌肤以惩恶，成康不式，四十馀年天下不犯，囹圄空虚。秦国用之，死者甚众，刑者相望，秏矣哀哉！

乌虖！朕夙寤晨兴，惟前帝王之宪，永思所以奉至尊，章洪

【今译】

王者应培养整饬的。这五种道能培养整饬好，就能得到天的保佑，鬼神也来赞助他接受祭祀，恩德就会普及到国外，扩大到一切生命。

汉武帝看了董仲舒的对策认为很不寻常，于是又策问大夫们说：

策问说：听说虞舜的时候，虞舜常常在宫殿的走廊里散步，没有什么作为，可是天下太平。周文王整天忙到日头偏西，连吃饭的空儿都没有，天下也很太平。帝王治理天下的道，难道没有共同的条理，一贯的主张吗？为什么安逸和劳苦有这样大的差别呢？

那些勤俭的帝王连黑色、黄色的旌旗也不制作。可是到了周朝，在宫门外筑了两座观望的台，乘坐用玉装饰的车，制造红色的盾和玉石做的斧柄，朝廷里排列着六十四人的舞蹈，到处响起歌颂的声音。帝王的道，难道意旨不一样吗？有人说："良玉不需要雕琢，"有人说"没有文采就不能辅助德行，"两种说法是不同的。

殷朝人制定五种刑法来防止奸诈，用毁伤身体的办法来惩戒邪恶。可是周成王和周康王放弃这些刑法四十多年，天下也没有犯法的。监狱空荡无人。秦国使用这些刑法，杀死的人很多，受刑的人接连不断，天下空虚，人口减少，真可哀呀！

唉！我晚睡早起，考虑先代帝王的法典，久久地思虑用什么来适合至尊的地位，光大祖宗的事业，我认为关键在于努力搞好

are strengthened, you can get the blessing of heaven, and rely on the spirits of the sacrifice gods. Your grace and virtue will reach to distant territory, spreading to all living things.

The Emperor was impressed by Dong's response. He then asked the grand masters a further policy question.

I heard that in the era of Yu and Shun, the monarch often took a walk along the high corridors of the palace. He did not need to lift a finger, but peace and harmony reigned. King Wen of Zhou was too busy to eat the whole day until the sun was in the west, and the world was also very peaceful. Is there no coherence and consistency in the Kings' Way of government ? Why is there such a big difference between ease and toil?

Those thrifty monarchs did not even make imperial black or yellow flags. But the House of Zhou built two watch towers outside the palace gate, rode in their huge carriages, made red shields and jade-handled axes, arranged eight by eight dancers in the court, and songs of praise could be heard everywhere. Was the Kings' Way of government differently purposed? Some people say: "Good jade need no carving," while others say: "Without literary grace we cannot assist virtue." The two statements are at odds.

Yin people developed five kinds of criminal punishment to check treachery, inflicting physical harm to punish evil. However, kings Cheng and Kang of Zhou suspended these forms for 40-odd years, and there were no offences under heaven. The prisons were empty. The State of Qin used such punishments, killed many people and penalized men one after another, so the world was depleted of population. What true sorrow

Alas! I stay up late and get up early, pondering the former emperors' laws. I always consider that the way to fit my supreme position and commend my ancestors' cause lies in efforts to improve agriculture and employ the talented. Now I

【原文】

业，皆在力本任贤。今朕亲耕藉田以为农先，劝孝弟，崇有德，使者冠盖相望，问勤劳，恤孤独，尽思极神，功烈休德未始云获也。今阴阳错缪，氛气充塞，群生寡遂，黎民未济，廉耻贸乱，贤不肖浑(淆)[殽]，未得其真，故详延特起之士，(意)庶几乎！今子大夫待诏百有馀人，或道世务而未济，稽诸上古之不同，考之于今而难行，毋乃牵于文系而不得骋(攱)[与]？将所繇异术，所闻殊方与？各悉对，著于篇，毋讳有司。明其指略，切磋究之，以称朕意。

仲舒对曰：

臣闻尧受命，以天下为忧，而未以位为乐也，故诛逐乱臣，务求贤圣，是以得舜、禹、稷、卨、咎繇。众圣辅德，贤能佐职，教化大行，天下和洽，万民皆安仁乐谊，各得其宜，动作应

【今译】

农业，任用贤人。现在我亲自耕种籍田为农民做榜样，鼓励百姓孝敬父母，友爱兄弟，尊敬有德行的人，并且派出很多使者，络绎不绝地去慰问劳苦人家，救济没有父母、没有子女的孤独的人，一切办法都想到了，但并没有收到大的成效和美好的德行。现在阴阳错乱，天地间充满了恶劣的气氛，许多生物得不到生长，人民陷在贫困的境地，廉洁的人和无耻的人混淆在一起，好人和坏人也分不清楚，得不到真实的情况，所以我广泛地邀请了特别杰出的士人来请教，目的也许可以达到吧！现在大夫们等待诏命的有一百多人，有的谈论当今的事情却不切实际，用古代历史来印证不相符合，用现在的情况来考察又难于实行，难道是因为受到文吏法令的牵累而不能任意发挥吗？还是因为学术的来源不同，所得的见解各异呢？每个人都可以尽意对答，写在篇上，不要害怕主管官吏，阐明你们的意旨和方略，进行切磋研究，以符合我的心意。

董仲舒对策说：

臣听说尧承受了天命，担忧天下不容易治理，没有拿处在天子的尊位作为欢乐，他诛杀、放逐扰乱国家的大臣，努力寻求贤圣的人，所以得到舜、禹、后稷、卨、咎繇。有众多圣明的人来帮助他提高德行，有许多贤能的人来辅助他恪尽职守，于是教化

personally cultivate my loan field as an example for farmers, encourage people to honor their parents and elder brothers, respect the virtuous people, and sent a constant stream of messengers to show sympathy for laboring people and relieve lonely people without parents or children. I rack my brains, but I have not had great success or achieved good virtue. Now yin *and* yang *are in disorder, and a miasma lies between heaven and earth: living things can hardly survive; people are not rescued from poverty; the incorruptible and the shameless are mixed together, the good undistinguished from the bad. The truth of the situation is hard to obtain, so I have invited a wide range of distinguished scholars to consult, with a view to achieving my purpose! Now over a hundred grand masters are waiting for an audience: some talk about contemporary affairs in ways that are impractical, cite ancient history to prove them unmatched and difficult to implement in accordance with the current situation. Is it because you are so bound by the law of civil officials that you cannot give play to your mind? Or because you come from different schools of thought, and heard different views? Every one of you can make responses freely, write them in volumes, and do not be afraid of the competent officials. Expound your main ideas, so that we may compare notes and study further, so as to satisfy my mind.*

Zhongshu's response was:

I heard that when Yao received the Mandate of Heaven, he was worried about the difficulties of rightly governing the world, he did not take pleasure in his elevated status as Son of Heaven; so he killed or banished his trouble-making ministers, and sought out sages and worthy talents, which is how he got Shun, Yu, Ji, Xie and Gaoyao. These sages helped him improve virtue, and many talented people assisted him in fulfilling the duties, so that moral education was widespread and peace

【原文】

礼，从容中道。故孔子曰“如有王者，必世而后仁”，此之谓也。尧在位七十载，乃逊于位以禅虞舜。尧崩，天下不归尧子丹朱而归舜。舜知不可辟，乃即天子之位，以禹为相，因尧之辅佐，继其统业，是以垂拱无为而天下治。孔子曰“《韶》尽美矣，又尽善(也)[矣]”，此之谓也。至于殷纣，逆天暴物，杀戮贤知，残贼百姓。伯夷、太公皆当世贤者，隐处而不为臣。守职之人皆奔走逃亡，入于河海。天下秏乱，万民不安，故天下去殷而从周。文王顺天理物，师用贤圣，是以闳夭、大颠、散宜生等亦聚于朝廷。爱施兆民，天下归之。故太公起海滨而即三公也。当此之时，纣尚在上，尊卑昏乱，百姓散亡，故文王悼痛而欲安之，是以日昃而不暇食也。孔子作《春秋》，先正王而系万事，

【今译】

大行，天下太平，人民都安于行仁，乐于行义，各得其所，行动合乎礼义，从从容容地在正确的道路上前进。所以孔子说：“假如有王者，必须经过三十年，才能实现仁政，”就是指这说的啊。尧在位七十年，就让位给虞舜。尧死后，天下人民没有归心于尧的儿子丹朱，却归心于舜。舜知道不可逃避，于是即位做了天子，用禹做宰相，继续任用尧所任用的人，继承了尧的传统和事业，所以垂衣拱手没有作为，就使天下太平。孔子说“《韶》乐十分美，又十分善啊”，就是这个意思。至于商纣，违背天意，残毁万物，杀害贤良聪慧的人，残害百姓。伯夷、姜太公都是当时的贤人，他们隐藏起来，不愿出来做官。在职为官的人，都逃亡到河边、海滨。天下黑暗混乱，人民不得安宁，所以天下的老百姓都背弃殷纣王，拥护周文王。周文王顺从天意治理万物，以贤良有德的人为教师并且起用他们，所以闳夭、大颠、散宜生等贤士都聚集在周的朝廷。仁爱施于人民，天下人都归顺他，所以姜太公从偏僻的海滨来投奔，后来做了周朝的三公。这时候，商纣王还在做天子，尊卑的次序混乱，百姓四散逃亡，周文王非常痛心，想让人民过上安定的生活，所以他整天忙得日头偏西还没时间吃饭。孔子写《春秋》，先写王作为正，然后记载各种事情，这表现了在下位而有德行的所谓素王的文章。这样看

prevailed, until the populace was content in benevolence and happy in righteousness. Each had his proper place, acted out of propriety, and followed leisurely in the path of the golden mean. This is what Confucius meant when he said: "If a truly royal ruler were to rise, it would still require 30 years before government by virtue would prevail." Yao reigned for 70 years before abdicating in favor of Shun. After Yao's death, the people did not pledge their loyalty to Yao's son Danzhu, but to Shun. Shun knew that he could not escape, so he ascended the throne as Son of Heaven, with Yu as the prime minister. He continued to employ Yao's assistants and inherited Yao's tradition and cause, so there were peace and harmony even though he needed not lift a finger. This is what Confucius meant when he said: "Shao music was perfectly beautiful, and also perfectly good." In the time of King Zhou of Yin, he ran contrary to Heaven and wasted things, killed virtuous and intelligent men and harmed the people. Boyi and Jiang Taigong were wise men of those times, but they chose to hide rather than serve as his officials. Officials fled to the rivers and hid by the sea. It was a world in chaos, and the people felt no peace, so all of them abandoned Yin in submission to King Wen of Zhou. King Wen of Zhou obeyed Heaven's will in governance of all things, learned from and employed virtuous men and sages, so Hong Yao, Taidian, Sanyi Sheng and other wise men gathered in his court. Love was administered to the multitudes, and people under heaven obeyed him, so Jiang Taigong joined him from his seaside refuge, and later became one of the three Dukes of Zhou. At this time, Zhou of Yin was still the King, the social hierarchy was upside down, and the people had fled to the four winds, so King Wen was grieved, and wanted to bring them peace; that was why he was too busy to eat until sundown. In the Spring and Autumn Annals, *Confucius first wrote of the king as being the first to link*

【原文】

见素王之文焉。繇此观之，帝王之条贯同，然而劳逸异者，所遇之时异也。孔子曰“武尽美矣，未尽善也”，此之谓也。

臣闻制度文采玄黄之饰，所以明尊卑，异贵贱，而劝有德也。故《春秋》受命所先制者，改正朔，易服色，所以应天也。然则宫室旌旗之制，有法而然者也。故孔子曰：“奢则不逊，俭则固。”俭非圣人之中制也。臣闻良玉不瑑，资质润美，不待刻瑑，此亡异于达巷党人不学而自知也。然则常玉不瑑，不成文章；君子不学，不成其德。

臣闻圣王之治天下也，少则习之学，长则材诸位，爵禄以养其德，刑罚以威其恶，故民晓于礼谊而耻犯其上。武王行大谊，平残贼，周公作礼乐以文之，至于成康之隆，囹圄空虚四十馀

【今译】

来，帝王的条理系统是一致的，但是勤劳和安逸不相同，是因为所遭逢的时代不一样。孔子说“《武》乐十分美，不够十分善啊”，就是这个意思。

臣听说制度文采和黑色、黄色的装饰，都是用来分别尊卑、区分贵贱和劝勉人们要有德行的。《春秋》是承受天命著述的，所以它首先制定的，就是改变历法和衣服的颜色，用这来顺应天。那么，宫室和旌旗的制度是有效法才那样的。所以孔子说：“奢侈了就不够谦逊，节俭了便简陋。”节俭并不是圣人适中的制度。臣听说好玉不雕琢，是因为它的质地本来就滑润美好，不需要再加以雕饰，这就好像项橐没有学习就能自己知道一样。可是普通的玉要是不雕刻，就不能成就美丽的花纹；君子不学习，就不能成就美德。

臣听说圣明的君王治理天下，对年轻的就教他们养成学习的好习惯，对年长的就授给职位察看他们的才能。用职位和俸禄来培养他们的德行，用刑罚来禁止他们作恶，所以人民都懂得礼义而耻于触犯他们的上级。周武王施行大义，平定残贼，周公作礼乐来加以文治，直到周成王和周康王时的盛世，牢狱空虚了四十

all kinds of things, he being the man displaying the qualities of a virtuous king although without his crown. It would appear from this that the monarchs' well-organized system is consistent, but the discrepancy between their diligence and ease came from the difference of the ages in which they lived. Confucius said: "Wu music was perfectly beautiful, but not perfectly good." This is what I mean.

I heard that the systems of patterns, and black or yellow decoration, were used to show hierarchy, to distinguish in status, and exhort the people to virtue. The Spring and Autumn Annals *was written in accordance with the Mandate of Heaven, so the first thing established was to change the calendar and the color of clothes, in order to comply with heaven. But, the system of palaces and flags followed some effective method. So Confucius said: "Extravagance leads to insubordination, and parsimony to meanness." Frugality was not the moderate system of the sages. I heard that good jade needs no carving, because it is too smooth and well-textured to need any further carving, which is no different from Xiang Tuo, knowing everything without having to learn. But if ordinary jade is not carved, beautiful patterns cannot be achieved; if a gentleman does not learn, he cannot achieve virtue.*

I heard that the sage king governed the world by teaching the young to develop good study habits, and appointing the seniors to positions according to their ability. Titles and salary were awarded to encourage their virtue, and penalties to awe them against evil, so people understood ritual and righteousness, being ashamed to go against their superiors. King Wu of Zhou implemented the grand righteous cause, putting down the residual enemy; and the Duke of Zhou created the ritual and music to rule through learning. In the prosperous times of kings Cheng and Kang, there were empty prisons for

【原文】

年，此亦教化之渐而仁谊之流，非独伤肌肤之效也。至秦则不然。师申商之法，行韩非之说，憎帝王之道，以贪狼为俗，非有文德以教训于(天)下也。诛名而不察实，为善者不必免，而犯恶者未必刑也，是以百官皆饰(空言)虚辞而不顾实，外有事君之礼，内有背上之心，造伪饰诈，趣利无耻；又好用憯酷之吏，赋敛亡度，竭民财力，百姓散亡，不得从耕织之业，群盗并起。是以刑者甚众，死者相望，而奸不息，俗化使然也。故孔子曰“导之以政，齐之以刑，民免而无耻”，此之谓也。

今陛下并有天下，海内莫不率服，广览兼听，极群下之知，尽天下之美，至德昭然，施于方外。夜郎、康居，殊方万里，说德归谊，此太平之致也。然而功不加于百姓者，殆王心未加焉。

【今译】

多年。这也是教化的感染和仁义的影响，不仅仅是毁伤身体的刑罚的功效。到了秦朝就不是这样，效法申不害、商鞅的办法，实行韩非的学说，憎恶古代帝王治理天下的道理，贪污成风，并不是用礼义来教化天下。秦只求名而不察实，行善的好人不一定能免罪，犯法的坏人也不一定就受到惩罚。所以百官都谎言欺诈，不务实际，表面上都表现出尊敬君上的礼貌，内心却怀着背叛君上的打算，弄虚作假来掩饰狡诈，追逐私利，没有羞耻；又总喜欢使用残忍刻毒的官吏，无限制地征收赋税，榨尽人民的财力，百姓四处逃亡，不能从事耕田和纺织工作，于是强盗到处起事。所以受刑的人很多，死的人一个接一个，但是做坏事的并没有停止，这是风俗教化所造成的。所以孔子说：“用政法来教导人民，用刑罚来制裁人民，人民苟且地要求免受惩罚却不知道羞耻。”就是这个意思。

现在陛下统一了天下，四海之内没有不顺服的。陛下广泛地观察，多方面听取，尽可能地吸取群下的智慧，具备了天下的美德，崇高的德行显耀普照，扩大到国外。远达万里的夜郎和康居悦服归心，就真是太平到来的景象啊。但是恩德并没有施加到普通百姓身上，大概是您还没有注意到这个问题吧。曾子说：“尊

40-odd years. This was due, not just to the effectiveness of physical punishment, but to the power of moral education and the influence of righteousness. But everything changed under the Qin Dynasty. They followed the laws of Shen Buhai and Shang Yang, and implemented Han Fei's theory. Hating the Way of ancient monarchs, they practiced corruption and cruelty, instead of educating their subordinates in propriety and virtue. They just punished the crime in name, without discerning it in reality. People doing good were not necessarily spared, while lawbreakers were not necessarily punished. So the officials lied, ignoring the actual facts, feigning respect and courtesy for the monarch on the surface, but with betrayal in their hearts. They falsified to conceal their cunningness, shamelessly seeking profits. And then cruel officials were preferred, to enforce unlimited collection of taxes, exhausting the people's wealth, so the people fled and scattered, unable to farm or weave. As a result, bandits appeared everywhere. Thus punishments were meted out in multitudes, and one corpse followed another, but there was no end to the evil doing, which had its source in debased custom. So Confucius said: "If the people be led by laws, and kept in line merely through punishments, they will try to avoid the punishment, but have no sense of shame." This is what I mean.

Your Majesty has now completely unified the world, meeting no disobedience within the four seas. You observe and listen widely, gathering as much as possible the courtiers' wisdom, and perfecting the beauty of the world, so your renowned noble virtues shine brightly, and extend abroad. Countries as far as Yelang and Kangju 10,000 li *away have been happy with virtue and reverted to righteousness, which means peace is really coming. Yet the benefits have not reached the common people, probably because you do not have it at*

【原文】

曾子曰："尊其所闻，则高明矣；行其所知，则光大矣。高明光大，不在于它，在乎加之意而已。"愿陛下因用所闻，设诚于内而致行之，则三王何异哉！

陛下亲耕藉田以为农先，夙寤晨兴，忧劳万民，思惟往古，而务以求贤，此亦尧舜之用心也，然而未云获者，士素不厉也。夫不素养士而欲求贤，譬犹不(瑑)[琢]玉而求文采也。故养士之大者，莫大(虐)[虖]太学；太学者，贤士之所关也，教化之本原也。今以一郡一国之众，对亡应书者，是王道往往而绝也。臣愿陛下兴太学，置明师，以养天下之士，数考问以尽其材，则英俊宜可得矣。今之郡守、县令，民之师帅，所使承流而宣化也；故师帅不贤，则主德不宣，恩泽不流。今吏既亡教训于下，或不承用主上之法，暴虐百姓，与奸为市，贫穷孤弱，冤苦失职，甚不

【今译】

崇自己所听到的道理，就高明了；实践自己所知道的道理，就光大了。高明光大，不在于别的，在于对这些注意罢了。"希望陛下采用所听到的道理，诚心诚意按那些道理去做，那么，跟三王又有什么不同呢？

陛下亲自耕种籍田来倡导农业，早起晚睡，为人民担忧，思念古代治世，用心寻求贤人，这也是尧舜的用心啊，可是没有得到贤人，这是因为平时对于士人没有鼓励劝勉的缘故。平时不培养人才却想寻求贤人，就好比不雕刻玉却要求玉有文采一样。所以培养人才没有比办好太学更重要的了，太学是产生贤士的地方，是教化的本源，现在各郡国的人都很多，可是有些郡国还没有应举贤良文学策问、作对策的人，这就是因为王道在那里经常断绝。臣希望陛下兴办太学。聘请高明的教师来教育培养天下的士人，经常考问他们而使他们充分发挥自己的才能，那么英俊的人才就可以得到了。现在的郡守、县令，就是百姓的老师和表率，是委派他们禀承君主的恩泽去宣扬教化的，师表不贤良，君主的仁德就得不到宣扬，恩泽就传布不到下面。现在官吏既然没有教育人民，或者不实行君主的法令，暴虐百姓，和坏人狼狈为

heart. Master Zeng said: "Respect the principle you have heard, and you become enlightened; practice the principle you already know and you will shine brighter. To be enlightened and bright shining requires only that you have these things at heart." I wish Your Majesty will apply the principles you have heard, having good faith in heart and practicing the knowledge. How then would you be different from the Three Kings?

Your Majesty personally cultivates the loan field as an example for farmers. You stay up late and get up early, worrying and wearied for the people, yearning for the ancient peace. And you try to seek the talented, as did Yao and Shun, but the worthy people have not materialized, because there is usually no encouragement or exhortation for scholars. To seek the talented without usually nurturing them, is akin to seeking good patterns in jade without carving it. Therefore, nothing is more important in producing such people than the Imperial College. The Imperial College is the place to produce talents, and the origin of enlightenment. And now people are plentiful in the prefectures and fiefs, but their policy responses do not conform to the classics, which is why in those places there are often stoppages in the Way. I hope Your Majesty will set up the Imperial College, and recruit wise teachers to train scholars from across the land, repeatedly examining them and giving full scope to their talents, so that you can get distinguished talents. Now the prefects and magistrates are teachers and examples for the people, assigned to carry on the good traditions with scholars and to practice moral education. If the teachers are not virtuous, then the monarch's benevolence is not made known, nor his grace permeate down to the people. Since the officials do not educate the people, or else do not implement the lord's decrees; they tyrannize the people instead, and trade with the unscrupulous for personal gains; the result is poverty

【原文】

称陛下之意。是以阴阳错缪，氛气充塞，群生寡遂，黎民未济，皆长吏不明，使至于此也。

夫长吏多出于郎中、中郎，吏二千石子弟选郎吏，又以富訾，未必贤也。且古所谓功者，以任官称职为差，非(所)谓积日絫久也。故小材虽絫日，不离于小官；贤材虽未久，不害为辅佐。是以有司竭力尽知，务治其业而以赴功。今则不然。(累)[絫]日以取贵，积久以致官，是以廉耻贸乱，贤不肖浑殽，未得其真。臣愚以为使诸列侯、郡守、二千石各择其吏民之贤者，岁贡各二人以给宿卫，且以观大臣之能；所贡贤者有赏，所贡不肖者有罚。夫如是，诸侯、吏二千石皆尽心于求贤，天下之士可得而官使也。遍得天下之贤人，则三王之盛易为，而尧舜之名可及也。

【今译】

奸，谋取私利，致使贫穷孤弱的人含冤受苦，流离失所，很不符合陛下的意愿。所以阴阳错乱，怨气充满，人民无法生活，在苦难中得不到救助，这都是郡守县令们不贤明，才造成这样的现象啊。

郡守、县令多数是出身于郎中、中郎，年俸二千石的大官的子弟选任郎官，又仗着有钱财，不一定贤明。而且古时候考核官吏的功劳，是按照做官是否称职来区分的，不以在任时间的长短为标准。所以才能小的人，虽然任职时间很长，还是小吏；有才能的人，虽然任职不久，并不妨碍他升迁为辅佐大臣。所以有职守的官吏，都竭尽自己的才能和智慧，努力做好工作，争取立功。现在却不是这样，官吏们积累时间就可以得到高位，日子一久，就可以升官，所以廉洁和无耻混淆，好人和坏人不分，真正的贤才就无法得到。臣愚蠢地认为让各位诸侯、郡守、二千石各自选择他们管辖下的官吏和百姓中的贤才，每年荐举两人，用他们在皇宫中值宿守卫，而且还可以拿这件事来观察大臣的能力，如果荐举的人贤能，就给予奖赏；要是荐举的人不好，就加以惩罚。如果像这样，诸侯、二千石官都尽心寻求贤才，天下有才能的人就可以得到，授给他们官职加以任用了。遍得天下的贤人，那么三王的盛世也就容易做到，尧舜的声名也就可以赶上了，

for the solitary without parents or children and for the weak, as well as homelessness and unemployment. Such suffering is quite contrary to Your Majesty's wishes. Now yin *and* yang *are in disorder, discontentment is rife and people cannot make a living, with no way out of their adversity; it is the benighted high officials who have caused this phenomenon.*

These prefects and magistrates mostly came from gentlemen of the interior, court gentlemen, or the children or siblings of 2,000-picul level high officials. They were chosen on the basis of money, not necessarily on virtue, whereas officials in ancient times were assessed on their competence, not on their length of service. So a man with little competence, no matter how long in post, remained a junior official; whereas there was nothing to stand in the way of promotion to a high minister for a real talent, although not in office long. Therefore, the officials in charge gave all of their ability and wisdom, so as to do a good job and acquire credit. This is not now the case, for officials can reach high positions purely by time serving. The incorruptible and the shameless are mixed together, the good are undistinguished from the bad. The real talented people cannot be had. Your humble servant thinks that the princes, marquises, governors, and 2,000-picul officials should be ordered to select worthy people among their own officials and people, each recommending two a year to the imperial court. Besides, this affords a chance to observe the ability of your ministers. Those who recommend wise people will be rewarded, and those who recommend bad people should be punished. Thus, the princes and 2,000-picul officials will do their utmost in seeking worthy people, the scholars can be obtained, and be awarded with official appointments. When the worthy men under heaven are all gathered, the Golden Age of the Three Kings will be easy to bring about, and Yao and Shun's reputation will be within

【原文】

毋以日月为功，实试贤能为上，量材而授官，录德而定位，则廉耻殊路，贤不肖异处矣。陛下加惠，宽臣之罪，令勿牵制于文，使得切磋究之，臣敢不尽愚。

于是天子复册之：

制曰：盖闻“善言天者必有徵于人，善言古者必有验于今”。故朕垂问乎天人之应，上嘉唐虞，下悼桀纣，寖微寖灭寖明寖昌之道，虚心以改。今子大夫明于阴阳所以造化，习于先圣之道业，然而文采未极，岂惑乎当世之务哉？条贯靡竟，统纪未终，意朕之不明与？听若眩与？夫三王之教所祖不同，而皆有失，或谓久而不易者道也，意岂异哉？今子大夫既已著大道之极，陈治乱之端矣，其悉之究之，孰之复之。《诗》不云乎：

【今译】

千万不要用做官时间的长短来计算功劳，实际考察官吏的贤能是上策，衡量了才能以后再授给官职，考察了德行以后再确定职位，那样，廉洁和无耻待遇不同，好人和坏人就能够区别了。陛下给臣恩惠，宽恕臣的罪过，教臣不要害怕主管官吏，使臣能够切磋研究，臣不敢不倾吐自己肤浅的见解。

于是天子又提出策问：

汉武帝策问道：听说“善言天的，一定能找到人事来印证，善说古的，一定能在现实中得到证明”。所以我问你们天人感应的关系，往上赞美唐尧虞舜，往下哀悼夏桀商纣，看到这些渐渐灭亡和逐步昌盛的道理，我要虚心改正错误。大夫们明晓阴阳的变化和作用，熟悉先代圣王的道术和事业，可是你们的文章并没有把这些充分表达出来，难道是你们对当代的政务有什么疑惑吗？有些道理没有系统整理和完整表达，大概是由于我不聪明，或是听话会迷惑吧？三王的教化，最初各不相同，却都有不足，有人说道是恒久不变的，这两种说法意思难道有什么不同吗？现在大夫们既然已经写出了大道的最高原则，陈述了治理乱世的方法，希望你们再说详细些、深刻些、周到些。《诗经》上不是说：“君子呀，不要苟且安息，神是听着你的，帮助你获得大

reach. Take no account of length of time served; the superior policy is to inspect their worthiness in reality. If you measure their ability before awarding official posts, and identify their virtue before determining their ranks, then the incorruptible and shameless are separated, the good and bad distinguished. Your Majesty is graceful enough to forgive my guilt, instructing me not to be bound by the law of civil officials, in order to discuss in depth. How could I refrain from pouring out my superficial views?

The Emperor posed a further question.

I heard that "Those good at expounding the Way of heaven are able to refer to its signs among men, and those good at describing ancient history can prove it in reality." So I condescend to ask you about the interaction between heaven and man; by praising Tang Yao and Yu Shun above and bewailing Jie and Zhou below I understand the process of decline and demise and rise and prosperity, and will sincerely seek to amend the wrongs. Now you grand masters are well versed in the changes of yin *and* yang, *familiar with the missions of yesteryear's sages, but your articles have not adequately expressed these. Is this because you have misgivings about politics in our current age? Is my lack of intelligence the reason for this lack of systematic ordering and complete expression? Or have I got confused in listening? The doctrines of the Three Kings were different at the start, each having its own inadequacy, but some say that the Way is eternal and immutable. Is there a conflict between these two statements? Now you grand masters have written about the highest principle of the Way, stating the method of governance in troubled times. I wish you repeat it in detail, in deeper and more considered fashion. Does not the* Book of Odes *say: "Gentlemen, do not rest idle. The gods are listening to you, helping to win great*

【原文】

"嗟尔君子，毋常安息，神之听之，介尔景福。"朕将亲览焉，子大夫其茂明之。

仲舒复对曰：

臣闻《论语》曰："有始有卒者，其唯圣人乎！"今陛下幸加惠，留听于承学之臣，复下明册，以切其意，而究尽圣德，非愚臣之所能具也。前所上对，条贯靡竟，统纪不终，辞不别白，指不分明，此臣浅陋之罪也。

册曰："善言天者必有徵于人，善言古者必有验于今。"臣闻天者群物之祖也，故遍覆包函而无所殊，建日月风雨以和之，经阴阳寒暑以成之。故圣人法天而立道，亦溥爱而亡私，布德施仁以厚之，设谊立礼以导之。春者天之所以生也，仁者君之所以爱也；夏者天之所以长也，德者君之所以养也；霜者天之所以杀也，刑者君之所以罚也。繇此言之，天人之徵，古今之道也。

【今译】

福。"我要亲自看你们的对策，大夫们要努力阐明你们的见解。

董仲舒又对策说道：

臣听《论语》上说："有始有终的，只有圣人啊！"很荣幸地承蒙陛下的恩惠，留心听取我们这些接受过传统学问的臣子的意见，又颁下高明的册书，切合其中的意义，并且彻底地研究圣德，这不是愚臣的能力所能详细陈述的。先前臣所上的对策，有些道理缺乏系统整理和完整的表达，辞句不清晰，意旨不明了，这都是我浅陋的罪过。

策问中说："善言天的，一定能找到人事来印证；善说古的，一定能得到现实的证明。"臣听说，天是万物之祖，所以天对万物普遍地覆盖着、包含着，没有偏颇。天造作日、月、风、雨来调和万物，通过阴、阳、寒、暑来生育万物。所以圣人效法天建立道，也是广施仁爱而没有一点私心，布施恩德和仁爱来厚待百姓，设立义理和礼制去引导人民。春季是天用来生育万物的，仁是人君用来爱护百姓的；夏季是天用来滋长万物的，德是人君用来养育人民的；秋霜是天用来诛杀万物的，刑法是人君用来惩罚罪犯的。由此说来，天和人的验证，是从古至今的道理。

blessing."? I will personally read your responses, so you grand masters must strive to articulate your views.

Dong responded:

I heard it said in The Analects of Confucius*: "Is it not the sage alone, who can unite in one the beginning and the consummation of learning!" Now Your Majesty obliges us with his grace, to listen carefully to those of us who have received the traditional knowledge, and has also issued a wise decree to bring home the meaning. But a thorough study of the virtue of sages is beyond your humble servant. It is my humble guilt that there was no systematic ordering and complete expression in my previous response, that my phrasing and my meaning were unclear.*

The question is: "Those good at expounding the Way of heaven are able to refer to its signs among men, and those good at describing ancient history can prove it in reality." As I heard, heaven is the origin of all things, so heaven covers and contains everything generally, with no bias. Heaven engenders the sun and the moon, wind and rain, to reconcile all things, complete through yin *and* yang*, winter and summer. So the sages established the Way following the moves of heaven, also with selfless universal love: they treated the people well by spreading virtue and benevolence, and guided the people by establishing righteousness and rites. As spring is when heaven brings birth to things, so benevolence is what the ruler uses to love the people; as summer is when heaven grows things, so virtue is what the ruler uses to cultivate the people; as frost is what heaven uses to kill things, so punishment is what the ruler uses to penalize criminals. Thus, it is the Way of ancient times and our current age to verify heaven's signs by reference to man.*

When Confucius compiled the Spring and Autumn Annals,

【原文】

孔子作《春秋》，上揆之天道，下质诸人情，参之于古，考之于今。故《春秋》之所讥，灾害之所加也；《春秋》之所恶，怪异之所施也。书邦家之过，兼灾异之变，以此见人之所为，其美恶之极，乃与天地流通而往来相应，此亦言天之一端也。古者修教训之官，务以德善化民，民已大化之后，天下常亡一人之狱矣。今世废而不修，亡以化民，民以故弃行谊而死财利，是以犯法而罪多，一岁之狱以万千数。以此见古之不可不用也，故《春秋》变古则讥之。天令之谓命，命非圣人不行；质朴之谓性，性非教化不成；人欲之谓情，情非度制不节。是故王者上谨于承天意，以顺命也；下务明教化民，以成性也；正法度之宜，别上下之序，以防欲也：修此三者，而大本举矣。人受命于天，固超然异于群生，入有父子兄弟之亲，出有君臣上下之谊，会聚相遇，则

【今译】

孔子作《春秋》，上度量天道，下验证人情，参看于古代，考察于今时。所以《春秋》所讥讽的，就是灾害所侵犯的；《春秋》所憎恶的，就是怪异所触及的。孔子写出了国家的过失和灾异的变化，从这里可以看出人们行为的好和坏，是和天地相通并且互相感应的，这也是谈天道的一种看法。古时候设立掌管教导训化的官，职责是用德和善来教化人民，人民大受感化以后，天下常常没有一个人在监狱里。现代废弃这种制度，没法教化人民，因此人民都不知道行义而死于追逐财利，所以违法犯罪的人就多了，一年之内，坐牢和诉讼的人竟有成千上万。由此可见，古时候的法度是不能不采用的，所以《春秋》遇到改变古代制度的事情就加以讥讽。天的命令叫做命，这个命不是圣人不能照着去做；生来的本性叫做性，这种性不是教化不能完成；人的欲望叫做情，这种情不用法度不能加以节制。所以做君王的，上面很谨慎地奉承天意来顺从天命；下面必须教化人民，使人民能够完成他们的性；建立应该遵循的法度，分清上下尊卑的次序，来防止贪欲；做好这三件事，国家的根本就奠定了。人承受了天命，本来是超群的，和其他生物不同。在家里有父子兄弟之亲，在外面有君臣上下的名分，大家聚会相遇，就有尊敬老人和分别长幼的

he conjectured the Way of heaven above, and verified against human conditions below, referring both to the ancient times and present day. Therefore, what is ridiculed in the Annals *was hit by disasters; what is hated in the* Annals *was touched by the weird. Confucius wrote down the country's faults, together with its changes of calamities and visitations, to show that good and bad extremes of behavior are connected to heaven and earth and mutually corresponding, which is one manner of describing the Way of heaven. In ancient times, officials in charge of teaching and training were appointed, charged with moral education of the people through virtue and moral good. Once this was widespread, there was often not a person in prison in the whole land. In this era, such a system was abolished, with nothing to educate the people, who then gave up practicing righteousness and die chasing profits. So people violate the law; there are more and more crimes, and tens of thousands of people are convicted every year. Thus, we must adopt the ancient system, this is why the* Annals *ridicule any changes to the ancient systems. The command of heaven is called giving the mandate, and only a sage can do this; innate quality is called one's nature, which cannot be perfected without moral education; human desire is called passion, which cannot be restrained without a system of law. Therefore, the monarchs would carefully carry out the gods' will above to follow the mandate; they must educate the people so that people can perfect their nature; they should establish appropriate laws, and distinguish the social hierarchy, to prevent greed: when these three things are in place, the country's foundation is laid. Man takes the mandate of heaven, placing him above the multitudes and thus different to other living things. At home, there are the relations of father, sons, and brothers, while outside there is a hierarchy of status like a monarch and subjects. When we meet,*

【原文】

有耆老长幼之施；粲然有文以相接，欢然有恩以相爱，此人之所以贵也。生五谷以食之，桑麻以衣之，六畜以养之，服牛乘马，圈豹槛虎，是其得天之灵，贵于物也。故孔子曰："天地之性人为贵。"明于天性，知自贵于物；知自贵于物，然后知仁谊；知仁谊，然后重礼节；重礼节，然后安处善；安处善，然后乐循理；乐循理，然后谓之君子。故孔子曰："不知命，亡以为君子。"此之谓也。

册曰："上嘉唐虞，下悼桀纣，寖微寖灭寖明寖昌之道，虚心以改。"臣闻众少成多，积小致钜，故圣人莫不以晻致明，以微致显。是以尧发于诸侯，舜兴乎深山，非一日而显也，盖有渐以致之矣。言出于己，不可塞也；行发于身，不可掩也。言

【今译】

规范，有明确的礼节相互接待，欢欣地有恩德地互相亲爱，这就是人可贵的地方。种植五谷作为食物，播种桑麻用来做衣，饲养六畜，驾牛骑马，圈豹槛虎，这就是人得到天的灵气，比万物可贵的表现。所以孔子说："天地所生，人是最可贵的。"人们明白了天性，就知道自己比万物可贵；知道自己比万物可贵然后知道礼义；知道礼义，然后注重礼节；注重礼节，然后安心处于善道；安心处于善道，然后乐于遵循道理做事；乐于遵循道理，然后叫做君子。所以孔子说"不知道命，不可以做君子"，就是这个意思啊。

策问说："往上赞美唐尧、虞舜，往下悲悼夏桀、商纣。看到这些渐渐灭亡和渐渐昌盛的道理，我要虚心改正错误。"臣听说积少就能成多，积小就能成大，因此圣人无不是积累暗淡的微明而达到光明，从微贱的地位一步步地达到显贵的。所以尧由诸侯而升为天子，舜从在深山中耕种兴起，都不是一天而尊显的，是逐渐达到的。话由自己说出，就不能再去堵塞；行为由自己做

there are norms for respecting the elderly and distinguishing between the young and old. There are clearly defined protocols for intercourse, and with kindness and virtue people are joyful as they love each other: this is why man is noble. We grow grains as food, plant mulberry and hemp for clothing, feed domestic animals, drive cattle and ride horses, raise caged leopards and tigers. We do this from the wit that heaven gives us, a demonstration of man's nobility compared with other living things. So Confucius said: "Of all creatures with their different natures produced by heaven and earth, man is the noblest." People understand the nature of all things, and know themselves to be nobler; when they know themselves nobler than other things, they know benevolence and righteousness; when they know benevolence and righteousness, they pay attention to etiquette; when they focus on courtesy, they are at peace in the good Way; when they are at peace in the good Way, they are willing to follow reason; willing to follow reason, they are called gentlemen. So Confucius said: "Without recognizing the ordinances of heaven, it is impossible to be a superior man." This is what I mean.

The question is: "by praising Tang Yao and Yu Shun above and bewailing Jie and Zhou below I understand the process of gradual decline and demise and rise and prosperity and will sincerely seek to amend faults. I heard that constant piling up of small things will mount up to something huge, so every sage accumulated minor glimmers of understanding to achieve illumination, rising step by step from a lowly position to become noble and distinguished. Therefore, Yao ascended from a vassal king, while Shun was a farmer's boy from the remote mountains. Their status was gradually achieved, not an overnight transformation. Their words came out of their own mouths, and could not be withdrawn; their deeds were their

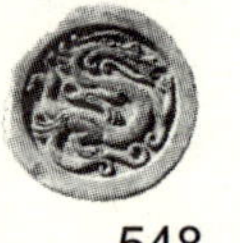

【原文】

行，治之大者，君子之所以动天地也。故尽小者大，慎微者著。《诗》云：“惟此文王，小心翼翼。”故尧兢兢日行其道，而舜业业日致其孝，善积而名显，德章而身尊，此其寖明寖昌之道也。积善在身，犹长日加益，而人不知也；积恶在身，犹火之销膏，而人不见也。非明乎情性察乎流俗者，孰能知之？此唐虞之所以得令名，而桀纣之可为悼惧者也。夫善恶之相从，如景鄉之应形声也。故桀纣暴谩，谗贼并进，贤知隐伏，恶日显，国日乱，晏然自以如日在天，终陵夷而大坏。夫暴逆不仁者，非一日而亡也，亦以渐至，故桀、纣虽亡道，然犹享国十馀年，此其寖微寖灭之道也。

册曰：“三王之教所祖不同，而皆有失，或谓久而不易者道

【今译】

出，也无法再来掩盖。言和行是治理国家最重大的条件，君子之所以能感动天地的也是言行。所以积小成大，谨慎注意细微的行为就会著名。《诗经》上说：“这文王啊，小心翼翼。”所以尧战战兢兢地每天实行他的治国之道，舜小心恐惧地每天尽他的孝道，做的好事积累多了，自然名声显达，德行彰著，自身也受人尊重，这就是渐渐昌盛的道理。积善在自己身上，就好像人日渐长大而自己不觉察；积恶在自己身上，好像灯火消耗油一样，人也不容易看出来。不是明晓情性和洞察世俗情况的人，谁能够懂得这种道理呢？这就是唐尧、虞舜得到美名，夏桀、商纣却使人伤痛恐惧的原因。善或恶的行为所得到的结果，好像影子跟随着人形，回响跟随着声音。所以桀、纣暴虐怠慢，谗恶的人都受到进用，贤良智慧的人都隐藏起来，于是桀、纣的罪恶一天比一天显著，国家也一天比一天混乱，可是他们却依旧安然怡得，自以为如太阳在天空一样，终于逐渐败坏以至于毁灭。那些残暴不仁的君主，并不是一下子就灭亡的，也是慢慢造成的。所以桀、纣虽然无道，都还在位十多年，这就是慢慢地衰微以至灭亡的道理啊。

策问说：“三王的教化，效法的各不相同，而且都有不足，

own, and could not be covered up. Words and deeds are the most important in governing, by which the gentleman is able to move heaven and earth. So by continuous accumulation of small parts, something huge is created; and careful attention to nuances of behavior will make you distinguished. According to the Book of Odes*: "This King Wen, how carefully he acted." So Yao was cautious in everyday implementation of his Way of governance, and Shun conscientious in everyday practice of his filial piety. Accumulated good deeds build a fine reputation, while conspicuous virtue brings respect, and this is the principle of gradual rise and prosperity. Good deeds accumulate in yourself, just as grow older day by day, without awareness of the process; evil deeds accumulate in yourself, like the flame consumes the candle, but you do not easily perceive it. Who can know this truth, except for those who are clear about current conditions and have insight into the ways of the people? This was how Tang Yao and Yu Shun became famous, and how Jie and Zhou became infamous, terrorizing their subjects. Good acts and evil both have consequences, like a shadow follows a body and an echo follows a sound. So Jie and Zhou's brutality and neglect resulted in the employment of slanderous crooks and the hiding of virtuous talents. Their evils became more egregious with every passing day, and the state fell into ever greater turmoil. But they remained complacent, thinking their position as assured as the sun's in the sky, but finally their corruption ended in their destruction. Those cruel and unscrupulous monarchs did not perish overnight; the end was slow in coming. So although Jie and Zhou were devoid of the Way, they were still on the throne for a dozen years, which is the way of gradual decline and demise.*

The question is: "The doctrines of the Three Kings were different at the start, each having its own inadequacy, but

【原文】

也，意岂异哉？”臣闻夫乐而不乱复而不厌者谓之道；道者万世亡弊，弊者道之失也。先王之道必有偏而不起之处，故政有眊而不行，举其偏者以补其弊而已矣。三王之道所祖不同，非其相反，将以捄溢扶衰，所遭之变然也。故孔子曰：“亡为而治者，其舜乎！”改正朔，易服色，以顺天命而已；其馀尽循尧道，何更为哉！故王者有改制之名，亡变道之实。然夏上忠，殷上敬，周上文者，所继之捄，当用此也。孔子曰：“殷因于夏礼，所损益可知也；周因于殷礼，所损益可知也；其或继周者，虽百世可知也。”此言百王之用，以此三者矣。夏因于虞，而独不言所损益者，其道如一而所上同也。道之大原出于天，天不变，道亦不变，是以禹继舜，舜继尧，三圣相受而守一道，亡救弊之政也，

【今译】

有人说道是永久不变的，这两种说法用意有什么不同吗？”臣听说享乐而不至于淫乱，反复实行而不厌倦的叫做道；道是万世都没有弊端的，出现弊端是由于违背了道。先王的道一定有偏颇不能实行的地方，所以在政治上也时有昏暗而行不通的，举出它的偏向，补救它的弊病就行了。三王的道虽然效法不同，可并不是相反的，都是为了补救过失，扶助衰败，之所以有所不同，是因为遇到的环境发生了变化。所以孔子说：“无所作为而能治理国家的，就是舜呀！”舜仅仅改变了历法，改换了车马、祭牲、服装的颜色，来顺承天命罢了，其他完全遵循尧的治国之道，为什么要改变呢！所以王者只改变制度的名称，没有改变道的实质。可是夏代注重忠，殷代崇尚敬，周朝尊崇文的原因，是因为朝代更替时，前代有过失存在，为了补救，应当这样做。孔子说：“殷朝根据夏代的礼制，有所增减，这是可以知道的；周朝根据殷朝的礼制，有所增减，也是可以知道的；其他承继周朝兴起的，虽然经历了百世，这也是可以知道的。”这就是说，百王所用的就是忠、敬、文这三者。夏朝沿袭虞舜，却独独不说增减，是因为夏朝和虞舜的道是一样的；夏崇尚的忠和虞舜是相同的。道的根本来自于天，天不变，道也不变，所以禹继承了舜的道，

some say that the Way is eternal and immutable. Is there a conflict between these two statements?" I heard that the Way is enjoyment without lust, and repetition without boredom; the Way is eternally without flaw; flaws come from turning one's back on the Way. The Way of the early Kings must have been patchily implemented in some places, so on occasions politics had its dark side and did not work. By adjusting the bias, and remedying the flaws, things would work. The doctrines of Three Kings varied, but they were by no means in opposition. They all intended to remedy the excesses and prevent the decline, and the reason for the differences is attributable to changes in the environment. So Confucius said: "May not Shun be instanced as having governed efficiently without exertion!" Shun just changed the calendar and altered the system of carriages, sacrifices and garment color, to follow the Mandate of Heaven. In all other matters he followed Yao's Way of governing. Why should he have done more? So the monarch reformed the system in names only, but did not change the Way substantively. But the Xia upheld loyalty, the Yin reverence and the Zhou esteemed writings, since it was necessary to remedy what was inherited from the preceding dynasty. Confucius said: "The Yin Dynasty followed the regulations of the Xia; wherein it took from or added to them may be known. The Zhou Dynasty followed the regulations of the Yin; wherein it took from or added to them may be known. Some other may follow the Zhou, but though it should be at the distance of a hundred ages, its affairs may be known." In other words, the hundred kings placed greatest importance on loyalty, reverence and writings. Xia followed Shun's regulations, but was alone in not adding or subtracting a word because its Way was the same as that of Shun and it upheld the same. The fundamental origin of the Way is heaven. The Way remains the same, as heaven is the same. So Yu

【原文】

故不言其所损益也。繇是观之，继治世者其道同，继乱世者其道变。今汉继大乱之后，若宜少损周之文致，用夏之忠者。

陛下有明德嘉道，愍世俗之靡薄，悼王道之不昭，故举贤良方正之士，论(谊)(议]考问，将欲兴仁谊之休德，明帝王之法制，建太平之道也。臣愚不肖，述所闻，诵所学，道师之言，廑能勿失耳。若乃论政事之得失，察天下之息秏，此大臣辅佐之职，三公九卿之任，非臣仲舒所能及也。然而臣窃有怪者。夫古之天下亦今之天下，今之天下亦古之天下，共是天下，古(亦)[以]大治，上下和睦，习俗美盛，不令而行，不禁而止，吏亡奸邪，民亡盗贼，囹圄空虚，德润草木，泽被四海，凤皇来集，麒麟来游，以古准今，壹何不相逮之远也！安所缪盭而陵夷若是？

【今译】

舜继承了尧的道，三位圣人互相传授，遵守一个道，没有救弊的措施，所以不说他们对道的增减。由此看来，继承治世的，他们的道是相同的；继承乱世的，他们的道是要改变的。现在汉朝承继大乱之后，应当减少周朝的文而用夏朝的忠。

陛下有圣明的德和美好的道，痛心世俗的衰薄，悲伤王道的不明，所以选举贤良方正的士人，议论考问，打算兴起仁义的美德，阐明帝王的法制，建立太平的治国之道。臣愚昧不肖，叙述曾听到的，背诵曾学过的，说的是老师教的道理，仅仅能够不忘记罢了。至于议论政事的得失，研究社会的兴盛和贫弱，这是大臣辅佐的职事，三公九卿的责任，不是臣下仲舒所能知道的。但是臣私下有感到奇怪的问题。古时候的天下也就是现在的天下，现在的天下也就是古时候的天下，同是一样的天下，古时候天下太平，上下和睦，习俗美好，不令而行，不禁而止，官吏没有奸邪，民间没有盗贼，牢狱空空，没有犯人，人主的恩德滋润了草木，普及到四海，凤凰飞来了，麒麟出现了，拿古时候的情况来衡量现在，怎么相差那么远呢？有什么错误致使衰落达到这样的

inherited the Way of Shun, and Shun's Way was inherited from Yao, and the three sages learned from each other to comply with the one Way, without remedy for political flaws. Hence one does not speak about them adding to or taking from the Way. Judging from this, those inheriting a time of good governance kept to the same Way; by contrast, those succeeding to disorder wanted to change the Way. Now that Han inherited times of chaos, it is better to slightly reduce reliance on the Zhou writings in favor of the Xia loyalty.

Your Majesty possesses sagacious virtue and a good Way. Pained at heart by the decline in people's usage, depressed by not understanding the kings' Way, you ordered that the worthy and excellent, straight and upright be recommended. By challenging and examination, you plan to promote the beautiful virtue of benevolence, clarify the imperial rule of law, and establish peaceful governance. Your humble and unworthy servant has simply recounted what I have heard, recited what I have learned, conveying what the teacher said, just managing to forget nothing. As for the discussion of the pros and cons of political affairs, the rise and decline of the world, this is the job of higher courtiers and the responsibility of the three dukes and nine chamberlains, not knowable by subjects like Zhongshu. But I have been curious about some issues privately. The ancient world is also the present world, and the present world is the ancient world. With the same world, in ancient times they enjoyed peace and stability, hierarchical harmony, good customs, spontaneous doing without orders given, spontaneous restraint without prohibitions, no treacherous officials, no thieves among the people, empty prisons, the monarch's grace nourishing vegetation and spreading to the four seas, the coming of the phoenix and appearance of kylin... Compared with the situation in ancient times, why is it so different today?

【原文】

意者有所失于古之道与？有所诡于天之理与？试迹之[于]古，返之于天，党可得见乎？

夫天亦有所分予，予之齿者去其角，傅其翼者两其足，是所受大者不得取小也。古之所予禄者，不食于力，不动于末，是亦受大者不得取小，与天同意者也。夫已受大，又取小，天不能足，而况人乎！此民之所以嚣嚣苦不足也。身宠而载高位，家温而食厚禄，因乘富贵之资力，以与民争利于下，民安能如之哉！是故众其奴婢，多其牛羊，广其田宅，博其产业，畜其积委，务此而亡已，以迫蹴民，民日削月朘，寖以大穷。富者奢侈羡溢，贫者穷急愁苦；穷急愁苦而上不救，则民不乐生；民不乐生，尚不避死，安能避罪！此刑罚之所以蕃而奸邪不可胜者也。故受禄之家，食禄而已，不与民争业，然后利可均布，而民可家足。此

【今译】

地步？我想也许是违背了古代的治国之道吧？也许是违背了天理吧？尝试考察过去的事情，追溯到天理，或许可以看出一些问题吧？

天对生物是分别给予的，给予利齿的就不再给角，给予翅膀的就只给两只脚，也就是接受了大的，就不能再取小的。古时候领取俸禄的，就不靠体力劳动来吃饭，也不谋取工商之利，这也是接受了大的，不能再取小的，和天意是相同的。假如已经得到了大的，又去取小的，天还不能那样给予，何况是人呢？这就是人民纷纷愁苦衣食不足的原因啊。那些受君主宠爱身居高位的人，家中衣食饱暖并且享有优厚的俸禄，依仗富厚的资产和势力，在下面和百姓争利，老百姓怎么能和他们比呢？所以那些人使用众多的奴婢，拥有众多的牛羊，扩大他们的田地住宅，扩充他们的产业，增加他们的积蓄，致力于这些而且没有止境，压迫百姓，使百姓感到惊惧，百姓天天受到剥削，渐渐走向穷困。富人奢侈浪费，穷人穷急愁苦；穷人穷急愁苦而处在上位的人却不救济，就会民不聊生；民不聊生，百姓就会连死都不怕，又怎会害怕犯罪！这就是刑罚繁多，奸邪却不能禁止的原因啊。所以享受俸禄的人家，应该只食俸禄就算了，不应当和百姓争夺谋利的产

What errors resulted in such decline? Perhaps it may be due to deviation from the ancient way of governance? Something may be contrary to divine justice? What if we try to examine the things of the past, and trace back to the way of heaven, maybe we can perceive some problems!

Heaven also differentiated in its giving, bestowing teeth on animals without horns, giving only two legs to those with wings. This means that those receiving something major cannot get something smaller in addition. In ancient times, those who received salary could not also engage in physical labor, nor pursue business interests, in other words those receiving something big were not entitled to something small on top – in line with the intention of heaven. To grant both large and small things is beyond the capacity of, heaven, let alone man! This is why the people are plagued with anxiety about not having enough to eat or wear. If those favored by the monarch with high positions, enjoying a comfortable home and generous salary, compete with the common people for commercial profits, exploiting their assets and power, how can ordinary people match them! So they use many serfs and maids, accumulate multitudes of cattle and sheep, increase their fields and homes, expand their industries and boost their savings, and incessantly at that, in such a way that they oppress the people. The people are being exploited every day, and gradually become impoverished. The rich are extravagant and wasteful, while the poor are in acute penury and anxiety. Those in acute poverty are wretched; if not relieved by the Emperor, they will be destitute; in hard times, the people will not even be afraid of death, so why would they fear to commit crimes! This is why the wide array of penalties cannot prevent evildoing. So the families who enjoy salary should be satisfied with salary only, and should not compete in profit-making industry with the people; this way

【原文】

上天之理，而亦太古之道，天子之所宜法以为制，大夫之所当循以为行也。故公仪子相鲁，之其家见织帛，怒而出其妻，食于舍而茹葵，愠而拔其葵，曰：“吾已食禄，又夺园夫红女利乎！”古之贤人君子在列位者皆如是，是故下高其行而从其教，民化其廉而不贪鄙。及至周室之衰，其卿大夫缓于谊而急于利，亡推让之风而有争田之讼。故诗人疾而刺之，曰：“节彼南山，惟石岩岩，赫赫师尹，民具尔瞻。”尔好谊，则民鄉仁而俗善；尔好利，则民好邪而俗败。由是观之，天子大夫者，下民之所视效，远方之所四面而内望也。近者视而放之，远者望而效之，岂可以居贤人之位而为庶人行哉！夫皇皇求财利常恐乏匮者，庶人之意也；皇皇求仁义常恐不能化民者，大夫之意也。《易》曰：“负且乘，

【今译】

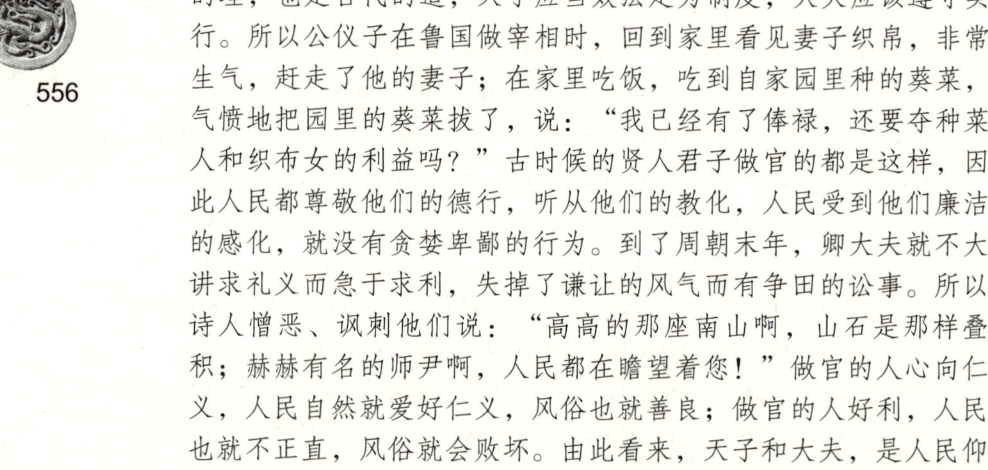

业，这样利益就可以平均分配，百姓也可以家用充足。这是上天的理，也是古代的道，天子应当效法定为制度，大夫应该遵守实行。所以公仪子在鲁国做宰相时，回到家里看见妻子织帛，非常生气，赶走了他的妻子；在家里吃饭，吃到自家园里种的葵菜，气愤地把园里的葵菜拔了，说：“我已经有了俸禄，还要夺种菜人和织布女的利益吗？”古时候的贤人君子做官的都是这样，因此人民都尊敬他们的德行，听从他们的教化，人民受到他们廉洁的感化，就没有贪婪卑鄙的行为。到了周朝末年，卿大夫就不大讲求礼义而急于求利，失掉了谦让的风气而有争田的讼事。所以诗人憎恶、讽刺他们说：“高高的那座南山啊，山石是那样叠积；赫赫有名的师尹啊，人民都在瞻望着您！”做官的人心向仁义，人民自然就爱好仁义，风俗也就善良；做官的人好利，人民也就不正直，风俗就会败坏。由此看来，天子和大夫，是人民仰望、效法的榜样，是远方的人遥望着模仿他们，怎么能够处在贤人的地位却去做出平民的行为呢？那些忙着谋取财利，常常担心穷困的想法，是平民的意向；忙着寻求仁义，时常忧虑不能教化人民的打算，是大夫的思想。《周易》上说：“背着东西又坐

benefits can be evenly distributed, and the common people can also become affluent families. This is the reason of heaven, and the ancient Way. The Son of Heaven should follow this in the system, and the grand masters should follow it when putting the system into practice. So when Mr. Gongyixiu was prime minister of Lu, he divorced his wife, enraged to see her weaving silk at home; eating at home, he found a dish of sunflowers from their own garden, and angrily uprooted the plants, saying: "I already have an official's salary, so how can I also grab the profits of vegetable growers and the weaving women?" The virtuous ancient officials or the gentlemen were all like this, so the populace had respect for their behavior, and listened to their doctrines. Influenced by their honesty the people did not behave in greedy or despicable fashion. But in the age of Zhou's decline, its highest officials were less avid for righteousness than for profits; they became litigious competitors to acquire farmland, losing the practice of humility. So poets despised and satirized this: "Tall is the South Mountain,/ Its rocks stack so on rock;/ Well-known is Precepter Yin,/ The people looking to you from afar!" If you uphold righteousness, the people naturally love benevolence, and their customs will also be good; if you like profits, the people will also be devious, and their customs will fall into corruption. For this reason, the Emperor and the grand masters are looked up to from below for moral example, and distant peoples look to them and copy. How can people in the position of worthy men have the behavior of commoners'! Those busy reaping financial benefits that habitually worry about poverty have the mindset of commoners; while those busy seeking justice and humanity, habitually worrying about their inability to educate the people have the thinking of grand masters. According to the Book of Changes*: "To travel by carriage but carry a burden on the shoulder is an invitation to*

【原文】

致寇至。”乘车者君子之位也，负担者小人之事也，此言居君子之位而为庶人之行者，其患祸必至也。若居君子之位，当君子之行，则舍公仪休之相鲁，亡可为者矣。

《春秋》大一统者，天地之常经，古今之通谊也。今师异道，人异论，百家殊方，指意不同，是以上亡以持一统；法制数变，下不知所守。臣愚以为诸不在六艺之科孔子之术者，皆绝其道，勿使并进。邪辟之说灭息，然后统纪可一而法度可明，民知所从矣。

对既毕，天子以仲舒为江都相，事易王。易王，帝兄，素骄，好勇。仲舒以礼谊匡正，王敬重焉。久之，王问仲舒曰：“粤王句践与大夫泄庸、种、蠡谋伐吴，遂灭之。孔子称殷有三仁，寡人亦以为粤有三仁。桓公决疑于管仲，寡人决疑于君。”仲舒对曰：“臣愚不足

【今译】

车，招致强盗的到来。”乘车是说处在君子的地位，负担东西是小人的事情，这就是说，处在君子的地位却做出庶人的行为，他的祸患一定会到来。如果处在君子的地位，做君子应当做的事，那么，除了像公仪休在鲁国做宰相那样，就没有别的可以做的了。

《春秋》推重统一，这是天地永恒的原则，是古今共通的道理。如今老师所述的道理彼此不同，人们的议论也彼此各异，诸子百家研究的方向不同，意旨也不一样，所以处在上位的人君不能掌握统一的标准，法令制度多次改变，在下的百姓不知道应当怎样遵守。臣认为凡是不属于六艺的科目和孔子学术的学说都一律禁止，不许它们同样发展。邪僻的学说消失，然后学术的系统可以统一，法令制度就可以明白，人民也知道服从的对象了。

对策结束后，汉武帝任命董仲舒为江都相，辅助易王。易王刘非，是汉武帝的哥哥，平素很骄横，喜欢勇武。董仲舒用礼义扶正易王，易王很敬重他。过了一段时间，易王问董仲舒说：“越王勾践和大夫泄庸、文种、范蠡密谋攻打吴国，后来终于灭了吴国。孔子说殷纣王有三位仁人，我认为越王勾践也有三位仁人。春秋时的齐桓公有

robbers." It is a gentleman's position to ride carriages, and it is a small man's task to carry burdens; this means that, if someone in a gentleman's position indulges in a commoner's behavior, his misfortune will surely come. If you are in the position of a gentleman, you should act befittingly, and what else can you do but act like Gongyixiu in the State of Lu?

The Spring and Autumn Annals *promotes grand unity as the eternal principle of heaven and earth and the common truth of ancient and modern times. Today, teachers state different ways, people deem differently, philosophers' approaches are divergent, and differently intentioned, so that the Emperor cannot maintain a uniform standard. The legal system keeps chopping and changing, so the people do not know what is to be observed. It is my humble opinion that those subjects not belonging to any of the Six Arts or the doctrine of Confucius should be prohibited, not allowed to develop in parallel. The heretical doctrines will disappear, and then the system can be unified, the legal system can be clarified, and the people will know what to obey.*

After the policy responses were finished, Emperor Wudi appointed Dong Zhongshu as prime minister of Jiangdu, to assist his older brother Prince of Yi, Liu Fei, an arrogant man by nature who loved martial deeds. Zhongshu set him on the right path with propriety and righteousness, so that the Prince respected him. After some time, the Prince asked Dong Zhongshu: "Goujian the King of Yue planned with his grand masters Xie Yong, Wen Zhong and Fan Li, to attack Wu and finally exterminated Wu. Confucius said that Yin possessed the three men of virtue. I think that Yue also possessed three men of virtue. In the Spring and Autumn Period. Duke Huan of Qi referred his doubts to Guan Zhong, I request that you perform the same role for me." Dong replied: "I am too ignorant to answer your questions. I heard that the monarch of Lu asked Liu

【原文】

以奉大对。闻昔者鲁君问柳下惠：‘吾欲伐齐，何如？’柳下惠曰：‘不可。’归而有忧色，曰：‘吾闻伐国不问仁人，此言何为至于我哉！’徒见问耳，且犹羞之，况设诈以伐吴乎？繇此言之，粤本无一仁。夫仁人者，正其谊不谋其利，明其道不计其功，是以仲尼之门，五尺之童羞称五伯，为其先诈力而后仁谊也。苟为诈而已，故不足称于大君子之门也。五伯比于他诸侯为贤，其比三王，犹武夫之与美玉也。”王曰：“善。”

仲舒治国，以《春秋》灾异之变推阴阳所以错行，故求雨，闭诸阳，纵诸阴，其止雨反是；行之一国，未尝不得所欲。中废为中大夫。先是辽东高庙、长陵高园殿灾，仲舒居家推说其意，中稿未上，主父偃候仲舒，私见，嫉之，窃其书而奏焉。上召视诸儒，仲舒弟子吕步舒不知其师书，以为大愚。于是下仲舒吏，当死，诏赦之。仲舒

【今译】

疑难的事让管仲解答，我有疑问请您解说。”董仲舒回答说：“臣愚昧不能解答您提出的问题。我听说春秋时鲁国国君鲁僖公问鲁国大夫柳下惠：‘我想攻打齐国，怎么样？’柳下惠说：‘不行。’他回家后面有忧色，说：‘我听说攻伐别的国家不问有仁德的人，国君想攻打齐国为什么问我呢！’柳下惠只不过被询问罢了，尚且感到羞愧，何况是设谋诈降来攻打吴国呢？由此说来，越国根本没有一位仁人。仁人端正他的义却不谋取私利，阐明他的道却不计较自己的功劳，所以在孔子的门徒里，即使是尚未成年的儿童也羞于谈论五霸，因为五霸推崇欺诈武力不注重仁义。越王君臣不过是实行不正当的诈术罢了，所以不值得孔子的门徒谈论。五霸比其他诸侯贤明，可是和三王相比，就好像似玉的石块和美玉相比一样啊。”易王说：“讲得好。”

董仲舒治理国家，是用《春秋》记载的灾异变化来推究阴阳错行的原因，所以求雨时，闭阳纵阴，他止雨时就闭阴纵阳。这种祈雨止涝的方法推行到江都全国，没有不随心所欲的。后来，董仲舒被废为中大夫。在这之前，辽东郡祭祀汉高祖的高庙和汉朝皇帝祭祖的地方长陵高园殿先后发生火灾，董仲舒在家里推论天降火灾和人世的关系，奏章草稿写好了没有上呈。主父偃来探望董仲舒，私自看了奏章草稿，他平素就嫉妒董仲舒，便把奏章草稿偷走，上交给汉武帝。汉武帝召集了很多儒生，让他们看董仲舒的奏章草稿。董仲舒的学生吕步舒不知道这个奏章草稿是他老师写的，认为非常愚昧。于是汉武帝

Xiahui: 'I want to attack Qi; what do you think?' Liuxia Hui said it would not do, but returned home worrying, saying: 'I heard that when a monarch is to attack another kingdom he will not ask people of benevolence. Why does he think to ask this question of me?' Liuxia Hui had only been asked his opinion, - very different from plotting to attack Wu by feigned surrender - yet he felt the taint of shame. Thus, there was no one man of benevolence at all in Yue. A benevolent man makes himself upright rather than pursuing his personal gain, clarifies his doctrine rather than quibbling about how much merit he deserves, so that among the disciples of Confucius, even small children were ashamed to talk about the Five Hegemons because they resorted to force and fraud before justice and humanity. Such improper treachery did not merit discussion among the disciples of the Great Sage. The Hegemons were more virtuous than the other princes, but compared to the Three Kings, they were near-jade as compared to fine jade." The Prince of Yi said: "Well said."

Dong Zhongshu governed the country on the basis of the *Spring and Autumn Annals*, deducing the disorder of *yin* and *yang* from the changes of calamity and visitation recorded in the classic; so in praying for rain, he closed *yang* to enhance *yin*, and reversed it when getting the rain to stop. This method was implemented throughout Jiangdu, not without getting what he desired. Later, he was demoted to the post of grand master of the palace. Prior to this, fire had struck first the Temple of Gaozu in Liaodong and then the Hall of Gaozu at Changling Mausoleum, and Dong Zhongshu had argued in a draft memorial about the significance of these events to the human world, but had not yet presented the memorial. Zhu Fuyan came to visit him, and secretly read the draft. Envious, he stole the memorial and presented it to Emperor Wudi, who summoned many Confucian scholars, and showed them the memorial. Dong's disciple Lü Bushu, unaware it was the work of his teacher, considered it very ignorant. The Emperor had Dong imprisoned and he was sentenced to death,

【原文】

遂不敢复言灾异。

仲舒为人廉直。是时方外攘四夷，公孙弘治《春秋》不如仲舒，而弘希世用事，位至公卿。仲舒以弘为从谀，弘嫉之。胶西王亦上兄也，尤纵恣，数害吏二千石。弘乃言于上曰："独董仲舒可使相胶西王。"胶西王闻仲舒大儒，善待之，仲舒恐久获罪，病免。凡相两国，辄事骄王，正身以率下，数上疏谏争，教令国中，所居而治。及去位归居，终不问家产业，以修学著书为事。

仲舒在家，朝廷如有大议，使使者及廷尉张汤就其家而问之，其对皆有明法。自武帝初立，魏其、武安侯为相而隆儒矣。及仲舒对

【今译】

把董仲舒交官问罪，判处死刑，汉武帝下诏赦免了他。董仲舒从此便不敢再谈论灾异变化。

董仲舒为人廉洁正直。当时汉朝正用兵周边少数民族，公孙弘研究《公羊春秋》的水平不如董仲舒，可是公孙弘迎合世俗，掌握大权，位至公卿。董仲舒认为公孙弘奉承谄媚，公孙弘嫉恨董仲舒。胶西王刘端也是汉武帝的哥哥，为人特别放纵，凶残蛮横，多次谋杀朝廷派去的二千石官。公孙弘就跟汉武帝说："只有董仲舒可以担任胶西王相。"胶西王刘端听说董仲舒是有名的儒家大师，待他还比较尊重。董仲舒害怕时间长了会遭到不测之罪，就以年老有病为由辞职回家了。董仲舒共计做过江都、胶西两国的相，都是辅佐骄横的诸侯王，他以身作则为下属做表率，多次上疏直言规谏，制定教令颁行国中，他所在的江都、胶西两国国都均治理得很好。到了去官归家后，他根本不管家庭产业，只是埋头诵读，专心著书。

董仲舒养病在家，朝廷如果讨论重大问题，就派使者和廷尉张汤到他家征询他的意见，董仲舒的解答都有根有据。从汉武帝初即位，魏其侯窦婴和武安侯田蚡先后做丞相，开始推崇儒学，到董仲舒对策，推尊宣扬孔子，抑黜百家。设立管理学校的官吏，州郡举荐茂材

but he was pardoned by imperial decree. After that, Zhongshu did not dare to talk about calamity and visitation.

Dong Zhongshu was a man of integrity and honesty. At the time, military forces were being used against the tribes on four frontiers, so although Gongsun Hong's mastery of the *Spring and Autumn Annals* could not compete with Dong Zhongshu's, the former directed himself to worldly affairs, and was promoted to the highest rank. Dong thought that Gongsun Hong was a sycophant, and the latter was jealous of Dong. The Prince of Jiaoxi Liu Duan was also a brother of Wudi, and he was particularly indulgent, cruel and unreasonable, even murdering 2,000-picul high officials dispatched by the court. Gongsun Hong advised the emperor, "Only Dong Zhongshu can act as the prime minister to the Prince of Jiaoxi." Aware of Dong's fame as famous Confucian master, the Prince treated him with some respect. But Dong feared it would be just a matter of time before things turned bad for him, so he resigned on the grounds of old age and ill health. Dong Zhongshu was prime minister of two princedoms, both times as assistant to arrogant princes. He set an example for subordinates to follow, presented many memorials of admonishment, and formulated regulations about moral education in the princedoms. So wherever he went, good government ensued. After he returned home upon retirement, he never did care about his family patrimony, concentrating exclusively on reading and writing books.

During Zhongshu's retirement at home, if there was a discussion of a major issue, a messenger and the Chamberlain of Law Enforcement Zhang Tang would come to seek his advice, and his responses were all well-founded. After Wudi ascended the throne, Marquis of Weiqi Dou Ying and Marquis of Wuan Tian Fen as the prime ministers praised Confucianism. And Dong Zhongshu answered with policy measures to promote Confucian doctrine, suppressing the other schools of thought. It was he who initiated the

【原文】

册，推明孔氏，抑黜百家。立学校之官，州郡举茂材孝廉，皆自仲舒发之。年老，以寿终于家。家徙茂陵，子及孙皆以学至大官。

仲舒所著，皆明经术之意，及上疏条教，凡百二十三篇。而说《春秋》事得失，《闻举》、《玉杯》、《蕃露》、《清明》、《竹林》之属，复数十篇，十馀万言，皆传于后世。掇其切当世施朝廷者著于篇。

赞曰：刘向称“董仲舒有王佐之材，虽伊吕亡以加，管晏之属，伯者之佐，殆不及也”。至向子歆以为“伊吕乃圣人之耦，王者不得则不兴。故颜渊死，孔子曰：‘噫！天丧余。’唯此一人为能当之，自宰我、子赣、子游、子夏不与焉。仲舒遭汉承秦灭学之后，《六

【今译】

孝廉，都是从董仲舒开始的。董仲舒老年在家里寿终。后来他家迁往茂陵县，他的儿子和孙子都凭学问做了大官。

董仲舒的著作，都是阐明儒家经学意旨的，加上奏疏教令，总共一百二十三篇。解说《春秋》记事的得失，及《闻举》、《玉杯》、《蕃露》、《清明》和《竹林》之类的文章，还有几十篇，十多万字，都流传到了后世。我挑选其中切合当今社会和朝廷的内容写在文章里。

赞曰：刘向称赞：“董仲舒有做君王辅佐的才干，即使是伊尹、吕望也不能超过他，管仲、晏婴之辈，是霸主的辅佐，怕是不如他吧。”刘向的儿子刘歆认为“伊尹、吕望是圣人的伴偶，王者得不到他们就不能兴起。所以颜渊死了，孔子说‘噫！天灭亡我。’只有颜渊一人能和伊尹、吕望相比，至于宰我、子贡、子游、子夏等人就不

appointment of school officials and recommendation of cultivated talents and the filial and incorrupt from local regions. He died of old age at home. Later, his family moved to Maoling County, and his son and grandchildren were made high officials because of their learning.

Dong Zhongshu's works were all written to clarify the intentions of the Confucian classics. These, plus the memorials to the throne and regulations with respect to moral education, total 123 articles in all. As to the notes on the pros and cons of events in the *Spring and Autumn Annals*, like "News of Recommendation", "Jade Cup", "Fan Lu", "Clear Bright" and "Bamboo Grove" and other articles, there are dozens, in hundreds of thousands of words, and they are handed down to future generations. I have selected some of these for their relevance to today's society and their use at Court.

Author's note: Liu Xiang praised "Dong had the capabilities of assisting kings, and even Yi Yin and Lü Wang did not surpass him; whereas Guan Zhong and Yan Ying, etc. were only good for the hegemons, and so inferior to him." Liu Xiang's son Liu Xin thought "Yi Yin and Lü Wang were companions to the sages, without whom the monarchs could not have risen. So when Yan Yuan died, Confucius said: 'Alas! Heaven is destroying me.' Only this one person was their equal. As to Zai Wo, Zigong, Ziyou, Zixia, they cannot be included in the same league. Dong Zhongshu appeared after Han picked up the pieces of Qin's destruction of scholarship, when the 'Six Classics' had fallen apart. So he studied conscientiously behind his curtain, devoted to the great cause of classical studies, to become the leading light of Confucians so that later scholars had the same understanding of the system. But when we investigated the origins of his mentors and friends, to see if they had influenced each other, we found Dong Zhongshu to be less learned than Ziyou and Zixia. Liu Xiang's opinion that Guan and Yan were not as good as he, or Yi and Lü no better is not correct."

【原文】

经》离析，下帷发愤，潜心大业，令后学者有所统壹，为群儒首，然考其师友渊源所渐，犹未及乎游夏，而曰管晏弗及，伊吕不加，过矣”。至向曾孙龚，笃论君子也，以歆之言为然。

——卷五十六《董仲舒传》第二十六

【今译】

能列入圣人之偶的行列了。董仲舒遭逢西汉承接秦朝焚灭学术之后，《六经》分崩离析，于是他下帷发愤钻研，潜心经学大业，使后来的学者对儒家学说有了系统一致的认识，成为群儒的首领。可是考察他的师友渊源，看他们彼此间的影响，董仲舒还赶不上子游、子夏，却说管仲、晏婴不如他，伊尹、吕望超不过他，这种看法是不对的。”刘向的曾孙刘龚则是善于确当评论人物的君子，他认为刘歆对董仲舒的评价是恰当的。

Liu Xiang's great-grandson Liu Gong was a gentleman who was known for his accurate assessment of people. He believed Liu Xin's comment on Dong Zhongshu was appropriate.

张骞传

【原文】

张骞，汉中人也，建元中为郎。时匈奴降者言匈奴破月氏王，以其头为饮器，月氏遁而怨匈奴，无与共击之。汉方欲事灭胡，闻此言，欲通使，道必更匈奴中，乃募能使者。骞以郎应募，使月氏，与堂邑氏奴甘父俱出陇西。径匈奴，匈奴得之，传诣单于。单于曰："月氏在吾北，汉何以得往使？吾欲使越，汉肯听我乎？"留骞十馀岁，予妻，有子，然骞持汉节不失。

居匈奴西，骞因与其属亡鄉月氏，西走数十日至大宛。大宛闻汉之饶财，欲通不得，见骞，喜，问欲何之。骞曰："为汉使月氏而为匈奴所闭道，今亡，唯王使人道送我。诚得至，反汉，汉之赂遗王

【今译】

张骞，汉中人，汉武帝建元年间为郎官。当时，投降汉朝的匈奴人说匈奴打败月氏王后，用月氏王的头作为饮酒的用具，月氏人逃走了并且很怨恨匈奴，但是没有人援助它共同打击匈奴。汉朝此时正打算消灭匈奴，听到这话，想派人出使月氏，但途中必经匈奴地区，于是就招募敢于出使月氏的人。当时张骞以郎官的身份应募。他出使月氏，带着姓堂邑氏的奴隶名叫甘父的，一道从陇西出发。在经过匈奴地区时，被匈奴人抓获，用专车送至单于处。单于说："月氏在我们的北面，汉朝为什么要向月氏派使者？我想派使者到南越，汉朝肯答应我的使者去吗？"就扣留了张骞十余年，还给他娶了妻子，有了孩子。可是张骞始终保留着汉朝出使用的符节，没有丢失。

张骞住在匈奴的西边，他乘机与部下向月氏方向逃去。他们向西逃了数十日，到达大宛。大宛人早就听说汉朝富庶，想和汉朝往来，但未能办到。这些人见到张骞来，就问张骞要到哪儿去。张骞说："是为汉朝出使月氏的，路上被匈奴所阻拦。如今逃出来，

Chapter 12

Biography of Zhang Qian

Zhang Qian, born in Hanzhong, was promoted to court gentleman in Emperor Wudi's Jianyuan reign period (ca. 140 BC). At that time, according to some surrendered Hun, after the Huns had defeated the King of Yuezhi they had made a drinking vessel out of its king's head. Yuezhi people had fled and hated the Huns, but they were without help to fight them. It happened that Han was planning to destroy the Huns, so at this news, they wanted to send an ambassador to Yuezhi, but the route would involve crossing through Hun territory. So the Emperor recruited one who dared take on the task. Zhang Qian enlisted in the capacity of court gentleman, to be ambassador to Yuezhi. He departed from Longxi, taking with him Gan Fu, a slave of the Tangyi clan. Passing through Hun territory, they were arrested, and taken to the Chanyu on a cart. The Chanyu said: "Yuezhi is to the north of us. How can Han send envoys there? If I wanted to send envoys to Yue in the far south, would Han allow me to?" Then they detained Zhang for more than 10 years, granting him a wife, who bore him children. However, Zhang Qian always retained his Han credentials, with no loss of his imperial ambassadorial staff.

Zhang Qian lived in the west of the Hun lands, so when the opportunity arose he escaped and fled in the direction of Yuezhi with his men. They traveled west for weeks, finally reaching Dayuan [Ferghana]. The people there had heard about the rich and fertile Han, and wanted to establish contact, but had not managed to do so. Delighted to see Zhang Qian, they asked where he was bound for. Zhang Qian said: "I am Han's envoy to Yuezhi, but on the road

【原文】

财物不可胜言。”大宛以为然，遣骞，为发译道，抵康居。康居传致大月氏。大月氏王已为胡所杀，立其夫人为王。既臣大夏而君之，地肥饶，少寇，志安乐，又自以远远汉，殊无报胡之心。骞从月氏至大夏，竟不能得月氏要领。

留岁馀，还，并南山，欲从羌中归，复为匈奴所得。留岁馀，单于死，国内乱，骞与胡妻及堂邑父俱亡归汉。拜骞太中大夫，堂邑父为奉使君。

骞为人强力，宽大信人，蛮夷爱之。堂邑父胡人，善射，穷急射禽兽给食。初，骞行时百馀人，去十三岁，唯二人得还。

骞身所至者，大宛、大月氏、大夏、康居，而传闻其旁大国五六，具为天子言其地形，所有。语皆在《西域传》。

【今译】

希望大王您派人做向导送我一下。果真到达大月氏的话，我回到汉朝，汉朝送给您的礼物会多得说不完。”大宛王认为张骞说得对，打发走张骞，并为他派了翻译和向导，送到康居。康居人又将他们送到大月氏。此时，大月氏王已为匈奴所杀，大月氏人拥立了王的夫人为王。他们已征服并占领了大夏，成为这里的君主。这里土地肥沃，很少有外来的侵扰，他们正在过安宁快乐的生活，又自认为远离汉朝而疏远了与汉朝的关系，根本没有报复匈奴之心。张骞从大月氏到大夏，一直没有得到结果。

张骞在那里停留了一年多，回来时，沿着昆仑山、阿尔金山和祁连山，想从羌族地区返回，可是又被匈奴人抓住。在匈奴被扣留了一年多，恰逢单于死，匈奴内部混乱，张骞便与他的匈奴妻子及堂邑父一起逃回汉朝。汉武帝授予他为太中大夫，堂邑父为奉使君。

张骞为人坚强而有毅力，宽宏大量，待人真诚，少数民族人喜欢他。堂邑父是匈奴人，善于射箭，在穷困危急的关头，就射取禽兽作为食物。当初，张骞出行时有一百余人，去了十三年，只有他和堂邑父两人回来。

张骞亲身所到过的地方，有大宛、大月氏、大夏、康居等国，他听说在这些国家的旁边还有五、六个大国，他一一向汉武帝讲述了这些国家的地形和物产。所说的内容都在《西域传》里。

I was obstructed by the Huns. Having now escaped from them, I hope Your Majesty will send a guide to show me to Yuezhi. If I really reach there, when I return to the Han Court, the gifts to Your Majesty will be more than words can describe." The King of Ferghana thought that Zhang Qian was right, so he put him on the road with a translator and guide, as far as Kangqu [Sogdiana], where people in turn escorted them to Great Yuezhi. Since the death of their king at the hands of the Huns, they had crowned his consort as Queen. They had conquered and ruled Bactria, a fertile land with little outside menace, so they were resolved upon leading a peaceful and happy life. Furthermore, since they were far away from Han, both in distance and relations, they had forgotten any wish to retaliate against the Huns. From Yuezhi, Zhang Qian went on to Bactria, without any positive result.

Zhang Qian remained there for more than a year, returning along the Kunlun and Qilian Mountains, planning a southern route via the area inhabited by the Qiang people, but he was again caught by the Huns. He was detained for more than a year, until the death of the Chanyu brought internal chaos. Then Zhang Qian fled with his Hun wife and Gan Fu to Han territory. Emperor Wudi granted him the title of Superior Grand Master of the Palace, and Gan Fu became Lord Envoy.

Zhang Qian was strong and persevering, generous and faithful, so the barbarians liked him. Gan Fu was a Hun, a fine archer able to hunt birds and animals for food at critical moments. Zhang's original party had been more than 100 strong, but after 13 years he and Gan Fu were the only ones to return.

Zhang Qian made first-hand visits to Ferghana, Great Yuezhi, Bactria, and Sogdiana, and heard about five or six more great powers that neighbored these countries. He described to the Son of Heaven the terrain and produce of these countries. The details are included in the "Annals of the Western Regions."

【原文】

骞曰："臣在大夏时，见邛竹杖、蜀布，问安得此，大夏国人曰：'吾贾人往市之身毒国。身毒国在大夏东南可数千里。其俗土著，与大夏同，而卑湿暑热。其民乘象以战。其国临大水焉。'以骞度之，大夏去汉万二千里，居西南。今身毒又居大夏东南数千里，有蜀物，此其去蜀不远矣。今使大夏，从羌中，险，羌人恶之；少北，则为匈奴所得；从蜀，宜径，又无寇。"天子既闻大宛及大夏、安息之属皆大国，多奇物，土著，颇与中国同俗，而兵弱，贵汉财物；其北则大月氏、康居之属，兵强，可以赂遗设利朝也。诚得而以义属之，则广地万里，重九译，致殊俗，威德遍于四海。天子欣欣以骞言为然。乃令因蜀犍为发间使，四道并出：出駹，出莋，出徙、邛，出僰，皆各行一二千里。其北方闭氐、莋，南方闭嶲、昆明。昆明

【今译】

张骞说："我在大夏的时候，见到邛那个地方的竹杖和蜀郡产的细布，问他们从哪儿得到这些东西，大夏国人说：'是我国的商人从身毒国买来的。身毒国在大夏东南，大约有数千里地。那里的风俗是过着定居的生活，和大夏相同，但地势低洼，潮湿，气候炎热。那里的人骑着大象打仗，国家滨临大水。'根据我的推测，大夏距离汉朝约有一万二千里，在汉朝的西南。现在身毒又在大夏东南数千里，有蜀郡的物产，这样看来，身毒距离蜀不远。现在出使大夏，从羌族地区经过，很危险，羌族人很厌恶汉朝；稍稍往北，则会被匈奴人俘获；如果从蜀郡走，当是方便的道路，又无侵扰。"汉武帝听说大宛和大夏、安息等国家都是大国，有许多奇怪的物产，又过着定居的生活，与汉朝的风俗相同。而兵力很弱，很看重汉朝的财物；其北方则是大月氏、康居等国，兵力强大，可以用赠送财物、给他们以好处的方法，诱使他们前来朝见汉天子。果真能够这样做并用道义的力量使他们归附汉朝，那么汉朝就可扩大疆土一万余里，有些民族的人到朝廷来，要经多重翻译才能通晓语言，一些奇风异俗的少数民族也前来归附，汉朝的威望德泽就可普及四海。汉武帝很高兴，认为张骞说得很有道理。于是下令通过蜀郡和犍为郡派遣探路的使者，分四路同时出发。一路从冉駹出发，一路从莋都出发，一路从徙和邛出发，一路从僰出发，各有一二千

Zhang Qian said: "When your humble servant was in Bactria, I saw bamboo canes from Qiong and fine cloth from Shu. When I asked where to get these things, the Bactrians said: 'Our merchants bought them from Hindu. Hindu is a country a few thousand *li* southeast of Bactria, and their custom is to live a settled life, as here in Bactria, but it is low-lying, hot and humid. People there fight their wars riding elephants, and the country is close to the Sea.' In my estimation, Bactria is about 12,000 *li* southwest of Han. So, if this Hindu is thousands of *li* southeast of Bactria, with produce from Shu, it seems that Hindu is not far from Shu. Now our envoy to Bactria must go through the Qiang's region. It is a very dangerous route, since Qiang people are most averse to us; further north, he will be captured by the Huns; but if he goes via Shu, the road should be straight, and without raiders." The Son of Heaven heard of Ferghana, Bactria, Parthia, and other lands as big countries, with many strange products, but living a settled life, as was the custom of the Middle Kingdom. However, militarily they were weak, and they valued Han products; while to their north lay Great Yuezhi, Sodgiana and other countries, with powerful military might. The former might be tempted with gifts of treasure and promised benefits to present themselves to the Emperor and come into allegiance with Han. With a combination of these things and the moral power of Han, it might be possible to bring them into allegiance; thus Han could expand its territory by 10,000 *li*; when the various peoples come to court, there would be needed many stages of translation; some peoples with their strange ethnic customs would join us, resulting in Han's prestige and might being universally felt. The Son of Heaven was very happy, thinking that Zhang Qian was right in his assessment. So he ordered that four groups of exploratory messengers be sent simultaneously via Shu and Qianwei, from Ranmang, Zuodu, Xi and Qiong, and Bo respectively, with each group traveling one or two thousand *li*. However, the northern routes were blocked by Di and

【原文】

之属无君长，善寇盗，辄杀略汉使，终莫得通。然闻其西可千馀里，有乘象国，名滇越，而蜀贾间出物者或至焉，于是汉以求大夏道始通滇国。初，汉欲通西南夷，费多，罢之。及骞言可以通大夏，乃复事西南夷。

骞以校尉从大将军击匈奴，知水草处，军得以不乏，乃封骞为博望侯。是岁元朔六年也。后二年，骞为卫尉，与李广俱出右北平击匈奴。匈奴围李将军，军失亡多，而骞后期当斩，赎为庶人。是岁骠骑将军破匈奴西边，杀数万人，至祁连山。其秋，浑邪王率众降汉，而金城、河西(西)并南山至盐泽，空无匈奴。匈奴时有候者到，而希矣。后二年，汉击走单于于幕北。

天子数问骞大夏之属。骞既失侯，因曰："臣居匈奴中，闻乌孙

【今译】

里路程。可是北方的通道为氐族和莋都夷所阻挡，南方的通道为巂和昆明所阻。昆明等少数民族没有君长，善于劫掠和盗窃。每每杀害过往的汉使，夺走财物，这条路终于没能打通。不过听说昆明西边大约千余里的地方，有乘象国，名叫滇越，蜀郡有些私自往来买卖货物的商人到过那儿。于是汉朝因寻求通往大夏的道路而开始与滇国往来。当初，汉朝想与西南夷通使，由于费用太多，停止了这项工作。及至张骞说可经西南夷通往大夏，汉朝才着手打通西南夷之路。

张骞以校尉的身份跟随大将军卫青出击匈奴，因为他了解水草分布的地方，军队才能不缺给养，于是封张骞为博望侯。这年是汉武帝元朔六年。两年以后，张骞作为卫尉，与李广将军一起从右北平出发抗击匈奴。匈奴包围李将军，汉军伤亡惨重，而张骞晚于约定的时间到达，按军法当处以斩刑，他用财物赎为平民。这一年，骠骑将军霍去病在西边打败匈奴，杀数万人，直至祁连山。秋天，匈奴浑邪王率领他的部众投降汉朝。于是，从金城、河西走廊，沿祁连山直至盐泽一带空无匈奴。匈奴时或有侦察兵前来，但也为数很少。又过了两年，汉朝击退匈奴单于并赶往漠北。

汉武帝多次向张骞询问大夏等国的情况。此时张骞已失去了侯的

Zuodu barbarians, and the southern route by Xi and Kunming. The Kunming and other peoples had no chieftain, and excelled in looting and theft. They would kill passing Han messengers and take their property, so Han failed to get through on this road. But there was talk of a place named Dianyue, a country where men rode elephants, a thousand *li* to the west of Kunming, which had been reached by some merchants from Shu selling secretly there. Thus it was that Han, seeking a route into Bactria began exchanges with the State of Dian. At first, when Han had wanted to make exchanges with barbarians in the southwest, the costs had put a stop to the idea. But when Zhang Qian said this way could lead into Bactria, dealings with the southwestern tribes were resumed.

In his capacity of commandant, Zhang Qian followed General-in-Chief Wei Qing in attacking the Huns, because he knew where to find water and plants, so the troops never went short of supplies; thus he was enfeoffed as Marquis of Bowang. This was year six of the Yuanshuo reign period (123 BC). Two years later, Zhang Qian as Chamberlain for the Palace Garrison, went together with Li Guang to attack the Huns from Youbeiping. General Li was surrounded by the Huns, and Han suffered severe casualties. Zhang Qian arrived later than scheduled, and was sentenced to decapitation, but he redeemed himself, losing his title to become a commoner. That year, Cavalry General Huo Qubing routed the Huns in the west, killing tens of thousands of them, and reached the Qilian Mountains. That autumn, the Hunye clan, led by their king, surrendered to Han. Thus, a whole swathe of territory - from Jincheng, Hexi, along the Qilian Mountains to the salt marshes of Lobnur Lake - became free of the Huns. There was an occasional Hun scout, but this was very rare. After another two years, Han had pushed back the Chanyu to Mobei, north of the Gobi Desert.

The Emperor Wudi, remaining curious about Bactria and other countries, frequently asked Zhang Qian about them. Zhang, having

【原文】

王号昆莫。昆莫父难兜靡本与大月氏俱在祁连、敦煌间，小国也。大月氏攻杀难兜靡，夺其地，人民亡走匈奴。子昆莫新生，傅父布就翎侯抱亡置草中，为求食，还，见狼乳之，又乌衔肉翔其旁，以为神，遂持归匈奴，单于爱养之。及壮，以其父民众与昆莫，使将兵，数有功。时，月氏已为匈奴所破，西击塞王。塞王南走远徙，月氏居其地。昆莫既健，自请单于报父怨，遂西攻破大月氏。大月氏复西走，徙大夏地。昆莫略其众，因留居，兵稍强，会单于死，不肯复朝事匈奴。匈奴遣兵击之，不胜，益以为神而远之。今单于新困于汉，而昆莫地空。蛮夷恋故地，又贪汉物，诚以此时厚赂乌孙，招以东居故地，汉遣公主为夫人，结昆弟，其势宜听，则是断匈奴右臂也。既连

【今译】

封号，就回答道："我住在匈奴的时候，听说乌孙王名昆莫。昆莫的父亲难兜靡本来和大月氏都住在祁连山、敦煌一带，是个小国。大月氏攻打杀害了难兜靡，强占他的地盘，乌孙人逃亡投奔匈奴。难兜靡的儿子昆莫那时刚出生不久，傅父布就翎侯抱着他逃亡，途中将他放在草丛中，去为他寻找食物。回来时，见狼正在给他喂奶，又有乌鸦衔着肉在旁边盘旋，以为昆莫是神，就抱着昆莫归附匈奴，单于喜欢他，将他抚养成人。昆莫长大后，单于把他父亲的民众交还给他，让他带兵打仗，昆莫屡次建立战功。那时，月氏已被匈奴打败，向西进攻塞王。塞王南巡迁往远方，月氏人便居住在塞王的地盘上。昆莫的力量壮大后，亲自请求单于允许他替父报仇，于是向西攻败大月氏。大月氏人再次西逃，迁往大夏人居住的地方。昆莫掠夺其民众，就留居在大月氏人的土地上，兵力逐渐强大起来，正好碰上匈奴单于死，于是不肯再入朝事奉匈奴。匈奴派军队攻打他，无法战胜，更认为昆莫是神而远离他。如今单于刚被汉朝打败，处于窘困的境地，而昆莫原来的地方无人居住。少数民族依恋故土，又贪心汉朝的财物，如果在此时多多地送些财物给乌孙，招引他们到东边来居住在原来的土地上，汉朝送公主给乌孙王作夫人，双方结为兄弟关系，根据以上对形势的分析，乌孙一定会听从我们的建议，那么这就等于切断了匈奴的右臂。联合了乌孙，

lost the title of marquis, replied: "When your humble servant lived among the Huns, I heard about King Kunmo of the Wusun. Kunmo's father Nandoumi originally lived in the Qilian Mountains and Dunhuang area together with Great Yuezhi, as a small state. Great Yuezhi attacked and killed Nandoumi and seized his territory, and the Wusun people fled to the Huns. Kunmo at the time was a babe-in-arms, so his godfather Bujiu, Marquis of Ling, cradled him as he made his escape. On the way, he placed the baby on the grass while he went to find food for him. When he came back, he saw a she-wolf suckling him, and a crow hovering nearby, meat in its beak, which made him believe Kunmo was a god. Holding Kunmo he pledged allegiance to the Huns; the Chanyu took a liking to him and brought him up. When Kunmo grew up, the Chanyu put his father's people under his generalship, and he went on to perform great military exploits. At that time, Yuezhi had been beaten by the Huns, so they turned their attack on the King of Sak in the west, forcing them to migrate to the distant south, their territory taken over by Yuezhi people. When Kunmo grew strong, he requested the Chanyu to allow him to avenge his father, so he attacked and overwhelmed Great Yuezhi in the west. The Yuezhi fled west once again, into Bactrian inhabited lands. Kunmo seized its people, and settled in the land. He began to build up military forces, and when the Chanyu died, he refused further allegiance to the Huns, who then sent troops against him. Their lack of success made them venerate Kunmo all the more and they left him alone. Now Chanyu has just been frustrated by the Han, and Kunmo's original place uninhabited. Attachment to their homeland is characteristic of the barbarians, and they are greedy for our products. Suppose we now send a lot more gifts to the Wusun, tempting them to move east back to their original land, and then marry a Han princess to their king, the two sides will become brothers. Based on this analysis, Wusun will follow our suggestions, and this will be tantamount to cutting off the Huns' right arm. An

【原文】

乌孙，自其西大夏之属皆可招来而为外臣。”天子以为然，拜骞为中郎将，将三百人，马各二匹，牛羊以万数，赍金币帛直数千钜万，多持节副使，道可遣之旁国。骞既至乌孙，致赐谕指，未能得其决。语在《西域传》。骞即分遣副使使大宛、康居、月氏、大夏。乌孙发译道送骞，与乌孙使数十人，马数十匹，报谢，因令窥汉，知其广大。

骞还，拜为大行。岁馀，骞卒。后岁馀，其所遣副使通大夏之属者皆颇与其人俱来，于是西北国始通于汉矣。然骞凿空，诸后使往者皆称博望侯，以为质于外国，外国由是信之。其后，乌孙竟与汉结婚。

初，天子发书《易》，曰“神马当从西北来”。得乌孙马好，名曰“天马”。及得宛汗血马，益壮，更名乌孙马曰“西极马”，宛马曰“天马”云。而汉始筑令居以西，初置酒泉郡，以通西北国。因益

【今译】

自乌孙以西的大夏等国，都可招来而为您的外臣。”汉武帝认为张骞说得对，授予张骞中郎将的官职，率领三百人，每人马各二匹，赶着上万计的牛羊，随身携带价值数千万万的黄金和礼物，还有许多持节副使随行，出使乌孙。道路方便的话，就派持节副使出使乌孙旁边的国家。张骞到达乌孙后，将汉武帝的礼物送给乌孙王并转达了汉武帝的旨意，但未能获得乌孙王的明确表态。具体内容记载在《西域传》里。张骞便分别派遣副使出使大宛、康居、月氏、大夏。乌孙王派翻译向导护送张骞。乌孙使者数十人，马数十匹随张骞回汉朝答谢汉武帝，趁机让他们察看汉朝的情况，了解到了汉朝的广大。

张骞返回汉朝，被授予大行官。一年多后，张骞去世。又过了一年多，他所派遣去通大夏等国的副使大都与这些国家的使节一同回到汉朝，于是西北各国开始了与汉朝的交通往来。不过由于张骞开辟了通往西域的道路，后来出使西域的人都仿效张骞，称博望侯，以此来取信于外国，外国人因此而信任他们。那以后，乌孙王终于与汉公主结婚。

当初，汉武帝打开《易》书占卜，说：“神马当从西北来。”得了乌孙马觉得好，给它起名为“天马”。等到又得了大宛汗血马，它比乌孙马更加膘壮，便将乌孙马改名为“西极马”，称大宛马为“天马”。并且汉朝开始从令居向西筑塞，新设酒泉郡，以便

alliance with the Wusun can attract Bactria and other countries west of Wusun to be your foreign subjects." The Emperor thought Zhang Qian was right, and appointed him leader of court gentlemen. Zhang Qian was to lead 300 people, each with two horses, plus tens of thousands of cattle and sheep, carrying gold and gifts worth billions of cash. He was accompanied by many deputy ambassadors with imperial tallies, who could peel off en route as envoys to Wusun's neighboring countries as required. Zhang Qian arrived, presented the gifts and conveyed the Emperor's wishes, but failed to get a clear decision from the King. The details are recorded in "Annals of the Western Regions." Then Zhang Qian sent his deputies on missions to Ferghana, Sogdiana, Yuezhi and Bactria. The King of Wusun sent a translator and guide to escort Zhang Qian, dispatching dozens of Wusun messengers with dozens of horses on a return trip to Han; this gave them the opportunity to witness its vastness.

Zhang Qian returned to Court, and was appointed Chief Messenger, to receive foreign guests, but he died over a year later. Then, another year on, most of the deputies he had sent to Bactria and other countries came back accompanied by the ambassadors of these countries. The countries of the northwest started ties with Han. Since it was Zhang Qian as Marquis of Bowang who opened up the route, later Han envoys referred to themselves as that, in order to win the trust and confidence of foreign countries. Subsequently, the King of Wusun did marry a Han princess.

At the start of his reign, Emperor Wudi opened the *Book of Changes* in divination, which said: "Divine horses should come from the northwest." He got a good Wusun horse and named it "Celestial Horse." Then he got a Ferghana horse, which was stronger. Then he renamed the Wusun horse "Western Extreme Horse," and the Ferghana horse "Celestial Horse." Han began to build fortresses west of Lingju County, establishing a new Jiuquan Prefecture, in order to facilitate access to the countries of the Western Regions.

【原文】

发使抵安息、奄蔡、犛靬、条支、身毒国。而天子好宛马，使者相望于道，一辈大者数百，少者百馀人，所赍操，大放博望侯时。其后益习而衰少焉。汉率一岁中使者多者十馀，少者五六辈，远者八九岁，近者数岁而反。

是时，汉既灭越，蜀所通西南夷皆震，请吏。置牂柯、越巂、益州、沈黎、文山郡，欲地接以前通大夏。乃遣使岁十馀辈，出此初郡，皆复闭昆明，为所杀，夺币物。于是汉发兵击昆明，斩首数万。后复遣使，竟不得通。语在《西南夷传》。

自骞开外国道以尊贵，其吏士争上书言外国奇怪利害，求使。天子为其绝远，非人所乐，听其言，予节，募吏民无问所从来，为具备人众遣之，以广其道。来还不能无侵盗币物，及使失指，天子为其习之，辄覆按致重罪，以激怒令赎，复求使。使端无穷，而轻犯法。其

【今译】

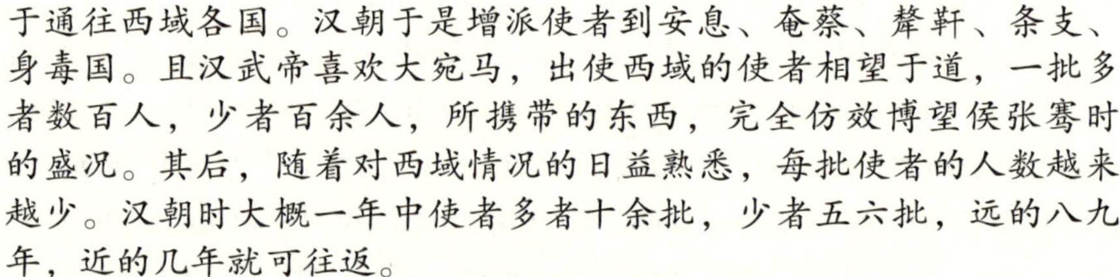

于通往西域各国。汉朝于是增派使者到安息、奄蔡、犛靬、条支、身毒国。且汉武帝喜欢大宛马，出使西域的使者相望于道，一批多者数百人，少者百余人，所携带的东西，完全仿效博望侯张骞时的盛况。其后，随着对西域情况的日益熟悉，每批使者的人数越来越少。汉朝时大概一年中使者多者十余批，少者五六批，远的八九年，近的几年就可往返。

这个时候，汉朝已灭了南越，与蜀郡相通的西南夷都很震动，他们请求汉朝在那儿设治并派官吏进行治理。汉朝在西南夷设置了牂柯、越巂、益州、沈黎、文山郡，想用在西南夷设郡的办法，地界相接，向前通往大夏。于是汉朝每年派使者十余批，从这些新设置的郡出发，但都再次被昆明夷所阻绝，汉使被杀、礼品遭劫。于是汉朝发兵出击昆明，斩首数万。后来又派使者，终不能通过。详情在《西南夷传》里。

自从张骞开辟了通往西域的道路而获得尊贵的地位，那些吏士争着上书谈论外国物产的稀奇古怪以及通使的利害关系，请求出使。汉武帝因为西域偏僻遥远，并非人人都乐意去，便接受他们的言论，给予出使的符节，招募官吏和百姓而不问应募者的身份资历，为这些人准备好随行人员打发他们出使，以此扩大出使西域人员的来源。这些人回来时，难免有劫掠和盗窃来的财物，以及执行使命时违背汉武帝的旨意，汉武帝因为他们熟悉西域的情况，就每每审查他们并致以重罪，以激发他们发奋去立功赎罪，再次请求出使西域。

The Dynasty sent additional envoys to Parthia, Alanorsi, Rome, Seleukia and Hindu. Since the Emperor loved Ferghana horses, the Han envoys were frequently seen along the road, their retinues numbering in the hundreds, carrying riches like in the time of the Marquis of Bowang. Later on, as familiarity with the Western Regions grew, the ambassadorial missions involved smaller entourages. There were between half a dozen and a dozen groups a year, on round trips of eight or nine years to faraway countries, or just a few years in the case of nearer ones.

By this time, Han had conquered the Southern Yue, and all the southwestern barbarians bordering Shu were awed into asking for Han commissioners to govern there. Han set up the prefectures of Zangke, Yuesui, Yizhou, Shenli, and Wenshan, intending to reach Bactria via these prefectures. So Han sent 10 ambassadorial parties a year, starting from these new prefectures, but still their way was blocked by the Kunming, who killed Han envoys and stole the gifts. Han sent troops against them, beheading tens of thousands. Later, it resumed sending envoys, but in the end none got through. The details are recorded in "Annals of Southwestern Barbarians."

Since Zhang Qian obtained noble status by opening up the international roads, officials and scholars vied with each other to write about the strange foreign customs and pros and cons of the foreign relations, requesting to be appointed to official missions. As the Western Regions were so remote, deterring many people, the Emperor accepted their words, and gave them mission tallies, regardless of the origins and qualifications of the recruited officials or commoners. He dispatched them complete with entourage, thereby greatly expanding the diversity of such ambassadorial groups. On their return, the Emperor's gifts had inevitably been plundered, and his mission instructions perhaps flouted, but considering their familiarity with Western Regions, the Emperor would interrogate them minutely and give them a heavy sentence; this was designed

【原文】

吏卒亦辄复盛推外国所有，言大者予节，言小者为副，故妄言无行之徒皆争相效。其使皆私县官赍物，欲贱市以私其利。外国亦厌汉使人人有言轻重，度汉兵远，不能至，而禁其食物，以苦汉使。汉使乏绝，责怨，至相攻击。楼兰、姑师小国，当空道，攻劫汉使王恢等尤甚。而匈奴奇兵又时时遮击之。使者争言外国利害，皆有城邑，兵弱易击。于是天子遣从票侯破奴将属国骑及郡兵数万以击胡，胡皆去。明年，击破姑师，虏楼兰王。酒泉列亭鄣至玉门矣。

而大宛诸国发使随汉使来，观汉广大，以大鸟卵及犛靬眩人献于汉，天子大说。而汉使穷河源，其山多玉石，采来，天子案古图书，名河所出山曰昆仑云。是时，上方数巡狩海上，乃悉从外国客，大都

【今译】

出使西域的缘由无穷无尽，且轻视犯法。那些吏卒也每每一再地推崇外国的物产，夸张程度大的，被给予符节，为正使，夸张程度小的为副使。故无稽之谈者及无良好品行之徒都争相仿效。使者们大都将天子送给西域各国的礼物据为己有，想以较低的价格卖出以从中牟利。外国人也厌恶汉使人人言语轻重不实，估计路远汉军不能到达，便断绝汉使的食物供应，使他们陷于困苦的境地。汉使生活穷困，谴责抱怨，以至于相互攻击。楼兰、姑师等小国，地处交通要道，攻击、劫掠汉使王恢等尤为厉害，且匈奴奇兵更是时时截击汉使。使者们争相谈论征服这些国家对汉朝有利，不讨伐它则对汉朝有害，这些国家都有城邑，军队战斗力弱，易于攻击。于是汉武帝派从票侯赵破奴，率领西域各属国骑兵及各郡兵力数万人反击匈奴，匈奴兵全部逃窜。第二年，赵破奴击败姑师，俘虏了楼兰王。汉朝从酒泉郡起布列了边防哨所，直至玉门关。

大宛诸国派使者随汉使来到汉朝，看到汉朝的广大，他们向汉朝献上驼鸟卵和犛靬的幻术家，汉武帝大喜。汉使穷尽黄河的源头，那里的山多玉石，汉使采来运回汉朝，汉武帝查考了古地图书籍，将黄河源头所出之山命名为昆仑山。这时，汉武帝正好多次到海边视察，身边竟全是外国客人跟随着。凡属大都市或人多的地方就打

to pressure them into requesting a further mission so as to make meritorious atonement for their faults. There were inexhaustible reasons for launching new missions, so the offenses were not taken seriously. The travelers would repeatedly praise foreign produce, and those with the most colorful, exaggerated tales were given ambassadorial tallies; the less colorful raconteurs became deputies. As a result, those who talked nonsense or misbehaved copied their superiors. Most of the envoys embezzled the gifts intended for the foreign rulers, and tried to profit by selling them cheaply. The foreigners also hated the bragging Han envoys, so they cut off their food supply to make them suffer, reckoning it was too far for Han troops to reach. The Han envoys were so hard up that they griped and groaned; they even attacked each other. Small countries like Loulan and Gushi, located on the traffic arteries, launched particularly damaging raids on Han envoys like Wang Hui, and the parties came under constant harrying by Hun detachments. Han envoys tried to outdo each other in talking about the pros and cons of conquering these countries, which had vulnerable towns and weak armies. So the Emperor sent Zhao Ponu the Marquis of Congpiao, at the head of vassal cavalry and troops from the Western Prefectures tens of thousands strong to attack the Huns, who all fled. The next year (108 BC), Zhao beat Gushi, and captured the King of Loulan. Han established border posts from Jiuquan up to Yumen Pass.

Ferghana and other countries sent envoys to accompany the Han missions back home, thus witnessing the vastness of Han. They presented to Court ostrich eggs and Roman magicians, delighting the Emperor. The outbound missions went as far as the source of the Yellow River, where the mountains contained jade. They brought jade back, and the Emperor examined the ancient books and maps, naming the mountains at the source of the Yellow River as the Kunlun,

At this time, the Emperor paid several inspections to the

【原文】

多人则过之，散财帛赏赐，厚具饶给之，以览视汉富厚焉。大角氏，出奇戏诸怪物，多聚观者，行赏赐，酒池肉林，令外国客遍观各仓库府臧之积，欲以见汉广大，倾骇之。及加其眩者之工，而角氐奇戏岁增变，其益兴，自此始。而外国使更来更去。大宛以西皆自恃远，尚骄恣，未可诎以礼羁縻而使也。

汉使往既多，其少从率进孰于天子，言大宛有善马在贰师城，匿不肯示汉使。天子既好宛马，闻之甘心，使壮士车令等持千金及金马以请宛王贰师城善马。宛国饶汉物，相与谋曰："汉去我远，而盐水中数有败，出其北有胡寇，出其南乏水草，又且往往而绝邑，乏食者多。汉使数百人为辈来，常乏食，死者过半，是安能致大军乎？且贰师马，宛宝马也。"遂不肯予汉使。汉使怒，妄言，椎金马而去。宛

【今译】

那儿经过，散发财物布帛进行赏赐，备办丰厚的礼物送给他们，以此来展示汉朝财力的雄厚。表演大角抵、奇戏等新奇的东西，引来众多的围观者，大行赏赐，酒池肉林。让外国客人遍观汉朝各仓库府藏的储积，想以此显示汉朝的广大，使他们对汉朝的强大既佩服又诧异。至于增加幻术家的技艺，角抵、奇戏花样的年年增变，它们的进一步兴起，就是从汉武帝时开始的。且外国使者不断地交替往来，络绎不绝。大宛以西的国家都自恃离汉朝遥远，还是骄傲放纵，汉朝没能使他们屈服，就用礼尚往来的方式与他们保持联系，出使这些国家。

汉朝出使到西域的人已很多，那些少年从使多用虚美的言辞怂恿汉武帝，说大宛有好马在贰师城，藏起来不肯让汉使看到。汉武帝喜欢宛马，听说后一心想得到它，他派壮士车令等带着千金和金马去请求大宛王送给贰师城好马。大宛国有许多汉朝财物，他们互相商量道："汉朝离我们很远，且人从盐泽一带经过每有死亡，从它的北面经过有匈奴的骚扰，从南面来则缺乏水草，加上沿途处处没有城邑，缺乏食物的情况经常发生。汉使一批数百人前来，常常缺乏食物。死者过半。这样的情况怎么能派大军来呢？况且贰师马是大宛的宝马啊。"终不肯给汉使。汉使大怒，痛骂一通，椎破金

seacoast, all followed by foreign guests. Where there were large cities with many people, he would go through, distributing cash and cloth to reward them, bestowing generous gifts on them, in order to impress by this demonstration of Han's wealth. Wonderful performances of wrestling and strange plays were staged, attracting massive crowds and accompanied by imperial rewards and feasting. Foreign guests were shown all the riches amassed in government stores, a demonstration of Han's greatness intended to make them wonder at and admire the powerful Han Dynasty. The number and variety of performances grew every year, with magic performances, wrestling and strange plays, the start of their future great popularity. A never-ending stream of foreign envoys came and went. The countries west of Ferghana counted on their distance from Han to protect their pride and indulgence, so Han was unable to make them submit. Instead, there was a policy of maintaining respectful contact, sending ambassadors to these countries.

So numerous were the Han missions to the Western Regions that many of the junior embassy followers curried favor with the Emperor, saying that Ferghana had a good horse in Ershi City, but was hiding it from Han envoys. Wudi, infatuated with this breed of horse, immediately wanted to possess it. He sent a warrior Cheling and his team, carrying heaps of gold and a golden horse in exchange for the Ferghana king's good horse at Ershi. Since Ferghana was already rich in Han treasures, they did not immediately agree, discussing thus: "The Han Empire is very far from us, and death along the salt marshes is a regular thing; in the north they have been harassed by the Huns, and in the south there is lack of water and plants. Besides, there is not a town to be found along the way, so food shortages are common. Hundreds of Han people come together, but often lack of food means that half of them die en route. So how can they send a large army? And anyway, the Ershi horse is a Ferghana treasure." So they finally refused to hand over

【原文】

中贵人怒曰："汉使至轻我！"遣汉使去，令其东边郁成王遮攻，杀汉使，取其财物。天子大怒。诸尝使宛姚定汉等言。"宛兵弱，诚以汉兵不过三千人，强弩射之，即破宛矣。"天子以尝使浞野侯攻楼兰，以七百骑先至，虏其王，以定汉等言为然，而欲侯宠姬李氏，乃以李广利为将军，伐宛。

骞孙猛，字子游，有俊才，元帝时为光禄大夫，使匈奴，给事中，为石显所谮，自杀。

——卷六十一《张骞李广利传》第三十一

【今译】

马而去。大宛国的贵臣们怒道："汉使太轻视我们了!"令汉使离开大宛国，又让东边的郁成王拦击他们，杀害汉使夺取他们的财物。汉武帝大怒。曾出使过大宛的姚定汉等人说："大宛兵弱，若用近三千的汉军，强弓劲弩向他们射击，便可打败他们。"汉武帝因曾派浞野侯赵破奴攻打楼兰，以七百骑兵先到楼兰，俘虏了楼兰王，故认为姚定汉等人言之有理，而想封宠姬李夫人的兄弟为侯，便以李广利为将军讨伐大宛。

张骞孙张猛，字子游，颇有才智，元帝时为光禄大夫，出使过匈奴，加官给事中，被石显陷害而自杀。

the horse. The ambassador was so furious he gave them a tongue lashing, smashed the golden horse and left. The Ferghana nobles said angrily: "Han envoys are too contemptuous!" They ordered the mission to leave the country, and had their eastern neighbor the King of Yucheng intercept the party, killing the envoys and seizing their property. The Emperor was furious. Former envoy to Ferghana Yao Dinghan and others said: "Ferghana troops are weak. All it would take to conquer them is 3,000 Han soldiers with strong crossbows." The Emperor had sent Marquis of Zhuoye (Zhao Ponu) to attack Loulan. With 700 cavalry arriving first at Loulan, they had captured its king, so he thought that Yao and others were right, and would like to ennoble the brother of his favorite concubine Madame Li. Accordingly, he appointed Li Guangli as the general to punish Ferghana.

Zhang Qian's grandson Zhang Meng, styled Ziyou, was quite intelligent and capable. Appointed Grand Master for Splendid Happiness by Emperor Yuandi (48-33 BC.) he was made ambassador to the Huns, and promoted to Palace Steward. He was framed by Shi Xian and committed suicide.

主父偃传

【原文】

主父偃，齐国临菑人也。学长短从横术，晚乃学《易》、《春秋》、百家之言。游齐诸子间，诸儒生相与排傧，不(客)[容]于齐。家贫，假贠无所得，北游燕、赵、中山，皆莫能厚，客甚困，以诸侯莫足游者，元光元年，乃西入关见卫将军。卫将军数言上，上不省。资用乏，留久，诸侯宾客多厌之，乃上书阙下。朝奏，暮召入见。所言九事，其八事为律令，一事谏伐匈奴，曰：

臣闻明主不恶切谏以博观，忠臣不避重诛以直谏，是故事无遗策而功流万世。今臣不敢隐忠避死，以效愚计，愿陛下幸赦而少察之。

【今译】

主父偃，齐国临菑人。他学的是长短纵横之术，晚年才学习《易》、《春秋》、百家之说。游学于齐国读书人之间，儒生们一齐排斥摒弃他，他在齐不能容身。家里很穷，无处借贷，于是他北游燕、赵、中山，都没有人厚待他，客居异乡，非常困窘。他认为诸侯们没有值得游说的，元光元年，便西入关中，谒见将军卫青。卫将军多次对皇上说起他，皇上一直没召见。主父偃无钱可用，在京城逗留时间久了，诸侯家的门客大都讨厌他，于是他就向朝廷上书。奏书早晨送到皇帝那里，晚上他就被召进宫中拜见皇帝。奏书中讲了九件事，其中八项是律令方面的问题，一项是谏阻征伐匈奴，文中说：

我听说圣明的君主不讨厌恳切的规劝来增广见识，忠臣不逃避严厉的责罚用直言诤谏，因此事无遗策而功名流传万世。现在臣下不敢隐藏忠言、逃避死罪，以奉献愚计，希望陛下赦臣冒昧之罪，并稍微鉴察一下我的见解。

Chapter 13

Biography of Zhu Fuyan

Zhu Fuyan was born in Linzi in the state of Qi. He studied political strategy, but it was only in his later years that he studied the *Book of Changes*, the *Spring and Autumn Annals*, and the hundred schools of philosophy. An itinerant student among Qi's scholars, he was rejected by the Confucians, so he could not find shelter in Qi. Being from a poor family, with no means of borrowing money, he drifted north to Yan, Zhao, and Zhongshan, without finding a welcome. A stranger in strange lands, he was in dire straits. Believing it a waste to try lobbying the princes, in year one of the Yuanguang reign period (134 BC), he traveled west through the Pass to request an audience with General Wei Qing. General Wei referred him to the Emperor on several occasions, but the Emperor did not summon him. Zhu Fuyan was hard up, and after a long stay in the capital, the followers of the princes were heartily sick of him, so he wrote a petition to the court. His memorial reached the Emperor in the morning, and he was summoned to an audience that same evening. He talked about nine issues, eight of them law-related, and one arguing against an expedition against the Huns. The text read

I heard the wise monarch does not object to those earnest exhortations that broaden his experience, and that the loyal courtier braves severe punishment with straightforward exhortations, so that nothing that should be done is left undone and his eternal fame will spread. Now your servant dares not to hide good advice in order to escape death, but will offer up this foolish plan. I hereby take the liberty of begging Your Majesty to kindly pardon my offense, and pay a little attention to my

【原文】

《司马法》曰："国虽大，好战必亡；天下虽平，忘战必危。"天下既平，天子大恺，春蒐秋狝，诸侯春振旅，秋治兵，所以不忘战也。且怒者逆德也，兵者凶器也，争者末节也。古之人君一怒必伏尸流血，故圣王重行之。夫务战胜，穷武事，未有不悔者也。

昔秦皇帝任战胜之威，蚕食天下，并吞战国，海内为一，功齐三代。务胜不休，欲攻匈奴，李斯谏曰："不可。夫匈奴无城郭之居，委积之守，迁徙鸟举，难得而制。轻兵深入，粮食必绝；运粮以行，重不及事。得其地，不足以为利；得其民，不可调而守也。胜必弃之，非民父母。靡敝中国，甘心匈奴，非完计也。"秦皇帝不听，遂使蒙恬将兵而攻胡，却地千里，以河为

【今译】

《司马法》说："国家虽大，好战必亡；天下虽然太平，忘战必危。"天下已经平定，天子的军队高奏还师振旅的《大凯》之乐，春猎秋狩以习武事，诸侯春季整军，秋天练兵，是为了不忘记战争。发怒是违逆之德，兵器是不祥之物，争斗是微末小节。自古以来人君一怒必定死人流血，所以圣明的君王慎行其事。务求打仗胜利、穷兵黩武的人，没有不招来悔恨的。

从前秦始皇凭藉战胜之威，蚕食天下，并吞列国，统一海内，功绩可比夏、商、周三代开国之主。他致力于打胜仗没有休止，要攻打匈奴，李斯谏阻说："不行。匈奴没有城郭居邑，没有积聚处所，流动迁徙像鸟一样飘忽不定，难以控制。轻兵深入，粮食必然接济不上；运粮而行，粮重难运，解决不了问题。夺取匈奴的土地，不能用来生利；俘获匈奴的民众，不能征调用来守卫。战胜匈奴必定要抛弃他们，这不是为民父母应做的事。使中国财力枯竭，而以攻打匈奴为乐，这不是完备之计。"秦始皇不听规劝，于是派蒙恬率兵攻打匈奴，拓地千里，以黄河为边

opinion.

According to Sima's Art of War, *"However great a state is, belligerence will lead inevitably to its demise; though the world is in peace, it will be dangerous to forget war." The world has been subjugated, and the triumphal music of the Emperor's armies still resounds. Spring and autumn hunting is practiced to exercise the arts of war: the princes prepare their army in the spring, do training in the autumn, in order not to forget war. Since anger runs counter to virtue and weapons are things of bad omen, to fight is a mean thing. Since ancient times, when the monarch gets angry death and bloody happenings ensue, so the sage king is cautious about it. Insisting on warfare as a means to win, and throwing all one's military strength at a problem is a certain way to invite future remorse. In the former times, the First Qin Emperor took advantage of his triumphant might, swallowing up the world, annexing the states, unifying the area within the seas; his exploits were comparable to those of the founding fathers of the Xia, Shang and Zhou. He was committed to waging non-stop war, wanting to attack the Huns, but Li Si dissuaded him: "No. The Huns have no cities or storehouses to defend, so they can fly hither and thither like birds, never settling, uncontrollable. If we send light troops to penetrate deep into their territory, our food supply lines will not reach them; nor will transporting it alongside work, since grain is heavy. When we capture their land, it cannot be used to make a profit; when we capture their people, we cannot draft them to keep guard. We defeat the Huns whom we must then abandon; this is not what we should do as their parents. To exhaust the resources of the Middle Kingdom and to attack the Huns as amusement is not a perfect plan." The Emperor ignored his advice, and dispatched Meng Tian to attack the Huns. His forces pushed 1,000* li *as far as the Yellow River at*

【原文】

境。地固泽卤，不生五谷，然后发天下丁男以守北河。暴兵露师十有馀年，死者不可胜数，终不能逾河而北。是岂人众之不足，兵革之不备哉？其势不可也。又使天下飞刍挽粟，起于黄、腄、琅邪负海之郡，转输北河，率三十锺而致一石。男子疾耕不足于粮饷，女子纺绩不足于帷幕。百姓靡敝，孤寡老弱不能相养，道死者相望，盖天下始叛也。

及至高皇帝定天下，略地于边，闻匈奴聚代谷之外而欲击之。御史成谏曰："不可。夫匈奴，兽聚而鸟散，从之如搏景，今以陛下盛德攻匈奴，臣窃危之。"高帝不听，遂至代谷，果有平城之围。高帝悔之，乃使刘敬往结和亲，然后天下亡干戈之事。

故兵法曰："兴师十万，日费千金。"秦常积众数十万人，

【今译】

境。那里本来就是盐碱地，不长五谷。随后，秦始皇又征发天下丁男戍守北河。军队在外驻守十几年，死者不可胜数，始终未能越过黄河北进。这难道是因为人马不足、装备不齐吗？是客观形势不允许啊！又使天下百姓急速运输粮草，从遥远的黄、腄、琅邪等靠海的郡县，转运到北河，一般发运三十钟粟，只有一石能运到。男子拼命耕种，满足不了粮饷之需，女子努力纺织，满足不了帷幕之求。百姓财穷力尽，孤寡老弱不能养活，路上死者相望，大概由于这个缘故天下开始反叛秦朝。

到高祖皇帝平定天下，略地到边境，听说匈奴聚集在代谷外，就要去攻打。御史成劝谏说："不行。匈奴行踪多变，一会儿像野兽聚合，一会儿又像鸟雀飞散，追赶他们如同捕捉影子。现在以陛下盛德去攻打匈奴，臣私下认为十分危险。"高祖皇帝不听，于是领兵进至代郡的山谷，果然发生了被围于平城的事。高祖皇帝很后悔，就派刘敬前往匈奴缔结和亲之约，然后天下才没有干戈纷争。

所以《孙子兵法》上说："兴师十万，日费千金。"秦朝时

the border. The land there had always been low and saline, unable to support grain. Subsequently, the emperor mobilized able-bodied men from across the empire to defend the North River. The troops were exposed in the wilderness for a dozen years, and countless men died, but they were never able to cross the Yellow River into the northern lands. Was this for lack of troops, or inadequate equipment? It was because the realities of the situation did not allow it! Once more the people across the land were ordered to rapidly ship fodder and grain supplies and they were to ship millet from the distant Huang, Chui, Langya and other counties near the coast way inland to the North River. In general, for 30 zhong of millet shipped, only one picul could be delivered. Hardscrabble farmers could not meet the demand for provisions, while women hard at weaving could not meet the demand for tents. The people were exhausted, unable to feed their elderly, widows and orphans; dead bodies littered the roads everywhere. Probably for this reason the world began to rebel against the Qin Dynasty.

When Emperor Gaodi conquered the land, and occupied the border, he wanted to attack the Huns after hearing they were massing outside the valley in Dai. But Censor Cheng remonstrated: "No, the Huns keep changing their whereabouts, sometimes gathering like beasts, sometimes flying away like birds; to try to follow them is like trying to catch a shadow. Now, motivated by high virtue, Your Majesty wants to attack the Huns but it seems to me very dangerous." Gaodi did not listen to him. He led the troops into the valley, and sure enough was besieged in Pingcheng. Gaodi regretted his action and sent Liu Jing to the Huns to negotiate a peace treaty by marrying one of his daughters to the Chanyu of Huns, and with this the world at last was free of warfare. Therefore, according to Master Sun's Art of War *"Mobilizing 100,000 soldiers, the daily cost is 1,000*

【原文】

虽有覆军杀将，系虏单于，适足以结怨深仇，不足以偿天下之费。夫匈奴行盗侵敺，所以为业，天性固然。上自虞夏殷周，固不程督，禽兽畜之，不比为人。夫不上观虞夏殷周之统，而下循近世之失，此臣之所以大恐，百姓所疾苦也。且夫兵久则变生，事苦则虑易。使边境之民靡敝愁苦，将吏相疑而外市，故尉佗、章邯得成其私，而秦政不行，权分二子，此得失之效也。故《周书》曰："安危在出令，存亡在所用。"愿陛下孰计之而加察焉。

是时，徐乐、严安亦俱上书言世务。书奏，上召见三人，谓曰："公皆安在？何相见之晚也！"乃拜偃、乐、安皆为郎中。偃数上

【今译】

经常在边境屯驻兵民数十万人，虽也有过歼灭敌军、斩杀敌将、俘获单于的功劳，恰好足以结怨匈奴，加深仇恨，却不能够抵偿天下的耗费。匈奴盗掠侵袭，是用以谋生的手段，天性本来如此。上自虞、夏、殷、周时代，就从来不向他们征课赋役，不加督察责罚，以禽兽看待他们，而不看作人类。上借鉴虞、夏、商、周时的经验，却往下因循近世的失误，这是臣深感忧惧之事，也是天下百姓痛苦之事。再者军队久居于外，就会发生变乱，所做的事太艰苦，人们就会思虑变革。使得边境上的百姓凋敝愁苦，将吏互相疑忌而与敌暗通，所以尉佗、章邯得以实现自己的野心，可是秦朝的政令却不能推行，因为权力被尉佗、章邯二人瓜分，这就是得和失的证明啊。所以《周书》说："天下安危在于天子发布什么样的号令，国家存亡在于天子使用什么样的人。"希望陛下认真研究这个问题并加以考察。

当时，徐乐、严安也都上书谈论国事。奏书送呈武帝，皇上召见三人，对他们说："诸位从前都在哪里呀？为什么我们相见这么晚啊！"于是任命主父偃、徐乐、严安都为郎中。主父偃多次上疏言

gold." The Qin Dynasty often kept hundreds of thousands of people at the border. Though they did on occasion wipe out the enemy troops, kill the enemy generals, and capture their Chanyu, these successes were just enough to deepen the Huns' enmity, but not to cover the cost to the empire. For the Huns, the looting and pillaging that follow their invasions is a way of earning a living; this is their nature. As early as the Yu, Xia, Shang and Zhou eras, they never imposed their rule on the Huns, taking them as animals rather than as human beings. Your servant is deeply apprehensive that we do not draw on the tradition of Yu, Xia, Shang and Zhou, but follow the mistakes of modern times, mistakes that bring misery to the common people. Besides, mutiny will occur among our armed forces when they are stationed far away from home for long, and the extreme hardship of work will cause disaffection. By making the people on the border depressed and miserable, making the generals and officials jealous of each other and enter into illicit relations with the enemy, Wei Tuo and Zhang Han did realize their own ambitions. But Qin imperial decrees were not implemented, because the power was divided between the two men. This is the proof of loss and gain. Therefore, according to Book of Zhou*: "The empire's safety or danger depends on what orders are issued, and its survival depends on the kind of person that is employed." I wish that Your Majesty will seriously study the problem and examine this.*

At that time, Xu Le and Yan An also submitted letters expounding their views on affairs of state. When the memorials were delivered to the throne, the Emperor summoned the three of them, and exclaimed: "Gentlemen, where were you in the former times? Why do we meet only now?" So he appointed Zhu Fuyan, Xu Le, Yan An as gentlemen of the interior. Zhu Fuyan submitted many memorials to recommend things, and was promoted to receptionist,

【原文】

疏言事，迁谒者，中郎，中大夫。岁中四迁。

偃说上曰：“古者诸侯地不过百里，强弱之形易制。今诸侯或连城数十，地方千里，缓则骄奢易为淫乱，急则阻其强而合从以逆京师。今以法割削，则逆节萌起，前日朝错是也。今诸侯子弟或十数，而適嗣代立，馀虽骨肉，无尺地之封，则仁孝之道不宣。愿陛下令诸侯得推恩分子弟，以地侯之。彼人人喜得所愿，上以德施，实分其国，必稍自销弱矣。”于是上从其计。又说上曰：“茂陵初立，天下豪桀兼并之家，乱众民，皆可徙茂陵，内实京师，外销奸猾，此所谓不诛而害除。”上又从之。

尊立卫皇后及发燕王定国阴事，偃有功焉。大臣皆畏其口，赂遗

【今译】

事，皇上下令迁升主父偃为谒者、中郎、中大夫。一年当中提升了四次。

主父偃向皇上进言说：“古时候，诸侯的土地不超过一百里，不论其强弱，局势都容易控制。现在，诸侯王有的连城数十座，土地方圆千里，平时骄纵奢侈，容易做出淫乱之事，危急时就会恃仗强大，联合起来反叛朝廷。现在如果用法令分割，削减他们的地盘，他们反叛的思想就会萌发，以前晁错就是主张削藩而引起吴、楚等七国之乱。现在诸侯王的子弟有的多达以十计算，只有嫡长子世代继承王位，其余的子弟虽然也是诸侯王的亲生骨肉，却没有尺寸之地的封国，这样仁孝之道就不能宣扬。希望陛下令诸侯王推恩分其土地给所有子弟，使他们都成为侯。他们人人喜得所愿，皇上用恩德布施，实际上却分割了诸侯王的封国，必然会渐渐自己衰弱下去。”于是皇上采纳他的谋议。主父偃又向皇上进言说：“茂陵刚置县，天下豪杰兼并之家，扰乱庶民，可以把他们都迁徙到茂陵，内可充实京师力量，外可消除奸猾之徒，这就是所谓不用诛杀而祸害消除。”皇上又采纳了他的意见。

尊立卫子夫为皇后以及揭发燕王刘定国的暗中犯罪活动，主父偃都有功劳。大臣们都害怕主父偃的嘴，贿赂和馈赠给他的钱财累

court gentleman, and grand master of the palace. He was promoted four times in a single year.

Zhu Fuyan suggested: "In ancient times, the princes had no more than 100 *li* of land. Regardless of their strength, it was easy to control the situation. Now, some princes rule dozens of towns together, in territory 1,000 *li* square; in times of peace they are often extravagant and dissipated, and in times of crisis they will rely on their power to unite in rebellion against the Court. Now if we split them by law, and cut their territory, rebellious thoughts will arise among them; one need only look to Chao Cuo's attempt to whittle down the vassal states, which prompted rioting in seven states like Wu and Chu. Now the children of the princes are dozens in number, but the throne passes down by primogeniture, via the eldest son of the first wife; although the rest of the children are also the prince's flesh and blood, they do not share an inch of the fief, so the way of benevolence and filial piety is not manifest. I suggest that Your Majesty decrees that the princes extend their grace to their children by sharing out their land with their offspring so that the children become marquises. They will all be happy to get what they want. The Emperor grants grace, but is actually splitting up the princes' power bases, and they are bound to gradually weaken of their own accord." The Emperor adopted his proposed plan.

Zhu Fuyan again advised: "Maoling has just become a county. All the gallants and monopolists disturbing the common people, they can be resettled in Maoling, with the dual purpose of building up strength within the capital and removing the unreliable elements outside. This is what is called eliminating the scourge without killing." The Emperor again accepted his advice.

Zhu Fuyan was instrumental and meritorious in designating Wei Zifu as Empress and exposing the clandestine affairs of Liu Dingguo the King of Yan. The ministers were afraid of his mouth, a fear that prompted bribes and gifts to him totaling 1,000 gold. Someone

【原文】

累千金。或说偃曰：“大横！”偃曰：“臣结发游学四十馀年，身不得遂，亲不以为子，昆弟不收，宾客弃我，我阸日久矣。丈夫生不五鼎食，死则五鼎亨耳！吾日暮，故倒行逆施之。”

偃盛言朔方地肥饶，外阻河，蒙恬筑城以逐匈奴，内省转输戍漕，广中国，灭胡之本也。上览其说，下公卿议，皆言不便。公孙弘曰：“秦时尝发三十万众筑北河，终不可就，已而弃之。”朱买臣难诎弘，遂置朔方，本偃计也。

元朔中，偃言齐王内有淫失之行，上拜偃为齐相。至齐，遍召昆弟宾客，散五百金予之，数曰：“始吾贫时，昆弟不我衣食，宾客不我内门，今吾相齐，诸君迎我或千里。吾与诸君绝矣，毋复入偃之门！”乃使人以王与姊奸事动王。王以为终不得脱，恐效燕王论

【今译】

计达千金。有人劝告主父偃说：“你太横行无忌了！”主父偃说：“我结发游学四十多年，自己不得志，父母不把我当儿子，兄弟不收留我，朋友离弃我，我穷困潦倒的日子太久了。再说大丈夫在世，生不能享用五鼎食，死就受五鼎烹刑算了！我日暮途穷，所以倒行逆施，不按常理做事。”

主父偃大谈朔方土地肥沃，物产丰饶，外有险阻黄河，蒙恬在那里筑城以驱逐匈奴，内有辗转运输和戍守漕运的人力物力，还能拓广中国的疆土，是消灭匈奴的根本所在。皇上看了他的奏议，下发给公卿大臣们讨论，大家都说不利。公孙弘说：“秦朝时曾征发三十万人在北河筑城，终究没有筑成，不久就放弃了。”朱买臣诘难并驳倒公孙弘，于是设置了朔方郡。这本来是主父偃的谋议。

元朔年间，主父偃向皇上汇报了齐王刘次景在王宫内淫乱放荡、行为邪僻的事，皇上任命主父偃为齐相。主父偃到了齐国，遍召兄弟朋友，散发五百金给他们，数落他们说：“当初我贫贱的时候，兄弟不给我衣食，朋友不让我进门，现在我做了齐相，诸君当中有人到千里外来迎接我。我现在和诸位断交了，请不要再进我的门！”于是他派人用齐王与其姐姐通奸的事惊动齐王。齐王感到最

remonstrated with him: "You are too lawless!"

Zhu Fuyan said: "I started traveling young, seeking learning for 40 years; but my lack of success meant my parents did not treat me as a son; my brothers did not accept me; the friends shunned me; the days of penury and pain were all too long. A real man of character, if not able to enjoy five-tripod feasts when alive, may get his recompense by being boiled in five tripods when dead! I am getting old, so just act perversely, not by convention."

Zhu Fuyan waxed lyrical about Shuofang's fertile land, beyond which lay the barrier of the Yellow River, where Meng Tian had built fortifications in order to drive out the Huns. From Shuofang, they could save the long-distance transportation of human and material resources. Besides, it could broaden China's territory, as a base for destroying the Huns. The Emperor saw his memorial, and referred it to his courtiers for discussion, but everyone talked about the difficulties. Gongsun Hong said: "In the Qin Dynasty, they sent 300,000 people to construct fortifications on the North River. In the end, it was not completed, and they soon gave up." But Zhu Maichen criticized and refuted Gongsun Hong, so Shuofang Prefecture was set up, along the lines of Zhu Fuyan's original proposal.

During the Yuanshuo reign period, Zhu Fuyan reported the promiscuous and incestuous debauchery in the palace of Prince of Qi, Liu Cijing, and the Emperor appointed Zhu Fuyan as Qi's prime minister. Zhu arrived in Qi, and summoned all his brothers and friends, and distributed 500 gold among them, before launching into his attack: "When I was poor and lowly, brothers did not give me food or clothing, and friends did not let me inside their doors. But now that I am the prime minister, some gentlemen have come to meet me from thousands of *li* away. I now sever relations with you. Please do not enter my door again!" Then he sent to alert the Prince of Qi that his adultery with his sister was known. The prince felt that he could not escape blame in the end, so, fearing the same death

【原文】

死，乃自杀。

偃始为布衣时，尝游燕、赵，及其贵，发燕事。赵王恐其为国患，欲上书言其阴事，为居中，不敢发。及其为齐相，出关，即使人上书，告偃受诸侯金，以故诸侯子多以得封者。及齐王以自杀闻，上大怒，以为偃劫其王令自杀，乃征下吏治。偃服受诸侯之金，实不劫齐王令自杀。上欲勿诛，公孙弘争曰："齐王自杀无后，国除为郡，入汉，偃本首恶，非诛偃无以谢天下。"乃遂族偃。

偃方贵幸时，客以千数，及族死，无一人视，独孔车收葬焉。上闻之，以车为长者。

——卷六十四上《严朱吾丘主父徐严终王贾传》第三十四上

【今译】

终不能逃脱罪责，害怕像燕王刘定国那样被判处死刑，就自杀了。

主父偃当初没当官还是平民时，曾游学燕、赵，等到贵为高官，就揭发了燕王犯罪的事情。赵王刘彭祖恐怕他成为赵国的祸患，想上书揭发他的阴事，因主父偃身在朝中，不敢发难。等到主父偃被任命为齐相，出了函谷关，赵王立即派人上书，告发主父偃接受诸侯王的金钱贿赂，因此诸侯王子弟多因行贿得以封侯。及至齐王自杀的消息传到京城，皇上闻报大怒，认为是主父偃威胁齐王而使其自杀的，就把主父偃召回，交给法官治罪。主父偃招认了接受诸侯王金钱贿赂的事实，但他的确没有威逼齐王使其自杀。皇上想不杀主父偃，公孙弘争辩说："齐王自杀没有后代继承王位，齐国被废为郡，归入朝廷。这件事主父偃是首恶，不杀主父偃，就无法向天下人交代。"于是武帝下令族灭主父偃。

主父偃正贵宠时，门客数以千计，及至他被族灭身亡，没有一个人肯收葬他，只有孔车把他收葬了。皇上听说这件事，认为孔车是位忠厚长者。

sentence meted out to the Prince of Yan, he committed suicide.

As a commoner Zhu Fuyan had traveled as a poor student in Yan and Zhao; now, as a high-rank official he exposed the Prince of Yan's criminal acts. The Prince of Zhao, Liu Pengzu, had wanted to write to the Emperor about Zhu's secret dealings, as he was afraid Zhu might become the scourge of Zhao, but he had not dared to send it since Zhu Fuyan was so well situated at Court. But as soon as Zhu Fuyan went out of Hangu Pass bound for Qi as its prime minister, the Prince of Zhao immediately wrote to the Emperor, detailing Zhu Fuyan's acceptance of money from the princes for the ennoblement of their children. When it was reported from Qi that the prince had committed suicide, the Emperor was furious, believing that Zhu Fuyan had coerced the prince into this. He recalled Zhu Fuyan, and had him handed over to the judge for punishment. Zhu confessed to accepting the princes' money, but not to forcing the Prince of Qi into committing suicide. The Emperor did not want to kill him, but Gongsun Hong argued: "The Prince of Qi died without issue, and the princedom is now reduced to a prefecture of Han. Zhu Fuyan is the principal culprit, and we shall be accountable to the people of the world if we do not kill him." Emperor Wudi then ordered the extermination of Zhu Fuyan's clan.

When Zhu Fuyan was in favor, he had thousands of hangers-on, but when he was terminated with his clan, no one was willing to bury him, except for Kong Che. When the Emperor heard about this, he thought Kong Che a kind and decent elder.

霍光传

【原文】

霍光字子孟，票骑将军去病弟也。父中孺，河东平阳人也，以县吏给事平阳侯家，与侍者卫少儿私通而生去病。中孺吏毕归家，娶妇生光，因绝不相闻。久之，少儿女弟子夫得幸于武帝，立为皇后，去病以皇后姊子贵幸。既壮大，乃自知父为霍中孺，未及求问。会为票骑将军击匈奴，道出河东，河东太守郊迎，负弩矢先驱，至平阳传舍，遣吏迎霍中孺。中孺趋入拜谒，将军迎拜，因跪曰："去病不早自知为大人遗体也。"中孺扶服叩头，曰："老臣得托命将军，此天力也。"去病大为中孺买田宅奴婢而去。还，复过焉，乃将光西至长安，时年十馀岁，任光为郎，稍迁诸曹侍中。去病死后，光为奉(常)

【今译】

霍光字子孟，是骠骑将军霍去病的弟弟。他的父亲中孺，是河东平阳人，以县吏的身份在平阳侯家供事，同侍女卫少儿私通而生下霍去病。中孺差事完成后回到家中又娶妻生下霍光，与卫少儿断了关系不通音信。过了一段时间，少儿的妹妹子夫得宠于汉武帝，被立为皇后，霍去病由于是皇后姐姐的儿子而地位尊贵并受到皇帝的宠幸。霍去病长大成人后，才知道自己的父亲是霍中孺，但一直未来得及探访。恰好霍去病被封为骠骑将军去攻打匈奴，路过河东，河东太守到城郊去迎接，背着弓箭在前面带路，到平阳侯家里的接待处休息。霍去病就派小吏去请霍中孺来相见。中孺急忙赶来很恭敬地晋见，霍去病上前迎接揖拜，跪下说："去病早先不知道自己是您的骨肉。"中孺伏地叩头说："老臣能把命运寄托给将军，这是上天所助啊。"去病为中孺买了大量的田地、房宅、奴婢后离开。还军的时候，霍去病又经过河东，于是就把霍光带到了长安，当时霍光才十几岁，就任命霍光为郎，不久就迁升为诸曹侍中。去病死后，霍光被封为奉车都尉

Chapter 14

Biography of Huo Guang

Huo Guang, styled Zimeng, was a younger brother of Cavalry General-in-Chief Huo Qubing. His father Huo Zhongru was born in Pingyang of Hedong Prefecture. He served in the house of the Marquis of Pingyang as a county clerk, where he had an illegitimate child Huo Qubing with a maid called Wei Shaoer. After completing his work Huo Zhongru returned home and took a wife, who gave birth to Huo Guang. Huo Zhongru then severed relations with Wei, and all communication ceased. After a time, Wei's younger sister Zifu, loved by Emperor Wudi, was established as Empress, so Huo Qubing as a nephew of the Empress was ennobled and favored by the Emperor. Huo Qubing was not informed until adulthood that his father was Huo Zhongru, but never had time to visit. It happened that Huo Qubing was commissioned to attack the Huns as Cavalry General-in-Chief, and as he passed through Hedong Prefecture, he was met in the outskirts by the Governor. Carrying Huo's bows and arrows, the Governor walked ahead to Marquis of Pingyang's official guesthouse. Huo Qubing then sent a clerk to Huo Zhongru with a request that he come see him. Zhongru shuffled in to bow respectfully, but his son the General stepped forward to kowtow. He knelt down saying: "Qubing did not know until recently that we are flesh and blood." In response Huo Zhongru bowed to the ground to kowtow, saying: "It is the working of Heaven that this veteran subject can trust his fate to the General." Qubing bought for his father a large amount of fields, houses, and serfs, and on his return from campaigning he passed through there again, and took his young half-brother Huo Guang, then a teenager, west to Chang'an. After

【原文】

[车]都尉光禄大夫，出则奉车，入侍左右，出入禁闼二十馀年，小心谨慎，未尝有过，甚见亲信。

征和二年，卫太子为江充所败，而燕王旦、广陵王胥皆多过失。是时上年老，宠姬钩弋赵倢伃有男，上心欲以为嗣，命大臣辅之。察群臣唯光任大重，可属社稷。上乃使黄门画者画周公负成王朝诸侯以赐光。后元二年春，上游五柞宫，病笃，光涕泣问曰：“如有不讳，谁当嗣者？”上曰：“君未谕前画意邪？立少子，君行周公之事。”光顿首让曰：“臣不如金日磾。”日磾亦曰：“臣外国人，不如光。”上以光为大司马大将军，日磾为车骑将军，及太仆上官桀为左将军，搜粟都尉桑弘羊为御史大夫，皆拜卧内床下，受遗诏辅少

【今译】

光禄大夫，皇帝出行则以奉车身份随驾，在宫内就侍奉左右，进出禁宫有二十多年，一直小心谨慎，未曾有过差错，很受皇帝的亲近信赖。

征和二年，卫太子被江充陷害所败，燕王刘旦、广陵王刘胥又都有很多过失。这时候皇上年老，宠姬钩弋赵婕妤生了一个男孩，皇上心中打算把皇位传给他，并命大臣来辅佐他。皇上观察群臣中只有霍光才可担当重任，辅助社稷。皇上于是就叫宫廷画师画了一张周公背着成王接受诸侯朝贺的画赐给霍光。后元二年的春天，皇上出游五柞宫，病得很厉害，霍光流泪问道：“如果皇上有不测，那当由谁来继位？”皇上说道：“难道您还不明白上次送给您的画的意思吗？立少子为帝，您当照周公辅佐成王那样行事。”霍光叩头，谦让说：“我比不上金日磾。”金日磾也说：“我是外国人，不如霍光。”皇上于是就任命霍光为大司马大将军，金日磾为车骑将军，以及太仆上官桀为左将军，搜粟都尉桑弘羊为御史大夫。他们都在天子卧室内的床

Qubing's death, Huo Guang became the Commander-in-Chief of Chariots, and a grand master for splendid happiness, attending the imperial chariot when the Emperor traveled and serving at court when the Emperor was in residence. He served in the inner palace for over 20 years, always careful and conscientious, never making mistakes, thereby winning the unshakeable trust of the Emperor.

In year two of the Zhenghe reign period, Crown Prince Wei met his downfall because of the slander of Jiang Chong and both Prince of Yan Liu Dan and Prince of Guangling Liu Xu had been very remiss in their behavior. At this time, the aging emperor's favorite concubine Lady of Handsome Fairness Zhao of Gouyi Palace gave birth to a son, whom the Emperor intended to designate as heir to the throne, and ordered the ministers to his assistance. Wudi's observations had convinced him that of his ministers only Huo Guang could take the responsible role of being entrusted with the state. The Emperor thus had the court painter paint a painting of the Duke of Zhou carrying King Cheng on his back to accept the audience of the vassal kings, and gave it to Huo Guang. In spring of year two of the Houyuan reign period (87 BC), the Emperor fell very ill en route to Wuzuo Palace, and Huo Guang asked in tears: "If things do not go well for Your Majesty, who will succeed to the throne?" The Emperor said: "Did you not understand what it meant when I gave you the painting? Establish the young son as heir, and you will assist him following the example of the Duke of Zhou." Huo Guang kowtowed, and said in humility: "I cannot compare to Jin Miti." But [the ethnic Hun] Jin Miti also said: "Being a foreigner, I cannot match Huo Guang." The dying Emperor then appointed Guang as Commander-in-Chief and General-in-Chief, Jin Miti as Chariot Horse General, and the Chamberlain for Imperial Stud Shangguan Jie as Left General, Defender in Charge of Searching for Millet Sang Hongyang as Censor-in-Chief. In front of the bed in their sovereign's bedchamber, the four all bowed in acceptance of

【原文】

主。明日，武帝崩，太子袭尊号，是为孝昭皇帝。帝年八岁，政事壹决于光。

先是，后元年，侍中仆射莽何罗与弟重合侯通谋为逆，时光与金日磾、上官桀等共诛之，功未录。武帝病，封玺书曰："帝崩发书以从事。"遗诏封金日磾为秺侯，上官桀为安阳侯，光为博陆侯，皆以前捕反者功封。时卫尉王莽子男忽侍中，扬语曰："帝(病)[崩]，忽常在左右，安得遗诏封三子事！群儿自相贵耳。"光闻之，切让王莽，莽鸩杀忽。

光为人沉静详审，长财七尺三寸，白皙，疏眉目，美须頿。每出入下殿门，止进有常处，郎仆射窃识视之，不失尺寸，其资性端正如此。初辅幼主，政自己出，天下想闻其风采。殿中尝有怪，一夜群臣相惊，光召尚符玺郎，郎不肯授光。光欲夺之，郎按剑曰："臣头

【今译】

前叩拜受职，接受遗诏辅佐年幼的君主。第二天，武帝驾崩，太子承袭皇位，称为孝昭皇帝。皇帝年仅八岁，政事全由霍光来决定。

在这以前，后元年时，侍中仆射莽何罗同他的弟弟重合侯莽通合谋反叛，当时霍光同金日磾、上官桀等人一起诛杀了这些叛逆，其功没有被记录颁赏。武帝病后，密封玺书说："我死以后打开玺书遵照从事。"遗诏封金日磾为秺侯，上官桀为安阳侯，霍光为博陆侯，都是按照以前捕杀叛逆的功劳来分封的。当时卫尉王莽的儿子王忽为侍中，在外面扬言道："帝崩的时候，我经常在他的身边，哪里会有遗诏封他们的事！这帮人是在自己抬高自己。"霍光听到这些话后，严厉责备王莽，王莽用毒酒杀死了王忽。

霍光性格沉静，思虑周到，身高只有七尺三寸，皮肤白皙，疏眉朗目，须髯很美。每当他出入殿门的时候，前进、停止的时候都有固定的位置。郎仆射暗中做记号来观察，发现不差分毫，他的资质就像这样端正。霍光辅佐幼主的时候，政令由自己发布，天下人都仰慕他的风采。宫殿中曾经有过鬼怪之事，整夜群臣都很惊慌，霍光召见掌管符玺的郎官，郎官不肯把玺给霍光。霍光想夺取符玺，郎官按剑说

the edict to assist the young lord. The next day, Wudi died, and the Crown Prince inherited the throne, as Emperor Zhao. The Emperor was only eight years old, and the administration of state affairs was totally entrusted to Guang.

Earlier, in the first year of the Houyuan reign period, when Supervisor of the Palace Attendants Mang Heluo plotted rebellion with his brother the Marquis of Chonghe Mang Tong, Huo Guang, Jin Miti, Shangguan Jie, and others had squashed the plot but their meritorious service had not been recorded or awarded. When Wudi fell ill, he sealed his edict and said: "When I am dead, open the edict and act in accordance with it." The posthumous edict acknowledged their meritorious action in apprehending the rebels and made Jin Miti Marquis of Du, Shangguan Jie Marquis of Anyang, and Huo Guang Marquis of Bolu. At that time, Chamberlain for the Palace Garrison Wang Mang's son Wang Hu was a palace attendant, and he threatened: "When Wudi was dying, I was never away from his side. Where was the posthumous edict to ennoble the three! That gang just ennobled themselves." Informed of this, Huo Guang severely remonstrated with Wang Mang, who killed Wang Hu by poison.

Guang was a quiet and thoughtful man, seven feet three inches tall, fair-skinned, with clearly defined eyebrows and a beautiful beard. Whenever he entered or left through the palace gate, he would always go forward and then stop at a fixed point. The supervisor of court gentlemen secretly marked and observed, and found that he missed not an inch, an indicator of the regularity of his character. When Huo Guang first assisted the young monarch as regent, the decrees released all emanated from him and the people across the land admired his strict rectitude. There had been frequent sightings of ghosts in the palace and all night the courtiers were alarmed, so Huo Guang summoned the court gentleman in charge of the Imperial Seal, but he refused to hand it over. Huo Guang wanted to seize it, but the gentleman brandished his sword and said: "My head you can

【原文】

可得，玺不可得也！”光甚谊之。明日，诏增此郎秩二等。众庶莫不多光。

光与左将军桀结婚相亲，光长女为桀子安妻，有女年与帝相配。桀因帝姊鄂邑盖主内安女后宫为倢伃，数月立为皇后。父安为票骑将军，封桑乐侯。光时休沐出，桀辄入代光决事。桀父子既尊盛，而德长公主，公主内行不修，近幸河间丁外人。桀、安欲为外人求封，幸依国家故事以列侯尚公主者，光不许。又为外人求光禄大夫，欲令得召见，又不许。长主大以是怨光。而桀、安数为外人求官爵弗能得，亦惭。自先帝时，桀已为九卿，位在光右。及父子并为将军，有椒房中宫之重，皇后亲安女，光乃其外祖，而顾事专制朝事，繇是与光争权。

【今译】

道：“我的头可以得到，但玺却不可为你所得!”霍光很敬佩郎官的行为。第二天，就下诏把这个郎官的官秩升了两级。众人没有不赞许霍光的这种行为的。

霍光与左将军上官桀是儿女亲家，关系亲密，霍光的大女儿嫁给上官桀的儿子上官安为妻。上官安有个女儿年龄同昭帝相当，上官桀就通过昭帝的姐姐鄂邑盖主把上官安的女儿纳进后宫当婕妤，几个月后就被立为皇后。皇后的父亲上官安就被任命为骠骑将军，封为桑乐侯。霍光有时休假出宫，上官桀就进宫代替霍光处理政事。上官桀父子位尊势盛之后，很感激长公主。长公主没有操行，亲近宠幸河间的丁外人。上官桀、上官安打算替丁外人请求封侯，希望按照国家以前只有列侯与公主配婚的惯例封侯，但霍光没有同意。他们又为丁外人求取光禄大夫之职，以期得到昭帝的召见，再次被霍光拒绝。长公主因此就对霍光非常怨恨。而上官桀、上官安因为几次为丁外人求取官爵没有成功，也感到很惭愧。在汉武帝的时候，上官桀已在九卿之列，官位在霍光之上，等到上官父子同为将军的时候，又有了宫中皇后的重要关系，皇后是上官安的亲生女儿，霍光只不过是她的外祖父，却反而独自专揽朝政，上官父子因此就与霍光争夺权力。

have, but not the Imperial Seal!" Huo Guang respected his conduct, and issued an edict next day upgrading this man by two official ranks. The common people approved of this action to a man.

Huo Guang was related by marriage to Shangguan Jie the Left General, having married his eldest daughter to the latter's son Shangguan An. The two men were on close terms. Shangguan An's daughter was the same age as Zhaodi, so Shangguan Jie asked the Emperor's elder sister Madame. Gai the Princess of Eyi, to get the daughter [his granddaughter] taken into the harem as a lady of handsome fairness. A few months later the young girl was established as Empress. Shangguan An was appointed Cavalry General-in-Chief, ennobled as Marquis of Sangle. Huo Guang sometimes took leave from the palace, so Shangguan Jie went there to deputize for him in administering imperial affairs. When the Shangguan father and son became noble and powerful, they were very grateful to the Elder Princess. The Princess did not behave morally and took Mr. Ding from Hejian outside the Pass as her lover. Shangguan Jie and his son intended to plead to have Ding ennobled, hoping to make him adjunct marquis as a princess consort in accordance with previous imperial practices, but Huo Guang vetoed this. They then wanted to plead for Ding to be made Grand Master for Splendid Happiness, in order to get him summoned to audience by the Emperor, but again Huo Guang refused. So the Elder Princess bore a mighty grudge against Huo Guang, and the Shangguan father and son felt humiliated by their repeated failures to get official posts for Ding. In the time of the late Emperor, Shangguan Jie had been a chief minister, superior in rank to Huo Guang. When the Shangguan father and son both became generals, with important relations in the Jiaofang palace in the person of the Empress, a power struggle with Huo Guang began, since he monopolized court affairs despite the Empress being Shangguan An's own daughter, whereas Huo Guang was her maternal grandfather only.

【原文】

燕王旦自以昭帝兄，常怀怨望。及御史大夫桑弘羊建造酒榷盐铁，为国兴利，伐其功，欲为子弟得官，亦怨恨光。于是盖主、上官桀、安及弘羊皆与燕王旦通谋，诈令人为燕王上书，言“光出都肄郎羽林，道上称趩，太官先置。又引苏武前使匈奴，拘留二十年不降，还乃为典属国，而大将军长史敞亡功为搜粟都尉。又擅调益莫府校尉。光专权自恣，疑有非常。臣旦愿归符玺，入宿卫，察奸臣变”。候司光出沐日奏之。桀欲从中下其事，桑弘羊当与诸大臣共执退光。书奏，帝不肯下。

明旦，光闻之，止画室中不入。上问：“大将军安在？”左将军

【今译】

燕王刘旦自以为是昭帝的哥哥，却没有继承帝位，就常抱有怨恨之心。还有御史大夫桑弘羊建议设立酒类专卖、盐铁官营的制度，为国家增加了财富，桑弘羊便居功自傲，打算为自己的子弟谋得官职，没有如愿，因此怨恨霍光。于是鄂邑盖主、上官桀、上官安以及桑弘羊这些人就与燕王刘旦一同设谋，假装让人替燕王来上书，说：“霍光出城演练郎官、羽林，行进在路上像皇帝出行那样设置威仪，而且还让太官提前准备饭菜。还有苏武以前出使匈奴，被拘留二十年没有投降，回来后只当了典属国，而大将军的长史杨敞没有功劳，却当了搜粟都尉。霍光又擅自调人来增加自己幕府的校尉。霍光专权放肆，恐怕他有不良的企图。臣刘旦愿交还燕王的符节玺印，入朝值宿守卫，审察奸臣的阴谋。”等霍光出宫休假的时候乘机上奏了此书。上官桀打算从宫内直接发下其事，桑弘羊就和其他大臣一起将霍光拘捕并解除他的职务。奏书交上去后，昭帝留住奏书不肯颁下。

第二天早晨，霍光听说了这件事，就留在殿前的画室中没有进去朝拜。皇上问道：“大将军在哪里？”左将军上官桀回答说：“因为

The Prince of Yan Liu Dan, as the elder brother of Zhaodi but not named the heir, was often a resentful soul. After Censor-in-Chief Sang Hongyang proposed the establishment of a liquor monopoly and government-run salt and iron system, and thereby increased national revenue, he boasted of his performance, counting on getting official positions for his children and brothers. So he too resented Huo Guang. So, Princess Eyi, the two Shangguans and Sang conspired with Prince of Yan Liu Dan. They had someone pretend to be Prince of Yan write a petition letter to the Emperor, saying: "Huo Guang went out of the city to drill the palace guard, and not only did he act in imperial fashion by banning pedestrians on the road before he marched on it, but also had the official provisioner prepare meals ahead." Then there is the case of Su Wu, an earlier envoy to the Huns who was detained by them for two decades, but did not surrender to them, eventually came back to become only Vassal Reception Officer; compare this with the case of Yang Chang the aide to General-in-Chief who was appointed Defender in charge of searching for millet (and in charge of the ministry of treasury) without any meritorious deeds to his credit. Huo Guang also made unauthorized transfers to reinforce the commandant of his secretariat. Huo Guang presumptuously monopolizes power, so I fear he has ulterior motives. Your servant Liu Dan would like to return the seal of Yan, and enter into the Court as imperial bodyguard to watch for the traitor's plot." On a day when Huo Guang was on leave, they took the opportunity to hand in the memorial. Shangguan Jie intended to refer the matter to the office in charge directly from the Inner Court, so that Sang Hongyang and the other ministers could arrest and force Huo's dismissal. But the Emperor Zhaodi kept hold of the petition, refusing to refer it downward.

The next morning, Huo Guang heard about this, and stayed in the Hall of Portraits without going to Court. The Emperor asked: "Where is the General-in-Chief?" Left General Shangguan Jie

【原文】

桀对曰："以燕王告其罪，故不敢入。"有诏召大将军。光入，免冠顿首谢，上曰："将军冠。朕知是书诈也，将军亡罪。"光曰："陛下何以知之？"上曰："将军之广明，都郎属耳。调校尉以来未能十日，燕王何以得知之？且将军为非，不须校尉。"是时帝年十四，尚书左右皆惊，而上书者果亡，捕之甚急。桀等惧，白上小事不足遂，上不听。

后桀党与有谮光者，上辄怒曰："大将军忠臣，先帝所属以辅朕身，敢有毁者坐之。"自是桀等不敢复言，乃谋令长公主置酒请光，伏兵格杀之，因废帝，迎立燕王为天子。事发觉，光尽诛桀、安、弘羊、外人宗族。燕王、盖主皆自杀。光威震海内。昭帝既冠，遂委任光，讫十三年，百姓充实，四夷宾服。

元平元年，昭帝崩，亡嗣。武帝六男独有广陵王胥在，群臣议所

【今译】

燕王告发他的罪行，所以不敢进来。"皇上就下诏召见大将军。霍光进来后，取下官帽，叩头谢罪，皇上说："将军请戴上帽子，朕知道这封奏书是假的，将军没有罪过。"霍光问道："陛下凭什么知道我没有罪呢？"皇上说道："将军到广明，演习郎官只是近来的事，调选校尉到现在也不过十天，燕王是怎么知道这些事的？况且将军要做非法的事，也不需要校尉的。"这时候昭帝年仅十四岁，尚书以及左右的大臣都很吃惊，而呈送书信的人果然逃走了，官府开始紧急搜捕。上官桀等人感到害怕了，就对皇上说这只是一件小事，不值得穷追究竟，皇上没有听从。

后来上官桀的党羽凡有说霍光的坏话的，昭帝就发怒道："大将军是忠臣，先帝所托付来辅佐朕的，敢有诽谤他的人就判他的罪。"从这以后，上官桀等人就不敢再说坏话了，他们就密谋让长公主摆酒席请霍光赴宴，准备埋伏士兵击杀他，乘机再废除昭帝，迎立燕王为天子。事情被发觉，霍光就将上官桀、上官安、桑弘羊、丁外人等人及家族全都诛杀了。燕王、盖主也都自杀。霍光的威势震动全国。昭帝成年后，就正式委任霍光执政，到昭帝十三年，百姓生活充裕厚实，四方的各少数民族都称臣归服。

元平元年，昭帝驾崩，没有继承人。汉武帝六个儿子中独有广陵王刘胥还活着。各位大臣商议所要立的人选，大家都主张立广陵王。

replied: "He is afraid to come in, since the Prince of Yan denounced his crime." The Emperor ordered the General-in-Chief to his presence. Huo Guang entered, removing his cap and kowtowing. But the Emperor said: "General, please replace your cap. I know that this letter is false, and the general is not guilty." Huo Guang asked: "How does Your Majesty know this?" Zhaodi replied: "The General went to Guangming, just for the testing of your subordinates. It is less than 10 days since you transferred the commandant. How did Prince of Yan know these things? Moreover, if you turned traitor, you would not require a commandant." The Emperor was just 14 years old at this time, so the imperial secretary and the courtiers were all surprised. Sure enough, the man who presented the memorial had fled, and the officials began an urgent hunt. The Shangguan Jie co-conspirators were afraid, and said it was only a trifle, not worth investigating, but the Emperor ignored them.

Later, when Shangguan Jie's partisans slandered their rival the Emperor would get angry and said: "The General-in-Chief is loyal, and the late Emperor entrusted him to assist me. Anyone who dares to slander him will be sentenced." From that point on, they dared not repeat their allegations. Then they came up with another plot, one that involved getting the Princess to hold a banquet for Huo Guang, but preparing soldiers to ambush and kill him, depose the Emperor, and enthrone the Prince of Yan as Son of Heaven. The coup conspiracy was discovered, and Huo Guang exterminated the Shangguan father and son, Sang, Ding and all their clans. The Prince of Yan and Princess Gai committed suicide. The whole realm trembled in awe of Huo Guang's power. Later, when Zhaodi came of age, he formally appointed Huo Guang until the 13th year of his reign. During these years the people lived in abundance, and the various barbarians remained submissive. In the first year of the Yuanping reign period, Zhaodi died without an heir, but only one of Wudi's six sons was still alive, namely the Prince of

【原文】

立，咸持广陵王。王本以行失道，先帝所不用。光内不自安。郎有上书言“周太王废太伯立王季，文王舍伯邑考立武王，唯在所宜，虽废长立少可也。广陵王不可以承宗庙”。言合光意。光以其书视丞相敞等，擢郎为九江太守，即日承皇太后诏，遣行大鸿胪事少府乐成、宗正德、光禄大夫吉、中郎将利汉迎昌邑王贺。

贺者，武帝孙，昌邑哀王子也。既至，即位，行淫乱。光忧懑，独以问所亲故吏大司农田延年。延年曰：“将军为国柱石，审此人不可，何不建白太后，更选贤而立之？”光曰：“今欲如是，于古尝有此否？”延年曰：“伊尹相殷，废太甲以安宗庙，后世称其忠。将军若能行此，亦汉之伊尹也。”光乃引延年给事中，阴与车骑将军张安

【今译】

广陵王本来因为行为有失道德，没有被先帝选用。霍光内心自感不安。有郎官上书说：“周太王废掉太伯而立王季，文王舍弃伯邑考而立武王，只要对国家有利，即使是废黜长子而立少子也是可以的。广陵王是不可以继承宗庙社稷的。”所说的正好同霍光心意相合。霍光就把这份奏书给丞相杨敞等人看，并且把这个郎官提升为九江太守，当天就奉皇太后的诏令，派遣代理大鸿胪事务的少府乐成、宗正刘德、光禄大夫丙吉、中郎将利汉去迎接昌邑王刘贺。

刘贺是汉武帝的孙子，昌邑哀王的儿子。他到宫中后，登上帝位，不久就行为淫乱。霍光忧虑气愤，独自以此事去问亲信的旧臣大司农田延年。田延年说：“将军作为国家的柱石，既然发觉这个人不可委以社稷，为什么不向太后建议禀报，另外选一个贤能之人立他为帝呢？”霍光说道：“我也想这么办，不知在古代有没有这样的先例？”田延年答道：“伊尹任殷朝丞相的时候，就废黜了太甲用来安定国家，后代的人都称赞他的忠诚。将军如果也能这样做，就是汉朝的伊尹了。”霍光就把田延年引荐为给事中，暗中同车骑将军张安世

Guangling Liu Xu. The courtiers deliberated and all supported the claim of the Prince of Guangling, despite his having been ruled out by the late Emperor on grounds of immoral behavior. Huo felt uneasy about this, and his misgivings were confirmed when one of the court gentlemen submitted a letter saying: "Taiwang, the founding father of Zhou chose King Ji instead of Taibo; King Wen abandoned Boyikao for King Wu. Provided the choice is appropriate to the interest of the state, it is possible even to depose the eldest son in favor of the junior. Prince of Guangling is not fit to inherit the ancestral temple." Guang showed this letter to Prime Minister Yang Chang and others, and upgraded that court gentleman to Governor of Jiujiang. On that day, they followed the edict of the Empress Dowager, and sent Shi Lecheng, Chamberlain for the Palace Revenue and acting Chamberlain for Dependencies, Liu De, Chamberlain for the Imperial Clan, Bing Ji, Grand Master for Splendid Happiness, and Li Han, Commander of Court Gentlemen, to meet with the Prince of Changyi Liu He.

Liu He, a grandson of Wudi, was the son of Prince Ai of Changyi. But after he came to the palace and ascended the throne, he was soon behaving like a libertine. Huo Guang was depressed, going alone to confer with his confidant Tian Yannian, former secretary and Chamberlain of the Imperial Treasury. Tian said: "The General, as the pillar of the country, finds that this person cannot be entrusted. Why do you not recommend to the Empress Dowager to select another person worthy to be emperor?" Huo replied: "This accords with my own thinking, but is there a precedent in ancient times for this?" Tian provided one: "When Yi Yin was prime minister of Yin, he deposed Taijia to stabilize the ancestral temple, and later people praised his loyalty. General, if you can do the same, you will be the Yi Yin of the Han Dynasty." Huo Guang recommended Tian as the Palace Steward, and planned secretly with Chariot Horse General Zhang Anshi; then he convened a consultation at Weiyang Palace,

【原文】

世图计，遂召丞相、御史、将军、列侯、中二千石、大夫、博士会议未央宫。光曰："昌邑王行昏乱，恐危社稷，如何？"群臣皆惊鄂失色，莫敢发言，但唯唯而已。田延年前，离席按剑，曰："先帝属将军以幼孤，寄将军以天下，以将军忠贤能安刘氏也。今群下鼎沸，社稷将倾，且汉之传谥常为孝者，以长有天下，令宗庙血食也。如令汉家绝祀，将军虽死，何面目见先帝于地下乎？今日之议，不得旋踵。群臣后应者，臣请剑斩之。"光谢曰："九卿责光是也。天下匈匈不安，光当受难。"于是议者皆叩头，曰："万姓之命在于将军，唯大将军令。"

光即与群臣俱见白太后，具陈昌邑王不可以承宗庙状。皇太后乃车驾幸未央承明殿，诏诸禁门毋内昌邑群臣。王入朝太后还，乘辇欲归温室，中黄门宦者各持门扇，王入，门闭，昌邑群臣不得入。王曰：

【今译】

谋划，于是就在未央宫召集丞相、御史、将军、列侯、中二千石、大夫、博士等一同商议。霍光说道："昌邑王行为昏聩淫乱，恐怕会危及国家，你们看怎么办？"众大臣大惊失色，不敢发言，只是唯唯诺诺而已。田延年离开座席走上前来，手按住长剑说道："先帝把年幼的孤儿托给将军，把天下交付给将军，是因为将军忠诚贤能，能够稳固刘氏的天下。如今群臣百姓鼎沸，国家将要倾覆。而且汉朝皇帝相传的谥号常用'孝'字，是为了长久地拥有天下，让宗庙永久享受祭祀。如今汉家将要断绝香火，将军即使以死谢罪，又有什么脸面到九泉之下去见先帝呢？今天的议事，应当即刻解决。群臣中如果有拖延回答的，臣下请求用这把剑斩了他。"霍光告罪说："九卿责备我是对的。天下骚动不安，我应当受到责罚。"于是参加议事的大臣都叩头说道："万民的性命都系在将军一人的身上，我们愿听将军的指示。"

霍光立刻同群臣一起谒见禀告太后，详细陈述昌邑王不能继承皇位的情况。皇太后于是乘车来到未央承明殿，诏令各个宫禁门卫不要放昌邑王的群臣进宫。昌邑王进宫朝见太后返回，准备坐辇车回到温室，宫中的黄门宦官各自手持门扇，等昌邑王进去后，就把宫门关上，昌邑王的群臣就进不来了。昌邑王问道："这是干什么？"大将

calling together the prime minister, censors, generals, adjunct marquises, full 2,000-picul officials, grand masters, and erudites. He addressed them: "Since the Prince of Changyi behaves in chaotic and promiscuous fashion, I fear he will endanger the state. What is your opinion of him?" The courtiers were all alarmed, afraid to speak, but just acquiesced. Tian Yannian rose from his seat and holding his sword, said: "The late Emperor entrusted the young orphans to the General, and placed the world with the General, because the General is loyal and worthy, able to stabilize the empire under the Liu clan. Now the courtiers are quarrelsome and confused, and the state is about to topple. Furthermore, the posthumous titles of Han emperors are commonly prefixed by the word 'filial,' in order to prolong its dominion, and to guarantee the ancestral temple eternal animal sacrifice. Now if sacrifices to the Han ancestral temple are cut off, even if the General were dead, what face would you have to see the late Emperor in the nether world? Today's discussion should be decided immediately. Should the courtiers delay in their responses, I request the order to behead them with my sword." Huo Guang apologized: "The chief ministers are right to blame me. There is unrest in the world, so I should be subject to censure." Then the participants in the proceedings all kowtowed and said: "The lives of the people are entrusted to the General, and we follow the General's instructions."

Guang immediately went with the courtiers to announce this to the Empress Dowager, and made a detailed statement that the Prince of Changyi could not inherit the throne. The Empress Dowager took the chariot to Chengming Hall in Weiyang Palace, ordering the palace guards not to admit Changyi's ministers. The Prince returned from the palace after kowtowing to the Empress Dowager, and was about to take the chariot back to the Warm Hall, but the yellow-door eunuchs of the palace held the doors shut behind the Prince of Changyi, preventing his ministers from entering. "What's going on?"

【原文】

“何为？”大将军跪曰：“有皇太后诏，毋内昌邑群臣。”王曰：“徐之，何乃惊人如是！”光使尽驱出昌邑群臣，置金马门外。车骑将军安世将羽林骑收缚二百馀人，皆送廷尉诏狱。令故昭帝侍中中臣侍守王。光敕左右：“谨宿卫，卒有物故自裁，令我负天下，有杀主名。”王尚未自知当废，谓左右：“我故群臣从官安得罪而大将军尽系之乎？”顷之，有太后诏召王。王闻召，意恐，乃曰：“我安得罪而召我哉！”太后被珠襦，盛服坐武帐中，侍御数百人皆持兵，期门武士陛戟，陈列殿下。群臣以次上殿，召昌邑王伏前听诏。光与群臣连名奏王，尚书令读奏曰：

丞相臣敞、大司马大将军臣光、车骑将军臣安世、度辽将军臣明友、前将军臣增、后将军臣充国、御史大夫臣谊、宜春侯臣谭、当涂侯臣圣、随桃侯臣昌乐、杜侯臣屠耆堂、太仆臣延年、

【今译】

军跪下说：“皇太后有诏令，不让昌邑王的群臣进来。”昌邑王说：“慢点来，为什么要弄得这么吓人!”霍光派人将昌邑王的群臣全部驱逐出宫，集中在金马门外。车骑将军张安世率领羽林骑士拘捕捆绑了二百多人，都交给廷尉关在诏令所规定的监狱内。并命令原昭帝的侍中、中常侍看守昌邑王。霍光告诫他们说：“你们要小心值班守卫，昌邑王如果突然死了或自杀，就会让我对不起天下人，背上杀害君王的罪名。”昌邑王这时还不知道自己要被罢黜，对身边的人说：“我原来的群臣随员有什么罪，而大将军全把他们关押起来了。”不久，太后下诏召见昌邑王。昌邑王听到要召见自己，心中开始害怕起来，于是说：“我犯了什么罪要召见我!”太后披着珍珠缀成的短袄，穿着盛装坐在布置兵器的帷帐中，几百名宫廷卫士都拿着武器，期门武士持戟守卫台阶，他们都排列在殿下。群臣按顺序走进殿来，叫昌邑王伏在前面听诏令。霍光同各位大臣一起联名奏劾昌邑王，尚书令宣读奏章道：

臣丞相杨敞、臣大司马大将军霍光、臣车骑将军张安世、臣度辽将军范明友、臣前将军韩增、臣后将军趟充国、臣御史大夫蔡谊、臣宜春侯王谭、臣当涂侯魏圣、臣随桃侯赵昌乐、臣杜侯

asked the Prince, at which the General knelt down and said: "The Empress Dowager has ordered that the Prince's ministers not be admitted." The Prince said: "Easy now, why make it so fearsome!" Huo Guang ordered the expulsion of all Changyi's ministers, assembling them outside the Jinma Gate. The Chariot Horse General Zhang Anshi led the Imperial Guard cavalry to arrest more than 200 people, who were handed over to Chamberlain of Law Enforcement and imprisoned under his jurisdiction. The late Zhaodi's palace attendant-in-ordinary was ordered to serve the Prince as his attendant-guard. Huo warned the attendants: "You must be careful in your guarding duty. If he suddenly dies or commits suicide, making me disappoint the world, I would bear the charge of regicide." The Prince, unaware he was being deposed, said to those around him: "What have my original entourage and ministers done to make the General-in-Chief detain them all?" Soon, the Empress Dowager issued a command summoning the Prince, which caused him to start getting fearful on his own account, saying: "What crime have I committed, to be summoned so?" The Empress Dowager, wearing a pearl decorated jacket, sat in formal dress in a military tent; there were hundreds of armed palace guards and Qimen warriors holding halberds guarding the steps, arranged in military formation. The courtiers entered the Hall in sequence, and the Prince of Changyi was called forward to listen to the edict on his knees. Huo Guang and the ministers jointly impeached the Prince, and the Director of Imperial Secretariat read the memorial:

Prime Minister Yang Chang, Commander-in-Chief and General-in-Chief Huo Guang, Chariot Horse General Zhang Anshi, Duliao General Fan Mingyou, Front General Han Zeng, Rear General Zhao Chongguo, Censor-in-Chief Cai Yi, Marquis of Yichun Wang Tan, Marquis of Dangtu Wei Sheng, Marquis of Suitao Zhao Changle, Marquis of Du Tuzhitang, Chamberlain for the Imperial Stud Du Yannian, Chamberlain

【原文】

太常臣昌、大司农臣延年、宗正臣德、少府臣乐成、廷尉臣光、执金吾臣延寿、大鸿胪臣贤、左冯翊臣广明、右扶风臣德、长信少府臣嘉、典属国臣武、京辅都尉臣广汉、司隶校尉臣辟兵、诸吏文学光禄大夫臣迁、臣畸、臣吉、臣赐、臣管、臣胜、臣梁、臣长幸、臣夏侯胜、太中大夫臣德、臣卬昧死言皇太后陛下：臣敞等顿首死罪。(大)[天]子所以永保宗庙总壹海内者，以慈孝礼谊赏罚为本。孝昭皇帝早弃天下，亡嗣，臣敞等议，礼曰“为人后者为之子也”，昌邑王宜嗣后，遣宗正、大鸿胪、光禄大夫奉节使徵昌邑王典丧。服斩缞，亡悲哀之心，废礼谊，居道上不素食，使从官略女子载衣车，内所居传舍。始至谒见，立为皇太子，常私买鸡豚以食。受皇帝信玺、行玺大行前，就次发玺不

【今译】

复陆屠耆堂、臣太仆杜延年、臣太常苏昌、臣大司农田延年、臣宗正刘德、臣少府史乐成、臣廷尉李光、臣执金吾李延寿、臣大鸿胪韦贤、臣左冯翊田广明、臣右扶风周德、臣长信少府傅嘉、臣典属国苏武、臣京辅都尉赵广汉、臣司隶校尉辟兵、臣诸吏文学光禄大夫王迁、臣宋畸、臣丙吉、臣赐、臣管、臣胜、臣梁、臣长幸、臣夏侯胜、臣太中大夫德、臣赵卬冒死罪禀告皇太后陛下：臣杨敞等人顿首死罪。天子之所以能够长久保持宗庙并拥有天下，是因为他能够以慈孝、礼义、赏罚分明作为根本。孝昭皇帝由于过早地离开人间，没有继承人，臣杨敞等人商议，根据礼所说的“做某人的继承人的人就是他的儿子”，昌邑王适于做继承人，于是便派遣宗正、大鸿胪、光禄大夫等官员奉持符节出使征召昌邑王来主持昭帝的丧事。昌邑王穿上丧服后，却没有悲哀的意思，而且还弃礼义于不顾，在路上不吃素食，派遣随从官吏抢掠女人，用遮蔽的车子把她们弄到他所住的驿馆。从刚开始到达京城谒见太后被立为皇太子起，就经常私下买鸡、猪来吃。在昭帝灵柩前接受信玺、行玺后，就在居丧的地方打开玺印不再

for Ceremonials Su Chang, Chamberlain of the Imperial Treasury Tian Yannian, Chamberlain for the Imperial Clan Liu De, Chamberlain for the Palace Revenues Shi Lecheng, Chamberlain of Law Enforcement Li Guang, Chamberlain for the Imperial Insignia Li Yanshou, Chamberlain for Dependencies Wei Xian, Guardian of the Left Tian Guangming, Guardian of the Right Zhou De, Steward of Empress Dowager Fu Jia, Supervisor of Dependent Countries Su Wu, Defender of the Capital Zhao Guanghan, Metropolitan Commandant Pi Bing, other officials, instructors, grand masters for splendid happiness Wang Qian, Song Ji, Bing Ji, Ci, Guan, Sheng, Liang, Changxing, Xiahou Sheng, Superior Grand Master of the Palace De, and Zhao Yang all risk their lives to memorialize Her Majesty the Empress Dowager: Yang Chang and others bow on pain of death. The reason that the Son of Heaven is able to maintain the ancestral temple forever and rule the world, is because he is dedicated to the fundamentals of love and filial piety, propriety and justice, reward and punishment. The Filial Zhaodi prematurely left the world without heirs, so Yang Chang and others made deliberations. According to the Rites: "A person's heir is his son." Prince of Changyi was a suitable heir, so they sent Chamberlain for the Imperial Clan, Chamberlain for Dependencies, and Grand Master for Splendid Happiness as messengers with tally to summon the Prince of Changyi to preside over the funeral. The Prince donned the hemp garments of mourning, but did not have the mind for grief; he flouted the rites and righteousness by not eschewing meat whilst en route; he sent officers of his retinue to abduct girls onto the covered carts and keep them in the posthouse where he stayed. From the day of reaching the capital and being received in audience with the Empress Dowager, he was established as Crown Prince, but he often secretly had chicken and pork purchased for him

【原文】

封。从官更持节，引内昌邑从官驺宰官奴二百馀人，常与居禁闼内敖戏。自之符玺取节十六，朝暮临，令从官更持节从。为书曰“皇帝问侍中君卿：使中御府令高昌奉黄金千斤，赐君卿取十妻”。大行在前殿，发乐府乐器，引内昌邑乐人，击鼓歌吹作俳倡。会下还，上前殿，击钟磬，召内泰壹宗庙乐人辇道牟首，鼓吹歌舞，悉奏众乐。发长安厨三太牢具祠阁室中，祀已，与从官饮啖。驾法驾，皮轩鸾旗，驱驰北宫、桂宫，弄彘斗虎。召皇太后御小马车，使官奴骑乘，游戏掖庭中。与孝昭皇帝宫人蒙等淫

【今译】

封上。随从的官员又拿着符节，带领昌邑王的从官、马官、官奴二百多人进宫，经常与他们在禁宫中玩耍游戏。亲自到保管符玺的地方取走十六根符节，早晚去灵柩前哭祭时，让随从的官员轮换着拿着符节跟着。还写信说：“皇帝问候侍中君卿：派中御府的长官高昌送去黄金一千斤，赐给君卿娶十个妻子。”孝昭皇帝的灵柩还停放在前殿，便叫人取出乐府的乐器，把昌邑国的乐人引进宫来，击鼓歌唱、吹奏乐器，扮演戏子。等到灵柩下葬返回，就到前殿去敲打钟磬，还把泰壹宗庙的乐人沿着辇道引到牟首，击鼓吹奏，载歌载舞，演奏各种音乐。从长安厨取出三副太牢供品，陈放在阁室中进行祭祀，祭祀完毕，就同随从的官员大吃大喝。驾着皇帝出行时专用的车马，车上蒙着虎皮，插着鸾旗，驱车跑到北宫、桂宫，追野猪，斗老虎。又召来皇太后用的小马车，叫官奴骑乘，在嫔妃居住的掖庭中嬉笑娱乐。还同孝昭

to eat. Before the coffin of Emperor Zhaodi he received the Seal of Emperor's Edicts and the Seal of Emperor's Commands, and at the mourning site he opened the seal cases, not to close them again. Besides, his entourage officials led more than 200 aides, stable-hands and official slaves from Changyi holding his credentials, often cavorting with them in the forbidden palace. He personally went to the imperial seal office and took 16 tallies. Morning and evening, he went to weep before the coffin, his entourage following by turns carrying the tallies. Also he wrote: "The Emperor's greetings to his palace attendant Junqing: tell the chief of the Palace Wardrobe Gao Chang to deliver to Junqing 1,000 catties of gold, so that he can take 10 wives." Filial Emperor Zhaodi's coffin was stationed in the front hall, but he called for musical instruments to be brought from the Music Bureau, and brought Changyi musicians into the palace to drum and sing, play reed and stringed instruments, perform skits and dances. After the coffin was interred, he returned to the front hall to beat bells and music stones, and he also summoned musicians from the Temple of Supreme God and Ancestral Temple along the Imperial Chariot Road to Mushou Pond, beating drums and playing flutes, singing and dancing, playing all varieties of ceremonial music. He took three full sacrifice offerings from Chang'an kitchen, performed sacrificial rituals in the room and as soon as the sacrifice was completed he began scoffing food and quaffing wine with members of his entourage. He drove the Imperial Sacrificial Chariot, covered with tiger skins and feathered flags, and went to the Northern Palace and Gui Palace, chasing boar and fighting tigers. He also summoned the Empress Dowager's pony carriage, to be driven by the official slaves; he entertained and amused himself in the harem. He had sex with Zhaodi's palace lady Meng and others, telling the harem chief that whoever dared leak rumors

【原文】

乱，诏掖庭令敢泄言要斩。

太后曰：“止！为人臣子当悖乱如是邪！”王离席伏。尚书令复读曰：

取诸侯王、列侯、二千石绶及墨绶、黄绶以并佩昌邑郎官者免奴。变易节上黄旄以赤。发御府金钱刀剑玉器采缯，赏赐所与游戏者。与从官官奴夜饮，湛沔于酒。诏太官上乘舆食如故。食监奏未释服未可御故食，复诏太官趣具，无关食监。太官不敢具，即使从官出买鸡豚，诏殿门内，以为常。独夜设九宾温室，延见姊夫昌邑关内侯。祖宗庙祠未举，为玺书使使者持节，以三太牢祠昌邑哀王园庙，称嗣子皇帝。受玺以来二十七日，使者旁午，持节诏诸官署征发，凡千一百二十七事。文学光禄大夫夏侯胜等及侍中傅嘉数进谏以过失，使人簿责胜，缚嘉系狱。荒淫

【今译】

皇帝的宫人蒙等行淫乱之事，下诏对掖庭令说，有敢泄露外传的人就要处以腰斩之刑。

太后说：“停一下！为人臣子怎么能这样糊涂放肆呢！”昌邑王离开席位伏在地上。尚书令又读道：

昌邑王取出诸侯王、列侯、二千石的绶带以及黑色、黄色绶带一起给昌邑国的郎官佩戴，把他们免为良人。将符节上的黄旄改为红色。把御府中的金子钱币，刀剑玉器，彩色绸缎赏给一同嬉游娱乐的人。同随从的官员以及没入官府的奴隶整夜聚饮，沉湎于酒中。下诏叫太官送上皇帝平时的膳食。食监奏道，没有除去丧服不可进用平日的饭菜，就下诏叫太官赶快准备，不要通过食监。太官不敢去准备，就派侍臣去宫外买来鸡和猪，下诏给宫殿门卫叫他们放行，以此作为常规。独自在夜晚于温室设九宾之礼，把他的姐夫昌邑关内侯请来相见。列祖列宗的祭庙还没有举行，就作玺书派使者拿着符节，用三副太牢祭祀昌邑哀王的陵园宗庙，自称为嗣子皇帝。接受皇帝玺印以来的二十七天中，使者往来不绝，拿着符节向各个官署下达诏令征索物品，共有一千一百二十七起。文学光禄大夫夏侯胜等以及侍中傅嘉几次为他的过失进言规劝，他就派人拿着文书责备夏侯胜，并把傅嘉绑

would face the punishment being cut through at the waist.

The Empress Dowager interrupted: "Stop! How can a courtier be so unruly and wanton!" The Prince left his seat and bowed to the ground, and the Director of Imperial Secretariat read on:

The Prince fetched the seal ribbons to denote the status of princes, adjunct marquises and 2,000-picul officials, and also black ribbons and yellow ribbons, and allowed the court gentlemen and freed slaves of Changyi to wear them. Yellow yak hair on the tallies was changed to red hair. He took the gold coins, swords, jade utensils, and colored silk from the Palace Wardrobe, awarding them to those with whom he disported himself. He caroused all night with his entourage officials and official slaves, abandoning himself in drink. He ordered the Provisioner to provide the regular diet of an emperor. The food supervisor reported: "Until the mourning garments are removed, the usual dishes are not allowed." But the Prince ordered the Provisioner to quickly prepare this, without it going through the supervisor. The Provisioner did not dare to prepare it, so he sent subordinates out to buy chicken and pork, and ordered the palace gatekeepers to admit them as routine. Alone at night in the Warm Hall he established the ceremony of nine relays, and invited his brother-in-law, Marquis of Guannei of Changyi, to meet here. Before even sacrificing at the Ancestral Temple, he sent a clay-sealed edict via an emissary holding the tally, to worship at Prince Ai of Changyi's grave and temple with three full offerings, claiming to be Emperor as eldest son and heir. In the 27 days since he received the Imperial Seals, his many messengers come and go without cease, carrying the imperial tally to order levies on the officials; in total 1,127 counts. Instructors and grand masters for splendid happiness Xiahou Sheng and others, as well as palace attendant Fu Jia have several times admonished him for his faults, but he sent

【原文】

迷惑，失帝王礼谊，乱汉制度。臣敞等数进谏，不变更，日以益甚，恐危社稷，天下不安。

臣敞等谨与博士臣霸、臣隽舍、臣德、臣虞舍、臣射、臣仓议，皆曰："高皇帝建功业为汉太祖，孝文皇帝慈仁节俭为太宗，今陛下嗣孝昭皇帝后，行淫辟不轨。《诗》云：'籍曰未知，亦既抱子。'五辟之属，莫大不孝。周襄王不能事母，《春秋》曰'天王出居于郑'，繇不孝出之，绝之于天下也。宗庙重于君，陛下未见命高庙，不可以承天序，奉祖宗庙，子万姓，当废。"臣请有司御史大夫臣谊、宗正臣德、太常臣昌与太祝以一太牢具，告祠高庙。臣敞等昧死以闻。

皇太后诏曰："可。"光令王起拜受诏，王曰："闻天子有争臣

【今译】

起来关进牢里。他荒淫昏乱，失去帝王的礼义，破坏了汉朝的制度。臣杨敞等人几次进言规谏，他都不改变过错，反而一天比一天厉害，恐怕要危害国家，天下不安。

臣杨敞等谨与博士孔霸、臣隽舍、臣德、臣虞舍、臣射、臣后仓商议，都说："高皇帝因为创建汉朝基业，所以称汉太祖，孝文皇帝因为仁慈节俭被称为太宗，如今陛下继承孝昭皇帝之后，行为放纵不合法度。《诗经》上说：'若说无知，也已抱子。'五刑的条文规定，罪孽没有比不孝更大的。周襄王不能侍奉好母亲，《春秋》就说'天王出居到郑国'，因为他不孝而被赶出京城，使他与天下人隔绝。宗庙比君王更重要，陛下没有到高庙接受大命，就不可以继承上天的意旨，奉祀祖宗宗庙，统治天下万民，应当废黜。"臣请求有关官员御史大夫蔡谊、宗正刘德、太常苏昌和太祝准备一副太牢供品，告祭高庙。臣杨敞等人冒死罪来奏报。

皇太后下诏说："准奏。"霍光就叫昌邑王起来跪拜接受诏令，昌邑王说道："听说天子只要有诤臣七个人，即使无道也不会失去天下。"

someone with a list to censure Xiahou Sheng, and had Fu Jia bound and jailed. He is dissolute and unruly, abandoning the propriety and righteousness expected of an emperor, destroying the system of the Han Dynasty. Yang Chang and others have remonstrated time and again, but he does not change his ways; indeed, he gets worse every day. We are afraid of endangering the state and making the world uneasy.

Yang Chang and others consulted with erudites Kong Ba, Juan She, De, Yu She, She and Cang, and they all said: "Gaodi founded the Han Dynasty, hence he was called Taizu, Wendi was Taizong because of his kindness and thrift. Now since His Majesty succeeded Zhaodi, he has acted out of indulgence, not conforming to the rules. According to the Book of Odes*: 'Maybe he was ignorant, but he already has a son.' Among the Five Punishments, there is not one offense greater than being unfilial. King Xiang of Zhou could not serve his mother, and the* Spring and Autumn Annals *says of this: 'The Son of Heaven was evicted to live in Zheng.' He was expelled because of his lack of filial piety, and was thus separated from the people of the world. The Ancestral Temple is more important than the monarch, and since His Majesty did not go to the Temple of Gaodi to accept the mandate he is not entitled to inherit it, or worship at the ancestral temple, or rule the people. He should be deposed." Your servant requests that the officials concerned, the Censor-in-Chief Cai Yi, Chamberlain for the Imperial Clan Liu De, Chamberlain for Ceremonials Su Chang and the Great Supplicant prepare a full offering, and pray at the Temple of Gaodi. Yang Chang and others risk their lives with this memorial.*

The Empress Dowager ordered: "The petition is sustained." When Huo Guang told the Prince to rise and bow down in acceptance of the edict, he protested: "I heard that the Son of

【原文】

七人，虽无道，不失天下。”光曰：“皇太后诏废，安得天子！”乃即持其手，解脱其玺组，奉上太后，扶王下殿，出金马门，群臣随送。王西面拜，曰：“愚戆不任汉事。”起就乘舆副车。大将军光送至昌邑邸，光谢曰：“王行自绝于天，臣等驽怯，不能杀身报德。臣宁负王，不敢负社稷。愿王自爱，臣长不复见左右。”光涕泣而去。群臣奏言：“古者废放之人屏于远方，不及以政，请徙王贺汉中房陵县。”太后诏归贺昌邑，赐汤沐邑二千户。昌邑群臣坐亡辅导之谊，陷王于恶，光悉诛杀二百馀人。出死，号呼市中曰：“当断不断，反受其乱。”

光坐庭中，会丞相以下议定所立。广陵王已前不用，及燕剌王反诛，

【今译】

霍光说：“皇太后已下诏令废黜，哪里还是天子!”于是上前抓住他的手，解下他身上的玺印绶带，捧上交给太后，扶着昌邑王下了宫殿，走出金马门，群臣跟着送行。昌邑王向西面拜道：“我愚昧不明事理，不堪担当汉朝的重任。”起身坐上皇帝侍从的车辆。大将军霍光把昌邑王送到昌邑邸后，霍光告罪道：“您的行为自绝于上天，臣下等怯懦无能，不能自杀来报答您的恩德。臣下宁可有负大王，不敢对不起国家。但愿大王能够自爱，臣下将再也不能见到您了。”霍光哭着离开了昌邑王。群臣又上奏说：“古代被罢黜放逐之人都流放到很远的地方，不使他干扰国家政令，我们请求把昌邑王刘贺迁到汉中房陵县。”太后下诏命刘贺回到昌邑，并赐给他收取赋税的私邑二千户。昌邑国的群臣由于没有尽辅佐教导君臣之谊，使王误入歧途而获罪。霍光就将他们全部杀了，共有二百多人。当这些人被拉出去处死的时候，都在街道中哭泣呼喊道：“当断不断，反受其乱。”

霍光坐在朝廷中，会同丞相以下大臣商议决定所立的人选。广陵王早在这之前就没有被选用，等到燕剌王谋反被诛，他的儿子也就不

Heaven, if he had seven ministers to remonstrate with him, would not lose possession of the empire even if he had not the Way." To this Huo Guang responded: "The Empress Dowager has decreed the deposition, so where is the Son of Heaven?" So he seized him by the hand, removed the ribbon of the Imperial Seal, lifted it to show the Empress Dowager, and led the Prince by the arm out of the hall, and out of Jinma Gate, followed by the ministers to escort them away. The Prince bowed to the west and said: "I am too ignorant, and inadequate for the responsibility of the Han Dynasty." He then boarded the chariot of the imperial entourage. General-in-Chief Huo Guang escorted him to Changyi Residence, and apologized to him: "Through your behavior you cut yourself off from heaven, and your servants were too cowardly and incompetent to die to repay your kindness. I would rather incur the blame of Your Highness than of the state. I hope that Your Highness will find self-respect. Your servant will never be able to see you again." Huo Guang left in tears. The ministers petitioned: "The ancients exiled the ousted person to a distant place, in order that he not interfere with state affairs. We request that Prince Liu He be moved to Fangling County in Hanzhong." The Empress Dowager decreed that Liu He go back to Changyi, and granted him a fief of 2,000 households for sacrificial ablutions. The ministers of Changyi were found guilty of dereliction of duty, not righteously assisting and advising, involving the Prince in evil ways, so Huo Guang had more than 200 persons executed. When these people were dragged out to die, crying in the streets they shouted: "We hesitated when decision was needed, and get into trouble instead."

Huo Guang, sitting in the court, consulted the Prime Minister and the other ministers to deliberate on the candidate for enthronement. The Prince of Guangling had already been passed over, and Prince Ci of Yan had been killed for rebellion, so his son could not be considered. The only person to receive unanimous

【原文】

其子不在议中。近亲唯有卫太子孙号皇曾孙在民间，咸称述焉。光遂复与丞相敞等上奏曰：“《礼》曰‘人道亲亲故尊祖，尊祖故敬宗。’(太)[大]宗亡嗣，择支子孙贤者为嗣。孝武皇帝曾孙病已，武帝时有诏掖庭养视，至今年十八，师受《诗》、《论语》、《孝经》，躬行节俭，慈仁爱人，可以嗣孝昭皇帝后，奉承祖宗庙，子万姓。臣昧死以闻。”皇太后诏曰：“可。”光遣宗正刘德至曾孙家尚冠里，洗沐赐御衣，太仆以軨猎车迎曾孙就斋宗正府，入未央宫见皇太后，封为阳武侯。已而光奉上皇帝玺绶，谒于高庙，是为孝宣皇帝。明年，下诏曰：“夫褒有德，赏元功，古今通谊也。大司马大将军光宿卫忠正，宣德明恩，守节秉谊，以安宗庙。其以河北、东武阳益封光万七千户。”与故所食凡二万户。赏赐前后黄金七千斤，钱六千万，杂缯三万匹，奴婢百七十人，马二千疋，甲第一区。

【今译】

在议论中了。近亲中现只有卫太子的孙子号称皇曾孙的还在民间，受到普遍称赞。霍光便又同丞相杨敞等大臣一同上奏说：“《礼》书中说‘为人之道能够亲爱亲人就能尊崇祖先，能够尊崇祖先就能够敬重宗庙’。如今大宗没有继承人，就应选择旁支子孙中贤能的人作为继承人。孝武皇帝的曾孙病已，武帝时有诏令在掖庭中抚养照看，到现在年已十八，从师学习《诗》、《论语》、《孝经》，身体力行节俭，仁慈爱人，可以继承孝昭皇帝的皇位，事奉祖先宗庙，统治万民。臣下冒死以告。”皇太后下诏说：“准奏。”霍光就派遣宗正刘德到曾孙家尚冠里，帮他洗梳沐浴，赐给他皇帝的衣服，叫太仆用轻便小车把曾孙接到宗正府进行斋戒，入未央宫谒见皇太后，被封为阳武侯。不久霍光就捧上皇帝的印玺，然后到高庙去拜谒，这就是孝宣皇帝。第二年，皇帝下诏说：“褒奖有德的人，赏赐有大功的人，是古今的常理。大司马大将军霍光守卫宫廷忠诚正直，宣扬道德彰明恩泽，保守节操秉行仁义，用来安定宗庙。将河北、东武阳的一万七千户加封给霍光。”加上他以前的封地一共有两万户。前后赏给他黄金七千斤，钱六千万，各色彩帛三万匹，奴婢一百七十人，马二千匹，上等住宅一处。

approbation among the surviving next of kin was the grandson of Crown Prince of Wei. He was now living as a commoner, and known as Imperial great-grandson. Huo Guang, Prime Minister Yang Chang and others petitioned as follows: "According to the *Book of Rites*: 'Those who can be dear to loved ones will be able to revere their ancestors, and those who revere their ancestors will be able to respect the clansman.' Now the clansman has no heirs, so we should choose the virtuous offshoot as heir. Emperor Wudi's great-grandson Bingyi, now 18 years old, was admitted in the reign of Wudi by imperial decree to be taken care of in the harem, to learn the *Odes*, *Analects*, and the *Book of Filial Piety*. He is painfully self-denying, benevolent and loving, thus suitable to inherit Zhaodi's throne, serve the ancestral temple and rule the people. We risk our lives to report this." The Empress Dowager then issued an edict: "Petition sustained." Huo Guang sent Chamberlain for the Imperial Clan Liu De to the home of the great-grandson in Shangguan Lane, to help with the ritual ablutions, and present the imperial robes, and the Chamberlain of the Imperial Stud took him in a two-wheeled carriage to fast at the Chamber of the Imperial Clan, and led him into Weiyang Palace for an audience with the Empress Dowager, who made him Marquis of Yangwu. Soon Huo Guang presented him Imperial Seal, and then took him to pay homage at the Temple of Gaodi, which made him Emperor Xuandi. The following year, the Emperor issued an edict: "It is a generally acknowledged truth of ancient and modern times that virtuous people are praised, and people who perform great service are rewarded. Commander-in-Chief and General-in-Chief Huo has always guarded the palace with loyalty, virtue, integrity, and righteousness to keep safe the ancestral temple. Let Huo Guang receive a further 17,000 households in Hebei and Dongwuyang counties as his fief." Add to what he already had, this brought his fiefdom to a total of 20,000 households. Before and after that, he was rewarded with 7,000 catties of gold, 60 million

【原文】

自昭帝时，光子禹及兄孙云皆中郎将，云弟山奉车都尉侍中，领胡越兵。光两女婿为东西宫卫尉，昆弟诸婿外孙皆奉朝请，为诸曹大夫，骑都尉，给事中。党亲连体，根据于朝廷。光自后元秉持万机，及上即位，乃归政。上谦让不受，诸事皆先关白光，然后奏御天子。光每朝见，上虚己敛容。礼下之已甚。

光秉政前后二十年，地节二年春病笃，车驾自临问光病，上为之涕泣。光上书谢恩曰："愿分国邑三千户，以封兄孙奉车都尉山为列侯，奉兄票骑将军去病祀。"事下丞相御史，即日拜光子禹为右将军。

光薨，上及皇太后亲临光丧。太中大夫任宣与侍御史五人持节护

【今译】

自昭帝时起，霍光的儿子霍禹以及霍光哥哥的孙子霍云都已是中郎将，霍云的弟弟霍山任奉车都尉、侍中，掌握胡、越兵权。霍光的两个女婿分别是东西宫的卫尉，霍光兄弟的女婿及外孙都有资格参加朝会，担当诸曹大夫，骑都尉，给事中的官职。党派亲族连成一体，盘根错节地占据了朝廷。霍光从后元以来一直总理朝政，等到皇上登基以后，才归还朝政。皇上谦让不肯接受，各种政事都要先请示霍光后，再上奏给天子。霍光每次上朝参见，皇上都谦恭严肃，对他十分恭敬礼让。

霍光执政前后达二十年，地节二年春他病得很厉害，皇上亲自去他家探望病情，为之流泪哭泣。霍光上书谢恩说："我愿把我封国食邑的三千户用来分封我哥哥的孙子奉车都尉霍山为列侯，以供奉我哥哥骠骑将军霍去病的祭祀。"皇上把此事交给丞相御史办理，当天就授任霍光的儿子霍禹为右将军。

霍光去世后，皇上及皇太后都亲自到霍光的灵堂去吊唁。太中大夫任宣和五个侍御史一同拿着符节操办丧事。中二千石的大臣在墓地

cash, 30,000 rolls of various colors of silk, 170 serfs, 2,000 horses, and a residence area of the highest level.

With the accession of Zhaodi, Guang's son, Huo Yu, and Huo Yun, his grandnephew, were already leaders of court gentlemen; Huo Yun's brother Huo Shan became Commandant-in-Chief of Chariots, palace attendant, in charge of the armies of the Western tribes and of Yue. Huo Guang's two sons-in-law were the Chamberlains of the Court at the East and West Palaces, and his brother's sons-in-law and grandsons were all eligible to attend Court, as grand masters, commandants of cavalry and palace stewards. His kin and relatives by marriage were inextricably fused together, a complex thicket of relationships occupying Court. Huo Guang had held onto the affairs of state since the Houyuan period (87 BC), so once the new emperor ascended the throne, he offered to return the reins of power. But Emperor Xuandi modestly refused to accept. So government affairs had to be reported first to Huo Guang, and then memorialized to the Emperor. Whenever Huo came to see his ruler, the Emperor became modestly serious, very respectful and courteous.

Huo controlled government for a total 20 years, but became very ill in the spring of year two of the Dijie reign period (68 BC). The Emperor himself took a chariot to his home to visit his sickbed, weeping with tears. Huo Guang wrote to thank the imperial favor: "I would like to share 3,000 households from my fief so as to enfeoff my brother's grandson Huo Shan the Commandant-in-Chief of Chariots as an adjunct marquis, to serve the sacrifice of my brother the Cavalry General Huo Qubing." The Emperor referred the matter to the prime minister and the scribe, and on that day Huo Guang's son Huo Yu was appointed Right General. The Emperor and Empress Dowager came in person to visit the body of Huo Guang in the hall of mourning, which was guarded by superior grand master of the palace Ren Xuan and five attendant censors, bearing the imperial tally. A full 2,000-picul official set up his command

【原文】

丧事。中二千石治莫府冢上。赐金钱、缯絮，绣被百领，衣五十箧，璧珠玑玉衣，梓宫、便房、黄肠题凑各一具，枞木外臧椁十五具。东园温明，皆如乘舆制度。载光尸柩以辒辌车，黄屋左纛，发材官轻车北军五校士军陈至茂陵，以送其葬，谥曰宣成侯。发三河卒穿复土，起冢祠堂，置园邑三百家，长丞奉守如旧法。

既葬，封山为乐平侯，以奉车都尉领尚书事。天子思光功德，下诏曰："故大司马大将军博陆侯宿卫孝武皇帝三十有馀年，辅孝昭皇帝十有馀年，遭大难，躬秉谊，率三公九卿大夫定万世册以安社稷，天下蒸庶咸以康宁。功德茂盛，朕甚嘉之。复其后世，畴其爵邑，世世无有所与，功如萧相国。"明年夏，封太子外祖父许广汉为平恩侯。

【今译】

上设置幕府办事。皇上还赐给金钱、帛绢丝绵，绣花棉被一百条，衣服五十箱，金镂玉衣，内棺、外椁、黄肠题凑各一副，随葬的外藏枞木椁十五副。东园制作的温明秘器，全都如同皇帝的规格。用辒辌车载着霍光的遗体，车上用黄缎覆盖，辕左插上羽饰大旗，派材官、轻车、北军五校士兵列队一直到达茂陵，来为霍光送葬。给他赐谥号为宣成侯。征发河东、河南、河内三郡的士兵挖掘墓穴，盖起陵墓祠堂，设置看护的园邑三百家，长史、丞掾按照旧法侍奉守护陵园。

霍光被安葬以后，宣帝就封霍山为乐平侯，以奉车都尉的身份兼管尚书的事务。天子追思霍光的功德，下诏令说："已故大司马大将军博陆侯在宫禁中侍奉孝武皇帝三十余年，辅佐孝昭皇帝又有十多年，中间遭遇到重大的灾难，挺身执仗正义，率领三公九卿大夫决定万年大计以安定国家，天下的黎民百姓才获得安康太平。他的功德无量，朕极为嘉许。决定免去他后代的徭役，子孙继承他的封爵食邑，世世代代不准改变，他的功劳与萧相国同等。"第二年夏天，宣帝封太子的外祖父许广汉为平恩侯。又下诏令道："宣成侯霍光在宫禁中

office in the cemetery. The Emperor also endowed money, silk, 100 embroidered quilts, 50 boxes of clothes, jade insignia, pearls, garments of jade sewn with gold thread, a funeral casket and coffin house, a yellow-core cypress enclosure, and 15 outer fir planks. The East Park procured burial lacquer ware, all according to the Emperor's specifications. The coffin was carried on an imperial funeral carriage, covered with yellow damask, a large feathered banner affixed to the left shaft. The funeral cortege was guarded by soldiers of strong archery, chariots, and five battalions of the North Guard lining the route to the Maoling Mausoleum, where Huo Guang was put to rest. He was given the posthumous title of Marquis of Xuancheng. Soldiers from the three He- prefectures were sent to dig the grave and build the tomb and ancestral hall. The Emperor set up a town of 300 households with magistrate and aides to serve as the guardians of the cemetery, following the old specifications for guarding a cemetery.

After the funeral obsequies, the Emperor made Huo Shan Marquis of Leping also responsible for the imperial secretariat in the capacity of Commander-in-Chief of Chariots. The Son of Heaven remembered Huo Guang's service in an edict: "The late Commander-in-Chief and General-in-Chief Marquis of Bolu guarded Emperor Wudi in the palace for more than 30 years and assisted Emperor Zhaodi for more than a decade. In the face of a major disaster, he came forward to assert justice, and led the great nobles and chief ministers, grand masters to decide on the plan for eternal peace and stability of the country, assuring peace and well-being for the common people across the land. His boundless virtue and merit were commendable in the extreme. From his offspring we shall remove the obligation of compulsory labor, and they shall inherit his title and fief, exempted from corvee for all generations, as his credit was equal to that of Prime Minister Xiao." The next summer, Xuandi made the Crown Prince's grandfather Xu Guanghan Marquis

【原文】

复下诏曰："宣成侯光宿卫忠正，勤劳国家。善善及后世，其封光兄孙中郎将云为冠阳侯。"

禹既嗣为博陆侯，太夫人显改光时所自造茔制而侈大之。起三出阙，筑神道，北临昭灵，南出承恩，盛饰祠室，辇阁通属永巷，而幽良人婢妾守之。广治第室，作乘舆辇，加画绣絪冯，黄金涂，韦絮荐轮，侍婢以五采丝辀显，游戏第中。初，光爱幸监奴冯子都，常与计事，及显寡居，与子都乱。而禹、山亦并缮治第宅，走马驰逐平乐馆。云当朝请，数称病私出，多从宾客，张围猎黄山苑中，使苍头奴上朝谒，莫敢谴者。而显及诸女，昼夜出入长信宫殿中，亡期度。

宣帝自在民间闻知霍氏尊盛日久，内不能善。光薨，上始躬亲朝政，

【今译】

侍奉天子忠诚正直，为国家辛勤操劳。褒奖善良的人应推及后代，此封霍光哥哥的孙子中郎将霍云为冠阳侯。"

霍禹继爵为博陆侯后，太夫人显改变了霍光生前自己设计的墓地规制而加以扩大。建起三个出口的门阙，修筑神道，北面靠近昭灵，南面越出承恩。大肆装修祠堂，辇车的专用道直通到墓穴中的永巷，又幽禁平民、奴婢、侍妾来守护。还大建住宅，制造乘坐的辇车，增加饰有图案的绣花坐垫、把手，并涂饰黄金，又用皮裹着丝絮包住车轮，侍从婢女用五彩的丝带拉着显所乘坐的车，在住宅中游戏取乐。当初，霍光宠爱家奴总管冯子都，常同他商量事情，等到显守寡独居时，她便和冯子都通奸。而霍禹、霍山也同时修缮住宅，常在平乐馆跑马追逐。霍云每当朝会的时候，多次称病私下外出，带着很多宾客，在黄山苑囿中张围打猎，却委派奴仆代为上朝谒见，没有人敢谴责。而且显和她的几个女儿，不分白天黑夜地进出长信宫的宫殿中，没有限度。

宣帝在民间时就听说并知晓霍氏尊贵强盛日子长久，心中并不认

of Pingen. He issued a further edict: "Marquis of Xuancheng Huo Guang always guarded the palace with loyalty and integrity, and worked hard for the country. Praise of the good person should extend to later generations, so the leader of court gentlemen Huo Yun, the grandnephew of Huo Guang is hereby made the Marquis of Guanyang."

Huo Yu inherited the title of Marquis of Bolu, and then Xian, Huo Guang's widow, changed the format of the cemetery Huo Guang had himself specified and expanded it extravagantly. Three memorial archways were built, the tomb passage constructed, stretching close to Zhaoling Hall in the north, and beyond Cheng'en Hall in the south. There was a grandiose renovation of the ancestral temple, making the chariot lane connect with the long tomb road, and they also sequestered civilians, slaves and concubines to guard it. They built residences everywhere, commissioned pompous light carriages, complete with embroidered cushions and handles, all finished in gold, their wheels wrapped in silk wadding covered over with leather. In Xian's mansion, her servants and maids were made to amuse her by giving her chariot rides, pulling the chariot along on multicolored silk ribbons. Earlier, Huo Guang had been fond of his butler Feng Zidu, and often discussed matters with him. When Xian was widowed, she committed adultery with Feng. Huo Yu and Huo Shan also refurbished their residences, often galloping and chasing each other in Peaceful Amusement Hall of the Imperial Forest Park. Even when Court was meeting, Huo Yun would repeatedly sneak out of the capital pleading ill health, followed by a lot of hangers-on, to go hunting in the imperial hunting grounds of Huangshan Palace, having delegated a servant to stand in for him at the Court audience. Not a soul dared condemn him. Furthermore, the widow Xian and several of her daughters haunted the hall of Changxin Palace day and night without constraint.

As a commoner before becoming Emperor, Xuandi had heard

【原文】

御史大夫魏相给事中。显谓禹、云、山："女曹不务奉大将军馀业，今大夫给事中，他人壹间，女能复自救邪？"后两家奴争道，霍氏奴入御史府，欲蹋大夫门，御史为叩头谢，乃去。人以谓霍氏，显等始知忧。会魏大夫为丞相，数燕见言事。平恩侯与侍中金安上等径出入省中。时霍山自若领尚书，上令吏民得奏封事，不关尚书，群臣进见独往来，于是霍氏甚恶之。

宣帝始立，立微时许妃为皇后。显爱小女成君，欲贵之，私使乳医淳于衍行毒药杀许后，因劝光内成君，代立为后。语在《外戚传》。始许后暴崩，吏捕诸医，劾衍侍疾亡状不道，下狱，吏簿问急，显恐事败，即具以实语光。光大惊，欲自发举，不忍，犹与。

【今译】

为这是一件好事。霍光去世后，宣帝才开始亲自治理朝政，让御史大夫魏相任给事中。显对霍禹、霍云、霍山等人说："你们这些人不努力继承大将军的遗业，如今大夫任给事中，一旦有人在中间挑拨，你们还能拯救自己吗？"后来霍、魏两家的奴仆争路，霍氏的奴仆就跑到御史大夫府中，要踢坏他府中的大门，御史为此叩头请罪，他们才离开。有人把这件事告诉了霍家，显等人才开始知道将有忧患。等到魏大夫担任丞相，经常在闲暇时被召见谈论政事。平恩侯和侍中金安上都能直接出入宫禁中。这时霍山仍旧兼领尚书的事务，但皇上叫官吏百姓可以密封奏章上报，不必通过尚书，群臣百官进见皇上可以独自往来，霍氏对此非常不满。

宣帝刚登基时，就册封卑贱而未显达时所娶的许妃为皇后。显很喜爱她的小女儿成君，想使她得到富贵，就暗自派产科医生淳于衍下毒药杀死许后，乘机劝霍光要宣帝娶成君，取代许后成为皇后。这些事《外戚传》中有记载。当时许后突然死亡之时，官吏逮捕了宫中所有医生，并弹劾淳于衍在治病过程中行迹可疑，不合常理，就把他关进了监狱。狱吏对他审问得很急迫，显害怕事情败露，就把实情告诉了霍光。霍光大吃一惊，想亲自去告发这件事又不忍心，正在犹豫。

of the Huo family's long enjoyment of honors and prosperity, and did not approve. After Huo Guang's death, he began to deal with affairs of state in person, making Censor-in-Chief Wei Xiang the palace steward. Xian said to Huo Yu, Huo Yun, and Huo Shan: "You do not work hard to inherit the legacy of General-in-Chief, and now that the Censor-in-Chief has become the palace steward, if someone was to sow discord in the middle, could you still save yourselves?" Later, the servants of Huo and Wei were in dispute over a right of way, and Huo's servant went to the residence of the Censor-in-Chief, intending to kick his gate, and only quit after the Censor-in-Chief kowtowed in apology. Someone told the Huo family about it. Xian and the others then knew they had cause to be concerned. When Censor-in-Chief Wei served as prime minister, he was often summoned to discuss state affairs when the Emperor was at leisure. The Marquis of Pingen and palace attendant Jin Anshang had direct access to the palace. At the time, Huo Shan was still in charge of the imperial secretariat, but the Emperor called the officials and the people to seal the memorials to be reported, without having to go via the secretariat. The ministers could have an audience with the Emperor, coming and going independently. The Huos hated it.

On Xuandi's accession to the throne, he elevated his humble wife Xu to the position of Empress. Xian loved her little daughter Chengjun, and aspired to make her a noble, so she secretly sent her obstetrician Chunyu Yan to kill Empress Xu with poison, and took the opportunity to persuade Huo Guang to marry Chengjun to the monarch, replacing Xu as Empress. Details of this can be found in "Biography of Emperors' In-Laws." Earlier, after the sudden death of Empress Xu, the officials arrested all the palace doctors, and they accused Chunyu Yan of questionable and unjustifiable treatment, and put him in jail. The warder's interrogation was very pressing, and Xian was afraid of the truth coming out, so she confessed her action to Huo Guang. Huo Guang was horrified and wanted to personally

【原文】

会奏上，因署衍勿论。光薨后，语稍泄。于是上始闻之而未察，乃徙光女婿度辽将军未央卫尉平陵侯范明友为光禄勋，次婿诸吏中郎将羽林监任胜出为安定太守。数月，复出光姊婿给事中光禄大夫张朔为蜀郡太守，群孙婿中郎将王汉为武威太守。顷之，复徙光长女婿长乐卫尉邓广汉为少府。更以禹为大司马，冠小冠，亡印绶，罢其右将军屯兵官属，特使禹官名与光俱大司马者。又收范明友度辽将军印绶，但为光禄勋。及光中女婿赵平为散骑骑都尉光禄大夫将屯兵，又收平骑都尉印绶。诸领胡越骑、羽林及两宫卫将屯兵，悉易以所亲信许、史子弟代之。

禹为大司马，称病。禹故长史任宣候问，禹曰："我何病？县官

【今译】

适逢此案的奏章上报，霍光就乘机批复对淳于衍不必再追究。霍光薨后，真相开始慢慢泄露出去。对这件事皇上只是刚听说到但不明虚实，就调动霍光的女婿度辽将军未央宫的卫尉平陵侯范明友任光禄勋，第二个女婿诸吏中郎将羽林监任胜出任安定太守。几个月后，又调出霍光姐姐的女婿给事中光禄大夫张朔任蜀郡太守，孙女婿中郎将王汉为武威太守。过了不久，又调霍光的大女婿长乐宫卫尉邓广汉任少府。再调霍禹任大司马，只戴小帽子，没有印章，撤销了他的右将军及所统辖的驻军官兵，只是让霍禹的官名与霍光一样，都是大司马。又收回范明友度辽将军的官印，只让他任光禄勋。还有霍光的三女婿赵平为散骑骑都尉光禄大夫统领驻军，又把赵平的骑都尉官印收回。所有统领的胡人、越人骑兵、羽林军以及两宫卫队所统领的士兵，都改为由宣帝所亲信的许、史两家子弟代为统领。

霍禹被任命为大司马后，就称说有病。霍禹原先的长史任宣来探

expose the matter but did not have the heart, and so hesitated. When the memorial of the case was reported, Huo Guang took the opportunity to approve the dropping of the case against Chunyu Yan. The truth of the matter began slowly to emerge once Huo Guang was dead. The Emperor only just heard of the matter, but did not know what the truth of it was, so he transferred Huo Guang's son-in-law Fan Mingyou, Duliao General, Chamberlain of the Garrison of Weiyang Palace, Marquis of Pingling, to be Chamberlain for Attendants, and his second son-in-law Ren Sheng, leader of court gentlemen and Supervisor of Palace Guard as Governor of Anding. A few months later, he transferred out Huo Guang sister's son-in-law Zhang Shuo, palace steward and grand master of splendid happiness as Governor of Shujun Prefecture, and the grandson-in-law Wang Han leader of court gentlemen as Governor of Wuwei Prefecture. Soon he transferred Deng Guanghan, Huo Guang's elder son-in-law, Chamberlain of the Garrison of Changle Palace, to be chamberlain for the palace revenues of Changxin Palace. Next he transferred Huo Yu as Commander-in-Chief, only wearing a small cap, with no seals, after the revocation of his Right General's overall control of the garrison officers and men, allowing him only the title, particular to Huo Guang, of Commander-in-Chief. Then he withdrew Fan Mingyou's seal of Duliao General, only letting him be Chamberlain for Attendants. Huo Guang's third son-in-law Zhao Ping was cavalier attendant, the commandant of cavalry, grand master of splendid happiness leading the garrison, and from him also the official seal of commandant was revoked. All commands of the Hu and Yue cavalry, palace guards, as well as the command of guard soldiers of the two palaces were replaced by the followers, children and brothers of the Xu, and the Shi families, who enjoyed the trust of Emperor Xuandi.

After Huo Yu was appointed Commander-in-Chief, he asked for sick leave. His former aide Ren Xuan came to ask after his health, to

【原文】

非我家将军不得至是，今将军坟墓未干，尽外我家，反任许、史，夺我印绶，令人不省死。”宣见禹恨望深，乃谓曰：“大将军时何可复行！持国权柄，杀生在手中。廷尉李种、王平、左冯翊贾胜胡及车丞相女婿少府徐仁皆坐逆将军(竟)[意]下狱死。使乐成小家子，得幸将军，至九卿封侯，百官以下但事冯子都、王子方等，视丞相亡如也。各自有时，今许、史自天子骨肉，贵正宜耳。大司马欲用是怨恨，愚以为不可。”禹默然。数日，起视事。

显及禹、山、云自见日侵削，数相对啼泣，自怨。山曰：“今丞相用事，县官信之，尽变易大将军时法令，以公田赋与贫民，发扬大将军过失。又诸儒生多窭人子，远客饥寒，喜妄说狂言，不避忌讳，大将军常雠之，今陛下好与诸儒生语，人人自使书对事，多言我家者。尝有上书言大将军时主弱臣强，专制擅权，今其子孙用事，昆弟

【今译】

望问候，霍禹说道：“我哪里有什么病？天子不是靠我家将军怎么能到现在的地步，如今将军的坟墓还没有干，他就一律疏远排斥我们家族，反而任用许、史两家的人员，还没收了我的官印，真让人死都弄不明白。”任宣见霍禹怨恨很深，就对他说道：“大将军的时代怎么还能再有！把持国家的权柄，生杀予夺操在手中。廷尉李种、王平、左冯翊贾胜胡以及车丞相的女婿少府徐仁都因冒犯大将军的意旨而被下狱处死。使乐成这样的小户人家子弟因为受到将军宠爱，官至九卿，爵为列侯。百官以下只事奉冯子都、王子方等人，根本不把丞相放在眼里。这是各自有自己的时代，如今许、史两家是天子的骨肉姻亲，得到尊贵正是理所当然。大司马如果因此而心怀怨恨，我认为不应该。”霍禹听后沉默不语。过了几天，霍禹又上朝处理事务。

显和霍禹、霍山、霍云眼看着自己的权势一天天被削夺，几次相对流泪啼哭，自相埋怨。霍山说：“现在丞相执政，受到皇帝信赖，全部改变大将军当时制定的法令，将公田授给贫民，以宣扬大将军的过失。又有诸位儒生，大多是穷人子弟，远道而来客居京城，衣食不保，却喜欢口出狂言，不避忌讳，大将军曾对这些人忌恨如仇，如今陛下却喜欢同众儒生交谈，又让他们自行上书答对政事，这些人就尽说我们家的事。曾经有人上书说大将军在时，主弱臣强，揽权独裁，

which Huo Yu responded: "How am I ill? How could the Emperor be where he is now if not for the General of my family, and now before the General's tomb is even dry he has alienated all of my family. He appoints the Xus and Shis instead and has confiscated my official seal. I really cannot understand it for the life of me." Seeing Huo Yu's deep resentment, Ren Xuan said: "How could the era of General-in-Chief happen a second time! He held the reins of power in the state, the arbiter of life and death. Chamberlain of Law Enforcement Li Zhong and Wang Ping, Guardian of the Left Jia Shenghu, and Prime Minister Ju's son-in-law Chamberlain for the Palace Revenues Xu Ren, were all guilty of violating the General's intention and were imprisoned and put to death. Shi Lecheng came from a humble family, but, due to the General's favor, he was made a chief minister and adjunct marquis. The various officials served only Feng Zidu, Wang Zifang, and the like, regarding the prime minister as inferior. For each there is a time, and now it is only natural that the Xu and Shi families, as flesh and blood of the Emperor, are being ennobled. For the Commander-in-Chief to be so embittered is not right in my opinion." Huo Yu had no comment to make, but after a few days, he returned to Court and to his duties.

Xian and Huo Yu, Huo Shan, Huo Yun, seeing their powers being whittled away with each passing day, wept among themselves often, with mutual recriminations. Huo Shan said: "The Prime Minister is ruling, trusted by the Emperor, changing all the laws enacted by the General. He has granted public land to the poor, in order to publicize the faults of the General. And the Confucian scholars are mostly from poor families, they come from afar, cold and hungry, but they like to blab their crazy ideas, without any taboo, so the General loathed these people. Now His Majesty likes to talk with all the Confucians, all and sundry are presenting proposals on state affairs, and our family is the subject of their comment. Someone has written to say that in the era of the General,

【原文】

益骄恣，恐危宗庙，灾异数见，尽为是也。其言绝痛，山屏不奏其书。后上书者益黠，尽奏封事，辄(使)[下]中书令出取之，不关尚书，益不信人。”显曰：“丞相数言我家，独无罪乎？”山曰：“丞相廉正，安得罪？我家昆弟诸婿多不谨。又闻民间讙言霍氏毒杀许皇后，宁有是邪？”显恐急，即具以实告山、云、禹。山、云、禹惊曰：“如是，何不早告禹等！县官离散斥逐诸婿，用是故也。此大事，诛罚不小，奈何？”于是始有邪谋矣。

初，赵平客石夏善为天官，语平曰：“荧惑守御星，御星，太仆奉车都尉也，不黜则死。”平内忧山等。云舅李竟所善张赦见云家卒卒，谓竟曰：“今丞相与平恩侯用事，可令太夫人言太后，先诛此两人。移徙陛下，在太后耳。”长安男子张章告之，事下廷尉。执金吾

【今译】

如今他的子孙当权，兄弟们更加骄横恣肆，恐怕将要危及宗庙社稷，灾异怪事频繁出现，都是因为这个缘故。他的话说得极其痛切，我就压下没有把此书上奏。后来上书的人更加狡猾，全都使用密封奏事，皇上就叫中书令出来取走，不通过尚书，皇上越来越不信任我了。”显问道：“丞相屡次说我家的事，难道就没有罪过吗？”霍山答道：“丞相廉洁正直，哪里能有罪？我家的弟兄们和各位女婿大多行为不慎。又听民间盛传说霍家用毒杀死了许皇后，真有此事吗？”显很害怕，就全部将实情告诉了霍山、霍云、霍禹。霍山、霍云、霍禹惊慌地说道：“像这等事情，为什么不早对我们说呢？天子离散斥逐我们家的几个女婿，是因为这个缘故啊。这是一件大事，处罚可不会轻，怎么办？”从此他们就开始有了邪谋。

当初，赵平的门客石夏知晓天文，他对赵平说：“荧惑守着御星，御星是太仆奉车都尉的星宿，他们不是被贬官就是被杀死。”赵平内心替霍山等人担忧。霍云的舅舅李竟的好友张赦见霍云家族岌岌可危，就对李竟说：“如今丞相与平恩侯当权，可以叫太夫人告诉太后，先把这两个人杀了。罢黜陛下，就在于皇太后。”长安男子张章

the monarch was weaker than the minister, who arrogated dictatorial powers, and now that his sons and grandsons are in power, the brothers are even more arrogant and unrestrained, which might threaten the ancestral temple. He claims this is the reason for frequent calamities and supernatural happenings. Because of his very cutting words, I suppressed this memorial. Later, the admonishers got craftier, sending the reports already sealed, and the Emperor told the Secretariat Director to come out for them, rather than them having to go through the secretary, so he trusts me less and less." Xian asked: "The Prime Minister has repeatedly reported on my family. Has he not done anything wrong himself?" Huo Shan replied: "The Prime Minister is incorrupt. There's no crime at all to find. Most of my brothers and your sons-in-law behave imprudently. I heard the common gossip that the Huo family poisoned Empress Xu. Is there any truth in this?" Xian was very afraid, and told the truth to Huo Shan, Huo Yun and Huo Yu. They panicked and said: "Why on earth didn't you tell us this before? It's because of this that the Emperor has scattered and expelled several of our sons-in-law. This is a big thing, the punishment cannot be light. What is to be done?" From then on, they began to plan their evil scheme.

Earlier, Shi Xia, a hanger-on of Zhao Ping, who could read the stars, told Zhao Ping: "Mars is violating the Charioteer Star, which refers to the Chamberlain of the Imperial Stud and Commander-in-Chief of Chariots, so they will be dismissed or killed." Zhao Ping was concerned about Huo Shan and others. When Zhang She, a friend of Huo Yun's uncle Li Jing, saw Huo Yun's family so anxious, he said to Li: "Today the Prime Minister and the Marquis of Pingen are in power. You can ask Huo Guang's widow to persuade the Empress Dowager, and first kill the two men. The removal of His Majesty is up to the Empress Dowager." Zhang Zhang, a man of Changan, informed about this, and Xuandi took the matter to the Office of Law Enforcement. The Chamberlain for the Imperial

【原文】

捕张赦、石夏等，后有诏止勿捕。山等愈恐，相谓曰：“此县官重太后，故不竟也。然恶端已见，又有弑许后事，陛下虽宽仁，恐左右不听，久之犹发，发即族矣，不如先也。”遂令诸女各归报其夫，皆曰：“安所相避？”

会李竟坐与诸侯王交通，辞语及霍氏，有诏云、山不宜宿卫，免就第。光诸女遇太后无礼，冯子都数犯法，上并以为让，山、禹等甚恐。显梦第中井水溢流庭下，灶居树上，又梦大将军谓显曰：“知捕儿不？亟下捕之。”第中鼠暴多，与人相触，以尾画地。鸮数鸣殿前树上。第门自坏。云尚冠里宅中门亦坏。巷端人共见有人居云屋上，彻瓦投地，就视，亡有，大怪之。禹梦车骑声正讙来捕禹，举家忧愁。

【今译】

告发了这件事，宣帝就把此事交给廷尉处理。执金吾拘捕了张赦、石夏等人，后来又有诏令制止，不准拘捕。霍山等人更加恐慌，相对说道：“这是天子看重太后的面子，所以没有深究。但是凶兆已显现，又有毒杀许后的事，陛下即使宽大仁厚，就怕他左右的人不听，时间久了仍然会追查，一旦查清就要被灭族，我们不如先动手。”于是就叫几个女儿各自回去告诉自己的丈夫，都说：“哪里还有地方避难呢？”

适逢李竟因与诸侯王勾结而致罪，供辞中涉及霍氏，宣帝就下诏说霍云、霍山不宜在宫中供职，免官回家。霍光的几个女儿对待太后无礼，冯子都数次犯法，皇上就一同加以责问，霍山、霍禹等人感到很害怕。显在梦中见到住宅中的井水溢出流到厅堂下，厨房里的炉灶挂在了大树上，又梦见大将军对显说：“你知道我们的儿子要被捕了吗？他们很快就会来捕人的。”住宅中的老鼠一下多了起来，与人相互碰撞，用尾巴在地上乱画。猫头鹰几次在殿前的树上叫唤。住宅的门无缘无故毁坏，霍云尚冠里住宅中的门也无缘无故地坏了。街巷口的人都看到有人坐在霍云的屋顶上，揭下瓦片扔到地上，到跟前去看，却又没有见到人，感到非常奇怪。霍禹梦中听到车马喧喧嚷嚷地来捕捉他，全家对这些怪事感到忧愁。霍山说道：“丞相擅自减少宗

Insignia arrested Zhang She, Shi Xia, etc. but a later edict stopped further arrests. Huo Shan and others were even more panicky, and said to each other: "It is out of the Emperor's consideration for the Empress Dowager, that they have not pursued the matter to the end. But an ill omen has appeared, and there is the matter of the poisoned Empress Xu. Even if His Majesty is inclined to be generous, I'm afraid that those around him will not listen. In the long run, it will be followed up, and that will mean the extermination of our clan. It is better to make the first move." So they told the daughters to go back and tell their husbands, who all said: "Where is there a place of refuge?"

It happened that Li Jing was guilty of colluding with the princes, and his confession implicated the Huos. The Emperor ordered that Huo Yun and Huo Shan should no longer serve in the palace, and dismissed them back to their home. Huo Guang's daughters treated the Empress Dowager rudely and Feng Zidu broke the law several times, so the Emperor blamed them together, to the great terror of Huo Shan, Huo Yu and others. Xian dreamed of water overflowing from a well onto the hall of her residence and the kitchen stove hanging in a high tree, and then dreamed of the General addressing her: "Do you know they want to arrest our sons? There will soon be an edict to take them." The house was overwhelmed by an infestation of rats, touching people, and scribbling with their tails on the ground. Owls in the trees in front of the hall hooted several times. The residence gate was destroyed for no reason whatsoever. The gates of Huo Yun's residence in Shangguan Lane were also broken. People at the end of the street all saw someone sitting on Huo Yun's roof, pulling off the tiles and throwing them to the ground, but could not see him when they approached to look, so they felt very strange. Huo Yu dreamed of the clatter of chariots and horses coming to take him, and the whole family was depressed. Huo Shan suggested: "The Prime Minister presumptuously allowed

【原文】

山曰："丞相擅减宗庙羔、菟、蛙，可以此罪也。"谋令太后为博平君置酒，召丞相、平恩侯以下，使范明友、邓广汉承太后制引斩之，因废天子而立禹。约定未发，云拜为玄菟太守，太中大夫任宣为代郡太守。山又坐写秘书，显为上书献城西第，入马千匹，以赎山罪。书报闻。会事发觉，云、山、明友自杀，显、禹、广汉等捕得。禹要斩，显及诸女昆弟皆弃市。唯独霍后废处昭台宫。与霍氏相连坐诛灭者数千家。

上乃下诏曰："乃者东织室令史张赦使魏郡豪李竟报冠阳侯云谋为大逆，朕以大将军故，抑而不扬，冀其自新。今大司马博陆侯禹与母宣成侯夫人显及从昆弟子冠阳侯云、乐平侯山诸姊妹婿谋为大逆，欲诖误百姓。赖(祖宗)[宗庙]神灵，先发得，咸伏其辜，朕甚悼之。

【今译】

庙供品的羔羊、兔子、青蛙，可以用这来定他的罪。"他们设谋叫太后为博平君设置酒席，把丞相、平恩侯以下的官员召来，让范明友、邓广汉奉太后的制令将这些人拉出去斩首，乘机罢除天子而立霍禹为帝。相约定的计划还没有实施，霍云就被任命为玄菟太守，太中大夫任宣被任命为代郡太守。霍山又因为抄写宫禁秘书犯法，显为此上书表示愿献出城西的宅第及一千匹马用以赎霍山的罪。宣帝在奏书上只批复知道了。刚好他们密谋的事被发觉，霍云、霍山、范明友自杀，显、霍禹、邓广汉等人被捕捉到。霍禹被腰斩，显及她的几个女儿兄弟都被处死。惟独霍后被废黜幽禁在昭台宫。与霍氏相牵连而被定罪诛杀灭族的有好几千家。

宣帝于是下诏说："不久以前东织室令史张赦指使魏郡的大户李竟给冠阳侯霍云回话，密谋犯上作乱，朕因为大将军的缘故，就将事情压住没有公开，希望他们能改过自新。如今大司马博陆侯霍禹和他的母亲宣成侯的夫人显以及堂弟的儿子冠阳侯霍云、乐平侯霍山和他们姊妹的女婿们阴谋造反，企图连累百姓。幸亏祖宗的神灵保佑，被事先发觉并捕获，全部都伏法处决。朕对这件事很痛心。所有被霍氏

reduction of the ancestral sacrifice offerings such as lambs, rabbits, frogs, and this can be used to convict him." They cooked up a plan to ask the Empress Dowager to hold a banquet for Lady Boping, to which would be invited the Prime Minister, the Marquis of Pingen and their subordinate officials, and order Fan Mingyou and Deng Guanghan to drag them out for beheading by order of the Empress Dowager, and then to depose the Son of Heaven in favor of Huo Yu. Before they could put the plan into action, Huo Yun was appointed Governor of Xuantu, and the superior grand master of the palace Ren Xuan was made Governor of Daijun. Huo Shan was guilty of copying a secret document in the palace, so Xian proposed that the crime be redeemed by presenting their mansion in the west of the city and 1,000 horses, but all Xuandi did in response was to acknowledge the offer. Just then their conspiracy was discovered, and Huo Yun, Huo Shan and Fan Mingyou committed suicide, while Xian, Huo Yu, Deng Guanghan, and others were captured. Huo Yu was cut in half at the waist, and Xian, her daughters, and brothers were killed in a public market. Only Empress Huo was put under house arrest in Zhaotai Palace after being deposed. Thousands of families related to the Huos were implicated and wiped out.

The Emperor so decreed: "Not long since, Zhang She, the clerk of East Weave Room, sent Li Jing the gallant from Wei Prefecture to report to Marquis of Guanyang Huo Yun in a conspiracy to rebel; for the sake of the late General-in-Chief, I suppressed it and did not disclose it in the hope that they could turn over a new leaf. And now the Commander-in-Chief Marquis of Bolu Huo Yu and his mother Lady Xian, widow of the Marquis of Xuancheng, and his cousin's son Marquis of Guanyang Huo Yun, Marquis of Leping Huo Shan and their sisters' husbands plotted rebellion, planning to embroil the people. Thanks to the ancestral gods, they were found out beforehand and apprehended, and all succumbed to execution for their crimes. The matter pains me to the heart. Those who are implicated by the

【原文】

诸为霍氏所诖误，事在丙申前，未发觉在吏者，皆赦除之。男子张章先发觉，以语期门董忠，忠告左曹杨恽，恽告侍中金安上。恽召见对状，后章上书以闻。侍中史高与金安上建发其事，言无入霍氏禁闼，卒不得遂其谋，皆雠有功。封章为博成侯，忠高昌侯，恽平通侯，安上都成侯，高乐陵侯。”

初，霍氏奢侈，茂陵徐生曰：“霍氏必亡。夫奢则不逊，不逊必侮上。侮上者，逆道也。在人之右，众必害之。霍氏秉权日久，害之者多矣。天下害之，而又行以逆道，不亡何待！”乃上疏言：“霍氏泰盛，陛下即爱厚之，宜以时抑制，无使至亡。”书三上，辄报闻。其后霍氏诛灭，而告霍氏者皆封。人为徐生上书曰：“臣闻客有过主人者，见其灶直突，傍有积薪，客谓主人，更为曲突，远徙其薪，不

【今译】

所连累的人，如果事情发生在丙申以前，还没有发觉报官在押的，一律赦免。男子张章先发觉了这件事，把它告诉了期门董忠，董忠又报告给左曹杨恽，杨恽报告给侍中金安上。杨恽被召见陈述情况，后来张章又上书报告。侍中史高与金安上建议告发这件事，说不准霍氏进入宫禁中，霍氏的阴谋才没有成功，他们都同样有功。特封张章为博成侯，董忠为高昌侯，杨恽为平通侯，金安上为都成侯，史高为乐陵侯。”

当初，霍氏生活奢侈，茂陵的徐生就说：“霍氏一定会灭亡。因为一旦骄奢就不会恭顺，不恭顺就必定要侮蔑皇上。侮蔑皇上是大逆不道的。在人之上，定会受到众人的忌恨。霍氏掌握权柄的日子很久，忌恨的人就多了。天下的人都忌恨他们，而他们又倒行逆施，不灭亡还等什么呢!”于是就上书进言道：“霍氏权势太盛，陛下即使很厚爱他们，也应该时时加以克制，不要让他们走上毁灭的道路。”上书三次，皇上只回复说知道了。后来霍氏被诛杀灭亡之后，凡是告发霍氏的人都得到封赏。有人替徐生上书说道：“臣听说有一个客人去拜访主人，看到主人家炉灶的烟囱是笔直的，旁边堆有柴草，客人就告诉主人，要他换个弯曲的烟囱，将柴草搬得远一点，不然将会有

Huos, if it happened before the 18th day of the seventh moon of year four of the reign of Dijie (66 BC) and they have not yet been found and taken into custody by the officers, let them be pardoned. The commoner Zhang Zhang was first to discover the plot, and told Qimen guard Dong Zhong, who reported to the Head of the Left Section Yang Yun, who reported to Palace Attendant Jin Anshang; Yang Yun was summoned to make a statement before the Emperor. Later, Zhang Zhang sent a memorial to report it. Palace Attendants Shi Gao and Jin Anshang suggested announcing the matter, and barring the Huos entry to the palace. Thanks to them the conspiracy failed, thus they were equally meritorious. Zhang Zhang is hereby made Marquis of Bocheng, Dong Zhong Marquis of Gaochang, Yang Yun Marquis of Pingtong, Jin Anshang as Marquis of Ducheng, and Shi Gao Marquis of Leling.

Earlier, the extravagance of the Huos caused Mr. Xu of Maoling to declare: "The Huo clan will surely perish. Once extravagant, you are not submissive; and disobedience will surely insult the Emperor. Insult to the Emperor is outrageous to the Way. Rising above the common people, you will surely be subject to their jealousy. The Huos have long exercised power and many are those who envy them. When the world envies you, and your acts run counter to the Way, what other outcome is there but to perish?" So he petitioned the Emperor: "The Huos are too powerful; even if Your Majesty loves them dearly, you should restrain them from time to time, not letting them take the road to perdition." It was submitted three times, receiving only an acknowledgment but no action. Later, when the Huos were exterminated, those who had denounced them were all enfeoffed. Someone wrote to the Emperor on behalf of Mr. Xu: "I heard that a guest visited the host, and noticed that his stove had a straight chimney, and next to it was a heap of firewood. He suggested to his host to change to a bent chimney and to move the firewood farther away, otherwise there would be a fire. The

【原文】

者且有火患。主人嘿然不应。俄而家果失火，邻里共救之，幸而得息。于是杀牛置酒，谢其邻人，灼烂者在于上行，馀各以功次坐，而不录言曲突者。人谓主人曰：‘鄉使听客之言，不费牛酒，终亡火患。今论功而请宾，曲突徙薪亡恩泽，焦头烂额为上客耶？’主人乃寤而请之。今茂陵徐福数上书言霍氏且有变，宜防绝之。乡使福说得行，则国亡裂土出爵之费，臣亡逆乱诛灭之败。往事既已，而福独不蒙其功，唯陛下察之，贵徙薪曲突之策，使居焦发灼烂之右。”上乃赐福帛十疋，后以为郎。

宣帝始立，谒见高庙，大将军光从骖乘，上内严惮之，若有芒刺在背。后车骑将军张安世代光骖乘，天子从容肆体，甚安近焉。及光身死而宗族竟诛，故俗传之曰：“威震主者不畜，霍氏之祸萌于

【今译】

火灾。主人默然不应。不久主人家果然失火，邻居街坊都来救火，幸而火被扑灭。于是主人杀牛摆酒，酬谢他的邻居，被烧伤的人安排坐在上座，其他的人按出力大小依次入座，惟独没有酬谢那个让他换个弯曲烟囱的人。有个人对主人说：‘如果当初你听客人的话，今天也就用不着破费杀牛置酒，而且始终不会有火灾。现在论功请客，对那位建议换弯曲的烟囱、将柴草搬开的人不作报答，怎么烧得焦头烂额的人反而成了上宾之客呢？’主人这才省悟而去请那位客人。现在茂陵的徐福几次上书说霍氏将有变故，应加以防患杜绝。假使当初徐福的建议得以采纳，国家就不会有割地封爵的花费，大臣就不会有谋反诛灭的祸败。往事已经过去，但只有徐福却有功未赏，望陛下明察，能够重视搬走柴草弯曲烟囱的良策，使其功在身体毛发被烧烂的人之上。”皇上于是就赐给徐福绢帛十匹，后来又任命他当了郎官。

宣帝刚登基时，去参拜高庙，大将军霍光与他同坐一辆车，皇上心里很害怕，好像有芒刺在背．后来车骑将军张安世代替霍光陪乘，天子就比较安逸自在，身体舒展自如，感到非常安全亲近。等到霍光死后，他的宗族也都被诛，因此民间就传说着：“威势震动君主的人

host was silent, unresponsive. Soon the house really did catch fire, but fortunately the neighbors all came to fight the fire, and it was extinguished. Afterwards, the host killed an ox and gave a feast to reward his neighbors. Those who had got burned were seated in the places of honor, and the others seated in turn according to their merit, but without reward to the person who had suggested changing the chimney. Someone said to the host: 'If you had listened to the words of your guest in the first place, you would not be spending money today on beef and wine, and you would never had had a fire at all. Now you treat the guests according to their merit, but show no gratitude to the person who recommended a different chimney or moving the wood. How can you treat those who got burned as the guests of honor?' The host woke up to reality and invited the guest. Now, Xu Fu from Maoling petitioned several times that something would happen to the Huos, and that precautionary measures should be taken to prevent it. If Xu Fu's recommendation had been adopted, the state would not have to cede fiefs and pay the cost of the new nobles, and the ministers would not have conspired to the ruination of their family. The matter is over and done with, but the only person not to have been rewarded for his merit is Xu Fu. I hope Your Majesty will see this clearly. Please recognize that the strategy of shifting the firewood and bending the chimney is superior in merit to people who get singed hair and scarred bodies." The Emperor thereupon gave Xu Fu 10 rolls of silk, and later appointed him a court gentleman.

Just after Xuandi's accession to the throne, he paid homage at the Temple of Gaodi and General-in-Chief Huo Guang sat with him in a chariot, but the Emperor was very tense, as if there was a thorn in his back. Later, when Chariot Horse General Zhang Anshi accompanied him instead of Huo Guang, the Son of Heaven felt quite at ease, his body relaxed, feeling secure and intimate. After the death of Huo Guang, his clan was terminated, and this gave rise

【原文】

骖乘。”

至成帝时，为光置守冢百家，吏卒奉祠焉。元始二年，封光从父昆弟曾孙阳为博陆侯，千户。

——卷六十八《霍光金日磾传》第三十八

【今译】

不会被容留，霍氏的祸患开始于陪乘。”

到成帝时，为霍光安置了一百家守墓的人，吏卒按时祭祀。元始二年，霍光堂兄弟的曾孙霍阳被封为博陆侯，赐食邑一千户。

to the folk saying: "He who has power and influence to shake the monarch will not be kept, and Huo's scourge began when keeping company in the imperial chariot."

In the reign of Chengdi, 100 families of grave keepers were allotted for Huo Guang, and officials and soldiers offered sacrifice. In year two of the Yuanshi reign period, Huo Yang, Guang's great grandnephew, was made Marquis of Bolu, with a fief of 1,000 households.

鲍宣传

【原文】

鲍宣字子都，渤海高城人也。好学明经，为县乡啬夫，守束州丞。后为都尉太守功曹，举孝廉为郎，病去官，复为州从事。大司马卫将军王商辟宣，荐为议郎，后以病去。哀帝初，大司空何武除宣为西曹掾，甚敬重焉，荐宣为谏大夫，迁豫州牧。岁馀，丞相司直郭钦奏："宣举错烦苛，代二千石署吏听讼，所察过诏条。行部乘传去法驾，驾一马，舍宿乡亭，为众所非。"宣坐免。归家数月，复征为谏大夫。

宣每居位，常上书谏争，其言少文多实。是时帝祖母傅太后欲与

【今译】

鲍宣，字子都，渤海高城人。勤奋好学，精通经义，先为县乡啬夫官，暂代束州县丞。后为都尉太守功曹，举孝廉被选任为郎，因病辞官，又为州从事。大司马卫将军王商曾征辟鲍宣，举荐他为议郎，后又因病离任。哀帝即位之初，大司空何武拜鲍宣为西曹掾，对他非常敬重，推荐他为谏大夫，又转任豫州牧。一年多后，丞相司直郭钦上奏说："鲍宣施政繁琐苛刻，他代替郡守任用官吏办理诉讼，所监察的问题超出了皇上所制定的条例。出去巡视考察时车乘规制也不遵典制，驾一匹马，夜宿乡亭，被众人所非议。"鲍宣因此而被免职。回家数月后，又被征召为谏大夫。

鲍宣在位为官时，常常上书进谏据理力争，他的话少有虚文，

Chapter 15

Biography of Bao Xuan

Bao Xuan, styled Zidu, was born in Gaocheng of Bohai. Studious, versed in the classics, at first he served as a bailiff for the county and township, acting as aide to the magistrate of Shuzhou. He served as Defender and then was in charge of the labor section for the commandery governor. He was recommended as filial and incorrupt to become a court gentleman, and later resigned due to illness, but then became an official retainer. Commander-in-Chief and General of Guards Wang Shang picked Bao Xuan and recommended him as court gentleman for consultation, but later he left office due to illness. In the first years of Emperor Aidi, the Grand Minister for Works He Wu appointed him as Administrator of the West Section. He respected Bao Xuan highly, and recommended him as a grand master of remonstrance and promoted him to Regional Governor of Yuzhou. More than a year later, Guo Qin, a rectifier to the prime minister petitioned: "Bao Xuan's measures are complicated and demanding, he handles litigation on behalf of the 2,000-picul officials and he examines questions beyond the regulations drawn up by the Emperor. When out on inspection he rides a level of carriage that does not conform to the Code, drives a one-horse cart, and lodges overnight at rural posts, attracting criticism from all parties." As a result, Bao Xuan was removed from office, but after staying home a few months, he was recalled, this time as a grand master of remonstrance.

Whenever Bao Xuan served as an official, he frequently sent memorials of remonstration; these avoided fancy verbosity, but went straight to the heart of things in plain words. At that time, Emperor

【原文】

成帝母俱称尊号，封爵亲属，丞相孔光、大司空师丹、何武、大司马傅喜始执正议，失傅太后指，皆免官。丁、傅子弟并进，董贤贵幸，宣以谏大夫从其后，上书谏曰：

窃见孝成皇帝时，外亲持权，人人牵引所私以充塞朝廷，妨贤人路，浊乱天下，奢泰亡度，穷困百姓，是以日蚀且十，彗星四起。危亡之征，陛下所亲见也，今奈何反覆剧于前乎！朝臣亡有大儒骨鲠、白首耆艾、魁垒之士；论议通古今，喟然动众心，忧国如饥渴者，臣未见也。敦外亲小童及幸臣董贤等在公门省户下，陛下欲与此共承天地，安海内，甚难。今世俗谓不智者为能，谓智者为不能。昔尧放四罪而天下服，今除一吏而众皆惑；古刑人尚服，今赏人反惑。请寄为奸，群小日进。国家空虚，用

【今译】

却朴实而切中时弊。当时哀帝的祖母傅太后想和成帝的母亲同称尊号，并为其亲属封官授爵，丞相孔光、大司空师丹、何武、大司马傅喜等人一开始就坚持正义，因此而违逆了傅太后的旨意，于是都被免官。丁、傅二氏外戚子弟都得以进升，董贤受宠幸而显贵，鲍宣以谏大夫的身份继孔光、师丹、何武、傅喜等人之后，上书进谏说：

我私下里看到孝成皇帝时，外戚掌权，人人都牵引自己所亲近的人充满了朝廷，堵塞了贤德之人的进升之路，使得天下一片混乱，奢侈无度，百姓穷困，因此，天上发生日食将近十次，彗星四次出现。那些危亡的征兆是陛下亲眼所见的，现在怎么反而又比以前更甚了呢？朝廷大臣中没有正直的儒学之士，没有老资格而富有经验的老人，没有健壮的武士；通晓古今历史，能够一呼百应，忧国忧民犹如饥渴而思饮食之迫切者，臣下也没有见到。倚重任用外亲小童及佞幸之臣董贤等在朝廷身居要职，陛下想和这些人一起奉天承运，安定天下，是很难办到的。现今世俗把缺少智慧的人称为能人，把有才智的人看作无能。过去唐尧将共工、驩兜、三苗、鲧四个罪人流放而天下臣服，今天拜授一个官吏而众人疑惑；古时施以刑罚而人还顺服，现在行以奖赏人

Aidi's grandmother Empress Dowager Fu contended for the honored title with Emperor Chengdi's mother, and both tried to enfeoff their own relatives. Prime Minister Kong Guang, the grand ministers of works Shi Dan and He Wu, and Commander-in-Chief Fu Xi, stuck to justice right from the start, running counter to the Empress Dowager Fu's will, so they were all dismissed. The relatives from the Ding and Fu clans were promoted in their stead, and Dong Xian got very favored treatment as a dignitary. Bao Xuan, as a grand master of remonstrance, and following the example of the dismissed ministers, wrote a memorial objecting, saying:

> *I saw that in the reign of Emperor Chengdi, the family of his wife had power, and everyone brought in people close to them to fill the court, thereby blocking the path to promotion for virtuous people, plunging the empire into confusion. Their inordinate luxury distressed the poor people, so the solar eclipse occurred nearly 10 times, and comets appeared in all corners. Your Majesty saw these signs of peril with your own eyes, so how is it that things have deteriorated even more? Among the courtiers there are no upright Confucians to provide backbone, no veteran and experienced graybeards, nor stouthearted warriors, I do not see anyone arguing with knowledge of ancient and modern history, sonorously moving us, concerned for the fate of our country like a hungry man avid for sustenance. With the childish in-laws and sycophants like Dong Xian enjoying preferment at Court, it is very difficult for Your Majesty to carry on the virtue of heaven and earth, and enjoy stability of the world whilst they are a factor. It is the current custom to call unwise people as capable, and intelligent people as incompetent. In antiquity, Yao exiled the four criminals to win the support of the world, but today, when an official is appointed the multitudes are bemused; in ancient times penalties were imposed and people showed obedience,*

【原文】

度不足。民流亡，去城郭，盗贼并起，吏为残贼，岁增于前。

凡民有七亡：阴阳不和，水旱为灾，一亡也；县官重责更赋租税，二亡也；贪吏并公，受取不已，三亡也；豪强大姓，蚕食亡厌，四亡也；苛吏繇役，失农桑时，五亡也；部落鼓鸣，男女遮迣，六亡也；盗贼劫略，取民财物，七亡也。七亡尚可，又有七死：酷吏殴杀，一死也；治狱深刻，二死也；冤陷亡辜，三死也；盗贼横发，四死也；怨仇相残，五死也；岁恶饥饿，六死也；时气疾疫，七死也。民有七亡而无一得，欲望国安，诚难；民有七死而无一生，欲望刑措，诚难。此非公卿守相贪残成化之所致邪？群臣幸得居尊官，食重禄，岂有肯加恻隐于细民，助陛下流教化者邪？志但在营私家，称宾客，为奸利而已。以苟容曲

【今译】

们反生疑虑。相互请托施行奸计，奸佞小人日益受到重用。国家府库空虚，费用不足。人民流亡，离开城郭，盗贼蜂拥而起，官吏残害百姓，一年比一年严重。

造成老百姓失业流离的原因有七：一、阴阳不和，水旱成灾；二、县官催以沉重的租税和更赋；三、贪官污吏侵吞公产，不断地进行搜刮；四、豪强大族蚕食无厌；五、苛暴之吏征发徭役，贻误了农时；六、乡间村落时时响起警戒盗贼的桴鼓之声，百姓不分男女都不得不出动围击追捕；七、盗贼抢劫掠夺百姓财物。这七种导致百姓流离失业的祸端尚且不说，又有七种导致百姓死亡的因素：一、被酷吏击杀；二、判案量刑过于严厉苛刻；三、冤枉陷害无辜；四、盗贼突然出现；五、结怨结仇者相互残杀；六、年景歉收，人遭饥馑；七、气候恶劣，疾病流行。百姓有七失而无一得，想要国家安定，实在是很难；人民有七死而无一生，想要搁置刑罚，也是很难的。这种状况难道不是公卿及郡守国相等地方官吏贪婪残酷成风所造成的吗？大臣们有幸身居高位，领取丰厚的俸禄，他们中又有谁能体恤百姓疾苦，辅佐陛下流布恩泽教化呢？他们的心思都只用在经营私家利益，招纳收买宾客，贪图不正当的利益而已。大家都以阿谀顺从为贤德，以明

but now rewarding people produces misgivings. Mutual favor-mongering brews devious schemes, crafty villains are promoted every day. The national treasuries are empty, and we cannot meet our costs. The people are forced to leave their homes, deserting their towns and cities, robber bands swarm up, and officials became cruel oppressors, more harsh with every passing year.

There are seven reasons why the people are displaced from their farmland and livelihoods: 1. yin *and* yang *are out of harmony, causing flood and drought; 2. heavy government taxation and corvee duties; 3. the corrupt officials embezzle public property, constantly receiving bribes; 4. insatiable encroachment of the gallants and big clans; 5. officials' harsh levying of corvee, with adverse impact on the farming season; 6. village alert drums constantly sounding, and both sexes mobilized to surround and hunt thieves; 7. thieves looting property. The seven causes of unemployment are as nothing, compared to the seven factors that cause people's death: 1. killing by ruthless officials; 2. excessively harsh sentences; 3. wrongful treatment or framing of the innocent; 4. sudden appearance of robbers; 5. feud killing; 6. poor harvests and famine; 7. extreme weather and epidemics. It is very difficult to aspire to national stability when the people have seven reasons for loss but not one for gain; it is also very difficult to lay aside penalties when the people have seven ways of dying but not one for living. Was this situation not caused by the greed and cruelty of the nobles, ministers, governors and the prime ministers of fiefs? The ministers are fortunate enough to hold high positions and receive a generous salary, so how can they be compassionate to the sufferings of common people, and assist Your Majesty to spread moral education? Their sole concern is the interests of their private operations or pleasing*

【原文】

从为贤，以拱默尸禄为智，谓如臣宣等为愚。陛下擢臣岩穴，诚冀有益豪毛，岂徒欲使臣美食大官，重高门之地哉！

天下乃皇天之天下也，陛下上为皇天子，下为黎庶父母，为天牧养元元，视之当如一，合《尸鸠》之诗。今贫民菜食不厌，衣又穿空，父子夫妇不能相保，诚可为酸鼻。陛下不救，将安所归命乎？奈何独私养外亲与幸臣董贤，多赏赐以大万数，使奴从宾客浆酒霍肉，苍头庐儿皆用致富！非天意也。及汝昌侯傅商亡功而封。夫官爵非陛下之官爵，乃天下之官爵也。陛下取非其官，官非其人，而望天说民服，岂不难哉！

方阳侯孙宠、宜陵侯息夫躬辩足以移众，强可用独立，奸人

【今译】

哲保身拱手默立只管领食俸禄为聪明，而把像我这样敢于直言的人看作是愚蠢。陛下您选拔大臣于山岩洞穴之中，实希望能对朝廷对国家有所帮助，难道陛下只是想让臣子们享受着高官厚禄锦衣玉食，以增添宫阙殿堂的威严吗？

天下是皇天的天下，陛下上为皇天之子，下为黎民父母，代替皇天统治养育众生，对他们当一视同仁，正如《诗经》中《尸鸠》一诗所说的那样。现在贫苦百姓食不裹腹，衣不蔽体，父子夫妇都无力相互保护，实在令人心酸。陛下不救助他们，他们将归附何处呢？为什么只厚待外戚和幸臣董贤，给他们的赏赐多以万数，以至于他们的奴婢侍从和门客都视酒肉为最普通低级的饮食，连奴婢侍从都跟着富裕起来了！这是违背天意的。至于汝昌侯傅商则无功而受封爵。官爵不是陛下的官爵，而是天下的官爵。陛下拿不属于自己的官爵授予不当受此官爵的人，却还指望天悦人服，又怎么可能呢？

方阳侯孙宠、宜陵侯息夫躬二人诡辩的口才足以打动众人，其势力强大足以独挡一面，他们是奸人中的枭雄，是最危险的人

of their hangers-on, seeking a dishonest advantage. Instant acquiescence and submission are regarded as virtue, and standing by in silence for the sake of a salary is seen as wisdom; but straight-talking individuals such as I are taken as idiots. Your Majesty promoted me from the rock cave, in the hope that I might help the Court and the country. Surely your Majesty's intention was not simply that the courtiers should enjoy the best of food and dress, and increase the majesty of the imperial palace hall?

The empire belongs to heaven, and Your Majesty is the Son of Heaven above, and the parent of the people below, shepherding the commoners on behalf of heaven, treating them with equal righteousness, as described in the ode "Cuckoos." Poor people now have neither food for their stomachs nor clothes for their backs; father and son, husband and wife cannot protect each other, and this is quite bitterly painful. What recourse have they if Your Majesty does not rescue them? Why favor only the in-law's family and the sycophant Dong Xian, rewarding them more than a million, so that even their serfs, servants and hangers-on regard wine and meat as cheap eating, and even their slaves and attendants have followed them into affluence! This is by no means the will of Heaven. Fu Shang Marquis of Ruchang was ennobled, without meritorious deeds to justify the elevation. The official rankings and titular honors are not the prerogative of Your Majesty, they belong to the empire. Your Majesty takes something that is not your own to give, and bestows it on an undeserving person. How do you still expect to please heaven and convince the people?

Sun Chong the Marquis of Fangyang and Xi Fugong the Marquis of Yiling argue eloquently enough to move the crowd, and are influential enough to work independently. They are the most ruthless and ambitious of a bunch of villains, the most

【原文】

之雄，或世尤剧者也，宜以时罢退。及外亲幼童未通经术者，皆宜令休就师傅。急征故大司马傅喜使领外亲。故大司空何武、师丹、故丞相孔光、故左将军彭宣，经皆更博士，位皆历三公，智谋威信，可与建教化，图安危。龚胜为司直，郡国皆慎选举，三辅委输官不敢为奸，可大委任也。陛下前以小不忍退武等，海内失望。陛下尚能容亡功德者甚众，曾不能忍武等邪！治天下者当用天下之心为心，不得自专快意而已也。上之皇天见谴，下之黎庶怨恨，次有谏争之臣，陛下苟欲自薄而厚恶臣，天下犹不听也。臣虽愚戆，独不知多受禄赐，美食太官，广田宅，厚妻子，不与恶人结仇怨以安身邪？诚迫大义，官以谏争为职，不敢不竭愚。惟陛下少留神明，览《五经》之文，原圣人之至意，深思天

【今译】

物，应当找机会及时将他们免退。至于那些不懂经术的外戚幼童，则应让他们都离任从师就学。应立即征召原大司马傅喜让他统领外戚。原大司空何武、师丹，原丞相孔光，原左将军彭宣，他们精通经义，都任过博士，且皆位历三公，他们的智谋威信，足以兴立教化、图谋国家存亡之大事。龚胜为司直，郡国都认真对待选举，京畿三辅委输官不敢投机取巧，可以委以大任。陛下先前因小有不快于心，不能忍受而罢免了何武等人，国人都很失望。您既然连那一大批毫无功德的人都能容忍，为何就不能容忍何武等人呢？治理天下者应当想天下人之所想，不能只凭一己之好恶行事。上有皇天谴责，下有黎民怨恨，还有敢于直谏的臣下奋起抗争，陛下就是想要减损自己的威德而增添恶人的势力，天下之人也不会听从的。我虽愚钝，难道不懂得多受俸禄和赏赐，做大官、吃美食，扩展田宅，厚养妻子儿女，不与恶人结怨以过安稳日子吗？实在是迫于大义而为，官以谏诤为天职，不敢不竭尽愚忠。希望陛下稍加留意，阅览《五经》的内容，探寻圣人至

dangerous, so we must find an early opportunity to dismiss them. As for those young in-laws ignorant of the classics, we should make them leave their posts and go study. Fu Xi the former Commander-in-Chief should be immediately summoned to command the in-laws. The former Grand Ministers for Works He Wu and Shi Dan, the former prime minister Kong Guang, the former Left General Peng Xuan, are all skilled in classics and were erudites, and were ennobled as the Three Excellencies; their resourcefulness and prestige are enough to establish moral education and plan for national survival. With Gong Sheng as Rectifier, the prefectures and fiefs are conscientious in their selection and recommendation of talents, and officials under the Three Metropolitan Guardians dare not be fraudulent, so Gong can be entrusted with great responsibility. Your Majesty previously dismissed He Wu and others because you could not tolerate some small dissatisfaction, and the people within the seas were disappointed. Since you tolerate a large number of people with no merit at all to speak of, why can you not be lenient to He Wu and the others? Rulers should think what the people are thinking, not act purely on the basis of their own likes and dislikes. Up above you have heaven's condemnation; down below is the resentment of the people, and the protesting remonstrators too. Even if Your Majesty wants to detract from your own virtue and increase the strength of evil ministers, the people of the world will not acquiesce to it. I am stupid, but who on earth doesn't want a stable life, with high salary and rewards, delicious food, expanses of fields and houses, wife and children well taken care of, and not incur hatred of evil men? I am forced to the righteous cause and it is the duty of officials to admonish. Duty-bound, I dare not withhold my foolish opinion. I hope that Your Majesty will spare a little attention to this, and read the texts of the "Five Classics," explore the

【原文】

地之戒。臣宣呐钝于辞，不胜惓惓，尽死节而已。

上以宣名儒，优容之。

是时郡国地震，民讹言行筹，明年正月朔日蚀，上乃征孔光，免孙宠、息夫躬，罢侍中诸曹黄门郎数十人。宣复上书言：

陛下父事天，母事地，子养黎民。即位已来，父亏明，母震动，子讹言相惊恐。今日蚀于三始，诚可畏惧。小民正月朔日尚恐毁败器物，何况于日亏乎！陛下深内自责，避正殿，举直言，求过失，罢退外亲及旁仄素餐之人，征拜孔光为光禄大夫，发觉孙宠、息夫躬过恶，免官遣就国，众庶歙然，莫不说喜。天人同

【今译】

诚至深之意，深思天地的告诫。臣鲍宣言语迟钝，感情恳切，尽忠守节而已。

皇上因鲍宣是名儒，因此对他很宽容，没有怪罪于他。

正在这时郡国发生了地震，民间谣言四起纷纷占卜求签，第二年正月初一出现日食，皇上于是征召孔光，罢免了孙宠、息夫躬，又罢退侍中诸曹黄门郎数十人。鲍宣又上书说：

陛下应当像侍奉父亲一样侍奉苍天，应像侍奉母亲一样侍奉大地，像养育自己的孩子一样养育黎民，陛下即位以来，苍天缺少光明，大地发生震动，百姓间谣言流传相互惊吓。如今日食出现于岁、月、日三始之时，确实令人畏惧。普通百姓在正月初一尚且怕毁坏器物，更何况太阳出现亏缺呢？陛下能深深自责，避开正殿，举用敢于直谏之士以检讨自己的过失，罢免外戚及您身边那些白食俸禄的无用之人，征拜孔光为光禄大夫，审察孙宠、息夫躬的过失和罪恶，让他们免官回到自己的侯国中去，众人和洽，无不欢欣鼓舞。天人同心，人心顺悦则天意和解。到二月丙

deep sincere meaning of the sages, and ponder the warnings of heaven and earth. My words lack eloquence, but my sincerity is inexhaustible, and my loyalty undying.

Because Bao Xuan had a famous reputation as a Confucian, the Emperor was very tolerant and did not punish him.

Just then there were earthquakes in the prefectures and fiefs, and rumors rose like wildfire; so people all worshipped the Queen Mother of the West and cast divination lots to her. On the first day of the first month of the next year there was a solar eclipse, so the Emperor did reinstate Kong Guang, and removed Sun Chong and Xi Fugong, and dismissed the palace attendants and gentlemen of the palace gate, dozens of them. Bao Xuan again petitioned:

Your Majesty should serve heaven as the father, serve earth as the mother, and raise the people as your own children; but there is lack of brightness in heaven since Your Majesty ascended the throne, the earth has shaken and trembled, and among the people panicky rumors spread. Now a solar eclipse has occurred at the start of the year, the month, the day. It is indeed enough to make one tremble. Ordinary people fear the destruction of vessels on the first day of the year: how much more should they fear the dimness appearing in the sun? Your Majesty was deep in remorse, avoiding the main hall; you selected courageous remonstrators to review your own fault, dismissed the in-laws and the useless parasites of your coterie. You appointed Kong Guang as Grand Master for Splendid Happiness, scrutinized the fault and crimes of Sun Chong and Xi Fugong, and dismissed them back to their own fiefs. The people were relieved and rejoiced to a man. Heaven and man are one heart, so when people are happy, the will of heaven is reconciled. On the 16th day of the second moon, a white rainbow violated the sun, and it was overcast but did not rain. This means heaven's melancholy is not yet resolved and the

【原文】

心，人心说则天意解矣。乃二月丙戌，白虹虷日，连阴不雨，此天有忧结未解，民有怨望未塞者也。

侍中驸马都尉董贤本无葭莩之亲，但以令色谀言自进，赏赐亡度，竭尽府藏，并合三第尚以为小，复坏暴室。贤父子坐使天子使者将作治第，行夜吏卒皆得赏赐。上冢有会，辄太官为供。海内贡献当养一君，今反尽之贤家，岂天意与民意邪！天(下)[不]可久负，厚之如此，反所以害之也。诚欲哀贤，宜为谢过天地，解仇海内，免遣就国，收乘舆器物，还之县官。如此，可以父子终其性命；不者，海内之所仇，未有得久安者也。

孙宠、息夫躬不宜居国，可皆免以视天下。复征何武、师丹、彭宣、傅喜，旷然使民易视，以应天心，建立大政，以兴太平之端。

高门去省户数十步，求见出入，二年未省，欲使海濒仄陋自通，远矣！愿赐数刻之间，极竭罜罜之思，退入三泉，死亡所恨。

【今译】

戌，白虹犯日，连阴不雨，这是天有忧结未释，人民心中尚有不满的征兆。

侍中驸马都尉董贤与皇室本没有任何亲戚关系，他却靠着巧言令色阿谀献媚而得以晋升，皇上对他的赏赐没有节制，用尽国库资财，合并三处宅第赐给他，尚嫌狭小，又将暴室之地赐予他。董贤父子坐在那里指使着天子的使者工匠修建宅第，为其府第巡夜打更的吏卒都能得到赏赐。他家上坟或有宴请聚会，都要少府太官供给物资，进行操办。全国各地进贡的物品，本是供养皇上的，现在反而都集中到董贤家里，这难道符合天意民心吗！天意民心不可长久辜负，如此厚待董贤，其实是在害他。陛下如果真的怜爱董贤，就应为他向天地谢罪，消除天下人士对他的怨恨，罢免他的官职，让他回归其封国，没收其所乘车舆和各种器物，还给县官。这样，尚可以使他们父子安度余生；否则，为天下人所仇恨者，是不可能长久过安稳日子的。

孙宠、息夫躬二人不宜身居要职，可罢免他们以示天下。再征用何武、师丹、彭宣、傅喜等人，使人民看到一个清明开朗的新气象，顺应皇天之心，建立完善的政治，以中兴天下太平之业。

高门距省户仅仅数十步，想要省视不过是一出一入的功夫而已，却尚且二年未省视了，在这种情况下，想要使天涯海角偏僻之地自行通达，太不可能了！希望陛下恩赐片刻时间，让我陈述我的浅见，然后，那怕是身葬黄泉，我也死而无憾了。

people are discontented and their hearts not satisfied.

Commandant-Escort within the palace Dong Xian is not related in the slightest way to the imperial family, but he was able to get himself promoted by means of clever flattery. His imperial rewards know no bounds. The resources of the state treasury have been exhausted for him; merging three houses was still too small for him, so the palace rooms were granted him too. Dong Xian and his son sat there ordering the emperor's messenger and craftsmen to build his mansion, and even his mansion watchmen could get some reward. He holds banquets even after visiting his family grave, everything being supplied courtesy of the official provisioner. The tribute from all over the country is meant for the Emperor, but now it is all diverted to Xian's home. Is this the will of heaven or the people? Heaven cannot be betrayed for long, so generosity towards Dong Xian is in fact to harm him. If you really love Dong Xian, you should apologize for him to heaven and earth, so as to relieve the world's hatred for him, dismiss him from office, have him return to his fief; confiscate his carriages and equipment for return to the throne. In this way, he and his son may spend their remaining days in peace. Otherwise, those hated by the people at large cannot count on a peaceful and stable life for long.

Sun Chong and Xi Fugong should not be administering the country. Both can be impeached to show the world. Re-employ He Wu, Shi Dan, Peng Xuan, and Fu Xi; this will unveil new, bright skies for the people, and conform to the will of heaven, establishing fine governance, for the cause of national resurgence and peace. The High Gate is only a dozen paces from the palace gate and it is but one short trip inside, but my requests for audience have been rejected for two years; how much less accessible therefore to those at the ends of the earth? I beg Your Majesty's grace of a moment's time to let me state

【原文】

上感大异，纳宣言，征何武、彭宣，旬月皆复为三公。拜宣为司隶。时哀帝改司隶校尉但为司隶，官比司直。

丞相孔光四时行园陵，官属以令行驰道中，宣出逢之，使吏钩止丞相掾史，没入其车马，摧辱宰相。事下御史中丞，侍御史至司隶官，欲捕从事，闭门不肯内。宣坐距闭使者，亡人臣礼，大不敬，不道，下廷尉狱。博士弟子济南王咸举幡太学下，曰："欲救鲍司隶者会此下。"诸生会者千馀人。朝日，遮丞相孔光自言，丞相车不得行，又守阙上书。上遂抵宣罪减死一等，髡钳。宣既被刑，乃徙之上党，以为其地宜田牧，又少豪俊，易长雄，遂家于长子。

【今译】

皇上对鲍宣所言大感惊异，于是采纳了他的意见，起用何武、彭宣，十天半月间都将他们复任为三公。拜鲍宣为司隶。这时哀帝改司隶校尉为司隶，官位级别相当于司直。

丞相孔光负责四时巡视园陵，其属官仗恃有皇帝的敕令而违反规制，乘车在驰道中行走，鲍宣外出正好遇见，鲍宣就让属吏扣留了丞相掾史，并没收其车马，羞辱丞相。此事被交到御史中丞那里处理，侍御史到司隶官衙处，想要逮捕鲍宣的随从官吏，鲍宣闭门不让其入内。鲍宣因此而犯了拒绝接纳使者、没有人臣之礼、大不敬、不守道义等罪过，被捕下廷尉狱。博士弟子济南人王咸举着一杆旗帜到太学门前，说："想救鲍司隶的人请集中在此旗帜下。"太学生聚集了一千余人。到了上朝之日，他们拦住丞相孔光自己说明情况，丞相的车马不能前行，又守候在宫阙门前，上书皇帝。皇帝于是将鲍宣的死罪递减一等，剃去头发，用铁圈束颈。鲍宣被判刑后，便举家迁徙到上党，他认为上党地区适于农耕和放牧，又少豪俊之士，容易为首称雄，于是就把家安在上党的长子县。

my humble view; this granted, even if I die and am buried in the underworld, I shall not regret it.

The Emperor, startled at Bao Xuan's remonstrance, adopted his advice to employ He Wu, Peng Xuan and re-appointed them as the Excellencies within two weeks. He appointed Bao Xuan as Metropolitan Commandant. Then the Emperor changed the office to metropolitan director, on the same level as Rectifier to the prime minister.

Kong Guang, the prime minister, was responsible for regular patrolling of the imperial mausoleums, but his subsidiaries, in violation of regulations rode in the middle of the Royal Road on the pretext of royal authority. Bao Xuan happened to see them on his way out and ordered to have the prime minister's aide detained and the carriage confiscated, in order to humiliate the prime minister. The case was submitted to the Censor-in-Chief, and an attendant censor went to the office of Metropolitan Director, wanting to arrest Bao Xuan's entourage, but Bao Xuan closed the gate to prevent their entry. He was thus thrown into prison of the Chamberlain of Law Enforcement for the crime of refusing entry to the messenger, for not observing ministerial protocol, for gross disrespect and not observing the Way. Erudite disciple Wang Xian from Jinan held a banner in front of the Imperial College, and said: "Those who want to save Metropolitan Director Bao, please gather under the banner." More than a thousand scholars assembled. On the day of the court audience, they stopped Prime Minister Kong's carriage to explain the situation and preventing his advance; and then, waiting at the palace gate, they sent a letter to the Emperor, who reduced the capital sentence by a degree. The lesser punishment was to have his head shaved and wear an iron yoke locked around the neck. Bao Xuan, thus sentenced, moved to Shangdang. He believed that the Shangdang region was suitable for farming and animal husbandry, and there were fewer gallants, thus easier for him to dominate, so he

【原文】

平帝即位，王莽秉政，阴有篡国之心，乃风州郡以罪法案诛诸豪杰，及汉忠直臣不附己者，宣及何武等皆死。时名捕陇西辛兴，兴与宣女婿许绀俱过宣，一饭去，宣不知情，坐系狱，自杀。

——卷七十二《王贡两龚鲍传》第四十二

【今译】

汉平帝即位后，王莽擅权，暗里有阴谋篡夺帝位之心，于是他暗示各州郡罗织罪名陷害诛杀豪杰之士，至于对汉朝忠诚正直不愿攀附自己的大臣，鲍宣及何武等人都被处死。当时通缉陇西人辛兴，辛兴与鲍宣的女婿许绀一起到鲍宣家，吃了一顿饭就离开了，鲍宣不知实情，受牵连被捕下狱，自杀而死。

settled his family in Changzi County.

When Emperor Pingdi ascended the throne, Wang Mang held political power, and secretly plotted to usurp the throne. So he hinted that each prefecture and fief cook up charges, to frame and kill the gallants. As for ministers of integrity who are loyal to Han and unaligned with Wang Mang, Bao Xuan, He Wu and others were put to death. At the time Bao Xuan was visited for a meal by his son-in-law Xu Gan, together with Xin Jing from Longxi, who happened to be a wanted man. The two left afterwards and though Bao Xuan was not in on things, he was implicated, arrested and imprisoned. He committed suicide.

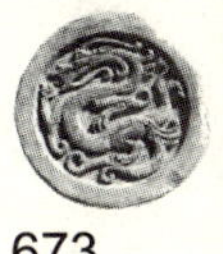

扬雄传赞

【原文】

赞曰：雄之自序云尔。初，雄年四十馀，自蜀来至游京师，大司马车骑将军王音奇其文雅，召以为门下史，荐雄待诏，岁馀，奏《羽猎赋》，除为郎，给事黄门，与王莽、刘歆并。哀帝之初，又与董贤同官。当成、哀、平间，莽、贤皆为三公，权倾人主，所荐莫不拔擢，而雄三世不徙官。及莽篡位，谈说之士用符命称功德获封爵者甚众，雄复不侯，以耆老久次转为大夫，恬于势利乃如是。实好古而乐道，其意欲求文章成名于后世，以为经莫大于《易》，故作《太玄》；传莫大于《论语》，作《法言》；史篇莫善于《仓颉》，作《训纂》；箴莫善于《虞箴》，作《州箴》；赋莫深于

【今译】

赞曰：这是扬雄的自序。起初，扬雄四十多岁时，从蜀来游京师，大司马车骑将军王音欣赏其文才，召作门下史，推荐扬雄待诏，一年多后，上奏《羽猎赋》，除官为郎，给事黄门，和王莽、刘歆并列。哀帝初，又和董贤同官。成、哀、平年间，王莽、董贤都作了三公，权过人君，推荐的人没有不提拔的，但扬雄三代不升官。到王莽篡位，论谈者用符命赞美其功德而被封爵的人很多，扬雄仍不被封侯，因年纪大而渐升为大夫，他就是如此淡泊势利。确实好古爱道，想以文章在后世扬名，认为经最大的是《易》，所以作《太玄》；传最好的是《论语》，所以作《法言》；史篇最好的是《仓颉》，所以作《训纂》，箴诫最好的是《虞箴》，所以作《州箴》；赋最深的是《离骚》，所以相背而推广它；辞最华丽的

Chapter 16

Author's Comments on Biography of Yang Xiong

Author's Comments: This is Yang Xiong's preface. Yang Xiong was in his forties when he came from Shu [Sichuan] to the capital. The Commander-in-Chief Wang Yin, a chariot horse general, appreciating Yang Xiong's literary talent, employed him as a scribe, and then recommended him as Gentleman in Attendance. More than a year later, he submitted "Rhapsody on Imperial Hunting," and was appointed a court gentleman, to serve as palace attendant together with Wang Mang and Liu Xin. Early in the reign of Emperor Aidi, he became a colleague of Dong Xian. In the reign of emperors Chengdi, Aidi and Pingdi, Wang Mang and Dong Xian were made great nobles of the realm, as powerful as the monarch himself. As a result, every person recommended by the two received promotion. Yang Xiong, however, was not promoted during the three reigns. When Wang Mang usurped the throne, many eloquent scholars who praised his merits citing signs of the Mandate of Heaven were knighted. Yang Xiong, however, was still not ennobled, but in consideration of his age, he gradually rose to a grand master. This shows his indifference to power. What he did value was antiquity and the Way, and he aspired to be renowned in later ages on account of his writings. Considering the greatest of the classics to be the *Book of Changes*, he wrote *Tai Xuan*, or the *Great Dark Mystery*; taking *The Analects of Confucius* as the best commentary, he wrote *Fa Yan*, or *Words to Live By*; thinking *Chang Jie* the best textbook, he wrote *Teachings Compiled*; no proverbs were better than *Yu's Proverbs*, so he wrote *Regional Proverbs*; the deepest rhapsody was *Encountering Sorrow*, so he analogized it to promote it; the flowery

【原文】

《离骚》，反而广之；辞莫丽于相如，作四赋：皆斟酌其本，相与放依而驰骋云。用心于内，不求于外，于时人皆曶之；唯刘歆及范逡敬焉，而桓谭以为绝伦。

王莽时，刘歆、甄丰皆为上公，莽既以符命自立，即位之后，欲绝其原以神前事，而丰子寻、歆子棻复献之。莽诛丰父子，投棻四裔，辞所连及，便收不请。时雄校书天禄阁上，治狱使者来，欲收雄，雄恐不能自免，乃从阁上自投下，几死。莽闻之曰："雄素不与事，何故在此？"间请问其故，乃刘棻尝从雄学作奇字，雄不知情。有诏勿问。然京师为之语曰："惟寂寞，自投阁；爰清静，作符命。"

雄以病免，复召为大夫。家素贫，耆酒，人希至其门。时有好事者载酒肴从游学，而钜鹿侯芭常从雄居，受其《太玄》、《法言》焉。

【今译】

是相如，所以作四赋：都探索本源，模仿发挥。用心在内，不求于外，当时人都轻视他；只有刘歆和范逡敬重他，而桓谭认为他无与伦比。

王莽时，刘歆、甄丰都做了上公，王莽既是假藉符命自立，即位之后想禁绝这种做法来使前事得到神化，而甄丰的儿子甄寻、刘歆的儿子刘棻又奏献符瑞之事。王莽杀了甄丰父子，流放刘棻到四裔，供辞所牵连到的，立即收系不必奏请。当时扬雄在天禄阁上校书，办案的使者来了，要抓扬雄，扬雄怕不能逃脱，便从阁上跳下，差点死了。王莽听到后说："扬雄一向不参与其事，为什么在此案中？"暗中查问其原因，原来刘棻曾跟扬雄学写过奇字，扬雄不知情。下诏不追究他。然而京师为此评道："因寂寞，自投阁；因清静，作符命。"

扬雄因病免职，又召为大夫。家境一向贫寒，爱喝酒，人很少到其家。当时有多事的人带着酒菜跟他学习，钜鹿侯芭常跟扬雄一起居住，学了《太玄》、《法言》。刘歆也曾看到，对扬雄说：

language of Sima Xiangru was the most gorgeous, so he wrote four *fu* rhapsodies. All his writings went back to explore the source, copy and celebrate the original. His exertions were all internal, not caring about outward appearances or success. His contemporaries despised him, only Liu Xin and Fan Qun respecting him. Huan Tan, however, thought him unparalleled.

In the reign of Wang Mang, Liu Xin and Zhen Feng were the greatest nobles of the realm. Wang Mang had had himself enthroned by faked indications of the Mandate of Heaven. Now, being in power, he wanted to stop this practice so as to get the previous events sanctioned by the gods. But Zhen Feng's son Zhen Xun and the son of Liu Xin Liu Fen wrote memorials to talk about the practice again. Wang Mang killed Zhen Feng and his son, and exiled Liu Fen to the borders. Those implicated in their confession were immediately imprisoned without appeal. Yang Xiong was collating books in the Tianlu Mansion when the law-enforcement messengers came to apprehend him. Afraid he would not get acquitted, he jumped out of the building and almost died. Wang Mang reacted to the news, saying: "Yang Xiong has never been involved in such matters; why is he implicated in this case?" Secret interrogation revealed that Liu Fen had learned from Yang Xiong how to write odd ancient Chinese characters, but Yang Xiong was not in on the conspiracy. Wang Mang ordered his prosecution to stop. However, people in the capital came up with the satirical lines: "Out of loneliness, he jumped from the mansion since; for quiet rectitude, he wrote the Heavenly Mandate."

Yang Xiong was excused from office due to illness, but was recalled as a grand master. He was never anything but poor, but he loved to drink, so very few people went to his home. Some busybody used to go with food and wine to study under him, and Hou Ba from Julu often went to stay with Yang Xiong, studying his *Great Dark Mystery* and *Words to Live By*. Also observing, Liu Xin

【原文】

刘歆亦尝观之，谓雄曰："空自苦！今学者有禄利，然尚不能明《易》，又如《玄》何？吾恐后人用覆酱瓿也。"雄笑而不应。年七十一，天凤五年卒，侯芭为起坟，丧之三年。

时大司空王邑、纳言严尤闻雄死，谓桓谭曰："子尝称扬雄书，岂能传于后世乎？"谭曰："必传。顾君与谭不及见也。凡人贱近而贵远，亲见扬子云禄位容貌不能动人，故轻其书。昔老聃著虚无之言两篇，薄仁义，非礼学，然后世好之者尚以为过于《五经》，自汉文景之君及司马迁皆有是言。今扬子之书文义至深，而论不诡于圣人，若使遭遇时君，更阅贤知，为所称善，则必度越诸子矣。"诸儒或讥以为雄非圣人而作经，犹春秋吴楚之君僭号称王，盖诛绝之罪也。自雄之没至今四十馀年，其《法言》大行，而《玄》终不显，然篇籍具存。

——卷八十七下《扬雄传》第五十七下

【今译】

"白白使自己受苦！现在学者有利禄，还不能通晓《易》，何况《玄》？我怕后人用它来盖酱瓿了。"扬雄笑而不答。活到七十一岁，在天凤五年死去，侯芭为他建坟，守丧三年。

当时大司空王邑、纳言严尤听说扬雄死了，对桓谭说："您曾称赞扬雄的书，难道能流传后世吗？"桓谭说："一定能够流传。但您和桓谭看不到。凡人轻视近的重视远的，亲眼见扬子云地位容貌不能动人，便轻视其书。从前老聃作虚无之论两篇，轻仁义，驳礼学，但后世喜欢它的还认为超过《五经》，从汉文帝、景帝及司马迁都有这话。现在扬子的书文义最深，论述不违背圣人，如果遇到当时君主，再经贤知阅读，被他们称道，便必定超过诸子了。"诸儒有的嘲笑扬雄不是圣人却作经，好比春秋吴楚君主僭越称王，应该是灭族绝后之罪。从扬雄死后到现在四十多年，他的《法言》大行于世，但《玄》到底未得彰显，但篇籍都在。

told Yang Xiong: "You make a rod for your own back, and to what end? Scholars nowadays are salaried, but they still don't understand the *Book of Changes* still less the *Great Dark Mystery*. I'm afraid future generations will use it to cover the sauce pot." Yang Xiong just laughed this off. He died at the age of 71 in the year five of the Tianfeng reign period. Hou Ba built his tomb, and kept mourning for three years.

When the Grand Minister of Works Wang Yi and Imperial Advisor Yan You heard that Yang Xiong had died, they said to Huan Tan: "You have praised Yang Xiong's books. Can these be handed down to posterity?" Huan Tan said: "They must be, but neither you or I will see it. Common people undervalue what is close at hand in favor of the distant. Seeing for themselves the unimpressive appearance and social status of Master Yang, they give scant regard to his books. Lao Dan wrote two articles on nothingness, slighting benevolence and righteousness, and refuting ceremonialism, but later people liked his works. No lesser persons than Han emperors Wendi and Jingdi, and Sima Qian commented that they believed them to surpass the Five Classics. Now the books by Mr. Yang are most profoundly meaningful, and the discussion does not violate the sages. If he met the then monarch, and he was read with approval by the wise, he would surely surpass the various schools of thinkers." Some Confucians ridicule Yang Xiong for writing classics without being a sage, a crime they deem comparable to that of the monarchs of Wu and Chu in the Spring and Autumn Period as pretenders to the throne, a crime punishable by extermination of the entire clan. Forty-odd years since Yang Xiong's death, his *Words to Live By* is very popular, The *Great Dark Mystery* remains obscure, but all the volumes are extant.

刘歆传

【原文】

歆字子骏，少以通《诗》、《书》能属文召，见成帝，待诏宦者署，为黄门郎。河平中，受诏与父向领校秘书，讲六艺传记，诸子、诗赋、数术、方技，无所不究。向死后，歆复为中垒校尉。

哀帝初即位，大司马王莽举歆宗室有材行，为侍中太中大夫，迁骑都尉、奉车光禄大夫，贵幸。复领《五经》，卒父前业。歆乃集六艺群书，种别为《七略》。语在《艺文志》。

歆及向始皆治《易》，宣帝时，诏向受《穀梁春秋》，十馀年，大明习。及歆校秘书，见古文《春秋左氏传》，歆大好之。时丞相史尹咸以能治《左氏》，与歆共校经传。歆略从咸及丞相翟方

【今译】

刘歆字子骏，小时候因通晓《诗》《书》能做文章被召见，见到成帝，在宦者署待诏，做黄门郎。河平年间，受诏和父亲刘向一起主持校定秘书，研究六艺传记，诸子、诗赋、数术、方技，没有不涉及的。刘向死后，刘歆又做中垒校尉。

哀帝刚即位，大司马王莽推举刘歆是有才德的宗室，做侍中太中大夫，升骑都尉、奉车光禄大夫，地位尊贵深受宠幸。又负责《五经》之事，完成父亲的遗业。刘歆便汇集六艺群书，分类编排为《七略》。《艺文志》有载。

刘歆和刘向开始都研究《易》，宣帝时，下诏让刘向学习《穀梁春秋》，十多年，已学得很精通。到刘歆校定秘书，看到古文《春秋左氏传》，他非常喜欢。当时丞相史尹咸因能研究《左氏》，和刘歆

Chapter 17

Biography of Liu Xin

Liu Xin, styled Zijun, was summoned as a child to see Emperor Chengdi because of his precocious knowledge of the *Book of Odes* and *Book of Documents* and his skill in writing essays. He became an expectant official at the Department of Eunuchs, as a palace gentleman. During the Heping reign period (28-25 BC), he and his father Liu Xiang were put in charge of collating the books of the secret library, to study notes of the Six Arts, philosophers, poetry and prose, divination, mystic techniques, leaving out nothing. After Liu Xiang's death, Liu Xin became a commandant of the capital garrison.

When Emperor Aidi had just ascended the throne, the Commander-in-Chief Wang Mang recommended Liu Xin as a virtuous and learned royal family member, to become superior grand master of the palace. He was promoted to defender of chivalry, defender of imperial chariot, grand master of splendid happiness, as a favorite of the emperor. Given the additional responsibility for the "Five Classics," he was to complete his father's unfinished work. Liu Xin would bring together books of the Six Arts, and catalogue the *Seven Books of Summary*. (See *Bibliographic Treatise*.)

Liu Xin and Liu Xiang studied the *Book of Changes* simultaneously at first. Later, Emperor Xuandi ordered Liu Xiang to learn Guliang's commentary on the *Spring and Autumn Annals*, and within 10 years he had a very proficient mastery of it. When Liu Xin collated the secret library, he saw the classic Zuo's Commentary on the *Spring and Autumn Annal*s, and admired it greatly. The then prime minister Shi Yinxian was able to study Zuo's Commentary, so

【原文】

进受，质问大义。初《左氏传》多古字古言，学者传训故而已，及歆治《左氏》，引传文以解经，转相发明，由是章句义理备焉。歆亦湛靖有谋，父子俱好古，博见强志，过绝于人。歆以为左丘明好恶与圣人同，亲见夫子，而公羊、穀梁在七十子后，传闻之与亲见之，其详略不同。歆数以难向，向不能非间也，然犹自持其《穀梁》义。及歆亲近，欲建立《左氏春秋》及《毛诗》、《逸礼》、《古文尚书》皆列于学官。哀帝令歆与《五经》博士讲论其义，诸博士或不肯置对，歆因移书太常博士，责让之曰：

昔唐虞既衰，而三代迭兴，圣帝明王，累起相袭，其道甚著。周室既微而礼乐不正，道之难全也如此。是故孔子忧道之不行，历国应聘。自卫反鲁，然后乐正，《雅》《颂》乃得其所；

【今译】

一起校订经传。刘歆大略跟尹咸和丞相翟方进学习，询问大义。起初《左氏传》多为古字古语，学者传解训诂而已，到刘歆研究《左氏》，引传文来解经，互相发明，从此也具备了章句义理。刘歆又沉静有谋略，父子都好古，博闻强记，超过别人。刘歆认为左丘明的好恶和圣人一样，亲眼见过夫子，而公羊、谷梁在七十子之后，听传闻和亲眼见，详略不同。刘歆多次向刘向发难，刘向不能责难他，却仍自己坚守着《谷梁》的义旨。等刘歆被皇上亲近，想把《左氏春秋》和《毛诗》、《逸礼》、《古文尚书》都立于学官。哀帝让刘歆和《五经》博士讲论其意旨，各位博士有的不肯和刘歆辩论，刘歆于是致书太常博士，责备他说：

从前唐虞衰亡，三代继起，圣帝明王，相承迭兴，大道显著。周室衰微礼乐不正，大道如此难以保全。所以孔子担心大道不通行，游历各国去应聘。从卫回鲁，之后音乐匡正，《雅》、

Liu Xin and he together collated the classics and made comments. Liu learned something from Shi Yinxian and the prime minister Zhai Fangjin, inquiring into the right meaning. Initially, Zuo's Commentary contained many classical words and old sayings, and scholars had been exegetic only. But when Liu Xin came to study Zuo's Commentary, he quoted the texts in the interpretive notes that threw light upon each other, so there were also complete chapters and theory. Liu Xin was composed and resourceful, and, like his father, loved the ancients, possessing encyclopedic knowledge and retentive memory surpassing other scholars. Liu Xin's view was that Zuo had the same likes and dislikes as the sages, having seen the Master Confucius himself, while Gongyang and Guliang came after the 70 disciples of the Master; so, listening to legend and seeing in person accounted for the different level of detail. Liu Xin quizzed his father several times, who did not blame him, but still adhered to the interpretation of Guliang's Commentary. When Liu Xin became closer to the Emperor, he tried to establish Zuo's *Spring and Autumn Annals* and "Mao's edition of the *Book of Odes*," "Lost edition of *Ceremony and Ritual*," and the classical *Book of Documents* in the government schools. Emperor Aidi ordered him to discuss its tenor with the erudites of "Five Classics," but some refused to engage in debate, so he wrote to the erudite of the chamberlain of ceremonials, taking him to task:

Formerly, Tang and Yu were in decline and the three dynasties rose, one following the other. The sage kings came, one succeeding the other, and their Way was brilliant. When the House of Zhou was in decline, the rites and music were not correct, which shows that the Way is so difficult to keep intact. Thus Confucius, concerned that the Way would not prevail, traveled to various states to offer his services. From Wei he returned to Lu, and then music was corrected. "Elegance" and "Odes" were well edited in the Book of Odes*; he revised the*

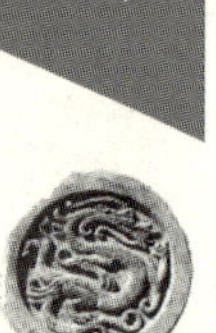

【原文】

修《易》序《书》，制作《春秋》，以纪帝王之道。及夫子没而微言绝，七十子终而大义乖。重遭战国，弃笾豆之礼，理军旅之陈，孔氏之道抑，而孙吴之术兴。陵夷至于暴秦，燔经书，杀儒士，设挟书之法，行是古之罪，道术由是遂灭。汉兴，去圣帝明王遐远，仲尼之道又绝，法度无所因袭。时独有一叔孙通略定礼仪，天下唯有《易》卜，未有它书。至孝惠之世，乃除挟书之律，然公卿大臣绛、灌之属咸介胄武夫，莫以为意。至孝文皇帝，始使掌故朝错从伏生受《尚书》。《尚书》初出于屋壁，朽折散绝，今其书见在，时师传读而已。《诗》始萌牙。天下众书往往颇出，皆诸子传说，犹广立于学官，为置博士。在汉

【今译】

《颂》各得其所；刊定《易》，作《书》序，著作《春秋》，来记载帝王之道。到夫子死而精微之言灭绝，七十子死而大义乖谬，又遇上战国纷争，摒弃笾豆的礼仪，着手军旅行阵，孔氏大道衰微，孙吴法术兴盛。逐渐衰落一直到了暴秦，烧经书，杀儒士，制定禁书法律，赞扬古代的被治罪，大道法术从此灭绝。汉兴起，离圣帝明王很远，仲尼大道又灭绝，法度无从因袭。当时只有一个叔孙通大致制定礼仪，天下只有卜书《易》，没有别的书。到孝惠时，废除禁书法律，但公卿大臣绛、灌等人都是披戴盔甲的武夫，不以为然。到孝文皇帝，开始让掌故晁错，跟伏生学习《尚书》。《尚书》刚从屋墙中取出，朽折散乱，现在那书仍在，当时师傅只是传解诵读而已。《诗》开始萌芽。天下出现了很多书，都是诸子的传释，尚且广泛立于学官，为它们设置

Book of Changes, *wrote a preface to the* Book of Documents, *and compiled the* Spring and Autumn Annals, *to record the Way of the Kings. When the Master died, the subtle essence of his words became extinct; after the deaths of his 70 disciples, the meaning of the classic interpretation also diverged. Then came the contentions of the Warring States and the abandonment of sacrifice ritual, to begin the mustering of armies and far campaigning. The Way of Confucius faded, whilst the art of war by Sun and Wu flourished. Gradual decline to the despotism of Qin culminated in the burning of the classics, killing of the Confucian scholars, the law banning private book collection and penalizing the offense of praising the ancients, and then both the Way and the arts became extinct.*

Even with the rise of Han, the sage kings were long ago and far away, and the Confucian Way was extinct, so there was no moral standard to follow. At that time, there was only one Shusun Tong to roughly formulate the rituals, and in the empire there was no other book than divination in the Book of Changes. *In the reign of Emperor Huidi, the law against private book collection was repealed, but the top nobles and chief ministers like Zhou Bo, Guan Ying and other officials were all military men, who cared not one jot about this. In the reign of Wendi, Chao Cuo, a clerk of anecdote, was sent to study the* Book of Documents *with Mr. Fu. But the* Book of Documents *had only just been taken from the wall of a house, and it was bent, scattered and decayed; nowadays that book still survives, only because it was passed on by the masters by word of mouth. Scholarship on the* Book of Odes *began to blossom. In the world there emerged numerous books, all commentaries on the philosophers, and widely included in the government schools, for which the system of erudites was set up. Of Confucians in the Han Dynasty, only Mr. Jia can count. In the reign of Emperor*

【原文】

朝之儒，唯贾生而已。至孝武皇帝，然后邹、鲁、梁、赵颇有《诗》、《礼》、《春秋》先师，皆起于建元之间。当此之时，一人不能独尽其经，或为《雅》，或为《颂》，相合而成。《泰誓》后得，博士集而读之。固诏书称曰："礼坏乐崩，书缺简脱，朕甚闵焉。"时汉兴已七八十年，离于全经，固已远矣。

及鲁恭王坏孔子宅，欲以为宫，而得古文于坏壁之中，《逸礼》有三十九，《书》十六篇。天汉之后，孔安国献之，遭巫蛊仓卒之难，未及施行。及《春秋》左氏丘明所修，皆古文旧书，多者二十馀通，臧于秘府，伏而未发。孝成皇帝闵学残文缺，稍离其真，乃陈发秘臧，校理旧文，得此三事，以考学官所传，经或脱简，传或间编。传问民间，则有鲁国（柏）[桓]公、赵国贯公、胶东庸生之遗学与此同，抑而未施。此乃有识者之所惜闵，

【今译】

博士。在汉朝的儒生，只有贾生而已。到孝武皇帝，之后邹、鲁、梁、赵常有讲解《诗》、《礼》、《春秋》的前辈老师，都兴起于建元年间。在这时，一人不能独自穷尽经书，有的通晓《雅》，有的通晓《颂》，大家相配合才能完成讲经。《泰誓》后出，博士收集并诵读。所以诏书说道："礼崩乐坏，书简脱缺，朕很担心。"当时汉兴起已七八十年，离开全部的经书，本来就很远了。

到鲁恭王发掘孔子旧宅，想建造宫室，在断墙中得到古文，《逸礼》有三十九篇，《书》有十六篇。天汉之后，孔安国献上它们，遇上巫蛊仓猝之祸，没来得及施行。至于左氏丘明所修的《春秋》，都是古文旧书，多的有二十多篇，藏在秘府，隐秘没有公布。孝成皇帝怜惜学术残缺，与原书相差很大，便公布旧藏，校订旧文，用这三种书，校订学官传授的经传，经有的脱简，传有的错编。传令询问民间，有鲁国桓公、赵国贯公、胶东庸生的传学与此相同，受压制没有施行。这是使有识者怜惜，士

Wudi, there were many of the early-generation teachers of the Odes, Rites *and* Spring and Autumn Annals *in Zou, Lu, Liang, Zhao, all of whom rose in the Jianyuan reign period. At this point, one person could not exhaust all the classics alone. So some specialized in "Elegance," and others in the "Odes," and they cooperated in order to complete the explanation of the classic. "Grand Pledge" was obtained later, and the erudites gathered to read it. So the edict said: "The rites are lost, and music destroyed, books incomplete, bamboo slips scattered. I am very sad about these things!" This was 70 or 80 years after the rise of Han, very far from the days when the classics were complete.*

When Prince Gong of Lu destroyed Confucius' old residence, wanting to build his palaces there, he found classical texts in a demolished wall, including 39 chapters missing from the Rites *and 16 chapters from the* Book of Documents. *After the Tianhan reign period, Kong Anguo offered them to the Emperor, but this was not implemented because of the disastrous campaign against witches. The* Spring and Autumn Annals *edited by Zuo Qiuming were old books written in ancient characters, 20 chapters and more, kept in the secret government library, hidden and not released. But Emperor Chengdi regretted this incomplete scholarship and severe loss of books, with much of the originals missing, and so he had the secret library publicized, the old texts cross-checked and revised to resurrect these three books, to compare against those transmitted by the government schools, only to find slips missing from some classics and some lost chapters from the notes. As to the folk notes, they found that those inherited from Mr. Huan of Lu, Mr. Guan of Zhao, and Mr. Yong of Jiaodong were the same as these, but they had been suppressed and not practiced. This was something men of insight deplored and that pained*

【原文】

士君子之所嗟痛也。往者缀学之士不思废绝之阙，苟因陋就寡，分文析字，烦言碎辞，学者罢老且不能究其一艺。信口说而背传记，是末师而非往古，至于国家将有大事，若立辟雍、封禅、巡狩之仪，则幽冥而莫知其原。犹欲保残守缺，挟恐见破之私意，而无从善服义之公心，或怀妒嫉，不考情实，雷同相从，随声是非，抑此三学，以《尚书》为备，谓左氏为不传《春秋》，岂不哀哉！

今圣上德通神明，继统扬业，亦闵文学错乱，学士若兹，虽昭其情，犹依违谦让，乐与士君子同之。故下明诏，试《左氏》可立不，遣近臣奉指衔命，将以辅弱扶微，与二三君子比意同力，冀得废遗。今则不然，深闭固距，而不肯试，猥以不诵绝之，欲以杜塞馀道，绝灭微学。夫可与乐成，难与虑始，此乃众

【今译】

君子痛心的事。以前做学问的人不考虑书的残缺，苟且因陋就寡，分析文字，言辞烦琐，学者到老不能研究通一艺。信口解说背诵传记，信奉低等的老师而责难以往的古事，至于国家要有大事，如立辟雍、封禅、巡狩的仪式，便糊涂不知应该怎样。仍要抱残守缺，带着怕被戳穿的私心，而没有服从善义的公心，或者心怀嫉妒，不思实情，雷同的便相追随，听声音附和是非，压抑这三种学问，认为《尚书》是完备的，说左氏没有传解《春秋》，不是很可悲的事吗！

现在圣上德通神明，继位承业，也怜惜文章错乱，学士们这么多，虽明白真情，仍然迟疑谦让，愿意和士君子一样。所以下发明诏，辩论《左氏》是否可立，派近臣奉上旨令，要来扶助微弱，和两三个君子同心合力，希望重立被废弃的经传。现在却并非如此，深藏坚拒，不肯论辩，苟且以不诵习而灭绝它，想来堵塞仅剩的大道，灭绝精微的学问。可以和他分享成果，难于和他

the superior gentlemen. Scholars in the past did not consider the deterioration of and missing parts of the books, making do with what little was available, and spent their time on textual analysis using verbose and impenetrable wording, unable to master even one of the arts before their dotage. They simply believed in the oral tradition, parroting it from memory, trusted the incompetent teachers and doubted the ancient events. When it came to a major state event, such as the formulation of the appropriate rites for the "imperial learning retreat," the "homage to Heaven and Earth at Mount Tai," and "imperial inspection," they were at a loss as to how things should be. They still stuck to the decayed fragments, selfishly afraid of having their ideas exposed, failing to observe the principle of the public good. They were too jealous to examine the facts, following echoes rather than the voice itself, suppressing the three kinds of knowledge, thinking that the Book of Documents *was complete, and asserting that Zuo did not comment on the* Spring and Autumn Annals. *Is that not lamentable?*

Now His Majesty is virtuously communicating with the gods, inheriting and strengthening the cause, and deploring the textual disarray. So many scholars, though understanding the truth, still hesitate most obligingly, happy to concur with the gentlemen. Hence the wise edict was issued to debate whether Zuo's Annals *can be presented at the official schools. Close courtiers were dispatched with the decree, to assist the weak scholarship, and work together with all of you in the hope that the abandoned and lost classics may be restored. Now it is not the case, people reject engagement; they refuse to debate by refusing to recite the classics, they want to terminate the scholarship; they think to stop the remaining Way and exterminate the significant knowledge. Then it is possible to share your achievements, but difficult to consider starting any*

【原文】

庶之所为耳，非所望士君子也。且此数家之事，皆先帝所亲论，今上所考视，其古文旧书，皆有征验，外内相应，岂苟而已哉！

夫礼失求之于野，古文不犹愈于野乎？往者博士《书》有欧阳，《春秋》公羊，《易》则施、孟，然孝宣皇帝犹复广立《穀梁春秋》，《梁丘易》，《大小夏侯尚书》，义虽相反，犹并置之。何则？与其过而废之也，宁过而立之。传曰："文武之道未坠于地，在人；贤者志其大者，不贤者志其小者。"今此数家之言所以兼包大小之义，岂可偏绝哉！若必专已守残，党同门，妒道真，违明诏，失圣意，以陷于文吏之议，甚为二三君子不取也。

其言甚切，诸儒皆怨恨。是时名儒光禄大夫龚胜以歆移书上疏深自罪责，愿乞骸骨罢。及儒者师丹为大司空，亦大怒，奏歆改乱旧

【今译】

考虑创业，这是老百姓的做法，不是名士君子所为。并且这几家的事，都是先帝亲自谈及，现在皇上考查，那些古文旧书，都有验证，内外相合，难道是苟且就能罢休的吗！

礼丧失则到民间去找，古文不是更胜于民间吗？以前博士《书》有欧阳，《春秋》有公羊，《易》则有施、孟，但孝宣皇帝还广泛设立《穀梁春秋》，《梁丘易》，《大小夏侯尚书》，虽然义旨不同，但仍然一起设置。为什么呢？与其因为它有错误而废弃它，宁可错误了而设立它。传解说："文武之道没有坠于地上，而在人间；贤人记大的方面，不贤的人记小的方面。"现在这几家的言论，是并有大小的义旨的，怎么能偏废呢！如果一定要独断守缺，同门结党，嫉妒真道，违背明诏，丧失圣意，被文官们的议论所淹没，我很希望这两三个君子不要这样做。

他的话非常深切，儒士们都很怨恨。这时名儒光禄大夫龚胜因刘歆致书向上陈述而深深自责，希望请求骸骨回家。至于儒者师丹

shared enterprise with them: this is the practice of common folk, and better behavior is expected of gentlemen. And these several classics were what the late Emperor himself talked about. They are what our current Emperor examined, and it is possible to verify them, by the consistency between the books in the imperial library and those kept by the ordinary people. Surely this is no mere coincidence!

When the rites are lost, we seek them among the people and are the classical texts not better sought there too? In the past, the Book of Documents *for erudites boasted Ouyang's Commentary, the* Spring and Autumn Annals *had Gongyang's Commentary, and the* Book of Changes *those by Shi and Meng; but Emperor Xuandi also established Guliang's Commentary on* Spring and Autumn Annals, *Liangqiu's* Book of Changes, *and Xiahou Sr. and Jr.'s* Book of Documents; *although different in their meaning, they were still juxtaposed. Why? Because it is better to err by establishing something than to err by abandoning it. According to the* Analects: *"The doctrines of Wen and Wu have not yet fallen to the earth. They are to be found among men. Men of talents and virtue remember the greater principles of these, and others, not possessing such talents and virtue, remember the smaller." Now that these several schools are what contain both greater and smaller meaning, how can we neglect it out of prejudice? If you must arbitrarily keep to the fragments, close ranks with your own partisans, jealous of the true Way, violating the wise edict and failing the imperial decree, overwhelmed by the talk of officialdom...I sincerely wish that these few gentlemen will ultimately cooperate.*

His words were so harsh that they incurred deep resentment from the Confucian scholars. The noted Confucian Grand Master of Splendid Happiness Gong Sheng was deeply remorseful because of Liu Xin's statements that he begged to retire on grounds of old

【原文】

章，非毁先帝所立。上曰："歆欲广道术，亦何以为非毁哉？"歆由是忤执政大臣，为众儒所讪，惧诛，求出补吏，为河内太守。以宗室不宜典三河，徙守五原，后复转在涿郡，历三郡守。数年，以病免官，起家复为安定属国都尉。会哀帝崩，王莽持政，莽少与歆俱为黄门郎，重之，白太后。太后留歆为右曹太中大夫，迁中垒校尉，羲和，京兆尹，使治明堂辟雍，封红休侯，典儒林史卜之官，考定律历，著《三统历谱》。

初，歆以建平元年改名秀，字颖叔云。及王莽篡位，歆为国师，后事皆在《莽传》。

——卷三十六《楚元王传》第六附

【今译】

是大司空，也大怒，上奏刘歆改乱旧章，毁谤先帝所立之学。皇上说："刘歆想推广道术，又怎能当作毁谤呢？"刘歆从此冒犯了执政大臣，被众儒诽谤，害怕被杀，请求出京补为官吏，做河内太守。因宗室不应主管三河，转为五原太守，后来又转到涿郡，共做过三郡太守。几年后，因病免官，从家中起用又做安定属国都尉。正逢哀帝崩，王莽主政，王莽年少时和刘歆都做黄门郎，器重他，禀告太后。太后留刘歆做右曹太中大夫，升中垒校尉，羲和，京兆尹，让他主管明堂辟雍，封为红休侯。主管儒林史卜官，考订乐律和历法，著《三统历谱》。

起初，刘歆在建平元年改名秀，字颖叔。到王莽篡位，刘歆做国师，后面的事都在《莽传》。

age. The Confucian Shi Dan served as Grand Minister of Works; also furious, he memorialized the Emperor that Liu Xin changed and disrupted the old rules, slandering what the late Emperor had established. The Emperor said: "Liu Xin wants to promote the Way and the arts. How can that be seen as slander?" Having offended a ruling minister, and being slandered by the Confucians, Liu Xin started to fear for his life. He applied to get out of the capital to be a provincial official and became Governor of Henei. A member of the imperial clan could not be in charge of the three He- prefectures, so he was transferred to be Prefect of Wuyuan, and later switched to Zhuojun, making him a three-time prefect. A few years later, he was removed because of illness, and then promoted from his home once more to be Defender of the Dependent States of Anding. After the death of Emperor Aidi, Wang Mang took over. When young, Wang Mang and Liu Xin had been palace gentlemen, and Wang Mang, thinking highly of him, recommended him to the Empress Dowager. She retained him as superior grand master of the Right Section, then promoted him to be Commandant of the Capital Garrison, Chamberlain of Imperial Treasury, Metropolitan Governor, put in charge of the Hall of Enlighten Rule, and made Marquis of Hongxiu. He was in charge of Confucian officials of scribes and diviners, regulating the music and calendar, as well as writing the Three-Entity Calendar. Earlier, Liu Xin was renamed Liu Xiu in the first year of the Jianping reign period, with the style Yingshu. When Wang Mang usurped the throne, Liu Xin became the National Preceptor, for details after this period, see the "Biography of Wang Mang."

儒林传序

【原文】

古之儒者，博学虖《六艺》之文。《六艺》者，王教之典籍，先圣所以明天道，正人伦，致至治之成法也。周道既衰，坏于幽厉，礼乐征伐自诸侯出，陵夷二百馀年而孔子兴，以圣德遭季世，知言之不用而道不行，乃叹曰："凤鸟不至，河不出图，吾已矣夫！""文王既没，文不在兹乎？"于是应聘诸侯，以答礼行谊。西入周，南至楚，畏匡戹陈，奸七十馀君。适齐闻《韶》，三月不知肉味；自卫反鲁，然后乐正，《雅》《颂》各得其所。究观古今之篇籍，乃称曰："大哉，尧之为君也！唯天为大，唯尧则之。巍巍乎其有成功也，焕乎其有文章(也)！"又(云)[曰]："周监于二(世)[代]，郁郁乎文

【今译】

古代的儒者，对《六艺》文章都广泛学习。《六艺》，是王教的经典，先圣用来明天道，正人伦，达到天下大治的成法。周道衰微，坏于幽厉之时，礼乐征伐出自诸侯，衰落二百多年后孔子兴起，因圣德遭逢末世，智言不被用，大道不能通行，于是慨叹道："凤鸟不来，河不出图，我算了吧！""文王已死，文章之事岂不在此乎？"于是应聘于诸侯，以答礼行义。向西入周，向南到楚，受惊于匡，断粮于陈，干谒七十多个国君。到齐听到《韶》乐，三月不知肉味；从卫返鲁，然后音乐得以修正，《雅》《颂》各得其所。探查古今篇籍，于是称赞道："尧做君主真伟大啊！只有天最大，尧效法它。他的成就多么高啊，他的礼乐法度多么美好啊！"又说："周追视二代，文章隆盛，我赞同周。"于是整述《书》便

Chapter 18

Preface to Biographies of Confucians

Ancient Confucian scholars studied the texts of "Six Arts" extensively. By the "Six Arts," we mean the classics of the Kings' moral education, the established laws that the earlier sages used to clarify the heavenly Way, rectify human relations and achieve perfect peace and order. After the Way of Zhou declined, it deteriorated so much in the reigns of King You and King Li that it was the vassal kings who decided ceremonies, music and military expeditions. The decline lasted over 200 years before the rise of Confucius, but his sagacious virtue met the last days of the reign, so his wise words were not used. The Way could not be practiced, hence the lament: "The phoenix bird does not come; the river sends forth no map; -- it is all over with me!" "After the death of King Wen, was not the cause of truth lodged here in me?" So he offered himself before the vassal kings, and practiced righteousness by answering questions on the rites. He went westward into Zhou, and south to Chu. But he was detained in Kuang and ran out of food in Chen, though he applied to more than 70 monarchs. In Qi he heard the music of Shao, and for three months did not know the taste of meat. He returned from Wei to Lu, and then corrected the music; "Elegance" and "Odes" both found their right place in the *Book of Odes*. He explored ancient and contemporary books and volumes, and so praised: "Great indeed was Yao as a monarch! It is only Heaven that is grand, and only Yao corresponds to it. How majestic were his accomplishments! How glorious the elegant regulations which he instituted!" He added: "Zhou had the advantage of viewing the two past dynasties. How complete and elegant are its documents! I follow Zhou." So when he

【原文】

哉！吾从周。”于是叙《书》则断《尧典》，称乐则法《韶舞》，论《诗》则首《周南》。缀周之礼，因鲁《春秋》，举十二公行事，绳之以文武之道，成一王法，至获麟而止。盖晚而好《易》，读之韦编三绝，而为之传。皆因近圣之事，目(音以)立先王之教，故曰：“述而不作，信而好古；”“下学而上达，知我者其天乎！”

仲尼既没，七十子之徒散游诸侯，大者为卿相师傅，小者友教士大夫，或隐而不见。故子张居陈，澹臺子羽居楚，子夏居西河，子贡终于齐。如田子方、段干木、吴起、禽滑氂之属，皆受业于子夏之伦，为王者师。是时，独魏文侯好学。天下并争于战国，儒术既黜焉，然齐鲁之间学者犹弗废，至于威、宣之际，孟子、孙卿之列咸遵夫子之业而润色之，以学显于当世。

及至秦始皇兼天下，燔《诗》、《书》，杀术士。六学从此缺

【今译】

从《尧典》开始，称乐便以《韶舞》为法，论《诗》则以《周南》为首。连结周礼，循鲁《春秋》，列举十二公的行事，用文武之道为标准，成为一统王法，到获麟为止。晚年喜欢《易》，读《易》次数太多而使连缀竹简的皮带断了好几次，为之作传。都是以近代圣王之事，来确立先王之教。所以说：“传承而不创新，诚信而好古；”“下学人事，上达天命，知道我的大概是天吧！”

仲尼死后，七十弟子散游诸侯，位高者为卿相师傅，位低者成为士大夫的师友，有的遁世隐身。所以子张在陈，澹台子羽在楚，子夏在西河，子贡死在齐。像田子方、段干木、吴起、禽滑氂等，都受业于子夏之辈，做王的老师。这时，只有魏文侯好学。战国时天下纷争，儒术被贬斥，然而齐鲁之地的学者还未废大道，到威、宣之际，孟子、孙卿等都遵循夫子的大业并加以润色，以学问著称于当世。

等到秦始皇兼并天下，焚烧《诗》《书》，杀害术士，六学便从此残缺了。陈涉称王时，鲁国的儒士拿着孔氏礼器去归依他，于是

narrated the *Book of Documents* he began with the "Classic of Yao." He took his lead from "Shao Dance" in speaking about music, and started with "South of Zhou" when talking about the *Book of Odes*. Linking the rites of Zhou, he went through Lu's *Spring and Autumn Annals*, citing the acts of 12 dukes of Lu, comparing them with the Way of King Wen and King Wu as the standard, as the dominant royal rule until the incident of capturing a kylin. In his old age, he liked to read the *Book of Changes*, so many times that the leather binding cord broke several times, and he became its biographer. He used the deeds of the modern sages to establish the moral education of the former Kings. So he said of himself: "A transmitter but not a creator, believing in and loving the ancients"; "I study human affairs in this world and communicate with the mandate of heaven. Perhaps it is heaven that knows me!"

After Confucius' death, his 70 disciples scattered to join the vassal kings, and the great scholars became the teachers of high nobles and prime ministers, while the small masters became friends and mentors of literati and officials; some were recluses who did not engage with the world. So Zizhang lived in Chen, Tantai Ziyu in Chu, Zixia in Xihe, but Zigong died in Qi. Tian Zifang, Duangan Mu, Wu Qi, Qin Guli, etc. had studied under Zixia and others and became the rulers' teachers. At this time, Marquis Wen of Wei was especially studious. The world was at war in the Warring States Period, and Confucianism was denounced. However, scholars of the land of Qi and Lu had not abandoned the path. In the reigns of King Wei and King Xuan, Mencius, Xunzi and others followed the Master's (Confucius) great cause and polished it, and were eminent in the contemporary world for their knowledge.

After the first Qin Emperor united the empire, there was the burning of the *Odes* and the *Book*, and the killing of scholars, and the learning of the Six Arts became incomplete. When Chen She rose as king, Confucians in Lu took Confucius' ritual utensils

【原文】

矣。陈涉之王也，鲁诸儒持孔氏礼器(而)[往]归之，于是孔甲为涉博士，卒与俱死。陈涉起匹夫，敺適戍以立号，不满岁而灭亡，其事至微浅，然而搢绅先生负礼器往委质为臣者何也？以秦禁其业，积怨而发愤于陈王也。

及高皇帝诛项籍，引兵围鲁，鲁中诸儒尚讲诵习礼，弦歌之音不绝，岂非圣人遗化好学之国哉？于是诸儒始得修其经学，讲习大射乡饮之礼。叔孙通作汉礼仪，因为奉常，诸弟子共定者，咸为选首，然后喟然兴于学。然尚有干戈，平定四海，亦未皇庠序之事也。孝惠、高后时，公卿皆武力功臣。孝文时颇登用，然孝文本好刑名之言。及至孝景，不任儒，窦太后又好黄老术，故诸博士具官待问，未有进者。

汉兴，言《易》自淄川田生，言《书》自济南伏生，言《诗》，于鲁则申培公，于齐则辕固生，燕则韩太傅；言《礼》，则鲁高堂生；言《春秋》，于齐则胡毋生，于赵则董仲舒。及窦太后崩，武

【今译】

孔甲成了陈涉的博士，最终和他一起死难。陈涉起身于匹夫，驱使谪戍而自立国号，不满一年就灭亡了，这本是很微浅的事，然而搢绅先生背着礼器委质为臣，是为什么呢？因为秦禁绝这项事业，心中积怒而依靠陈王来发泄。

等到高皇帝杀项籍，率兵围鲁，鲁地儒士还在讲诵习礼，弦歌之声不断，难道不是圣人遗化的好学之国吗？于是诸儒才能开始修习经学，讲习大射、乡饮之礼。叔孙通制作汉礼仪，因此做了奉常，诸弟子一起参与制定的人，都成为选首，然后学术喟然而兴。然而仍有战事，要平定四海，也没有来得及兴办庠序之事。孝惠、高后时，公卿们都是武力功臣。孝文时稍有进用，但孝文本来喜好刑名之学。到了孝景，不任用儒生，窦太后又喜好黄老之术，所以诸博士备官待问，没有进用的。

汉兴起后，淄川田生讲《易》；济南伏生讲《书》；讲《诗》，在鲁是申培公，在齐是辕固生，在燕是韩太傅；讲《礼》，则是鲁高堂生；讲《春秋》的，在齐是胡毋生，在赵是董仲舒。等到窦太

and threw in their lot with him, so Kong Jia became Chen She's erudite, and they finally died together. Chen She started life as a commoner, driven on the road as an exile soldier. He established himself as king, but perished in less than a year. His cause was a very slight event, however, the literati and officials carrying their ritual utensils came to make themselves his subjects. Why was that? Because Qin had cut off their cause, and the accumulated grievances of their hearts found an outlet with King Chen. When Gaodi killed Xiang Yu, and surrounded Lu with his army, the Confucians there were still lecturing on the Master's thought and chanting the *Odes*, learning the rituals, so the sound of the music instruments and singing were heard constantly. Is it not a studious state where the sage left behind his doctrines? So the Confucians could at last attend studies of the classics, teaching archery contestation and the rural drinking ceremony. Shusun Tong formulated the Han rituals, and so was made officer in charge of imperial sacrifices. All his disciples who participated in its finalization became the chosen masters of sacrifices, and thereafter learning took off in a big way. However, wars still continued in the efforts to pacify the land, allowing no time to initiate schools at local level. Under Emperor Huidi and Empress Gaodi, the highest nobles and chief ministers were all war heroes. Emperor Wendi promoted quite a few Confucians but at heart he preferred the Legalist school. Emperor Jingdi did not appoint Confucian scholars, and Empress Dowager Dou was keen on the Taoist teachings of the Yellow Emperor and Laozi. So the erudites were all candidates to be consulted, but none were promoted.

After the rise of Han, Mr. Tian advocated the *Book of Changes* in Zichuan; Mr. Fu talked about the *Book of Documents* in Jinan; as to the *Book of Odes* there was Mr. Shen Pei in Lu, Mr. Yuan Gu in Qi, and Grand Mentor Hann in Yan; Mr. Gao Tang in Lu talked on the *Book of Rites*; for the *Spring and Autumn Annals*, there was Mr. Huwu in Qi, and Dong Zhongshu in Zhao. After Empress Dowager

【原文】

安君田蚡为丞相，黜黄老、刑名百家之言，延文学儒者以百数，而公孙弘以治《春秋》为丞相封侯，天下学士靡然鄉风矣。

弘为学官，悼道之郁滞，乃请曰：“丞相、御史言：制曰：‘盖闻导民以礼，风之以乐。婚姻者，居室之大伦也。今礼废乐崩，朕甚愍焉，故详延天下方闻之士，咸登诸朝。其令礼官劝学，讲议洽闻，举遗兴礼，以为天下先。太常议，予博士弟子，崇乡里之化，以厉贤材焉。’谨与太常臧、博士平等议，曰：闻三代之道，乡里有教，夏曰校，殷曰庠，周曰序。其劝善也，显之朝廷；其惩恶也，加之刑罚。故教化之行也，建首善自京师始，繇内及外。今陛下昭至德，开大明，配天地，本人伦，劝学兴礼，崇化厉贤，以风

【今译】

后崩，武安君田蚡做丞相，排斥黄老、刑名百家言论，延用文学儒士数百人，公孙弘因研究《春秋》而做了丞相封侯，天下学士纷纷效仿。

公孙弘是学官，伤心大道的衰微，于是奏请说：“丞相、御史说：制书说‘听说要以礼指导人民，以乐施行教化。婚姻，是居室的大伦。现在礼崩乐坏，朕很感伤，所以延用天下有道博闻之士，都录用于朝廷。应当令礼官劝学，讲释经义，广博见闻，举求遗逸，兴盛礼仪，作天下的榜样。太常建议，授予博士弟子，崇尚乡里教化，以劝勉贤才。’谨与太常臧、博士平等商议道：听说三代之道，乡里有教育之所，夏称校，殷称庠，周称序。劝勉善行，使之昭显于朝廷；惩治恶行，便施以刑罚。所以教化的实行，建立首善从京师开始，由内及外。现在陛下昭明至德，开大明，配天地，

Dou died, Lord Wuan Tian Fen became prime minister, and he excluded the teachings of the Yellow Emperor and Laozi and those of Legalism etc., in favor of hundreds of Confucian instructors. Thus, Gongsun Hong became the prime minister and a marquis for his command of the *Spring and Autumn Annals*. Scholars across the land followed suit in a universal vogue.

Gongsun Hong was an official in charge of education. Lamenting the decline of the Way, he petitioned:

> *"The prime minister and the censor say: The edict reads, 'I heard about the guidance of the people with rites and moral education through music. Marriage is the great ethic of a man and wife living together. Nowadays, the rites are wasted and music is in disarray. This pains me, so scholars with integrity in the Way and well-read in the world shall all be invited and hired in the court. The erudites shall exhort people to study, speaking of doctrines from their extensive knowledge; they shall seek out lost classics, promoting the rites as examples for the world. The chamberlain for ceremonials recommended that disciples be bestowed on the erudites, advocating moral education in rural schools, so as to encourage the production of worthy talents.' I seriously discussed with the chamberlain for ceremonials Kong Zang, the chief erudite, and others. And they said: 'We heard that it was the way of the three ancient dynasties to establish village education units: under Xia these schools were called* xiao*; under Yin they were called* xiang*; and under Zhou they were called* xu*. They encouraged good deeds so that they were represented at Court; they punished evil, and would impose penalties. So the practice of moral education began with the establishment of pre-eminence in the capital city, from inside the palace, spreading to the world outside.' Now Your Majesty has shown the ultimate virtue, opened the great enlightenment to correspond to heaven and earth, and base your rule on*

【原文】

四方，太平之原也。古者政教未洽，不备其礼，请因旧官而兴焉。为博士官置弟子五十人，复其身。太常择民年十八以上仪状端正者，补博士弟子。郡国县官有好文学，敬长上，肃政教，顺乡里，出入不悖，所闻，令相长丞上属所二千石。二千石谨察可者，常与计偕，诣太常，得受业如弟子。一岁皆辄课，能通一艺以上，补文学掌故缺；其高第可以为郎中，太常籍奏。即有秀才异等，辄以名闻。其不事学若下材，及不能通一艺，辄罢之，而请诸能称者。臣谨案诏书律令下者，明天人分际，通古今之谊，文章尔雅，训辞深厚，恩施甚美。小吏浅闻，弗能究宣，亡以明布谕下。以治礼掌故

【今译】

以人伦为本，劝学兴礼，崇尚教化，勉励贤才，来教化四方，这是太平的本源。古代政教没有普遍，礼仪不完备，请利用旧学官而兴起它。为博士官设置弟子五十人，免除其徭役。太常选择十八岁以上仪容端庄的人，补充博士弟子。郡国县官有爱好文献经典，敬重长上，恭守政教，顺行乡里，出入不违礼的，听说后，县令国相县长县丞报告所属的二千石。二千石谨慎察看，认为可以的，就与推荐的官吏一起，到太常去，就能够像弟子一样受业。第一年都专学一门，能通学一艺以上，补充文学掌故的空缺；高第可以为郎中，太常编选名册奏上。如果有奇异的人才，便单独具名上奏，那些不事学问的下才，以及不能精通一艺的，便免去资格，再请求能胜任的。臣谨案所颁发的诏书律令，分明天人之别，沟通古今道理，文章雅正，训辞深厚，恩泽宏美。小吏见闻浅薄，不能深刻宣传，无

human relations; by exhorting people to study and raising up the rites, advocating moral education and encouraging worthy talent, you aim to educate all quarters, and this is the source of peace. In ancient times, governance and moral education were not universal, nor were the rites complete; now I beg that you use the old school officers to effect a resurgence. Let the officials allocate for the erudites 50 disciples who shall be exempted from corvee. The chamberlain for ceremonials shall select as disciples young men of dignified appearance over the age of 18. In prefectures, fiefs, counties, whenever there is word of persons well versed in the classics, respectful to elders, strict in governance and moral education, who are well received in their villages and who observe the rituals, then the magistrates, prime ministers, and deputies in the localities shall report such people to the local 2,000-picul officials. These officials shall in their turn cautiously examine those suitable, and send them in together with fiscal officials to the chamberlain for ceremonials, to be taught as disciples. They will all be tested once a year, and those who master more than one of the Six Arts shall be appointed to fill vacancies among instructors and anecdote clerks; those who excel in the examinations can become palace gentlemen, to be listed in the memorial of the chamberlain for ceremonials. Those with a singular talent shall be individually named, while those of lower caliber who do not dedicate themselves to learning, and those unable to master one of the arts, shall be removed from eligibility, and then more competent candidates will be requested. Your humble servant has studied the edict and laws issued, that clearly demarcates heaven and man and communicates ancient and modern truth with elegant and perfect text, deep admonition and beautiful grace. The petty clerks are too ill-informed to ensure that this is communicated in fullest depth, or to implement promulgation to

【原文】

以文学礼义为官，迁留滞。请选择其秩比二百石以上及吏百石通一艺以上补左右内史、大行卒史，比百石以下补郡太守卒史，皆各二人，边郡一人。先用诵多者，不足，择掌故以补中二千石属，文学掌故补郡属，备员。请著功令。它如律令。”

制曰：“可。”自此以来，公卿大夫士吏彬彬多文学之士矣。

昭帝时举贤良文学，增博士弟子员满百人，宣帝末增倍之。元帝好儒，能通一经者皆复。数年，以用度不足，更为设员千人，郡国置《五经》百石卒史。成帝末，或言孔子布衣养徒三千人，今天子太学弟子少，于是增弟子员三千人。岁馀，复如故。平帝时王莽

【今译】

法明白颁布晓谕下民。因治礼掌故之官本以有文学习礼义为职，应该迁擢留滞的人才。请选择其俸禄相当二百石以上以及吏百石精通一艺以上者补左右内史、大行卒吏，相当百石以下的补郡太守卒史，都是每郡二人，边郡一人。先录用诵经多的，不足，就选择掌故来补中二千石属，文学掌故补郡属，以配足名额。请著于功令。其他的一如律令。”

昭帝时举荐贤良文学，增加博士弟子满一百人，宣帝末年又增加了一倍。元帝喜好儒学，能精通一经的都免除徭役。数年后，因为用度不足，改为设员一千人，郡国设置《五经》百石卒史。成帝末年，有人说孔子以平民身份养弟子三千人，现在天子太学弟子太少，于是增加弟子至三千人。一年多后，又恢复旧制。平帝时王莽

their inferiors. The ritual clerks for anecdotes are charged with the tasks of official governance of instruction and ceremony, so I recommend you to promote those talents who have long stagnated in lower positions. Please select those with a salary of 200 piculs or above as well as officials of 100 piculs proficient in at least one of the Six Arts to serve as clerks of Left and Right Chamberlain for the Capital and the Chamberlain for Dependencies; officials below 100 piculs to serve as clerks of the Prefecture Governors, two clerks for each office, but one for each outlying prefecture. Give priority to those who can chant the more classics; if not sufficient, just select clerks of anecdote to fill the clerks for officials of full 2,000-piculs, and instructors and anecdote clerks to serve as prefecture clerks, to fill the quota of places. Please make it clear in the recruitment decree. The other matters should be conducted according to the existing law."

The edict said: "Approved." Since then, more and more dukes of the realm and ministers of the state, grand masters, and lower officials were learned scholars.

In the reign of Emperor Zhaodi, the worthy, excellent and learned were recommended, and the number of erudites' disciples increased to a full hundred; by the end of the reign of Emperor Xuandi, the number had doubled again. Emperor Yuandi championed Confucianism and those who were proficient in one of the Arts were exempted from corvee. A few years later, because of budget difficulties, it was changed to a quota of 1,000, and the prefectures and fiefs set up clerks of the Five Classics at 100 piculs a year. At the end of Emperor Chengdi's reign, it was asserted that Confucius as a private man kept 3,000 disciples, and that the current number of Imperial College disciples was too low, so the number was raised to 3,000. But after a year or so they reverted to the old system. In the reign of Emperor Pingdi, when Wang Mang

【原文】

秉政，增元士之子得受业如弟子，勿以为员，岁课甲科四十人为郎中，乙科二十人为太子舍人，丙科四十人补文学掌故云。

——卷八十八《儒林传》第五十八

【今译】

执政，增加元士的子弟可以像弟子一样受业，不算作定员数中，岁课甲科四十人做郎中，乙科二十人做太子舍人，丙科四十人补文学掌故。

was in power, sons of imperial scholars were added to be taught as disciples, but out-of-quota. Every year, 40 top-scoring examinees were appointed as palace gentlemen, 20 second-level examinees as housemen of the Crown Prince, and 40 third-level examinees as instructors and clerks of anecdote.

原涉传

【原文】

原涉字巨先。祖父武帝时以豪桀自阳翟徙茂陵。涉父哀帝时为南阳太守。天下殷富，大郡二千石死官，赋敛送葬皆千万以上，妻子通共受之，以定产业。时又少行三年丧者。及涉父死，让还南阳赙送，行丧冢庐三年，繇是显名京师。礼毕，扶风谒请为议曹，衣冠慕之辐辏。为大司徒史丹举能治剧，为谷口令，时年二十馀。谷口闻其名，不言而治。

先是涉季父为茂陵秦氏所杀，涉居谷口半岁所，自劾去官，欲报仇。谷口豪桀为杀秦氏，亡命岁馀，逢赦出。郡国诸豪及长安、五

【今译】

原涉，字巨先。其祖父在汉武帝时以豪杰的身份从阳翟县迁徙来到茂陵。他的父亲在汉哀帝时作了南阳郡太守。那时，天下富足，大郡太守死在任上的，所收到人家送来助办丧事的钱财都在千万以上，家属全数得到这笔钱，便可以用来置办产业。而当时又很少有人能够为死者守丧三年的。而到了原涉父亲死后，原涉不仅退还了南阳郡人赠送的助丧钱财，还住进了冢庐，为父亲守丧三年，因此他在京城就出了名。守丧礼刚一完毕，请他去作郡府议曹的使者就像疾风一样地赶来了，仰慕他的士大夫也从四面八方聚了过来。由于受到大司徒史丹的推荐，说他有处理繁难事务的才干，原涉便当上了谷口县令，那时他年仅二十多岁。谷口县人早就听到过原涉的名声，所以不需要他开口发令，地方上就已经一派井然了。

早先，原涉的叔父被茂陵的秦氏杀害，原涉在谷口呆了半年多，因为自己去审理了此案而被免官，于是打算报仇。谷口的豪杰替原涉杀了秦氏，原涉因此逃亡在外一年多，遇上了大赦，才又重新露面。

Chapter 19

Biography of Yuan She

Yuan She was styled Juxian. His grandfather migrated from Yangdi County to Maoling as a gallant in the reign of Emperor Wudi, and his father was governor of Nanyang Prefecture during the reign of Emperor Aidi. At that time, the country was prosperous and a 2,000-picul official in a large prefecture who died in office received more than 10 million cash in levies that people sent to help with funeral expenses. The family got the money in full, which could be used to establish a business. At the time, few people observed mourning rites for three full years after the death of a father, but when Yuan's father died he not only refunded Nanyang's mourning gift, but also observed three years mourning, living in the tomb cottage. As a result his name became known in the capital. When the observation of mourning was over, the Guardian of the Right in the capital invited him to be his aide, and gentry who admired him gathered around him. By recommendation of the secretary of the Grand Minister of Education, who praised his ability to handle convoluted matters, he was appointed magistrate of Gukou, when he was still in his twenties. His name was already known there, so it needed no pronouncements or edicts to restore law and order, everyone fell into line automatically.

Earlier, Yuan's youngest uncle had been killed by Mr. Qin of Maoling. After he spent about six months in Gukou, he excused himself and gave up his government post, intent on taking revenge. A gallant in Gukou killed Mr. Qin for him, went in exile for more than a year until under a general amnesty, he was able to resurface. The gallants in prefectures and fiefs, and men of integrity in Changan

【原文】

陵诸为气节者皆归慕之。涉遂倾身与相待，人无贤不肖阗门，在所闾里尽满客。或讥涉曰："子本吏二千石之世，结发自修，以行丧推财礼让为名，正复仇取仇，犹不失仁义，何故遂自放纵，为轻侠之徒乎？"涉应曰："子独不见家人寡妇邪？始自约敕之时，意乃慕宋伯姬及陈孝妇，不幸壹为盗贼所污，遂行淫失，知其非礼，然不能自还。吾犹此矣！"

涉自以为前让南阳赙送，身得其名，而令先人坟墓俭约，非孝也。乃大治起冢舍，周阁重门。初，武帝时，京兆尹曹氏葬茂陵，民谓其道为京兆仟。涉慕之，乃买地开道，立表署曰南阳仟，人不肯从，谓之原氏仟。费用皆印富人长者，然身衣服车马才具，妻子内困，专以振施贫穷赴人之急为务。人尝置酒请涉，涉入里门，客有道涉所知母病避疾在里宅者。涉即往候，叩门。家哭，涉因入

【今译】

郡县和诸侯国的豪杰以及长安、五陵等地有气节的义士都倾慕他，于是原涉也对他们竭诚相待，不论品行好的还是不好的人都来结交原涉，一时间宾客盈门，连他家所居住的街巷也挤满了来客。有人讥讽原涉说："你本是郡太守的后人，年轻时就能自我修养，后来因为为父亲守丧三年又退还了财产及为人谦恭而出名，即使因报仇而结仇，仍不失为一个仁义君子，又何必就放纵自己，去做那种轻薄的侠义之徒呢？"原涉回答道："你就没见到民间的寡妇吗？起初自我约束的时候，心里想的是宋伯姬和陈孝妇的榜样，一旦遭遇不幸，被盗贼奸污，就会放荡起来，虽然明知违反礼教，但已不能回复到洁身自处的时候去了。我便是这样的啊！"

原涉自以为从前退还了南阳人送来的助葬礼金和物品，固然获取了名声，但这却使父亲的坟墓简陋异常，而有失孝道。于是他便大修坟墓，并在墓旁建筑房舍，在阁楼四周建造重门。当初武帝时，京兆尹曹氏安葬在茂陵，人民都称他的墓道为"京兆仟"。原涉羡慕它，就买地开墓道，建立表帜，题署为"南阳仟"，人们不肯跟着这样叫，就称之为"原氏仟"。这一切的费用都依靠有钱有势的人供给，而原涉自身只备有必需的衣物和车马，家中妻儿还生活在困苦之中。原涉专门做一些救济穷人、为人排忧解难的事。一次，有人置办酒宴请原涉，原涉刚走进里门，宾客中就有人告诉他

and the five mausoleum areas admired him greatly, and Yuan also treated them well, regardless whether their conduct had been good or bad and they flocked to him. Thus hangers-on filled his door, and even the vicinity of his home was crowded with visitors. Someone mocked Yuan: "You are the descendant of a 2,000-picul official, engaged in self-cultivation as a young man, and are famous for three-years mourning for your father and the modest act of returning the mourning expenses gift. Even if you engaged in a vendetta, you are still regarded as a virtuous gentleman. Why do you let yourself go in this manner, as a light-weight, would-be gallant?" Yuan replied: "Don't you see the widows in the neighborhood? At first, they had self-restraint and stayed chaste, admiring the examples set by the Count of Song's Concubine and Filial Widow Chen. But then they had the misfortune to be raped and defiled by thieves, and they let themselves go. They are fully aware that they are in violation of decency and propriety, but cannot return to the time that they were chaste. Thus it is with me!"

Yuan thought to himself, though the return of the Nanyang funeral gifts had, of course, won him a reputation, his father's humble grave was in fact a dereliction of filial duty. He then overhauled the grave, encircling the tomb with continuous buildings and installing double gates on each side. Earlier, in Emperor Wudi's reign, Mr. Cao the Metropolitan Governor was buried in Maoling, and people called the path to his grave the "Metropolitan Footpath." Yuan envied it and bought land to create an approach to the tomb, setting up a monument inscribed "Nanyang Footpath." People refused to comply and simply called it "Yuan's Footpath." All these costs were covered by donations from the rich and the seniors, while he himself just had essential clothing and a horse-drawn cart; his wife and children lived in hardship at home. He made a point of providing relief to the poor, and solving problems for others. Once, someone prepared a banquet for him. He had just entered the gate to

【原文】

吊，问以丧事。家无所有，涉曰：“但絜埽除沐浴，待涉。”还至主人，对宾客叹息曰：“人亲卧地不收，涉何心鄉此！愿彻去酒食。”宾客争问所当得，涉乃侧席而坐，削牍为疏，具记衣被棺木，下至饭含之物，分付诸客。诸客奔走市买，至日昳皆会。涉亲阅视已，谓主人：“愿受赐矣。”既共饮食，涉独不饱，乃载棺物，从宾客往至丧家，为棺敛劳徕毕葬。其周急待人如此。后人有毁涉者曰“奸人之雄也”，丧家子即时刺杀言者。

宾客多犯法，罪过数上闻。王莽数收系欲杀，辄复赦出之。涉惧，求为卿府掾史，欲以避客。文母太后丧时，守复土校尉。已为

【今译】

说，他所知道的母亲有病的那一家，现在因病避居在里中，原涉随即便去登门探望，叩门。听见家中有哭丧声，原涉就进去吊唁，又询问治丧的情况。见到其家中一无所有，他便说：“请把屋子打扫干净，给死者洗一个澡，等着我回来。”原涉回到置办酒席的主人处，对宾客们叹息道：“人家母亲去世了，躺在地上不能收殓，我哪有心思享用这些酒食啊！请撤掉酒席吧。”宾客们抢着询问应当买些什么，原涉便按着哀怜丧家的礼节，侧身席地而坐，削好木简开出了一份购物清单，详细地列出了要购买的寿衣、被褥、棺木，以至死者嘴里含的葬物等物品，分交给各位宾客去置办。宾客们分头奔走购买，直到日头偏西才都又回来会集。原涉亲自检视完毕，对主人说：“现在可以接受赐宴了。”大家一同饮酒进食，而惟独原涉没有吃饱，于是就用车装载着棺木等物，领着宾客来到死者家里，为死者入殓，并劝勉宾客等安葬完毕再离去。原涉就是这样急人之难、诚心待人的。后来有人诋毁原涉，说他是“奸人之雄”，死者的儿子立即就去把说这话的人刺杀了。

原涉的宾客多有犯法的，朝廷也多次听说他们的罪行。王莽几次拘捕并要杀掉这些人，但又总是把他们赦免释放了。原涉很害怕，便谋求到卿府去做属官，想藉此回避宾客。正逢文母太后的丧事，原涉临时充任了复土校尉。以后做了中郎，不久又被免官。原涉想

the quarter, when one of the guests told him that one of his friends was hiding away there because of a sick mother. He immediately went to visit, knocking on the door. He heard the sound of weeping inside, went in to offer condolences, and asked in passing about the funeral arrangements. Seeing they had absolutely nothing, Yuan said: "You just clean the house, and wash the body of the departed. I'll be back." Back at the banquet, he sighed to the guests: "The mother is dead, lying on the ground without a coffin to rest in. How can I be in the mood to enjoy this food and wine! Please clear away the feast." The guests vied with each other in asking what they should buy. Yuan sat on the floor sideways, according to the etiquette of a bereaved family, cut open good wooden slips and used them to write a detailed list of which guest should buy which item: the shroud, blankets, a coffin, as well as the grain and shell funerary objects to be placed in the mouth of the dead. They went off to make their purchases, to reassemble late in the afternoon. Yuan personally inspected them completed and said to the host: "Now I will accept your banquet." After they finished eating, only Yuan did not eat his fill. Then they loaded the coffin and other items onto a cart and Yuan led the guests to the deceased's home. There her body was placed in the coffin, and he persuaded the guests to stay until the burial was completed. This was how he helped the needy, and sincerely treated others. Later, someone slandered Yuan, calling him "an outlaw," but the son of the dead woman immediately knifed the slanderer to death.

Many of Yuan's hangers-on broke the law, and the Emperor heard of their crimes many times. Wang Mang arrested them several times and wanted them killed, but they were always pardoned and released. Very afraid, Yuan sought to become the assistant to the government minister and wanted to give the slip to his unwelcome entourage. During the mourning service for the Empress Dowager Wenmu, he acted as the Commandant of the Excavated Soil. After

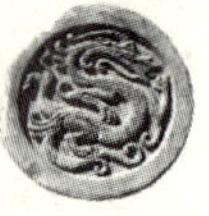

【原文】

中郎，后免官。涉欲上冢，不欲会宾客，密独与故人期会。涉单车敺上茂陵，投暮，入其里宅，因自匿不见人，遣奴至市买肉，奴乘涉气与屠争言，斫伤屠者，亡。是时，茂陵守令尹公新视事，涉未谒也，闻之大怒。知涉名豪，欲以示众厉俗，遣两吏胁守涉。至日中，奴不出，吏欲便杀涉去。涉迫窘不知所为。会涉所与期上冢者车数十乘到，皆诸豪也，共说尹公。尹公不听，诸豪则曰："原巨先奴犯法不得，使肉袒自缚，箭贯耳，诣廷门谢罪，于君威亦足矣。"尹公许之。涉如言谢，复服遣去。

初，涉与新丰富人祁太伯为友，太伯同母弟王游公素嫉涉，时为县门下掾，说尹公曰："君以守令辱原涉如是，一旦真令至，君复单车归为府吏，涉刺客如云，杀人皆不知主名，可为寒心。涉治

【今译】

到冢舍去住，不想会见宾客，只与老朋友秘密约会。他独自驾车去茂陵，天快黑时，进入里中住宅，于是藏在家里不肯见人。一天，原涉派奴仆到集市上去买肉，奴仆仗着原涉的气焰，与卖肉的争吵起来，并砍伤了卖肉者，然后逃跑了。这时，代行茂陵县令的尹公新上任，而原涉却没去拜会，尹公知道后便大为恼怒。他深知原涉是有名的豪侠，就想藉这件事来显示威严，严肃风纪。他派了两个差役守候在原涉的家门两侧。到了中午时分，见买肉的那个奴仆还不出来，差役就想杀掉原涉而去。原涉处境窘迫，不知该怎么办才好，正巧这时他所约好的要一同上坟的友人乘着几十辆车到了，他们都是当地的豪杰，便一起去劝说尹公。尹公不听劝说，豪杰们便说："原巨先的家奴犯了法，不能缉拿归案，那就让原巨先本人脱衣自缚，双耳插箭，到官门前来谢罪吧，这样对于维护您的威望也就足够了。"尹公这才答应。于是，原涉照着豪杰们所说的办法去谢罪，尹公让他仍穿着衣服回家去了。

当初，原涉与新丰的富豪祁太伯是朋友，而太伯的同母弟弟王游公却一向嫉恨原涉。王游公这时在县府做属官，就向尹公进言道："您凭着一个代理县令就如此羞辱原涉，一旦正式县令到任，您依旧驾着单车回郡府去做府吏，而原涉的宾客朋友中刺客如云，杀了人都不知是谁干的，我真为您担心。原涉修筑坟墓和房舍，

that he became a palace gentleman, but was dismissed before long. Yuan thought of living by the family grave to avoid his gang of hangers-on, only meeting up with his old friends in secret. He was alone driving his cart to Maoling, and entered a local house at dusk, where he hid himself away refusing all company. He sent a servant to the market to buy meat, but the servant, throwing his weight about because of the connection with Yuan, quarreled with the butcher, wounded him, and ran away. At this time, Mr. Yin, the acting magistrate of Maoling, had just taken office, and Yuan had not paid a courtesy call; Yin was infuriated at the news. Aware of Yuan's fame as a gallant, Yin wanted to make a conspicuous show of his authority and make a public spectacle of Yuan. He sent two officers to wait on both sides of the gate of Yuan's house. At noon, seeing that the servant did not come out, the officers wanted to kill Yuan and leave. Yuan She was at a loss, not knowing how to extricate himself. It happened that he had arranged with friends to come and visit the tomb together, and they came riding on a dozen carts. They were all local gallants, and went to persuade Magistrate Yin. The Magistrate would not listen, but the gallants said: "The servant of Yuan Juxian is guilty, but he cannot be brought to justice, so let the master strip off his clothing and get bound, with arrows piercing his ears, to make an apology in front of the office. This will be enough to maintain your prestige." Magistrate Yin agreed. Thus, Yuan apologized in this fashion, and he was allowed home wearing his clothes.

Earlier, Yuan was friends with Qi Taibo, a rich man of Xinfeng County, whose younger stepbrother Wang Yougong had always been jealous of Yuan. Wang was a clerk in the county and said to Yin: "As an acting magistrate, you so humiliated Yuan She. Once the real magistrate comes, you will go back to being a county official, back to driving a single-horse cart. But there are very many assassins among Yuan's friends, killing people without being found

【原文】

家舍，奢僭逾制，罪恶暴著，主上知之。今为君计，莫若堕坏涉家舍，条奏其旧恶，君必得真令。如此，涉亦不敢怨矣。”尹公如其计，莽果以为真令。涉繇此怨王游公，选宾客，遣长子初从车二十乘劫王游公家。游公母即祁太伯母也，诸客见之皆拜，传曰“无惊祁夫人”。遂杀游公父及子，断两头去。

涉性略似郭解，外温仁谦逊，而内隐好杀。睚眦于尘中，(独)[触]死者甚多。王莽末，东方兵起，诸王子弟多荐涉能得士死，可用。莽乃召见，责以罪恶，赦贳，拜镇戎大尹。涉至官无几，长安败，郡县诸假号起兵攻杀二千石长吏以应汉。诸假号素闻涉名，争问原尹何在，拜谒之。时莽州牧使者依附涉者皆得活。传送致涉长安，更始西屏将军申屠建请涉与相见，大重之。故茂陵令尹公坏涉冢舍者

【今译】

奢侈过分，超越了法制，罪恶显著，这些皇帝也都知道。现在为您着想，不如把原涉修筑的坟墓和房屋捣毁，然后将他以往的罪恶分条上奏，您就一定会做得成正式县令。这样一来，原涉也就不敢怀恨了。”尹公照着他的计谋行事，王莽果真任命尹公做了正式县令。原涉因此而怨恨王游公，便挑选宾客，让长子原初领着二十乘车去抢劫王游公的家。王游公的母亲也就是祁太伯的母亲，宾客们见到她都俯首跪拜，并传原涉的话说：“不得惊动祁夫人。”于是杀死了王游公和他的生父，把二人的头割下来，然后离去。

原涉的性情有一些像郭解，外表温和仁厚谦逊，内中却藏着好杀之心。在尘世中多有怨恨，因触犯他而被他杀死的人很多。王莽末年，东方起兵反叛，有许多王府的子弟向王莽推荐原涉，称他能笼络人心，人家都乐于为他卖命，可以任用。王莽于是召见原涉，因他所犯的罪恶而责备他，接着又赦免了他，并任命他为镇戎大尹。原涉到任不久，长安兵败，附近郡县的一些豪强假藉名号纷纷起兵，攻杀郡守长官，响应汉军。那些假藉名号者早就听说原涉的大名，便都争相打听原涉的住处，前往拜见。当时王莽任用的州牧和使者凡是依附原涉的也都保全了性命。原涉被他们用驿车送到长安，更始帝的西屏将军申屠建请求原涉与他相见，对原涉大为器重。

out. I am worried on your behalf. Yuan constructed his extravagant tombs and houses exceeding the limits laid down by law; it is a conspicuous crime, and the Emperor knows it. Now for your own sake, you'd better have his tombs and houses destroyed, then submit a memorial about his previous crimes too, then you will become the real magistrate for sure. If you handle things this way, Yuan will not dare bear a grudge." Magistrate Yin acted on this advice, and Wang Mang did appoint him to the permanent position. Yuan thus hated Wang Yougong, and then he selected some of his gang, telling his eldest son Yuan Chu to lead 20 carts to rob the house of Wang Yougong. Wang's mother was also the mother of Yuan's friend Qi Taibo, and the hangers-on bowed down to her when they saw her, conveying Yuan's words: "Do not disturb Lady Qi." But they killed Wang Yougong and his father, and left with their two heads.

Yuan was somewhat like Guo Xie in disposition: moderate, compassionate and humble in appearance, but blood-thirsty at heart. He harbored many resentments in the course of life, and many of those who offended him met an early death at his hands. At the end of the reign of Wang Mang, an army rebelled in the east, and many of the royal children recommended Yuan, saying he could win over people to sacrifice their lives for him, and should thus be used. Wang Mang summoned him, berated him for his crimes, then pardoned him, and appointed him governor of Zhenrong. Shortly after Yuan's appointment the capital Chang'an was defeated. Some impostors in the nearby counties rose with an army in another's name, assaulting 2,000-picul officials in response to Han's appeal. Long aware of Yuan's reputation, the impostors vied to find the location of Governor Yuan's residence, and went to kowtow to him. All Wang Mang's governors and envoys who had attached themselves to Yuan had preserved their lives. They escorted Yuan to Chang'an in a carriage, and Emperor Gengshi's Xiping General Shentu Jian requested to meet with him, regarding him highly.

【原文】

为建主簿，涉本不怨也。涉从建所出，尹公故遮拜涉，谓曰：“易世矣，宜勿复相怨！”涉曰：“尹君，何壹鱼肉涉也！”涉用是怒，使客刺杀主簿。

涉欲亡去，申屠建内恨耻之，阳言：“吾欲与原巨先共镇三辅，岂以一吏易之哉！”宾客通言，令涉自系狱谢，建许之。宾客车数十乘共送涉至狱。建遣兵道徼取涉于车上，送车分散驰，遂斩涉，县之长安市。

自哀、平间，郡国处处有豪桀，然莫足数。其名闻州郡者，霸陵杜君敖，池阳韩幼孺，马领绣君宾，西河漕中叔，皆有谦退之风。王莽居摄，诛钽豪侠，名捕漕中叔，不能得。素善强弩将军孙建，莽疑建藏匿，泛以问建。建曰；“臣名善之，诛臣足以塞责。”莽

【今译】

曾经捣毁原涉坟墓房舍的那个原茂陵县令尹公，现在做了申屠建的主簿。原涉本已不再仇视尹公。当他从申屠建的官府出来时，尹公故意迎上去拦住拜见原涉，对原涉说：“改朝换代啦，不应当再怀着怨恨了！”原涉说：“尹君，你为何专把我当成鱼肉任意宰割啊！”原涉因此而被激怒，便派宾客去刺杀了主簿尹公。

原涉打算逃走，申屠建觉得蒙受了耻辱因而对原涉怀恨在心。他假意说：“我要和原巨先共同镇抚三辅一带，怎么会因死了一个小吏就改变主意呢！”宾客把此话传告给原涉，并让他去自首投狱，向申屠建谢罪。申屠建同意这样办。于是，宾客们便乘着几十辆车一同送原涉去监狱。申屠建派兵途中拦截，在车上将原涉拘捕，护送的车辆一时分头疾驰逃散，于是当即就将原涉问斩，头颅被悬挂到了长安市上。

自哀帝、平帝年间，郡国处处都有豪杰之士，然而数量却无法统计。其中闻名于州郡的，有霸陵的杜君敖、池阳的韩幼孺、马领的绣君宾、西河的漕中叔等，他们都有谦逊礼让的风尚。王莽摄政，要杀尽除光豪侠之士，指名捉捕漕中叔，却没有逮到。漕中叔一向与强弩将军孙建亲善，王莽怀疑孙建窝藏了他，就询问孙建藏了没有。孙建说：“臣下我与漕中叔亲善，杀了我足以顶替他了。”王

Yin, the former Maoling Magistrate who had destroyed Yuan's tomb-site accommodation, was by now the secretary general of Shentu, but Yuan was no longer hostile to him. When Yuan came out from the Shentu official residence, Magistrate Yin deliberately stopped him and greeted him: "The regime has changed! There is no longer reason to be resentful!" Yuan said: "Mr. Yin, why do you specifically victimize me!" He was so enraged that he sent his hangers-on to kill Yin.

Yuan intended to escape, but Shentu Jian felt humiliated and thus bore him a grudge. Masking his true intention, he said: "I want to control the three metropolitan posts together with Yuan, so how can the death of a petty clerk change my mind!" His hangers-on conveyed the remark to Yuan, and told him to give himself up in prison, to apologize to Shentu for his offense. Yuan agreed to this. So, the hangers-on rode on a convoy of dozens of carts to escort Yuan to prison. Shentu sent soldiers to intercept him en route and arrested him as he rode. The escort vehicles fled to the four winds, Yuan was immediately beheaded, and his head was hung up in the market of Chang'an.

From the reigns of Emperors Aidi and Pingdi, gallants appeared everywhere in prefectures and fiefs, however, it is an impossible task to say how many their numbers totaled. Among the well-known in the regions and prefectures, there were Du Jun'ao in Baling, Hann Youru in Chiyang, Xiu Junbin in Maling, Cao Zhongshu in Xihe; all had a humble and courteous manner. Wang Mang as regent killed and eliminated the gallants; he put Cao Zhongshu on the wanted list, but failed to catch him. Cao was always friendly with Crossbow General Sun Jian, and Wang Mang, suspecting Sun of sheltering him, brought up the subject casually. Sun Jian said: "I am known

【原文】

性果贼，无所容忍，然重建，不竟问，遂不得也。中叔子少游，复以侠闻于世云。

——卷九十二《游侠传》第六十二

【今译】

莽性情狭隘，毫无容忍之心，但很重视孙建，便不再追问，终于没有捉到漕中叔。漕中叔的儿子漕少游，后又以豪侠身份闻名于世。

for my friendship with Cao, and having me killed is just the same as killing him." Wang Mang's temperament was narrow, intolerant, but he attached too great importance to Sun to ask further, and finally did not catch Cao Zhongshu. Later, Shaoyou, Cao's son, also became known as a gallant.

匈奴传赞

【原文】

赞曰：《书》戒“蛮夷猾夏”，《诗》称“戎狄是膺”，《春秋》“有道守在四夷”，久矣夷狄之为患也。故自汉兴，忠言嘉谋之臣曷尝不运筹策相与争于庙堂之上乎？高祖时则刘敬，吕后时樊哙、季布，孝文时贾谊、朝错，孝武时王恢、韩安国、朱买臣、公孙弘、董仲舒，人持所见，各有同异，然总其要，归两科而已。缙绅之儒则守和亲，介胄之士则言征伐，皆偏见一时之利害，而未究匈奴之终始也。自汉兴以至于今，旷世历年，多于春秋，其与匈奴，有脩文而和亲之矣，有用武而克伐之矣，有卑下而承事之矣，有威服而臣畜之矣，诎伸异变，强弱相反，是故其详可得而言也。

【今译】

赞曰：《书经》告诫“蛮夷少数民族扰乱中原”，《诗经》称赞“勇敢地面对戎狄”，《春秋》上说“有道之君四边的少数民族也拥护”，夷狄为害中原由来已久。所以自从汉朝建立，那些忠言直谏、计谋深远的大臣们，何尝不是费尽心机，出谋划策，在朝廷上争论如何对付夷狄？高祖时有刘敬，吕后时有樊哙、季布，孝文帝时有贾谊、晁错，孝武帝时有王恢、韩安国、朱买臣、公孙弘、董仲舒，人们坚持己见，有相同的，有不同的，然而归纳起来，也就是两种意见。缙绅儒士坚持与匈奴和亲，披甲戴胄的武士则坚持讨伐攻打匈奴，都是只顾某一时期有利或有害的偏执之见，却没有深入考察匈奴自始至终的历史。从汉朝建立直到现在，经历了很多年代，比《春秋》纪年还多，汉朝与匈奴的关系，既有崇尚文治而实行和亲的时候，也有使用武力征伐战斗的时候；既有谦卑恭顺侍奉匈奴的时候，也有用武力征服而把他们当臣子奴才对待的时候。有屈有伸，变化不同，或我强、或你弱，地位相反，所以我们可以谈论一下其中详情。

Chapter 20

Author’s Comments on Annals of the Huns

Author's comment: The *Book of Documents* cautioned against “the barbarian minorities disrupting the Central Plains,” the *Book of Odes* praised “containment of the Northwestern barbarians,” and the *Spring and Autumn Annals* had “Sagacious rulers with the proper Way have the support of the barbarians on four sides.” The barbarians have long been a thorn in the side of the Central Plains! Since Han was established, have there not been ministers with loyal advice and far-reaching stratagems, arguing with each other at Court on how to deal with them? There was Liu Jing in the reign of Gaozu; Fan Kuai and Ji Bu in the era of Empress Gaozu; Jia Yi and Chao Cuo under Emperor Wendi; Wang Hui, Han Anguo, Zhu Maichen, Gongsun Hong, and Dong Zhongshu under Emperor Wudi. They had decided opinions, but whatever the nuanced differences, they could be summed up as belonging to either of two categories. Gentry Confucian courtiers insisted on peace-making with the Huns through imperial marriages, whereas the armored warriors favored military expeditions to attack invading Huns. Their views tended to swing according to the benefits or damage in a particular period, but none was based on an in-depth study into the Huns’ history overall. From the rise of Han to the present day, more time has elapsed than the period chronicled in the *Spring and Autumn Annals*, and the relationship between us and the Huns has included ritual governance of peace-making by marriage and conquest by force of arms; there have been times of humble service and times of coercive vassal subjugation. Below we discuss in detail the shifts between submission and assertion, weakness and restoration of dominance.

【原文】

昔和亲之论，发于刘敬。是时天下初定，新遭平城之难，故从其言，约结和亲，赂遗单于，冀以救安边境。孝惠、高后时遵而不违，匈奴寇盗不为衰止，而单于反以加骄倨。逮至孝文，与通关市，妻以汉女，增厚其赂，岁以千金，而匈奴数背约束，边境屡被其害。是以文帝中年，赫然发愤，遂躬戎服，亲御鞌马，从六郡良家材力之士，驰射上林，讲习战陈，聚天下精兵，军于广武，顾问冯唐，与论将帅，喟然叹息，思古名臣，此则和亲无益，已然之明效也。

仲舒亲见四世之事，犹复欲守旧文，颇增其约。以为“义动君子，利动贪人，如匈奴者，非可以仁义说也，独可说以厚利，结之于天耳。故与之厚利以没其意，与盟于天以坚其约，质其爱子以累

【今译】

以往提倡与匈奴和亲的言论，是由刘敬开始的。当时天下刚刚安定，汉朝刚经历了在平城被匈奴围困的灾难，所以皇帝听从了他的建议，与匈奴商议和亲，送给单于金银粮棉，希望能够使边境安定。孝惠帝、高后的时候听从匈奴，不敢违抗，匈奴的侵掠却一点儿也没减少或停止，而单于反而更加骄狂。到了孝文帝时，与匈奴互通贸易，开放边境市场，把汉朝公主嫁给单于，增加送给匈奴的财物，每年要花一千金子，匈奴却屡次违反和约，汉朝边境屡遭侵害。所以文帝到了中年以后，发愤图强，亲自穿起戎装，骑上战马，率领六郡的精壮勇猛的战士，在上林苑练习骑马射箭，演练战阵，调集天下的精兵强将，驻扎在广武城。文帝向冯唐询问，和他谈论将帅，感叹思慕古代的名臣。因此与匈奴和亲毫无益处，已然是十分明了的了。

董仲舒亲眼见到了汉初四朝的那些事情，却还是想遵从过去的章程，大大增重与匈奴的规约。他认为“仁义能够感动君子，利益能够鼓动贪婪的小人，像匈奴人那样的，是不能用宣教仁义来使他们明白的，只能用厚利金钱使他们高兴，和他们向天发誓，结下盟约。所以应该多送给他们金银财物以消弭他们凶暴的攻击意识，与他们对天盟誓从而使双方缔结的盟约更牢固，让单于的爱子来汉朝

The theory of peace-making by marriage was advocated in the past by Liu Jing. At that time, the empire had not long been at peace under Han and the Dynasty had just experienced disaster at the hands of the Hun by being besieged in Pingcheng, so the Emperor listened to his proposal, and negotiated for peace by marriage alliance, sending sumptuous gifts to the Chanyu, in the hope of pacifying the border. Huidi and Empress Gaozu deferred to and appeased the Huns, but the raids and plundering neither abated nor stopped, and the Chanyu became more arrogant than ever. In the reign of Emperor Wendi, cross-border trade was opened, and a Han princess was married to their Chanyu, and gifts increased to 1,000 gold a year; but the Huns repeatedly violated their commitment and our border suffered repeated infringement. Therefore, though now a middle-aged man, Emperor Wendi enraged and resolved, donned military uniform, and took personal leadership of the fiercest fighters from military families of the six prefectures to drill in the Imperial Forest Park. There they trained in horseback archery and were briefed on battle formations. With the mobilization of the empire's crack troops, they were stationed in Guangwu. The Emperor consulted Feng Tang, talking about the generals and lamenting the absence of the famous ministers of old. It was already very clear that the peace-through-marriage policy had been no use whatsoever.

Dong Zhongshu witnessed those things over the reigns of four Han emperors, but still wanted to significantly increase the commitment to the Huns to comply with the decree of the past. He believed that "righteousness moves the gentleman, while profit is the spur for the greedy and low. People like the Huns are immune to persuasion by virtue, but can be made happy with lucrative gains, and bound by swearing to heaven. So we should give them money and goods galore so as to turn their minds from savage depredations, enter into vows to heaven with them to affirm their commitment, and use the Chanyu's beloved son as a hostage to influence any

【原文】

其心，匈奴虽欲展转，奈失重利何，奈欺上天何，奈杀爱子何。夫赋敛行赂不足以当三军之费，城郭之固无以异于贞士之约，而使边城守境之民父兄缓带，稚子咽哺，胡马不窥于长城，而羽檄不行于中国，不亦便于天下乎！”察仲舒之论，考诸行事，乃知其未合于当时，而有阙于后世也。当孝武时，虽征伐克获，而士马物故亦略相当；虽开河南之野，建朔方之郡，亦弃造阳之北九百馀里。匈奴人民每来降汉，单于亦辄拘留汉使以相报复，其桀骜尚如斯，安肯以爱子而为质乎？此不合当时之言也。若不置质，空约和亲，是袭孝文既往之悔，而长匈奴无已之诈也。夫边城不选守境武略之臣，脩障隧备塞之具，厉长戟劲弩之械，恃吾所以待边寇，而务赋敛于民，

【今译】

做人质从而使他下决心时受到牵累。即使匈奴想要辗转边塞，攻击汉朝，也没有办法不顾及到要失去金钱厚利、会欺骗上天、爱子会被杀死，从而无法举措。为向匈奴送礼而征收的钱财，比不上出动三军征伐匈奴所花费的军费；防御匈奴的坚固的城郭的效用，与派行为贞正的人与匈奴订立的盟约的效用也没有什么两样。而这样做，却能够使边塞城池中防卫边境的人们解下铠甲，得以轻松，使他们的孩子能够平安地吃口饭。使匈奴的骑兵不再窥视侵袭汉朝的长城，刀枪弓箭不再在中原流行，对于天下人民来说不是很便利的事情吗！”然而考察一下，董仲舒的言论，与当时的事实情势比较一下，就会知道他说的那些在当时是不合时宜的，对后世来说也有不正确的地方。在孝武帝的时候，虽然攻打匈奴，所获甚多，然而士兵、战马死去的数目与获得的也大致差不多；虽然开辟了河套以南的原野，建筑了朔方郡，可是也抛弃了造阳以北的地方九百多里。匈奴的百姓时时来投降汉朝，单于也总是扣留汉朝使者做为报复，他们桀骜不驯的性格还是原来那样，又怎么肯把自己的爱子交给汉朝做人质呢？这就是董仲舒言论不合当时时宜的地方。如果不能做到让匈奴人来做人质，和亲的盟约就是白纸一张，这就重犯了孝文帝过去的错误，而助长匈奴没完没了的欺诈行为。不选拔能够保卫国境的武将驻守边境上的城池；不修亭障、筑小路，准备保卫

decision that he makes. Even if the Huns are tempted to renege and attack us, they will not contemplate giving up on huge profits, or deceiving heaven, or causing the death of the beloved son. Thus, the taxation and levies to raise gifts to the Huns will cost us less than launching military expeditions against them; there is no difference in effectiveness between the strong walls and fortresses built against the Huns and the commitments brought back from them by our envoys of integrity. But by this course of action, we can give respite to our border people in the frontier fortresses so that the men can put aside their arms and relax and the children eat in safety, so that the Hun cavalry no longer spy along the Great Wall for a chance to attack, and the Central Plains no longer witness streams of arms and soldiers. Is that not much less vexatious for our people!" However, if we look at Dong Zhongshu's theory in the light of the actual situation, we will know that what he said was outdated at the time, and incorrect for future generations too. In the reign of Emperor Wudi, though the expeditions resulted in the conquering of wide areas, the loss of soldiers and horses was more or less equivalent; though they opened up Hetao, the wilderness within the Loop of the Yellow River, and constructed Shuofang Prefecture, they abandoned the 900-*li* area north of Zaoyang. Whenever the Hun population came to surrender to Han, the Chanyu would always detain Han envoys as payback. Obstinate and recalcitrant by nature, how was he willing to send his own beloved son as hostage? This is how Dong Zhongshu's remarks were off the mark. If the Huns cannot be prevailed upon to provide a hostage, a marriage alliance for peace is empty, which is to repeat Emperor Wendi's past mistakes, while contributing to the Huns' endless fraudulent behavior. Suppose we do not select frontier military commanders to defend the border cities, do not build castle beacons and get ready the means to defend the fortresses, do not sharpen halberds and prepare crossbows ready, so as to have something to rely on against the invaders. Suppose we

【原文】

远行货赂，割剥百姓，以奉寇雠，信甘言，守空约，而几胡马之不窥，不已过乎！

至孝宣之世，承武帝奋击之威，直匈奴百年之运，因其坏乱几亡之阸，权时施宜，覆以威德，然后单于稽首臣服，遣子入侍，[三]世称藩，宾于汉庭。是时边城晏闭，牛马布野，三世无犬吠之警，藜庶亡干戈之役。

后六十馀载之间，遭王莽篡位，始开边隙，单于由是归怨自绝，莽遂斩其侍子，边境之祸构矣。故呼韩邪始朝于汉，汉议其仪，而萧望之曰："戎狄荒服，言其来服荒忽无常，时至时去，宜待以客礼，让而不臣。如其后遂逃窜伏，使于中国不为叛臣。"及孝元时，议罢守塞之备，侯应以为不可。可谓盛不忘衰，安必思危，远

【今译】

边塞的手段；不把长戟磨锋利、把劲弓准备好，使我们有所凭藉、有所依靠，却一味向百姓横征暴敛，跑了好远去赂遗匈奴，剥夺百姓的财产，去送给我们的敌人。相信虚假的好话，信守空无一用的盟约，却期望匈奴人不来入侵，这不也太过分了吧！

到孝宣帝的时候，上承武帝奋勇攻击匈奴的余威，正碰上匈奴百年不遇的厄运，趁机利用他们的国内混乱，几乎亡国的灾祸，灵活地对待当时的情况，采取相适宜的方法，再加上对匈奴恩威并用，然后单于才向天子叩头，表示臣服，派儿子入朝侍奉，三代人做汉朝的外藩之臣，宾服于汉朝廷。当时边境城市安宁，牛马遍野，三代没有狗儿狂叫之类的警报，百姓不服兵役。

以后的六十多年的时间里，汉朝被王莽篡夺了江山，王莽开始挑起了边境争端，单于因此埋怨新朝，与中原断绝关系。王莽杀了单于入侍的儿子，边境上的祸端就这样开始了。所以呼韩邪单于起初到汉朝朝拜的时候，汉朝商议对待他的礼仪方式，萧望之就说："戎狄荒服，说的就是匈奴人来臣服于汉朝荒忽不定，没有常规，时而来了，时而去了，应当以待客人的礼节对待他，予以辞让，不让他做臣子。如果他的后代背叛了汉朝，远远地逃走了，也可以对于汉朝来说不成为臣子背叛。"到了孝元帝时，朝廷商议撤销边塞上守卫的军队，侯应认为不可以。他的见解可以称得上是在兴盛时

focus instead on imposing levies and taxes on our people to bribe the Huns to keep their distance. That amounts to depriving our own people to give to our enemies. If we believe in sweet words, and abide by empty treaties, still expecting the Huns not to make incursions, is this not too much?!

In the reign of Emperor Xuandi, benefiting from the after-effects of Wudi's courageous attacks and on the rare occasion of a Hun disaster, we took advantage of the domestic chaos of the Huns who had almost been destroyed. We treated the situation flexibly, taking the appropriate method of kindness coupled with severity, and only then did the Chanyu kowtow as a subject, sending his son to serve the Emperor. They remained allegiant to the Han imperial court for three generations. Back then, the border city gates did not close until very late at night, and oxen and horses were spread everywhere in the wilds; three generations were free of dogs barking warnings and the common people were free of conscription.

Within the following 60-odd years, Wang Mang usurped the throne and began to provoke discord in the border regions. This angered the Chanyu, who consequently severed relations with the new regime. Wang Mang killed the Chanyu's son who was then serving at Court, thus setting in motion calamity for the border regions. So, when the Chanyu of the Huhanye was beginning to pay homage to Han, the Han court deliberated what ritual to accord him, Xiao Wangzhi said: "Rong and Di are remote and barely subjugated, meaning that the Huns' allegiance to Han was fickle and uncertain, one minute there the next minute not, so we should treat them as guests in courtesy, but politely decline to admit them as our courtiers. If their descendants were to rebel against Han and flee far, then they would not in Han eyes count as insurgent courtiers." Under Emperor Yuandi, there was some discussion of recalling the army guards on the frontier, but Hou Ying advised against this. His long-sighted, clear-focused views can be called "in prosperity, not forgetting

【原文】

见识微之明矣。至单于咸弃其爱子，昧利不顾，侵掠所获，岁钜万计，而和亲赂遗，不过千金，安在其不弃质而失重利也？仲舒之言，漏于是矣。

夫规事建议，不图万世之固，而媮恃一时之事者，未(必)[可]以经远也。若乃征伐之功，秦汉行事，严尤论之当矣。故先王度土，中立封畿，分九州，列五服，物土贡，制外内，或脩刑政，或昭文德，远近之势异也。是以《春秋》内诸夏而外夷狄。夷狄之人贪而好利，被发左衽，人面兽心，其与中国殊章服，异习俗，饮食不同，言语不通，辟居北垂寒露之野，逐草随畜，射猎为生，隔以山谷，雍以沙幕，天地所以绝外内也。是故圣王禽兽畜之，不与约誓，不就攻伐；约之则费赂而见欺，攻之则劳师而招寇。其地不可

【今译】

不忘衰落，居安思危，看得细，有远见之明。到单于咸的时候，抛弃了他在汉朝的爱子，贪得重利，不顾其他，侵盗掠夺所得到的财物，一年里就数以万计，可是和亲所带来的，不过千金，他怎么会不抛弃做人质的儿子而去追逐重利呢？董仲舒的言论，从这里可以看出很大漏洞。

考虑事情，提供建议，不从谋求万世之固的眼光出发，而苟且地依赖某一时的情势，那样的建议是不能够用来治理长远以后的事情的。至于用武力征伐匈奴的功效，秦朝、汉朝为对付匈奴所做的事情的长短，严尤的议论是很正确的。所以先王规划度量国土，在中原地带设立王畿国都，天下划分为九州，王畿京都周围的地方划分为五服，向朝廷上贡各地物产，因五服的远近差异而制定不同的制度。在有的地方尚用刑法，有的地方昭明文治，是因为地理位置的远近，情势不同所决定的。因此《春秋》中说：把中原各族看作内部关系，把夷狄看作外族。夷狄的人贪婪好利，披发左衽，人面兽心。他们与中原人服饰制度不同，风俗也不一样，吃的东西也不同，言语不通；居住在偏僻的北部边陲，暴露于荒野寒露之中，逐水草而放牧，随牲畜而迁徙，以射鸟猎兽为生计；被山谷分隔开，被沙漠所壅塞，这是天地自然把他们与中原断绝开，外内不同啊。所以圣明的君王像对待禽兽一样对待他们，不与他们立约盟誓，也

decline; enjoying peace but preparing for danger." When Chanyu Xian abandoned his beloved son in the Han court, he was fixated on profit to the exclusion of all else. What he seized in invasion and plunder amounted to millions a year, compared to a paltry thousand gold that marriage peace brought. Why would he not abandon his son as hostage in favor of heavy profits? Dong Zhongshu's reasoning really did not hold water!

In planning and advising, if we do not seek permanent solidity, but are swayed according to the temporary situation, the proposal will not be a durable one. As for the discussion in the Qin and Han dynasties of the pros and cons of military campaigns against the Huns, Yan You's opinion on the issue was totally right.

So the early Kings, in measuring land, established their capital in the Central Plains area, and divided the world into nine regions in a range of five rings, categorized for their tribute of local produce, and developed different systems for the outer and inner rings. In some places, they established a code of laws and penalties; in others, they ruled by civil example, the difference reflecting the different geographical situation. Therefore, in the *Spring and Autumn Annals* it says: "All peoples of the Central Plains area are regarded as native, while barbarian peoples are aliens. The barbarians are greedy and profit-grabbing, brutish at heart, wearing their hair long and buttoning their garments to the left. They are different from the Central Plains people in their costume, customs, food, and language; living in the remote northern border, exposed to cold dew in the wilderness, they live nomadically, follow their grazing herds and hunting for a livelihood; they are separated by mountains and valleys, and blocked by deserts. And by such means did heaven and earth cut them off from the Central Plains and separate the inner world from the outside. Thus the sage kings treated them like they would livestock, neither entering into treaties with them, nor engaging in war with them; to make treaties with them would be to

【原文】

耕而食也，其民不可臣而畜也，是以外而不内，疏而不戚，政教不及其人，正朔不加其国；来则惩而御之，去则备而守之。其慕义而贡献，则接之以礼让，羁靡不绝，使曲在彼，盖圣王制御蛮夷之常道也。

——卷九十四下《匈奴传》第六十四下

【今译】

不去从事战争，攻打他们；与他们立盟约就会既花费钱财贿赂，又被欺骗，攻打他们就会使军队疲惫，又招来他们的侵袭。他们那里的土地不能耕种从而提供食物，他们的人民不能做为臣子从而抚养他们，所以要排斥而不接纳他们，疏远而不亲近他们，政治教化不顾及到他们的百姓，正朔历法不对他们使用；他们来进攻就杀伤、抵御他们，他们离去就防备他们，守住边塞。他们向慕仁义，来朝拜天子贡献礼品，那么就按礼节接待他们，笼络他们，不主动与他们断绝关系，使理亏的一方在他们那一边，这大概就是圣明的君王制服、驾御匈奴蛮夷的常道。

waste bribe money and get deceived; to attack them would exhaust the army and invite an invasion. Their land could not grow food, and their people could not be raised as subjects, so they excluded rather than absorbed them, kept them at a distance rather than close; politics via moral education was not applied to their people, nor our standard calendar to their region. If they attacked us, we killed and resisted them; when they left we prepared against the next time and guarded our fortresses. If they paid tributes to Court out of admiration for our righteousness, we accepted them with complaisance proper to the rules of propriety, conciliating rather than breaking relations with them, so that they would always be the side at fault. Thus, not engaging was the sage kings' preferred method of controlling the barbarians."

西域传序赞

【原文】

西域以孝武时始通，本三十六国，其后稍分至五十馀，皆在匈奴之西，乌孙之南。南北有大山，中央有河，东西六千馀里，南北千馀里。东则接汉，阸以玉门、阳关，西则限以葱岭。其南山，东出金城，与汉南山属焉。其河有两原：一出葱岭山，一出于阗。于阗在南山下，其河北流，与葱岭河合，东注蒲昌海。蒲昌海，一名盐泽者也，去玉门、阳关三百馀里，广袤三百里。其水亭居，冬夏不增减，皆以为潜行地下，南出于积石，为中国河云。

自玉门、阳关出西域有两道。从鄯善傍南山北，波河西行至莎车，为南道；南道西逾葱岭则出大月氏、安息。自车师前王廷随北山，波河西行至疏勒，为北道；北道西逾葱岭则出大宛、康居、奄蔡焉(耆)。

【今译】

西域从汉武帝时开始与中原交通，那里本来有三十六国。后来渐分为五十余国，都分布在匈奴以西，乌孙以南。西域南北有大山，中央有河流，东西宽六千余里，南北长一千余里。它的东面连接汉朝，以玉门关和阳关为险塞，西边以葱岭为界。它的南山，东面起于金城郡，与汉朝的南山相连。它的河有两个源头：一个发源于葱岭山，一个发源于于阗。于阗在南山下，河向北流，与葱岭河汇合后，向东注入蒲昌海。蒲昌海又名盐泽，东距玉门关和阳关三百余里，湖面长宽约三百里。湖水稳定，冬夏不增减，湖水在地下潜流，向南从积石山冒出，就是中原地区的黄河。

从玉门关、阳关到西域有两条道路。从鄯善沿着南山北面，顺塔里木河西行至莎车，为南道；南道西越葱岭可到大月氏、安息。自车师前王廷沿着北山南面，顺塔里木河西行至疏勒，为北道；北道西越葱岭可到大宛、康居、奄蔡。

Chapter 21

Preface and Author's Comments on Annals of the Western Region

It was in the reign of Emperor Wudi that the Western Regions became accessible from the Central Plains and at the time there were 36 kingdoms, which later divided into more than 50, all of them located to the west of the territory of the Huns, and to the south of the Wusun people. High mountains rise both north and south, and a river flows through the middle; the lands stretch 6,000 *li* from east to west, and over 1,000 *li* from north to south. Its eastern boundaries are contiguous with the Han empire, with frontier posts at Yumen and Yangguan passes; it is delimited by the Congling Mountains to the west. Its Nanshan (South Mountain) has its eastern extremity in Jincheng Prefecture, and joins with Han's Nanshan. The river has two sources: one in Congling Mountains, the other in Khotan. Khotan is situated at the foot of Nanshan, and the river flows north to the confluence of the Congling River, continuing eastward to empty into Puchang Lake. Puchang Lake is also known as Salt Marshes, 300-odd *li* from Yumen and Yangguan, and the lake is 300 *li* in length and width. Its size is constant, neither increasing in winter nor shrinking in summer. The river then flows underground, emerging at Jishi to the south. This is the Yellow River that flows through our Central Plains. From Yumen Pass and Yangguan Pass two routes take you into the Western Regions. From Shanshan along the north side of Nanshan, we go westbound following the Tarim River to Yarkand, that is, the Southern Route; traveling west on this route, we cross Congling Mountains to Greater Yuezhi and Parthia. From the former royal capital of Jushi, we go along the North Mountain, following the Tarim westward to Shule (Kashgar), that is, the

【原文】

西域诸国大率土著，有城郭田畜，与匈奴、乌孙异俗，故皆役属匈奴。匈奴西边日逐王置僮仆都尉，使领西域，常居焉耆、危须、尉黎间，赋税诸国，取富给焉。

自周衰，戎狄错居泾渭之北。及秦始皇攘却戎狄，筑长城，界中国，然西不过临洮。

汉兴至于孝武，事征四夷，广威德，而张骞始开西域之迹。其后骠骑将军击破匈奴右地，降浑邪、休屠王，遂空其地，始筑令居以西，初置酒泉郡，后稍发徙民充实之，分置武威、张掖、敦煌，列四郡，据两关焉。自贰师将军伐大宛之后，西域震惧，多遣使来贡献，汉使西域者益得职。于是自敦煌西至盐泽，往往起亭，而轮

【今译】

西域各国大多过着定居生活，有城郭、田地、牲畜，和匈奴、乌孙的风俗不同，从前都受奴役并隶属于匈奴。匈奴西部的日逐王设置僮仆都尉，管理西域，经常驻在焉耆、危须、尉黎等地，向各国征收赋税，很富足。

自周朝衰落以后，戎、狄等族杂居在泾水、渭水以北。到了秦始皇时，赶走了戎、狄，修筑长城，为中原国家的边境，但秦的西边不超过临洮县。

西汉建立到武帝时，经营四周民族地区，宣扬威德，于是张骞开始开通西域之路。以后骠骑将军霍去病击败匈奴右地，浑邪王、休屠王投降，右地遂无匈奴，汉开始在令居以西筑烽燧，开始设酒泉郡，稍后，征发民众来到这里居住，又设置武威、张掖、敦煌，共四郡，并据守玉门、阳关二关。自从贰师将军李广利伐大宛以后，西域各国都很骇怕，多数国家派使者来长安进贡，汉朝到西域的使者越来越得到赏赐、升官。于是从敦煌西到盐泽，到处建立亭障，在轮台、渠犁都有屯田卒数百人，汉设使者校尉领导监护屯田事，

Northern Route; heading west on this route we cross the Congling Mountains to Dayuan, Kangqu, and Alani.

The people of the Western Regions mostly live a sedentary life, with castles and walls, farmland and livestock. Their ways are very different from those of the Huns and Wusun, but formerly they were enslaved and annexed by the Huns. In the western areas of Hun territory their King Rizhu set up a Commandery of Servants, to rule over the Western Region, often stationed in the areas of Yanqi, Weixu and Yuli, collecting taxes from these kingdoms, and getting very rich.

After the decline of Zhou, the Rong and Di peoples lived sporadically north of the Wei and Jing rivers. When the First Emperor of Qin got rid of the Rong and Di by building the Great Wall as the borders of the Central Kingdom, the western limit of Qin power did not extend past Lintao.

When the Han Dynasty reached the reign of Wudi, the Emperor operated on the barbarian areas neighboring the empire, to promote his influence and virtue; and then Zhang Qian opened up the route to the Western Regions. After that, Cavalry General Huo defeated the Huns on their right-hand area, so that King Hunye and King Xiutu surrendered and left the area unpopulated. Han began building outposts to the west of Lingju and set up Jiuquan Prefecture. Later, migrants were moved here to fill the place; Wuwei, Zhangye, and Dunhuang were also established, making a total of four prefectures, and troops were garrisoned at Yumen and Yangguan passes. After Ershi General Li Guangli conquered Dayuan, the kingdoms of the Western Regions were frightened and most states sent envoys to Chang'an bearing tribute. The gifts given to Han envoys sent to the Western Regions became ever more sumptuous. So, from west of Dunhuang to the Salt Marshes, fortresses sprang up in great number, and both in Luntai and Quli were stationed hundreds of soldiers in state farm camps. Envoy commandants were established for leading

【原文】

台、渠犁皆有田卒数百人，置使者校尉领护，以给使外国者。

至宣帝时，遣卫司马使护鄯善以西数国。及破姑师，未尽殄，分以为车师前后王及山北六国。时汉独护南道，未能尽并北道也，然匈奴不自安矣。其后日逐王畔单于，将众来降，护鄯善以西使者郑吉迎之。既至汉，封日逐王为归德侯，吉为安远侯。是岁，神爵三年也。乃因使吉并护北道，故号曰都护。都护之起，自吉置矣。僮仆都尉由此罢，匈奴益弱，不得近西域。于是徙屯田，田于北胥鞬，披莎车之地，屯田校尉始属都护。都护督察乌孙、康居诸外国动静，有变以闻。可安辑，安辑之；可击，击之。都护治乌垒城，去阳关二千七百三十八里，与渠犁田官相近，土地肥饶，于西域为中，故都护治焉。

至元帝时，复置戊己校尉，屯田车师前王庭。是时匈奴东蒲类王

【今译】

并供应汉朝到外国的使者的生活。

到宣帝时，派卫司马负责监护鄯善以西几个国家。到了打败姑师的时候，并未全部消灭他们，只是将他们分为车师前王、车师后王和山北六国。当时汉朝只监护南道，没有全部兼并北道，可是匈奴已经感到很不安了。以后，日逐王背叛单于，率领部众来降汉朝，汉的护鄯善以西使者郑吉迎接日逐王。到了汉朝，汉封日逐王为归德侯，郑吉为安远侯。这一年是神爵三年。汉就使郑吉并护北道，所以号称“都护”。都护之设置从郑吉开始。匈奴原设在西域的僮仆都尉从此罢掉，匈奴更弱了，不能靠近西域。于是汉迁徙百姓屯田在北胥鞬，分莎车之地，从此屯田校尉开始属于都护。都护侦察乌孙、康居等外国的情况，如有动静，立即报告皇帝。可以安抚的就安抚；需要打击的就打击。都护驻乌垒城，东到阳关二千七百三十八里，和渠犁的屯田官接近，土地肥沃，在西域的中央，所以都护驻在这里。

到元帝时，又设置戊己校尉，屯田于车师前王庭。这时，匈奴东

and guarding them, and for providing supplies to Han envoys to the foreign countries.

In the reign of Xuandi, the Protector Commandant was sent, to keep watch over several states to the west of Shanshan. After routing the Gushi, we did not wipe them out completely, but just divided them as the Front and Rear Kingdoms of Jushi, and the six states north of the mountains. At that time, Han only guarded the Southern Route, having not yet annexed the whole Northern Route, but the Huns were feeling very uneasy. Later, King Rizhu turned his back on the Chanyu, and led his clan to surrender to Han, so Zheng Ji, the Han envoy protector of the area west of Shanshan, went to escort him. When they arrived in Court, King Rizhu was appointed Marquis of Guide (Return to Virtue) and Zheng Ji was made Marquis of Anyuan (Making Safe the Remote Area). This happened in year three of the Shenjue reign period (59 BC). Then Zheng Ji was given responsibility for the Northern Route also, together with the corresponding title of "Protector General." Zheng Ji was the first Protector General and the position endured. The Commandery of Servants was canceled and the Huns were weakened, being prevented from coming near the Western Regions. So the Han peoples relocated the state farm to Beixujian, divided the land of Yarkand and reverted their commandants to the jurisdiction of the Protector General. The Protector General closely monitored the movements of Wusun, Kangqu and other foreign states, and immediately reported any developments to the Emperor. When they could be appeased, he did so; when fighting was called for, he attacked them. The Protector General was based in the City of Wulei, 2,738 *li* from Yangguan Pass, and close to the state farm office in Quli, chosen for its fertile land and central position in the Western Regions.

In the reign of Yuandi, Wuji Commandant was also established, with his state farm based at the court of the Front King of Jushi. At this time, Dongpulei King Zilizhi of the Huns led 1,700 men of his

【原文】

兹力支将人众千七百馀人降都护，都护分车师后王之西为乌贪訾离地以处之。

自宣、元后，单于称藩臣，西域服从，其土地山川王侯户数道里远近翔实矣。

赞曰：孝武之世，图制匈奴，患其兼从西国，结党南羌，乃表河(曲)[西]，列(西)[四]郡，开玉门，通西域，以断匈奴右臂，隔绝南羌、月氏。单于失援，由是远遁，而幕南无王庭。

遭值文、景玄默，养民五世，天下殷富，财力有馀，士马强盛。故能睹犀布、玳瑁则建珠崖七(部)[郡]，感枸酱、竹杖则开牂柯、越巂，闻天马、蒲陶则通大宛、安息。自是之后，明珠、文甲、通犀、翠羽之珍盈于后宫，蒲梢、龙文、鱼目、汗血之马充于黄门，钜象、师子、猛犬、大雀之群食于外囿。殊方异物，四面而至。于是广开上林，穿昆明池，营千门万户之宫，立神明通天之台，兴造甲乙之帐，落以随珠和璧，天子负黼依，袭翠被，冯玉几，而处其

【今译】

蒲类王兹力支率领部众一千七百余人投降都护，都护分车师后王西面的土地为乌贪訾离国，安排兹立支部居住。

自宣帝、元帝以后，匈奴单于向汉称藩臣，西域也服从汉朝，西域的土地、山川、王侯、户口、道里远近，都得以详实记载下来。

赞曰：汉武帝时，力图制服匈奴。但匈奴胁从西域各国，又联合南羌，构成汉朝的大患。汉武帝就设河西四郡，开玉门关，通于西域，以切断匈奴的右臂，隔开与南羌、月氏的联系。单于失去了西域各国和羌人的支援，从此向远方逃去，沙漠以南没有匈奴的王庭了。

经历文景无为而治，休养生息五代，天下富庶，财力有余，兵马强盛。所以汉武帝能见到犀、象、玳瑁就开建了珠崖等七郡，有感于枸酱、竹杖就开设了牂柯、越巂等郡，听说天马、葡萄就打通了大宛、安息之路。从这以后，明珠、玳瑁、通犀、翠羽等珍宝积满了后宫，蒲梢、龙文、鱼目、汗血各种骏马充满了黄门，大象、狮子、猛犬、鸵鸟成群地游食于苑囿中。远方的珍奇异物自四面而来。于是汉武帝扩大上林苑，开掘昆明池，建千门万户之宫，筑神明通天之台，制甲乙之帐，系随珠和璧，武帝列彩绣之屏风，

tribe to surrender to the Protector General, who divided the western territories of Jushi's Rear King as Wutanzili Kingdom, so as to accommodate them.

Author's Comment: In the reign of Emperor Wudi, Han tried to subjugate the Huns, but the latter coerced the kingdoms of the Western Regions into cooperation and also allied with the Southern Qiang, creating a nightmare scenario for Han. Emperor Wudi marked the boundary in Hexi and set up four prefectures, opening Yumen Pass to the Western Regions, in order to cut off the right arm of the Huns, and cut their contact with the Southern Qiang and Yuezhi. Without this support, the Chanyu then fled to a remote area, so that south of the desert there was no royal base for the Huns.

The reigns of Wendi and Jingdi were characterized by non-intervention and recuperation for five generations; the empire was prosperous and rich, financial resources more than adequate, and the army strong. So Wudi set up the seven prefectures of Zhuya, etc. when he wanted to lay his hands on rhinos, elephants, and hawksbills; and opened Zangke and Yuexi when he missed Japanese raisin sauce and bamboo canes; and communicated with Dayuan and Parthia when he heard of Ferghana horses and grapes. After that, treasures like pearls, tortoiseshell, rhinoceros horn, and peacock feathers filled his harem, and horses like Pushao, Dragon-pattern, Fisheye, and Ferghana filled the Imperial Palace; herds of elephants, lions, bulldogs, and ostriches fed in the enclosure. Distant exotic articles came from every direction. So Wudi expanded the Imperial Forest Parkland, dug Kunming Pool, built the palace of one thousand doors, and the Shenming and Tongtian terraces, as well as Tent Jia and Tent Yi hung with Marquis of Sui luminous bead and Mr. He's jade. The Son of Heaven lived surrounded by screens with ax patterns, with outer garments of peacock feathers, and reclined on couches ornamented with jade. The Emperor entertained barbarian

【原文】

中。设酒池肉林以飨四夷之客，作《巴俞》都卢、海中《砀极》、漫衍鱼龙、角抵之戏以观视之。及赂遗赠送，万里相奉，师旅之费，不可胜计。至于用度不足，乃榷酒酤，筦盐铁，铸白金，造皮币，算至车船，租及六畜。民力屈，财用竭，因之以凶年，寇盗并起，道路不通，直指之使始出，衣绣杖斧，断斩于郡国，然后胜之。是以末年遂弃轮台之地，而下哀痛之诏，岂非仁圣之所悔哉！且通西域，近有龙堆，远则葱岭，身热、头痛、縣度之阸。淮南、杜钦、扬雄之论，皆以为此天地所以界别区域，绝外内也。《书》曰“西戎即序”，禹既就而序之，非上威服致其贡物也。

西域诸国，各有君长，兵众分弱，无所统一，虽属匈奴，不相亲附。匈奴能得其马畜旃罽，而不能统率与之进退。与汉隔绝，

【今译】

披翠羽之外衣，依玉饰之几案。武帝住在这里，设酒池肉林招待四周少数民族客人；表演《巴俞》之舞，都卢、海中《砀极》，鱼龙幻术，化装角抵等戏。还有赏赐送礼，万里供给，军队花费，不计其数。财政不够使用，就国家专卖酒，专营盐铁，铸白金造皮币为钱，征收车船六畜之税。民力屈尽，财用枯竭，再加之荒年歉收，寇盗并起，道路不通，于是武帝命直指使者暴胜之等穿绣衣，持斧钺，到各郡国进行镇压，然后取得胜利。到武帝末年，放弃了轮台屯田，下了沉痛诏书，这不是仁人圣者所悔悟的事吗！况且通西域的道路上，近的有白龙堆，远的有葱岭，还有身热、头痛、县度等险要地区。淮南王刘安、杜钦、扬雄的议论，都认为这是天地设置来划分区域的，以隔绝内外。《尚书》说“西戎即序”，是说禹在治洪水、划九州之后，把西戎各国划在一定的范围之内，不是靠皇上的威武来让他们进贡的。

西域诸国，各有自己的君长，军队分散力弱，不能统一。虽曾属于匈奴，但与匈奴并不亲密。匈奴能得到他们的马畜氈罽，但不能统率他们进攻或退却。他们与汉朝隔绝，道路遥远，得到他们不算

guests with ponds of wine and forests of meat, with performances of Ba and Yu dances, Dulu acrobatics, Dangji music from the sea, circus, and wrestling bouts. His rewards and gifts were presented across tens of thousands of *li*, and military spending was beyond counting. When government coffers could not cope, this led to the state monopoly on wine and control of salt and iron production, cast silver was made and leather coin instituted, and the taxes were levied on carts, boats and domestic animals. The people were at the end of their tether, and government resources were drained dry; add to this poor harvests in the years of famine, and there was a consequent rise of bandits and impassable roads. So Emperor Wudi ordered out the straight-pointer envoys, in fine embroidered garb and bearing a symbolic ax to suppress the despots in the prefectures and fiefs, and won a violent victory. In the last years of his reign, Emperor Wudi gave up the Luntai state farm, and issued the painful edict. Was this not something to be repented by the benevolent sage! Moreover, when the route to the Western Regions was opened, as near as the White Dragon Terraces or as far as Congling Mountains, the way was beset by dangers of fevers, headaches, and suspended crossings. The Prince of Huainan Liu An, Du Qin, and Yang Xiong voiced their opinions, all thinking this was the boundary region where the world was divided, in order to isolate the inner world from the beyond. The *Book of Documents* said: "They are all set west of the Rong." This means that after King Yu controlled the flood and divided the land into nine *zhou*, he divided up the kingdoms of West Rong into spheres of influence, and that country was not designated as a zone that paid tribute to the awesome majesty of the Emperor.

The kingdoms of the Western Regions all had their own monarchs or chiefs, but their armies were too dispersed and weak to be unified. Although they had been subjugated by the Huns, they were not close to them. The Huns could get their horses, livestock, and felt carpets, but could not command them to attack or retreat.

【原文】

道里又远，得之不为益，弃之不为损。盛德在我，无取于彼。故自建武以来，西域思汉威德，咸乐内属。唯其小邑鄯善、车师，界迫匈奴，尚为所拘。而其大国莎车、于阗之属，数遣使置质于汉，愿请属都护。圣上远览古今，因时之宜，羁縻不绝，辞而未许。虽大禹之序西戎，周公之让白雉，太宗之却走马，义兼之矣，亦何以尚兹！

——卷九十六上、下《西域传》第六十六上、下

【今译】

有益，抛弃他们不算损失。汉朝的盛德是我们自己创造的，并不依靠他们得来。所以自光武帝建武以来，西域各国思念汉朝的威德，都愿意内属。只有小国如鄯善、车师地近匈奴，还受到匈奴的控制。其他大国如莎车、于阗等，数次派使者送质子来汉朝，并希望允准他们属于都护。光武帝考察古今历史，根据当时的形势，采取羁縻政策，不同意派出西域都护，亦遣回各国的质子。虽然大禹划定西戎之区域，周公不收越裳氏之白雉，汉文帝不收千里马，都是古圣贤之美事，但光武帝之所为都兼有此义，没有比这一做法更高明的了。

Isolated from Han, their roads are far away. To have them was no great advantage and it was no great loss to abandon them. The flourishing virtue Han was of our own creation, not at all dependent on them. Therefore, since the Jianwu reign of Emperor Guangwu, the Western Region states, missing our might and virtue, became willing to align with us of their own accord. Only a few small places, such as Shanshan and Jushi, whose territory is near to the Huns, are still controlled by the Huns. But their big kingdoms, like Yarkand and, Khotan, on several occasions sent envoys and left their hostages with Han, and consented to come under our Protector General. But the Emperor, having consulted ancient and recent history, adopted a policy of engagement according to the current circumstances, so he declined to admit them to the protectorate and sent the hostages away. Though King Yu demarcated the zone of West Rong, the Duke of Zhou declined the tribute of a white pheasant, and the Han Emperor Wendi returned the fast steed. These were noble deeds of the ancient sages, but Emperor Guangwu was equal in this virtue, and there was no loftier approach than his.

外戚传序

【原文】

自古受命帝王及继体守文之君，非独内德茂也，盖亦有外戚之助焉。夏之兴也以涂山，而桀之放也用末喜；殷之兴也以有娀(又)[及]有㜪，而纣之灭也嬖妲己；周之兴也以姜嫄及太任、太姒，而幽王之禽也淫褒姒。故《易》基《乾》、《坤》，《诗》首《关雎》，《书》美釐降，《春秋》讥不亲迎。夫妇之际，人道之大伦也。礼之用，唯昏姻为兢兢。夫乐调而四时和，阴阳之变，万物之统也，可不慎与！人能弘道，末如命何。甚哉，妃匹之爱，君不能得之臣，父不能得之子，况卑下乎！既欢合矣，或不能成子姓，成子姓矣，

【今译】

自古以来，那些创业的帝王以及继承皇位遵循先王成法的君主，并非只凭自己美好的德行，也与外戚的帮助分不开。夏朝的兴起与涂山氏有关，而桀遭到放逐则是起因于末喜；殷代的兴起离不开有娀氏和有㜪氏，而纣的灭亡则是由于宠信妲己；周朝的兴起有赖于姜嫄、太任和太姒，而幽王被戎狄擒捉则是因为与褒姒淫乐。因此《易》从《乾》《坤》二卦开始，《诗经》以《关雎》为第一篇，《尚书》赞美唐尧把两个女儿嫁给虞舜，《春秋》讽刺鲁隐公娶妻而不亲自迎娶。夫妇关系是人伦之大事。礼法中婚姻之事要谨慎而行。音乐和谐，四时才能和谐。阴阳的变化，生成天地万物，又怎么能够不慎重呢！人可以弘扬大道，对待天命却无可奈何。配偶之间的感情是超过一切的，即使凭着君父地位之尊，也无法勉强臣下子女，更何况低贱之辈呢！夫妻之爱欢乐融洽，有些人却不能生儿育女，而生养了儿女，却又不能得到善终，这些难道不正是天命吗！

Chapter 22

Preface to Biography of Emperors' In-Laws

Since ancient times, monarchs who received the Mandate of Heaven, or inherited the throne and followed their predecessors' laws, relied not just on their great virtue, but also on the help of the consort's family. The rise of the Xia was related to the Tushan clan, while Jie was exiled because of Moxi; the rise of Yin would not have been possible without the Yousongs and the Youshens, while Zhou's demise was due to his favoritism for Lady Daji; the rise of the Zhou Dynasty depended on Jiang Yuan, Tairen and Taisi, while King You was captured by Rong and Di tribes because he was indulging in carnal pleasures with Baosi. Thus, the *Book of Changes* starts with the trigrams "qian" (masculine) and "kun" (feminine), the first in the *Book of Odes* is "Fishhawk Singing," the *Book of Documents* praises how King Yao married his two daughters to King Shun, while the *Spring and Autumn Annals* mocks how Duke Yin of Lu did not receive his wife in person. The relationship of husband and wife is the major ethics of humanity. In the practice of rite, great caution must be exercised in the matter of marriage. Only when music is harmonious will the four seasons be in harmony too. Changes of *yin* and *yang* generate the continuum of all things. How can we not be careful about it! A man can enlarge the Way which he follows, but he is helpless before destiny. The emotion of spousal love surpasses all, a love that even a monarch cannot force from subjects, nor can a father get from his children, not to mention the inferior people! After joyous consummation, some people may not bear children; and there are those who, despite producing children, may not enjoy married love right to the end. Are these things not in the hands of fate!

【原文】

而不能要其终，岂非命也哉！孔子罕言命，盖难言之。非通幽明之变，恶能识乎性命！

汉兴，因秦之称号，帝母称皇太后，祖母称太皇太后，適称皇后，妾皆称夫人。又有美人、良人、八子、七子、长使、少使之号焉。至武帝制倢伃、娙娥、傛华、充依，各有爵位，而元帝加昭仪之号，凡十四等云。昭仪位视丞相，爵比诸侯王。倢伃视上卿，比列侯。娙娥视中二千石，比关内侯。傛华视真二千石，比大上造。美人视二千石，比少上造。八子视千石，比中更，充依视千石，比左更。七子视八百石，比右庶长。良人视八百石，比左庶长。长使视六百石，比五大夫。少使视四百石，比公乘。五官视三百石。顺常视二百石。无涓、共和、娱灵、保林、良使、夜者皆视百石。上家人子、中家人子视有秩斗食云。五官以下，葬司马门外。

——卷九十七上《外戚传》第六十七上

【今译】

孔子很少谈论天命，大概是由于难以讲述清楚。不懂得阴阳变化，又怎么能知晓性命呢！

汉朝沿袭秦朝的称号，皇帝的母亲称为皇太后，祖母称为太皇太后，嫡妻称为皇后，妾都称为夫人。又有美人、良人、八子、七子、长使、少使等称号。到汉武帝时，设婕妤、娙娥、傛华、充依，各有一定的爵位，元帝时又加设昭仪的称号，共有十四个等级。昭仪的禄秩相当于丞相，爵位与诸侯王相当。婕妤相当于上卿，爵位与列侯相当。娙娥相当于中二千石，爵位与关内侯相同。傛华相当于真二千石，爵位与大上造相同。美人相当于二千石，爵位与少上造相同。八子相当于千石，爵位与中更相同。充依相当于千石，爵位与左更相同。七子相当于八百石，爵位与右庶长等同。良人相当于八百石，爵位与左庶长等同。长使相当于六百石，爵位与五大夫等同。少使相当于四百石，爵位与公乘等同。五官相当于三百石。顺常相当于二百石。无涓、共和、娱灵、保林、良使、夜者都相当于百石。上家人子、中家人子相当于有秩禄的斗食。五官以下的等级，死后埋葬在司马门之外。

Confucius rarely talked about destiny, probably because it is difficult to describe. Without knowledge of the changes of *yin* and *yang*, how can we know our life and the nature of living!

The Han Dynasty followed the Qin system of titles, so that the emperor's mother was called the empress dowager, and his grandmother, known as the grand empress dowager, his consort was called empress and his concubines madames. Other court lady titles were beauty, virtuous lady, eighth lady, seventh lady, senior chamber lady and junior chamber lady. In the reign of Emperor Wudi, new titles were established: lady of handsome fairness, jing'e, ronghua, chongyi, each with a certain rank. Emperor Yuandi added the title of lady of bright deportment, making a total of 14 ranks. The allowance of the lady of bright deportment was equivalent to that of the prime minister, and her title equivalent to that of a prince. The lady of handsome fairness was equivalent to the superior chamberlain, and, in title, to an adjunct marquis. The jing'e was equivalent to a full 2,000-picul official, and, in title, to Marquis of Guannei. The ronghua was equivalent to an almost 2,000-picul official, and, in title to a major *shangzao*. The beauty was equivalent to a 2,000-picul official, and, in title, to a minor *shangzao*. The eighth lady was equivalent to a 1,000-picul official, and, in title, to a center *geng*. The chongyi was equivalent to a 1,000-picul official, and, in title, to a left *geng*. Seventh lady was equivalent to an 800-picul official, and, in title, to a right *shuzhang*. The virtuous lady was equivalent to an 800-picul official, and in title, to a left *shuzhang*. The senior chamber lady made the equivalent of 600 piculs, and her title was equivalent to the *wudafu*. Junior chamber lady made the equivalent of 400 piculs, and her title was equivalent to *gongcheng*. The *wuguan* is the equivalent of 300 piculs. The *Shunchang* the equivalent of 200 piculs. *Wujuan*, *gonghe*, *yuling*, *baolin*, *liangshi*, and *yezhe* were all equivalent to 100 piculs. Upper family girl and medium family girl were equivalent to the petty official with rank. Ladies below the rank of *wuguan* were buried outside the Outer Palace Gate.

李夫人传

【原文】

孝武李夫人，本以倡进。初，夫人兄延年性知音，善歌舞，武帝爱之。每为新声变曲，闻者莫不感动。延年侍上起舞，歌曰：“北方有佳人，绝世而独立，一顾倾人城，再顾倾人国。宁不知倾城与倾国，佳人难再得!”上叹息曰：“善！世岂有此人乎？”平阳主因言延年有女弟，上乃召见之，实妙丽善舞。由是得幸，生一男，是为昌邑哀王。李夫人少而蚤卒，上怜闵焉，图画其形于甘泉宫。及卫思后废后四年，武帝崩，大将军霍光缘上雅意，以李夫人配食，追上尊号曰孝武皇后。

初，李夫人病笃，上自临候之，夫人蒙被谢曰：“妾久寝病，形貌毁坏，不可以见帝。愿以王及兄弟为托。”上曰：“夫人病甚，

【今译】

孝武帝李夫人，原本是作为歌伎进宫的。起初，李夫人的哥哥李延年精通音律，擅长歌舞，武帝很喜欢他。李延年每次作出新的乐曲，听到的人没有不受感动的。他为武帝跳舞，唱道：“北方有个美人，风华绝代，举世无双。回眸一笑，倾覆邦国。回眸再笑，倾覆国家。不是不爱惜城与国，只是美人难以再得。”皇上叹息说：“好！世上难道真有这样的人吗？”平阳公主就说李延年有个妹妹，武帝就召见她，确实美貌善舞。因此得到武帝宠爱，生了一个儿子，也就是昌邑哀王。李夫人年轻却早死，武帝非常惋惜，就画了她的肖像挂在甘泉宫。卫思后被废四年之后，武帝去世，大将军霍光按照武帝的心意，让李夫人在宗庙配享，并追赠尊号为孝武皇后。

当初，李夫人病重，武帝亲自去看望她，夫人用被子蒙住脸说：“我卧病日久，相貌丑陋，不能拜见皇上。请皇上好好照顾我的儿子和兄弟。”武帝说：“夫人病得厉害，大概是要不行了。和我见

Chapter 23

Biography of Madam Li

Madam Li, Wudi's concubine, originally came to the palace as a singsong girl, via the influence of her brother Li Yannian, a favorite of the Emperor for his musical expertise, and his talent at singing and dancing. Whenever Li Yannian wrote new music or variations, all who heard were moved. For Emperor Wudi he danced, and sang: "There is a beauty in Northern China/ with unmatched beauty/ unique in the world. One turn of her smiling face/ and she overturns a city. A second look back/ and she overturns a kingdom. Not because they were not valued/ But a beauty is difficult to come by." The Emperor sighed: "Good! Is there really such a person in the world?" Princess Pingyang said Li had a younger sister, and the Emperor summoned her. Indeed she was an enchanting beauty, and a good dancer too. Thus she captivated Wudi and gave him a son, Prince Ai of Changyi. Madam Li died young and the Emperor was very distressed, and commissioned her portrait to hang in Ganquan Palace. Four years after Empress Wei was deposed, Emperor Wudi died, and General-in-Chief Huo Guang, in line with Wudi's last wishes, arranged for Madam Li to share sacrifices with Wudi in the ancestral temple, and gave her the posthumous appellation of Empress Wudi.

Earlier, when Madam Li was terminally ill, the Emperor went to see her on her sickbed, but she hid her face beneath the quilt, and said: "I am confined to bed too long, and my features are too ugly to have an audience with the Emperor, but I beg that Your Majesty will take care of my son and brothers." The Emperor replied: "You are seriously ill, and may never get up again. Would it not make you

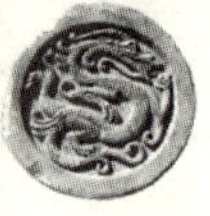

【原文】

殆将不起，一见我属托王及兄弟，岂不快哉？”夫人曰：“妇人貌不修饰，不见君父。妾不敢以燕媠见帝。”上曰：“夫人弟一见我，将加赐千金，而予兄弟尊官。”夫人曰：“尊官在帝，不在一见。”上复言欲必见之，夫人遂转鄉歔欷而不复言。于是上不说而起。夫人姊妹让之曰：“贵人独不可一见上属托兄弟邪？何为恨上如此？”夫人曰：“所以不欲见帝者，乃欲以深托兄弟也。我以容貌之好，得从微贱爱幸于上。夫以色事人者，色衰而爱弛，爱弛则恩绝。上所以挛挛顾念我者，乃以平生容貌也。今见我毁坏，颜色非故，必畏恶吐弃我，意尚肯复追思闵录其兄弟哉！”乃夫人卒，上以后礼葬焉。其后，上以夫人兄李广利为贰师将军，封海西侯，延年为协律都尉。

上思念李夫人不已，方士齐人少翁言能致其神。乃夜张灯烛，设

【今译】

上一面，嘱托儿子和兄弟的事情，难道不高兴吗？”夫人说：“女子没有梳妆打扮，不能见君父。我不敢仪容不整地见皇上。”武帝说：“夫人只要和我见上一面，就赏赐给你千金，并且给你的兄弟加官晋爵。”夫人说：“加官晋爵是皇上决定的，不在于和我见上一面。”武帝又说一定要见她，夫人就转过脸去抽泣，不再说话。于是武帝很不高兴地走了。夫人的姐妹埋怨她说：“您难道就不能和皇上见上一面嘱托一下兄弟的事吗？为什么对皇上如此怨恨？”夫人说：“我之所以不想见皇上，正是要藉此来嘱托兄弟的事。我靠着美貌，能够从微贱之人得到皇上的宠幸。凭藉容貌侍奉别人的人，容貌衰老情谊就浅了，情谊变浅恩惠也就断了。皇上之所以还深情地眷念着我，正是由于我原来的容貌。现在如果见到我容貌丑陋，一定会又害怕又厌烦，嫌弃于我，哪里还能再怀念怜悯我、优待我的兄弟呢！”夫人死后，武帝用皇后的礼节将她安葬。然后，武帝封李夫人的哥哥李广利为贰师将军，海西侯，封李延年为协律都尉。

武帝一直对李夫人念念不忘，方士齐人少翁说能招徕李夫人的魂魄。就在夜里点上灯烛，挂上帷帐，摆上酒肉，让武帝到别的帐篷

happy to discuss entrusting the son and brother to my care while looking at my countenance?" Madam Li declined: "A woman who is not groomed cannot see the monarch. I dare not see the Emperor in such a disheveled state." The Emperor said: "Madam, just grant me one look and you will immediately be granted 1,000 gold; and I will promote your brothers to esteemed offices." Madam Li said: "The promotion of officials should be decided by the Emperor, not by a meeting with myself." The Emperor insisted on seeing her, but Madam turned away sobbing, no longer speaking. Disconsolate, the Emperor left. Madam Li's sisters blamed her: "Surely you could have seen the Emperor and ensured the future of your brothers. Why be so horrible to the Emperor?" Madam said: "The reason I did not want to see him is that I wanted to entrust my brothers in a binding way. It was on account of my beauty that I became the Emperor's love and rose from a humble position. A woman who finds favor with a man by virtue of her good looks will find that passion cools as beauty ebbs away, and her privileges and favors will be cut in the fullness of time. The reason the Emperor loves me deeply is because of my original appearance. If he sees me ugly, and my good looks gone, he will turn from me in fear and disgust. I will be repugnant to him. How could he still yearn for me and give preferential treatment to my brothers!" At Madam Li's death, Emperor Wudi honored her with funeral rites befitting an Empress. Then, Wudi promoted Madam's brother Li Guangli to Ershi General, the Marquis of Haixi, and Li Yannian to Director of Imperial Music.

Wudi was obsessed with the memory of Madam Li, and the necromancer Shaoweng from Qi said that he could summon her spirit. Candles were lit by night in a tent, meat and wine were put out, and the Emperor was told to sit in another tent. He saw in the distance a beautiful woman who looked like Madam Li. She sat down in this tent, and then rose up, walking slowly. But she could not be approached to look at, so the Emperor missed his love all the

【原文】

帷帐，陈酒肉，而令上居他帐，遥望见好女如李夫人之貌，还幄坐而步。又不得就视，上愈益相思悲感，为作诗曰：“是邪，非邪？立而望之，偏何姗姗其来迟！”令乐府诸音家弦歌之。上又自为作赋，以伤悼夫人，其辞曰：

美连娟以脩嫮兮，命樔绝而不长，饰新宫以延贮兮，泯不归乎故乡。惨郁郁其芜秽兮，隐处幽而怀伤，释舆马于山椒兮，奄修夜之不阳。秋气(潜)[憯]以凄泪兮，桂枝落而销亡，神茕茕以遥思兮，精浮游而出畺。托沉阴以圹久兮，惜蕃华之未央。念穷极之不还兮，惟幼眇之相羊。函菱荴以俟风兮。芳杂袭以弥章，的容与以猗靡兮，缥飘姚虖愈庄。燕淫衍而抚楹兮，连流视而娥扬，既激感而心逐兮，包红颜而弗明。欢接狎以离别兮，宵寤梦之芒芒，忽迁化而不反兮，魄放逸以飞扬。何灵魂之纷纷兮，哀裴回以踌躇，势路日以远兮，遂荒忽而辞去。超兮西征，屑兮不见。浸淫敞克，寂兮无音，思若流波，怛兮在心。

【今译】

里去，武帝远远看到一个美女，正像李夫人的样子，在帐中坐下，又起身徐徐而行。可是不能走近去看，武帝就更加思念李夫人，心中感伤，为她作了一首诗说：“是不是你呢？我站在那儿望着你，却为何偏偏走得如此从容缓慢！”命令乐府的那些乐师配上曲子演唱。武帝又自己写了一篇赋，用来悼念李夫人，是这样写的：

你的姿容孅弱美好啊，可叹性命短暂不长久，装饰了新宫久久期待着你啊，你却消失了身影不再回归故乡。荒草丛生一片凄凉景象啊，你身处幽暗之地令我神伤，把车马停在陵墓旁啊，长夜漫漫何时天明？秋气寒凉令我心中惨痛啊，那可人的桂枝玉陨香销，我的灵魂孤独地思恋着远方的你啊，精神脱离躯体四方漫游。长期寄情于地下的你啊，痛惜你花容如繁华早逝，天的尽头大概并不遥远啊，我想念你那翩翩徜徉的身姿。花蕊绽放等待着春风啊，沁人的芬芳愈加浓郁，明亮的面容婉顺安详啊，飘摇于风中却更加端庄。燕儿飞去飞来栖止于楹梁啊，你美目流盼娥眉轻扬。我如有所感心中追寻着你啊，你却将红颜深深地掩藏。相会欢愉亲热又终于分离啊，我深夜从梦中惊醒心下茫然，你忽然逝去再也不回转啊，魂魄放任无拘自在逍遥。思绪飘渺无定啊，你徘徊驻足我心哀戚，道路越来越远啊，恍惚中你飘然离去。如同红日西坠，霎时不见了踪迹。一切渐渐朦胧起来，静悄悄地再也没有了声音，我对你的思念如流水不绝，心里永远凄怆伤怀。

more. Heartbroken, he wrote this poem for her: "You? Not you?/ I stood there looking at you./ But why did you go so calmly and slowly!" He commanded the musicians of the Music Bureau to sing it to a lyre accompaniment. The Emperor also wrote a *fu* rhapsody in her memory. It goes like this:

Alas, beautiful, and slender you were, but your life was not long. A new palace is decorated and is waiting for you, but you slipped away and does not return to the homeland. Dismal and dreary is the wasteland, and that you now are in the nether world pierces my heart. I stopped the chariot next to the tomb, and will the long night never dawn? The autumn air chills my aching heart, and the lovely cassia lets fall its fragrant stems and dies. Left alone, my soul longs for you, now far away, and my spirit leaves the nation, roaming. Long committed to the ground, alas, before your youth was halfway spent. The end of the horizon is not far away, how I miss your graceful dancing postures. The petals spread, waiting for the spring breeze, and their intoxicating fragrance intensifies. Your perfect, lustrous face betokens calm and auspice, your leisurely figure sways in the wind, but all the more elegant. Flying swallow lingers to perch on the beams, your bewitching glances arch your lovely brows. Excited, my heart goes in search for you, but you hide your rosy cheeks from me. Our meeting again in joyful intimacy is broken up again; in deepest night I awake from the dream, and am perplexed; you suddenly perished, never to return, your soul released and free of care. My thoughts wander aimlessly, but your wandering steeps my heart in sorrow. The road moves farther off and farther; in my trance you float above, leaving me. Then, like the setting sun on the horizon, you vanish in an instant. Gradually all grows dim, quiet and silent. My yearning for you is like a constant flowing stream, and my heart is forever sad.

In conclusion: A brilliant beauty withers like a red flower; how can jealous low creatures match you! In the prime of your

【原文】

乱曰：佳侠函光，陨朱荣兮，嫉妒阘(葺)[茸]，将安程兮！方时隆盛，年夭伤兮，弟子增欷，洿沫怅兮。悲愁于邑，喧不可止兮。向不虚应，亦云已兮。嫶妍太息，叹稚子兮，恻栗不言，倚所恃兮。仁者不誓，岂约亲兮？既往不来，申以信兮。去彼昭昭，就冥冥兮，既下新宫，不复故庭兮。呜呼哀哉，想魂灵兮！

其后李延年弟季坐奸乱后宫，广利降匈奴，家族灭矣。

——卷九十七上《外戚传》第六十七上

【今译】

结语说：佳丽光彩照人，却如鲜花般凋零；那些嫉妒卑贱之辈，如何能与你相匹敌！正当鼎盛年华，却夭折而亡，兄弟小儿哭个不休，涕泪交流。悲愁郁结于中，哀声不绝于耳。我们的哀痛你无法知晓，真令人无可奈何。可叹你忧伤瘦损，又哀怜年幼的小儿，你哀怆不语，心中定是有所希冀。仁者不必发誓，难道对待亲戚还要誓言。你虽从此一去不复返，我还是要表白自己的诚意。你远离光明的人世，前往昏暗的阴间，降临到了新宫，不再去往日的庭园。可悲啊可叹，我终日想念着你的魂灵！

后来李延年的弟弟李季因在后宫淫乱而获罪，李广利又投降了匈奴，李氏一家就被灭族了。

beauty you died; your brothers and child wept endlessly, their sad tears mingling. Wretched in grief, they could not stop weeping. Our appeals you do not respond to, rendering us helpless. You were pitifully thin but were concerned only for your son, sad and not speaking, but in your heart hoping for your dependents. The benevolent person does not have to swear an oath; surely there is no need for such with relatives. You are gone forever, but I still must declare my loyal love. You went away from the bright world of man to the dark underworld. Come to the New Palace, and return no more to the garden of the past. Such being my sorrow, alas, I shall miss your soul forever!

Later, Li Ji, the younger brother of Li Yannian was convicted of promiscuity in the palace and Li Guangli surrendered to the Huns, so the whole Li clan was exterminated.

图书在版编目(CIP)数据
汉书选：汉英对照 /（东汉）班固著；王之光译.
-- 北京 : 外文出版社，2015
（大中华文库）
ISBN 978-7-119-09408-3
Ⅰ.①汉… Ⅱ.①班… ②王… Ⅲ.①英语–汉语–对照读物
②汉书–译文 ③中国–古代史–西汉时代–纪传体
Ⅳ.①H319.4 ②K234.104.2
中国版本图书馆CIP数据核字(2015)第056165号

出版策划： 胡开敏
责任编辑： 杨春燕　曹晓娟　刘芳念
英文审定： Sue Duncan　贺　军

大中华文库
汉书选
（汉）班固　著
安平秋　张传玺　今译
王之光　英译

出 版 人： 徐　步
出版发行：
外文出版社
(中国北京百万庄大街24号)
邮政编码 100037
http://www.flp.com.cn
电话：008610-68320579（总编室）
008610-68995852（发行部）
008610-68327750（版权部）
制　　版：
北京杰瑞腾达科技发展有限公司
印　　刷：
深圳市佳信达印务有限公司
开　　本： 960mm × 640mm　1/16　**印　　张：** 50.25
2015年4月第1版第1次印刷
（汉英）
ISBN 978-7-119-09408-3
（精装）
定价：160.00元（全2卷）
